CASES IN
ALLIANCE
MANAGEMENT

THE IVEY CASEBOOK SERIES
A SAGE Publications Series

Series Editor
Paul W. Beamish
Richard Ivey School of Business
The University of Western Ontario

Books in This Series

CASES IN ALLIANCE MANAGEMENT
Building Successful Alliances
Edited by Jean-Louis Schaan and Micheál J. Kelly

CASES IN BUSINESS ETHICS
Edited by David J. Sharp

CASES IN ENTREPRENEURSHIP
The Venture Creation Process
Edited by Eric A. Morse and Ronald K. Mitchell

CASES IN OPERATIONS MANAGEMENT
Building Customer Value Through World-Class Operations
Edited by Robert D. Klassen and Larry J. Menor

CASES IN ORGANIZATIONAL BEHAVIOR
Edited by Gerard H. Seijts

CASES IN THE ENVIRONMENT OF BUSINESS
International Perspectives
Edited by David W. Conklin

Forthcoming

MERGERS AND ACQUISITIONS
Text and Cases
Edited by Kevin K. Boeh and Paul W. Beamish

JEAN-LOUIS SCHAAN
The University of Western Ontario

MICHEÁL J. KELLY
University of Ottawa

CASES IN ALLIANCE MANAGEMENT

Building Successful Alliances

SAGE Publications
Thousand Oaks ▪ London ▪ New Delhi

For information:

Sage Publications, Inc.
2455 Teller Road
Thousand Oaks, California 91320
E-mail: order@sagepub.com

Sage Publications Ltd.
1 Oliver's Yard
55 City Road
London EC1Y 1SP
United Kingdom

Sage Publications India Pvt. Ltd.
B-42, Panchsheel Enclave
Post Box 4109
New Delhi 110 017 India

Printed in the United States of America

Library of Congress Cataloging-in-Publication Data

Schaan, Jean-Louis.
Cases in alliance management : building successful alliances / Jean-Louis Schaan, Micheál J. Kelly.
    p. cm.
Includes bibliographical references.
ISBN 1-4129-4029-X or 978-1-4129-4029-0 (pbk.)
    1. Strategic alliances (Business) I. Kelly, Micheál J. II. Title.
HD69.S8S315 2007
658′.044—dc22

                        2006011065

This book is printed on acid-free paper.

06 07 08 09 10 10 9 8 7 6 5 4 3 2 1

Acquisitions Editor:	Al Bruckner
Editorial Assistant:	MaryAnn Vail
Production Editor:	Libby Larson
Copy Editor:	Gillian Dickens
Typesetter:	C&M Digitals (P) Ltd.
Proofreader:	Mary Meagher
Cover Designer:	Candice Harman

CONTENTS

INTRODUCTION TO THE
IVEY CASEBOOK SERIES

As the title of this series suggests, these books all draw from the Ivey Business School's case collection. Ivey has long had the world's second largest collection of decision-oriented, field-based business cases. Well more than a million copies of Ivey cases are studied every year. There are more than 2,000 cases in Ivey's current collection, with more than 6,000 in the total collection. Each year approximately 200 new titles are registered at Ivey Publishing (www.ivey.uwo.ca/cases), and a similar number are retired. Nearly all Ivey cases have teaching notes available to qualified instructors. The cases included in this volume are all from the current collection.

The vision for the series was a result of conversations I had with Sage's Senior Editor, Al Bruckner, starting in September 2002. Over the subsequent months, we were able to shape a model for the books in the series that we felt would meet a market need.

Each volume in the series contains text and cases. "Some" text was deemed essential in order to provide a basic overview of the particular field and to place the selected cases in an appropriate context. We made a conscious decision to not include hundreds of pages of text material in each volume in recognition of the fact that many professors prefer to supplement basic text material with readings or lectures customized to their interests and to those of their students.

The editors of the books in this series are all highly qualified experts in their respective fields. I was delighted when each agreed to prepare a volume. We very much welcome your comments on this casebook.

—Paul W. Beamish
Series Editor

PREFACE

Alliances have become an essential vehicle for firms around the world in their quest to sustain or improve their competitiveness.

The book is designed to respond to the growing need to train savvy alliance managers in business schools.

The text part of the casebook is a four-part series on building strategic alliances that work. The chapters are intended to help you understand the cornerstones of success to building a strategic alliance.

Each chapter concentrates on the central activities and issues surrounding a unique phase of the alliance process. These phases include: creating the strategic rationale for an alliance, selecting a partner, negotiating the deal, and implementing the relationship.

At the conclusion of each section, you will be provided a helpful set of diagnostic questions to aid you in determining a company's strength and suitability of achieving success through alliances. These tools can be a healthy way of reviewing the quality of an alliance, indicating where intervention may be required.

The orientation of the book, through the text and the cases, is decidedly practical. Each chapter begins with an overview of central activities and issues surrounding a specific

The Partnering Process

Strategic Rationale	Partner Selection	Negotiation	Implementation
Objective assessment of whether or not an alliance is the best choice for the organization	Identification and ranking of potential partners based on rigorous criteria	Preparation and conduct of alliance negotiations based on lasting relationship fundamentals	Planning, supporting, monitoring, and continuous learning for successful results

Figure 0.1   The Partnering Process

phase of the alliance process. The overviews draw on state-of-the-art academic research about alliances and our own studies with executives involved in alliance management over more than a decade. They provide tools designed to help managerial decision making.

Each chapter includes a number of case studies that were selected to cover alliances in a variety of industry sectors and regions of the world. Because they are rich in content and integrate management issues as managers face them, a number of the cases could be used to illustrate phases of the alliance process other than the ones they were categorized under.

ACKNOWLEDGMENTS

We wish to thank Paul Beamish, Director of Ivey Publishing, and Al Bruckner, Senior Editor at Sage, for their encouragement and support in this alliance. Our thanks to Ms. Andrie Nel, who edited our initial text and designed the summary flowcharts at the end of each chapter. We would like to extend our gratitude to our colleagues and case writers who produced the case materials. Finally, we would like to thank the executives who contributed the original insights, which shaped our own thinking about alliances.

INTRODUCTION

Firms are looking to create and maintain a competitive edge in a business climate where the abilities to adapt and respond are critical to survival. Increasingly, this search involves radically rethinking traditional organizational boundaries and business models. Emerging models emphasize cooperative strategies and relationship-based organizational structures that are highly flexible, capable of responding to rapid and sometimes radical changes in the marketplace and technology.

It has been estimated that over the past decade, the rate of alliance formation has increased at a rate of 25% annually. Numerous studies in recent years involving different industries and countries have pointed to the importance of alliances in the competitive strategies of contemporary firms.

Despite the strategic and financial benefits, there is also a substantial body of evidence pointing to the difficulties that firms have in achieving their alliance objectives. It is clear that, when managed well, alliances can create tremendous value. If poorly managed, however, they can be very costly distractions wasting resources, destroying morale, and resulting in a loss of competitiveness. Studies have consistently shown that the wrong alliance can be a black hole for management time and resources.

Strategic alliances and alliance-based business models will play an increasingly important role in the competitive environment of the next decade and beyond. The ability to form, implement, and manage them successfully will become a key source of competitive advantage. Partnering, however, is not an exact science. There is no simple recipe or formula for what makes a successful relationship. Every alliance has its own idiosyncrasies, its own unique attributes and ingredients that arise from specific circumstances and people.

1. The material presented in the text provides a context for assessing the value of alliances to a business and its ability to pursue them. It also provides a structured and disciplined approach to the key issues involved in creating and executing alliances as well as practical guidance to the key steps in the alliance process. In particular, it highlights some of the major problems that companies typically run into in their efforts to create and manage alliances. However, it is only designed as a guide, and the material in it should be interpreted in the context of the individual situation.

2. Alliances are not a quick-fix solution to a company's strategic problems or resource deficiencies. Successful alliances take work and commitment and a great deal of trust and goodwill among the parties involved in order to overcome the numerous problems that will likely arise over the life of the venture. This being said, successful alliances can bring extraordinary benefits to the companies involved. In particular, they provide excellent opportunities for companies to increase their knowledge base and develop new skills in core areas.

Given the importance that partnering will likely play in the future of any business, now is the time to start preparing by evaluating its partnering capabilities and assessing its partnering options.

This book is dedicated to our wives, Claudia and Marjolaine. We thank them for their love and their support.

1

STRATEGIC RATIONALE

Should a Firm Build a Strategic Alliance?

In Brief

Today's business environment has changed. Amid rapid and dramatic change heavily driven by globalization, increased business complexity, diversified customer needs—and simply speed—companies need to respond and adapt accordingly if they are going to survive and grow. Alliances serve as an important business strategy to respond to the business environment, and they increasingly define the structure of entire industries, as is the case in the multimedia, telecommunications, automobile, and biotechnology industries.

And they work. Companies that successfully embrace alliance strategies consistently perform better than those that do not. These companies benefit from alliances in a variety of ways, including sharing cost and risk, pooling their respective strengths, and leveraging complementarities. How much importance and stake is placed in forming an alliance should be directly proportionate to the degree to which the alliance supports a company's overriding business strategy. Simply stated, if it is going to be instrumental in achieving its long-term business objectives, the company managers will want to put into it suitable time and resource commitment to ensure its success. In contrast, if it is not as strategically important, prudence needs to be exercised in making a commitment.

Deciding to commit is only part of the readiness question. It is essential to take a close look at the internal structure, policy, and culture of the organization to make sure the internal machinery is indeed setting the company up for success. Sometimes, managers may discover they must first get their house in order before they should entertain forming an alliance with another organization because those alliances that are not managed well can prove to be very costly!

Firms of all sizes are looking to create and maintain a competitive edge in a business climate where the abilities to adapt and respond are critical to survival. Traditional organizational boundaries and business models have been redefined, with more emphasis being placed on alliances. Among large companies, alliances have become the norm, with companies engaging in anywhere from 30 to 100 alliances each.[1] Why? The belief is that alliance models are highly flexible, are generally lower risk, and enable companies to respond to rapid and sometimes radical changes in the marketplace and technology.

WHAT ARE STRATEGIC ALLIANCES?

A strategic alliance is a formal and mutually agreed to commercial collaboration between companies. The partners *pool, exchange,* or *integrate* specific business resources for mutual gain. Yet partners remain separate businesses.[2] Alliances can be either equity or non-equity based and typically start with one cooperative agreement that evolves into a portfolio of arrangements built over time.

Alliances are not risk free, however, and many studies cite 40% to 50% success rates.[3] Other research points out these rates are not dissimilar to alternative strategies, including wholly owned subsidiaries,[4] but the bottom line is *there is much opportunity for improvement.* Managers are well served to invest effort in managing their alliances well. If poorly managed, they can be very costly distractions wasting resources, destroying morale, and resulting in a loss of competitiveness. Even ventures that ultimately succeed are seldom problem free, and at least half can expect to see serious operational challenges within the first 2 years.

In spite of this sobering rate, enthusiasm for alliances continues to grow. A 2004 PriceWaterhouseCoopers study of 201 senior finance executives finds that nearly two thirds of respondents were more willing to strike alliances than they were 3 years earlier.[5] Another study of *Fortune* 500 companies shows that the top 25 that successfully embrace alliance strategies consistently performed better than those that do not.[6]

Why alliances? Alliances are viewed as an excellent vehicle to obtain market growth amid market conditions that are rapidly and dramatically changing worldwide. Globalization, the growing complexity of the business environment, increasingly diverse customer needs, and the need for speed and momentum are the underlying factors. In this climate, alliances are an excellent way for organizations to share risks, pool strengths, and integrate business operations for their mutual benefit.

While growth and profitability are typically the common end goal, alliances satisfy a variety of needs for individual companies and can be a valuable tool across a company's entire business system, as indicated below. Moreover, alliances have been increasingly used to construct broader business systems by linking a company's internal core competencies with the "best of breed" capabilities of allies.

Partnering for Growth

Ask Jeeves is a highly popular Internet site that allows visitors to type questions in ordinary language and receive relevant answers. The core strength of the Web site is the company's natural language search technology. In 2000, the company enjoyed a strong brand within a competitive search engine space. Management wanted to capitalize on their leadership position and swiftly expand into the lucrative enterprise market. Using alliances as a vehicle to achieve market growth, Ask Jeeves announced partnerships with several customer support outsourcing companies already serving *Fortune* 1000 companies. While alliance partners gained access to leading-edge search technology to improve their outsourcing solutions, Ask Jeeves gained accelerated entry, forecasting a 20% increase in its customer base over the next 12 months as a result of the alliances.

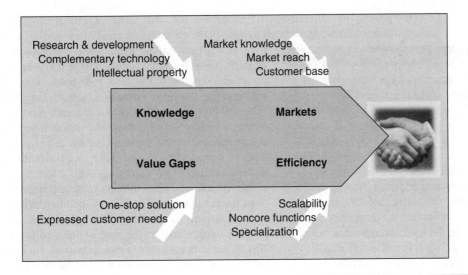

Figure 1.1   Why Cooperate?

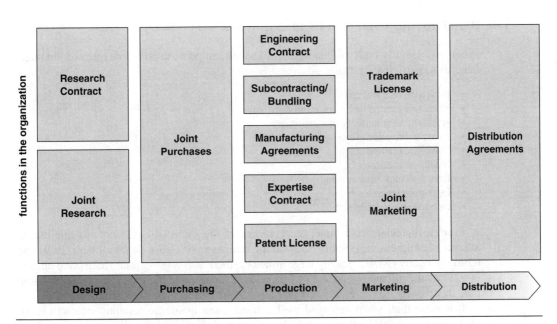

Figure 1.2   Where You Might Cooperate

Source: Sabine Urban and Serge Vendemini, *European Strategic Alliances: Cooperative Strategies in the New Europe* (Oxford, UK: Blackwell, 1992), 131.

The growth of alliance-based businesses has led some experts to conclude that competition is becoming as much a battle between competing and often overlapping coalitions as it is between individual firms. Alliance networks, or business webs, increasingly define the very structure of an industry, as is the case with industries including multimedia, telecommunications, networking, automobile, and biotechnology. Cisco, Dell, and, more recently, Nortel are examples of *virtual integration,* where noncore competencies in the value chain are distributed across alliance partnerships. For smaller companies, this means understanding—and targeting—the ideal ecosystem within which they want to participate and understanding what the resulting implications of membership are.

Outsourcing is another form of alliance that has evolved particularly in the area of information systems (IS). What is remarkable is that industries, such as banking, are choosing to outsource IS while they consider it to be a core competency that, intuitively, one expects would not be outsourced.[7] In these instances, the strategic drivers, which include changing organizational boundaries, organizational restructuring, and risk mitigation, supersede the traditional view.

> ### Competing Industry Alliances
>
> Juniper Networks develops high-performance networking products for the growing Internet market. The Mountain View, California, firm has directed its technology at the heart of Cisco in the Internet core. In 1998, it raised venture financing and partnered with a number of Cisco competitors, including Ericcson, Nortel, the Siemens/Newbridge alliance, 3Com, Lucent, VVNET Technologies Inc., and ATT Ventures. For Juniper, this represented a partnership with companies that collectively represented more than $75 billion in annual sales to virtually every major networking customer. These alliances provided a foundation for the delivery of Juniper's technology around the world. Its partners had the opportunity to integrate Juniper's leading-edge technology with their existing product lines and services worldwide.

THE BENEFITS AND CHALLENGES OF STRATEGIC ALLIANCES

When successfully built and managed, alliances can provide both strategic and financial benefits to participating firms:

- Reduced costs and risks
- Access to needed technology and distribution
- Access to new markets and customers
- Faster acceptance of new technology
- Enhanced credibility
- Increased investment
- Boost in stock market value
- Opportunities to learn
- Opportunity to build new skills

From a financial perspective, the evidence of the impacts on the bottom line due to alliances is impressive, pointing to substantial impacts on return on investment (ROI) and return on equity (ROE). Among large alliances, there was a substantial share price change in 52% of the alliances, and 70% of these were share price increases. It is interesting to note that this figure represents substantially higher effects than from acquisitions.[8]

It is clear that, when managed well, alliances can create tremendous value. In terms of revenue, in a 2002 International Data Corporation study, 90% of survey respondents reported their alliances contributed between 5% and 50% of corporate revenue.[9]

So although there are cautionary statistics on alliance failures, there is also evidence of significant potential. Alliances will remain a strategic business model. The fundamental question therefore becomes, What drives successful alliances for both large and small companies?

Problematic alliances can be the result of many factors, including industry dynamics (e.g., regulatory changes), new technologies, new entrants, or economic cycles. The ability to weather external forces as well as maximize internal alliance potential is heavily driven by establishing a solid alliance foundation that includes experience, mutual trust, strong relationships, and sound business rationale.

UNDERSTANDING WHAT A FIRM REALLY NEEDS FROM AN ALLIANCE

The rationale for a strategic alliance needs to be firmly grounded in a clear strategic understanding of a company's current capabilities and those it will need to be successful in the future. First, managers need to establish their company's strategic objectives and then evaluate their resources and capabilities to see if they are capable of executing on their own. The clearer the significance of the alliance for the success of a company's future strategy, the more committed it will be to work at its success.

The process starts by developing a realistic appraisal of what resources are required to meet a company's long-term strategic goals; that is, what capabilities will provide a competitive advantage in 3 to 5 years?

These capabilities might include credibility, geographical presence, distribution, technology, or money. Then managers need to objectively state what their firm's current capabilities really are.

	What Is Needed?	Measure Gap	Current Capability?
What **market strengths** are needed? (e.g., credibility, channels, offering, customer & industry relationships, etc.)	1. 2. 3.	1. 2. 3.	1. 2. 3.
What **human resources and expertise** are needed? (e.g., technical skills, industry experience, etc.)	1. 2. 3.	1. 2. 3.	1. 2. 3.
What **financial resources** will be required? (e.g. capital investments, working capital, etc.)	1. 2. 3.	1. 2. 3.	1. 2. 3.
What kind of **infrastructure** will be required? (e.g., manufacturing capacity, service fleet processes, etc.)	1. 2. 3.	1. 2. 3.	1. 2. 3.
What other competencies are of crucial importance to achieving our company objectives?	1. 2. 3.	1. 2. 3.	1. 2. 3.

Figure 1.3   Analyzing Current Capabilities

An understanding of the gap between what a company might be able to accomplish internally and what it needs helps to develop the profile of the best partner (if any). With this undertaking, managers begin to establish their criteria for rating partnership opportunities if this is an option they choose.

ALLIANCE OR ACQUISITION?

Managers also need to assess their company's readiness to embark on an alliance. The process should involve an evaluation of various alternatives and the pros and cons of each. In many cases, a strategic alliance may not be the most appropriate vehicle for meeting a company's strategic needs. Studies show that alliances work best for companies entering new geographic markets or related industries. Acquisitions, which should be viewed as an alternative to alliances, are more likely to be effective in core business areas or existing, highly competitive markets.[10] Make note, however, that a study by McKinsey & Company found that using an alliance to hide a weakness—as opposed to leveraging strength—was rarely a successful strategy.[11]

IDENTIFY THE REAL COSTS

Before deciding that an alliance is the way to go, the potential costs involved need to be considered—for example, technology transfer, coordination, and management costs, which can be particularly high in international alliances. Potential costs can also include reduced control, reduced flexibility in optimizing global production and marketing efforts, lost opportunity costs, or even creating or strengthening a competitor. Moreover, if differing operational and financial structures exist, an alliance may strain a company's ability to deal with more pressing internal, competitive, or operational issues that need attention. Managers need to ask themselves what they are *not* going to be able to do if they pursue an alliance.

IS THE ORGANIZATION ALLIANCE FRIENDLY?

One of the greatest determinants of alliance success is the experience one or both companies have in managing them. Experienced organizations know what it will take and will likely have gotten their own house in order to support additional alliances. If this is its first alliance, a company should look carefully at its internal policies and practices and evaluate to what degree they will help or hinder an alliance. For instance, an organization with shaky internal communications practices or with incentive programs focused on individual performance can place significant strain on an alliance relationship. It is best to modify internal practices as necessary before introducing a third party.

Even if the review shows a firm that it is not capable of managing an alliance right now, it should clarify what capabilities it needs to develop, what capabilities the firm brings to the table, and the timeframe that it needs to achieve a specific partnering goal.

In the end, alliances are only one strategic approach. They make most sense when other internal options are not viable or when it would be foolish to go it alone. In today's environment, however, it is frequently the case that going it alone is less and less a viable option.

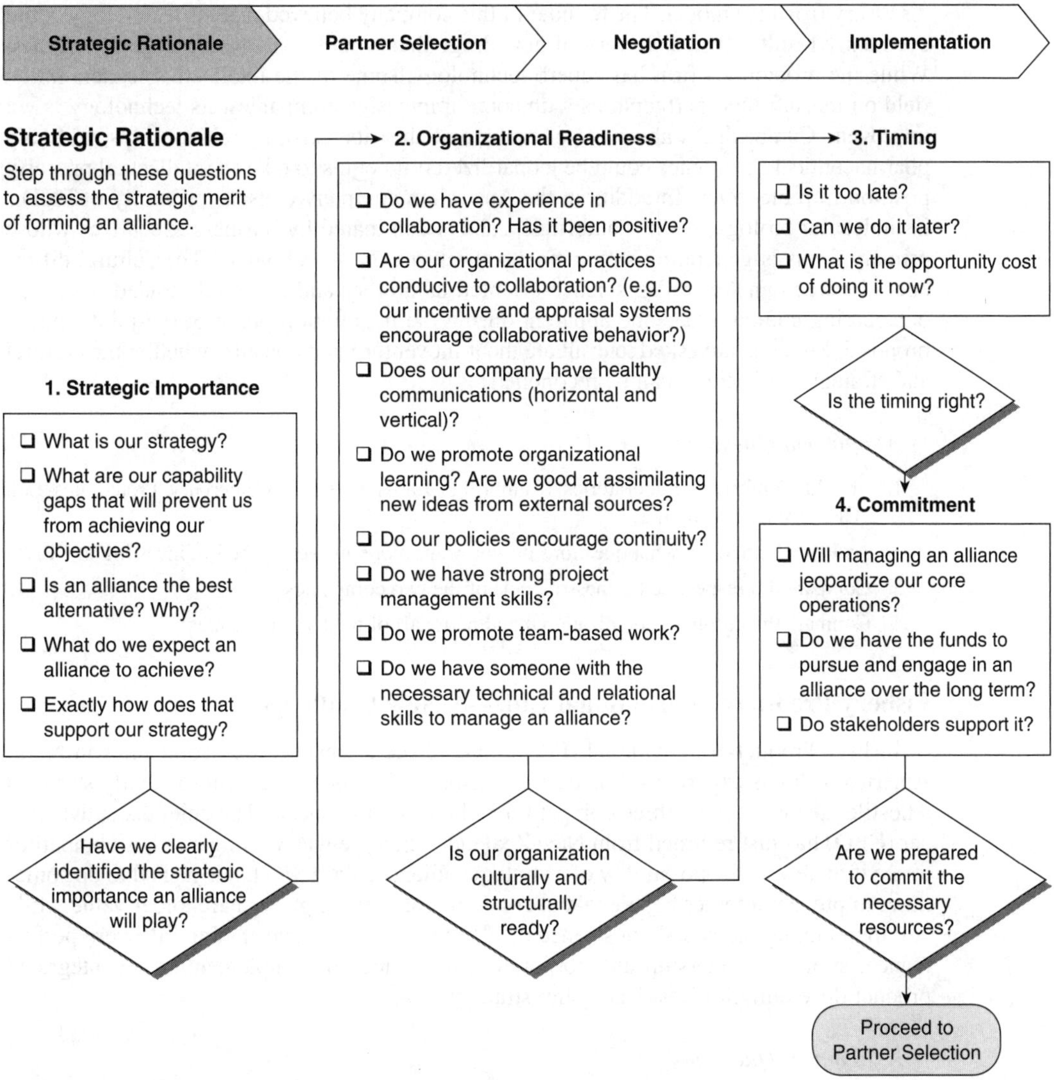

| Strategic Rationale | Partner Selection | Negotiation | Implementation |

Strategic Rationale

Step through these questions to assess the strategic merit of forming an alliance.

2. Organizational Readiness

❏ Do we have experience in collaboration? Has it been positive?

❏ Are our organizational practices conducive to collaboration? (e.g. Do our incentive and appraisal systems encourage collaborative behavior?)

❏ Does our company have healthy communications (horizontal and vertical)?

❏ Do we promote organizational learning? Are we good at assimilating new ideas from external sources?

❏ Do our policies encourage continuity?

❏ Do we have strong project management skills?

❏ Do we promote team-based work?

❏ Do we have someone with the necessary technical and relational skills to manage an alliance?

3. Timing

❏ Is it too late?

❏ Can we do it later?

❏ What is the opportunity cost of doing it now?

Is the timing right?

1. Strategic Importance

❏ What is our strategy?

❏ What are our capability gaps that will prevent us from achieving our objectives?

❏ Is an alliance the best alternative? Why?

❏ What do we expect an alliance to achieve?

❏ Exactly how does that support our strategy?

4. Commitment

❏ Will managing an alliance jeopardize our core operations?

❏ Do we have the funds to pursue and engage in an alliance over the long term?

❏ Do stakeholders support it?

Have we clearly identified the strategic importance an alliance will play?

Is our organization culturally and structurally ready?

Are we prepared to commit the necessary resources?

Proceed to Partner Selection

Figure 1.4 Strategic Rationale Flowchart

CASES

Cambridge Laboratories: Proteomics

Cambridge Laboratories is essentially a fee-for-service provider of laboratory tests. It spends less than 0.5% of revenues on research and development and holds relatively few patents for a biotech company. It now has an opportunity to invest $5 million to establish a joint venture with an Australian proteomics company that operates on a drug discovery (royalty) model. The founder of this company believed that his technology could eventually result in the discovery of new drugs that would generate significant royalties. While the proteomics firm has superb technology, some of the intellectual leaders in the field on its staff, and partnerships with some impressive companies, its technology is yet unproven. Cambridge Labs is also concerned that its existing relationships with big pharmaceutical companies could be jeopardized if it begins to take an intellectual property position in proteomics. In addition, the Australian company consists primarily of Ph.D.s in molecular biology, while Cambridge Labs is dominated by business executives whose primary focus is generating strong financial returns for shareholders. The cultural differences between an Australian science-oriented laboratory and a publicly traded American outsourcing company become apparent during the negotiation phase of the joint venture proposal. Students are asked to evaluate the joint venture and consider whether the cultural and strategic differences can be reconciled.

Assignment Questions

1. Should Cambridge Laboratories (Cambridge Labs) invest in Canterbury Proteomics Ltd. (CPL)? Why or why not?
2. As Paul Henderson, what questions do you want more answers to before investing in CPL?
3. Compare the respective business models of the two companies.
4. Compare the cultures (organizational and national) of the two companies.

Fishery Products International Ltd.—A New Challenge

Fishery Products International (FPI) is one of the largest seafood companies in North America. FPI has experienced its best performance in a decade and has recently survived a hostile takeover bid by three competitors who acted in concert. The chief executive officer (CEO) has just returned from New Zealand, where he was visiting a major competitor to see if there was the possibility of a strategic alliance. The CEO knew he had to do something to prevent another hostile takeover and to continue to grow shareholder value while still maintaining the social conscience of FPI. Some of the issues facing FPI were performance, strategic leadership and corporate governance, and implementing an integrated product differentiation/cost leadership strategy.

Assignment Questions

1. Complete an analysis using the value chain and Value, Rareness, Imitation, Organization (VRIO) framework (see table on page 11 in Barney, 2002) and discuss FPI's sources of sustainable competitive advantage (SCA). Refer to Barney's VRIO framework.[12]
2. Sources of SCA include legitimacy and reputation, strategic leadership, quality image/reputation, and brand loyalty (see table on page 11 in Barney, 2002). How would you describe FPI's performance? Why hasn't FPI been able to create shareholder value?
3. FPI's performance is comparable with its competitors' performances—below the industry's in some respects and below other industries. The most significant challenges in creating shareholder value include industry difficulties in the early 1990s (stock depletion, quota restrictions) and the nature of the industry (overcapacity, volatility of natural resource supply, uncertain pricing). As Vic Young, what business and/or corporate strategies might you consider? Which would you select and why?

NonStop Yacht, S.L.

NonStop Yacht, S.L. is a Web site that provides e-commerce service to the mega-yacht industry. Originally, the founder had planned to run NonStop Yacht (NSY) as an Internet business. However, success with this business model is proving elusive, and investors are growing restless as performance continues to fall short of the business plan. Substantial pressure to improve the company's performance had the founder considering a variety of alternative business models that would enable him to more effectively capture value from the concept of nonstop parts procurement for high-end yachts. These options involve key decisions about the strategic positioning of the company and the relative advantages and disadvantages of pursuing strategic alliances with players at different points in the industry value chain.

Assignment Questions

1. What is NSY's strategy?

2. Why didn't the NSY Web site receive a positive market response?

3. What are the key success factors in the parts procurement segment of the mega-yacht industry?

4. Does NSY have the basis for competitive advantage?

5. Which business model makes the most sense for NSY?

6. To what extent does your answer differ if you are evaluating these options from the perspective of Metcalf? His investors?

Strategic Direction at Quack.com (A)

Quack.com was in dire straits. An early entrant in the voice portal market, Quack was quickly running out of money. The company's management team had just returned from a road show for a second round of venture financing, but they had been unsuccessful. To exacerbate this issue, Quack's two major competitors had each received substantial funding. At the current burn rate, Quack could survive on its bridge financing for only 3 more months. Moreover, after the first few months of running the voice portal, Quack's business-to-consumer (B2C) model for voice portals was already showing signs of weakness. Quack's management believed the failure of its road show could be related to its B2C focus. The company was facing many major decisions that would reshape and dictate the future of the firm.

Assignment Questions

1. Where do you see the market unfolding, and where do you see each of the major players on the industry value chain?

2. How should Quack deal with its financing issues?

3. What strategic direction should Quack take? Specifically, on which products and market should it focus?

4. What do you foresee as the best and worst scenarios for Quack?

5. What is your contingency plan?

Pharma Technologies Inc.

A new biotechnology firm, Pharma Technologies, has developed a competing method for the treatment of erectile dysfunction that promises significant advantages over Pfizer's blockbuster drug, Viagra. With deep-pocketed pharmaceutical companies also pursuing product development efforts, the president of Pharma Technologies is charged with deciding how to leverage his company's superior proprietary technology into a viable product before the window of opportunity closes. Students can explore the trade-offs in pursuing internal versus external development of new technology, the strategic implications of in-licensing and out-licensing, and the criteria used in identifying potential alliance partners to expedite the commercialization of new technology.

Assignment Questions

Assume the position of Blair Glickman, president of Pharma Technologies, Inc. (PTI). Develop a plan for commercializing Factor X as a treatment for male erectile dysfunction. Your plan should include the following:

- A clear explanation of PTI's strategy for taking the technology to market, in terms of the role that in-licensing, out-licensing, and/or partnering should play in moving forward, including whether you would make any trade-offs in the other areas of technology development the company is pursuing
- A detailed set of action priorities that will support your strategy, including timeframes for their execution
- An estimate of the resource implications of your intended strategy

ALPES S.A.: A Joint Venture Proposal (A)

The senior vice-president for Corporate Development for Charles River Laboratories (CRL) must prepare a presentation to the company's board of directors requesting up to $2 million investment in a Mexican joint venture with a family-owned animal health company. However, the chief executive officer views the proposed joint venture as a potential distraction while his company continues to expand rapidly in the United States. He is also worried about the risks of investing in a country such as Mexico and about the plan to partner with a small, family-owned company. Moreover, the Mexican partner is unable to invest any cash in the joint venture, which would need to be fully funded by Charles River Laboratories.

Assignment Questions

1. As a member of the CRL's Board of Directors, should CRL go ahead with this proposed joint venture? Why or why not? Be prepared to argue your position.

2. As Alejandro Romero, why do you want this joint venture? Are there realistic market opportunities? What issues or problems do you foresee?

3. If the board approves the joint venture, what advice would you give Dennis Shaughnessy as to how to proceed?

NOTES

1. Jim Bamford and David Ernst, "Measuring Alliance Performance," *The McKinsey Quarterly,* Web Exclusive, October 2002.

2. Jordan Lewis, *Partnerships for Profit: Structuring Alliances* (New York: Free Press, 1990).

3. Marloes Borker, Ard-Pieter de Man, and Paul Weeda, "Embedding Alliance Competence: Alliance Offices," 2004, http://www.cgcpmaps.com/papers/embeddingalliance.pdf.

4. Andrew Delios and Paul W. Beamish, "Joint Venture Performance Revisited: Japanese Foreign Subsidiaries Worldwide," *Management International Review* 44, no. 1 (2004): 69–91.

5. "PricewaterhouseCoopers Research Findings: CFOs Embrace Strategic Alliances as Major Growth Tool and Alternative to Higher-Risk M&A," *Business Wire,* May 7, 2004, http://www.business wire.com/photowire/pw.050704/241285485.shtml.

6. Gabor Garai, "Strategic Alliances: The Path to Success or Disaster," *Corporate Board Member Magazine,* April 2001.

7. Kerry McLellan, Barbara L. Marcolin, and Paul W. Beamish, "Financial and Strategic Motivations Behind IS Outsourcing," *Journal of Information Technology* 10, no. 4 (1995): 299–321.

8. David Ernst and Tammy Halevy, "When to Think Alliance," *The McKinsey Quarterly* 1 (2000): 47–55.

9. Nicole Gallant, Marilyn Carr, and Stephen Graham, *Measuring the Financial Impact of Strategic Alliances: An Evaluation Framework,* Document 28635 (Framington, MA: International Data Corporation, 2002).

10. Jeffrey H. Dyer, Prashant Kale, and Harbir Singh, "When to Ally & When to Acquire," *Harvard Business Review* 82, no. 9 (2004): 109–17.

11. J. Bleeke and David Ernst, "The Way to Win in Cross Border Alliances," in *Collaborating to Compete* (New York: John Wiley, 1993), 21–2.

12. Jay Barney, *Gaining and Sustaining Competitive Advantage,* 2nd ed. (Upper Saddle River, NJ: Prentice Hall, 2002).

CAMBRIDGE LABORATORIES: PROTEOMICS

Prepared by David Wesley under the supervision of Professors Henry W. Lane and Dennis Shaughnessy

Paul Henderson scanned the headlines of *The Boston Globe* before beginning his Monday morning commute to Cambridge, Massachusetts, where he served as senior vice-president for corporate development and general counsel for Cambridge Laboratories (Cambridge Labs). What caught his eye this morning was a headline titled, "Midsize Biotech Firms Take Hit, Many Struggling to Raise Cash."[1]

As Henderson scrutinized the newspaper article, he could not help but notice the contradictions. On the one hand, the paper rightly pointed out that biotech firms "are struggling to raise cash, and many are trading at a small fraction of what they were worth just two years ago during the biggest boom in the industry's history." Yet, "there's been a resurgence of interest . . . in early-stage companies," an industry analyst was quoted as saying. The journalist added, "Investors are placing a premium on companies that are focused on producing drugs."

The Globe article reiterated much of what Henderson already knew: namely, that many genomics and proteomics firms had benefited from a short-lived "irrational exuberance"[2] that created spectacular valuations and allowed some laboratories to raise significant capital through public offerings. Investors eventually realized that drug discovery was a long process and that many years would pass before most of these companies would ever recognize revenues. As suddenly as they had risen to prominence, many labs had become pariahs of Wall Street. Meanwhile, researchers remained optimistic about the potential to revolutionize health care by treating disease at the molecular level.

As head of his company's mergers and acquisitions, Henderson reviewed many potential biotech partnerships and acquisitions. Recently, he had received a joint venture proposal from Canterbury Proteomics Ltd. (CPL), a small Australian proteomics firm that wanted to enhance its drug discovery research by establishing a presence in the United States. Canterbury Proteomics had patented technology that the company's founders believed would eventually lead to the discovery of blockbuster drugs. In exchange for start-up capital amounting to US$5 million,[3] CPL promised millions of dollars in downstream drug royalties for Cambridge Labs.

Although CPL's managers seemed confident in their ability to deliver a competitive product, Henderson wondered if a drug development "premium" was really warranted. Was proteomics another scientific fad that consisted of more hype than substance, or would it usher in a new and unprecedented age of discovery leading to the development of new drugs to treat everything from infectious disease to cancer? The Cambridge Labs management team constantly received investment proposals from high-potential firms, but only invested in five per cent to 10 per cent of the proposals reviewed. Henderson wondered if Canterbury Proteomics should be one of them, and if so, under what terms.

CAMBRIDGE LABORATORIES

Founded in 1947, Cambridge Laboratories provided laboratory services for use in drug discovery research and the development and testing of new pharmaceuticals. At the height of the technology stock market bubble, Cambridge Labs launched an initial public offering (IPO) that raised $257 million, facilitating further expansion (Financial summaries are provided in Exhibits 1–3). When the economy began to falter in 2001, Cambridge Labs remained one of the few companies that continued to grow.[4]

Cambridge Labs served hundreds of laboratories in more than 50 countries worldwide. These were primarily large pharmaceutical companies, including the 10 largest pharmaceutical companies (based on 2001 revenues). Together with biotechnology firms, pharmaceutical companies accounted more than 75 per cent of the company's sales. The remaining customers included animal health, medical device and diagnostic companies, as well as hospitals, academic institutions and government agencies. The company did very little of its own research and development in the creation of new laboratory services.[5] Instead, most of the company's technology was licensed or purchased from third parties, or developed through collaboration with universities and biotechnology firms.

As a result of its leadership position in the laboratory outsourcing services, Cambridge had not lost any of its 20 largest customers in more than 10 years, while its largest customer accounted for less than three per cent of total revenues. The company maintained 78 facilities in 16 countries and had nearly 5,000 employees, including approximately 250 with advanced degrees such as DVM, PhD or MD.

The Cambridge Labs publicly announced its strategic growth objectives to grow its existing businesses by between 12 per cent and 15 per cent annually and its entire business by 20 per cent. This left a "strategic growth gap" of five per cent to eight per cent each year. Cambridge Labs then pursued technology platform acquisitions, joint ventures, technology licensing and strategic partnerships to fill the gap. Henderson commented:

Period Ending	2001	2000	1999
Total Revenue	$465,630,000	$306,585,000	$219,276,000
Cost of Revenue	(298,379,000)	(186,654,000)	(134,592,000)
Gross Profit	$167,251,000	$119,931,000	$84,684,000
Operating Expenses			
Selling General and Administrative Expenses	(68,315,000)	(51,204,000)	(39,765,000)
Other Operating Expenses	(8,653,000)	(3,666,000)	(1,956,000)
Operating Income	90,283,000	65,061,000	42,963,000
Total Other Income and Expenses Net	2,465,000	1,715,000	489,000
Earnings Before Interest and Taxes	92,748,000	66,776,000	43,452,000
Interest Expense	(22,797,000)	(40,691,000)	(12,789,000)
Income Before Tax	69,951,000	26,085,000	30,663,000
Income Tax Expense	(27,095,000)	(7,837,000)	(15,561,000)
Minority Interest	(2,206,000)	(1,396,000)	(22,000)
Net Income From Continuing Operations	$40,650,000	$16,852,000	$15,080,000
Nonrecurring Events			
Extraordinary Items	(5,243,000)	(28,076,000)	2,044,000
Net Income	$35,407,000	$(11,224,000)	$17,124,000

Exhibit 1   Cambridge Laboratories Income Statement (for years ending December 31)

If we were satisfied with just growing our existing business we would be too risk averse. Our investors have come to expect that we will deliver on our commitment each quarter, which creates additional pressure to perform particularly when the stock price reached $40 in 2002 from an IPO price of $16.

In 2001, Cambridge Labs increased revenues to $465 million, a 50 per cent improvement over the previous year, and enjoyed a profit margin of about 20 per cent. Much of the company's growth was due to two large acquisitions that enhanced revenues by $100 million. The company was also the recipient of numerous accolades and honors from prominent business journals and newspapers.

Laboratory Services Division

Laboratory Services was Cambridge Labs' largest and fastest growing division (a summary of other services offered by the company is provided in Exhibit 4). By employing technologies that were licensed or purchased from universities and biotechnology firms, Laboratory Services sought to predict the potential success of new drug candidates. Laboratory service firms, such as Cambridge Labs, expanded in order to meet demand from biotechnology and pharmaceuticals firms. The company's chief executive officer (CEO) commented on the impact this was having on Cambridge Labs:

Laboratory Services is our fastest growing business, which is well in excess of 40 per cent annually. Much of this expansion is driven by genomics, which is a field that is growing worldwide, and we expect to see this growth continue for the foreseeable future. Our facilities here, as well as in California, Japan and France have all had to expand to meet demand.

Pharmaceutical clients were interested in outsourcing many routine trials as long as laboratory service firms were able to provide quality,

Period Ending	2001	2000	1999
Net Income	$35,407	$(11,224)	$17,124
Cash Flow Operating Activities			
Depreciation	28,578	25,370	15,643
Adjustments To Net Income	$28,246	$28,928	$7,723
Changes in Operating Activities			
Changes In Accounts Receivables	(27,505)	(843)	5,346
Changes In Liabilities	13,227	(1,965)	(3,547)
Changes In Inventories	(3,762)	(2,343)	133
Changes In Other Operating Activities	(2,893)	(4,155)	(4,854)
Cash Flows From Operating Activities	$71,298	$33,768	$37,568
Cash Flow Investing Activities			
Capital Expenditures	(36,406)	(15,565)	(12,951)
Other Cash Flows From Investing Activities	(55,515)	989	(21,217)
Cash Flows From Investing Activities	$(91,921)	$(14,576)	$(34,168)
Cash Flow Financing Activities			
Dividends Paid	(729)	—	—
Sale Purchase Of Stock	118,954	235,964	102,993
Net Borrowings	(70,995)	(235,182)	323,086
Other Cash Flows From Financing Activities	—	—	(437,583)
Cash Flows From Financing Activities	47,230	782	(11,504)
Effect Of Exchange Rate	$(1,465)	$(1,855)	$(1,697)
Change In Cash And Cash Equivalents	$25,142	$18,119	$(9,801)

Exhibit 2   Cambridge Laboratories Cash Flow Statement (for years ending December 31) ($000s)

reliable service. Cambridge Labs prided itself on that ability as Henderson commented, "We can conduct these trials faster and cheaper than pharmaceutical companies can internally, and without sacrificing quality."

With demand for outsourced laboratory services continuing to grow, expanding existing facilities became a priority, and Cambridge Labs could not hope to meet that demand alone. The company's CEO explained:

We absolutely need several players to service the outsourcing trend. We have backlogs of several months across the board in our toxicology business and a lot of that is contractual in nature, contracts lasting from 90 days to a year. In response,

we continue to add space, as do other companies. It's clear that biotech companies want to continue outsourcing these services. And as long as they have good companies to outsource to, I'm sure they will.

DRUG DISCOVERY

The Role of Chemistry

The growth of the pharmaceutical industry depended on its ability to develop new drugs. Thus, drug companies spent from 10 per cent to 20 per cent of revenues on R&D, or some $50 billion a year industry-wide. Despite

Period Ending	2001	2000	1999
Current Assets			
Cash and Cash Equivalents	$58,271	$33,129	$15,010
Net Receivables	107,179	48,087	38,158
Inventory	39,056	33,890	30,534
Other Current Assets	5,648	4,631	6,371
Total Current Assets	210,154	119,737	90,073
Long-term Assets			
Long-term Investments	3,002	2,442	21,722
Property Plant And Equipment	155,919	117,001	85,413
Goodwill	90,374	41,893	36,958
Other Assets	18,673	16,529	13,315
Deferred Long-term Asset Charges	93,240	113,006	115,575
Total Assets	571,362	410,608	363,056
Current Liabilities			
Payables And Accrued Expenses	75,389	58,685	58,550
Short-term And Current Long-term Debt	933	412	3,543
Other Current Liabilities	22,210	5,223	7,643
Total Current Liabilities	98,532	64,320	69,736
Long-term Debt	155,867	202,500	382,501
Other Liabilities	14,465	13,531	2,469
Deferred Long-term Liability Charges	—	—	4,990
Minority Interest	12,988	13,330	304
Total Liabilities	281,852	293,681	460,000
Stockholders' Equity			
Redeemable Preferred Stock	—	—	13,198
Common Stock*	442	359	198
Retained Earnings	(283,168)	(318,575)	(307,351)
Capital Surplus	588,909	451,404	193,742
Other Stockholders' Equity	(16,673)	(16,261)	(9,929)
Total Stockholders' Equity	289,510	116,927	(110,142)
Net Tangible Assets	$199,136	$75,034	$(147,100)

*Outstanding shares numbered approximately 46 million.

Exhibit 3   Cambridge Laboratories Balance Sheet (for years ending December 31) ($000s)

generous increases in annual R&D budgets, few new drugs reached the market, while the cost of bringing a single drug to market increased to more than $800 million in 2001 from $230 million in 1987.[6] Jim York, a senior scientist from Cambridge's Discovery Services division, explained:

The industry is in a well-publicized R&D productivity trough, and hence there is great interest in small companies that are well along in the development of new compounds. The lack of R&D productivity has also led to the increased valuations for those small companies with well-developed compounds to serve as stopgaps for large Pharma's pipeline woes.

Pharmacokinetic and Metabolic Analysis conducted pharmacokinetic studies to determine the mechanisms by which drugs function in mammalian systems to produce therapeutic effects, as well as to understand how drugs may produce undesirable or toxic effects. Metabolic studies also revealed how drugs are broken down and excreted, and the duration that drugs or their byproducts remain in various organs and tissues. These studies were often performed as part of the drug screening process to help identify lead compounds, as well as later in the development process to provide information regarding safety and efficacy.

Bioanalytical Chemistry Services supported all phases of drug development from discovery to non-clinical studies and clinical trials. Researchers designed and conducted projects, developed and validated methods used to analyse samples, conducted protein studies and performed dose formulation analysis.

Pharmacologic Surgery studied drugs designed to be administered directly to a precise location within the body using surgical techniques. The development of these and certain other drugs required the use of surgical techniques to administer a drug, or to observe its effects in various tissues.

Specialty Toxicology Services were undertaken by a team of scientists that included toxicologists, pathologists and regulatory specialists who designed and performed highly specialized studies to evaluate the safety and toxicity of new pharmaceutical compounds and materials used in medical devices.

Medical Device Testing provided a wide variety of medical device testing required by the Federal Drug Administration (FDA) prior to the introduction of new materials. Cambridge Labs maintained state-of-the-art surgical suites where custom surgery protocols were implemented on behalf of medical device customers.

Pathology Services identified and characterized pathologic changes within tissues and cells as part of the determination of the safety of new compounds.

Biotech Safety Testing determined if human protein drug candidates were free of residual biological materials. The bulk of this testing work was required by the FDA before new drugs could be approved. As more biotechnology drug candidates entered development, Cambridge expected demand for these services to increase.

Biopharmaceutical Production Services maintained production facilities for the development and manufacture of drugs in small quantities for clinical trials.

Exhibit 4   Other Services Offered by Cambridge Laboratories

Meanwhile the expiration of patents led to pricing pressures as more generic drugs entered the market. Even when drug companies lowered prices, they often saw their market share decline by as much as 80 per cent during the first year following the launch of an equivalent generic brand.

In the past, drug discovery was focused on chemistry, as researchers attempted to identify compounds that could target specific diseases. Improved instrumentation allowed the number of compounds being reviewed to increase substantially in the 1980s and 1990s. Nevertheless,

higher throughput did not deliver many promising drug prospects. Henderson recalled a recent visit by a lead scientist from a major pharmaceutical company:

This person was in charge of 400 chemists all working on identifying new drugs. In more than 20 years, his team has yet to identify one candidate for a new drug. He seemed discouraged by the fact that 20 years of work had been wasted. And his experience was not unusual. In the last 50 years, drug companies have only brought 500 new drugs to market, and most of those have been improvements on drugs that already existed.

The Shift Toward
Genomics and Proteomics

In the 1990s, drug discovery began to move away from its roots in chemistry to rely increasingly on biological research. Advances in genetics, for example, gave researchers new hope that the foundation for many diseases could be found in a person's genes. They sought to identify measurable changes in biological systems, known as biomarkers, which increased the propensity for disease. High cholesterol, for example, would be considered a biomarker for heart disease. In this case, cholesterol reduction through medication and diet could help patients to reduce the risk of heart attack. Genetic biomarkers worked on the same principle. By identifying differences between healthy individuals and diseased individuals at the molecular level, new drugs could be developed to specifically target key genes and proteins. Some chemical compounds that could be used to treat disease probably already existed in large pharmaceutical laboratories around the world, but had yet to be matched with appropriate biomarkers.[7]

The greatest challenge for researchers was to process the massive amounts of data encoded in living cells.[8] Cataloguing that data in large relational databases consumed all the resources of many of the most advanced computers available.[9] One such process was the sequencing of the human genome, which began in earnest in 1988 as a government-funded project administered by the National Institutes of Health (NIH) and the Department of Energy (DOE). By 1998, advances in computer systems[10] allowed a privately funded company, known as Celera Genomics, to enter the fray with a promise to sequence the entire human genome by 2001. With great fanfare, both organizations published their results in February 2001.

Amazing as this feat was, it represented a small (but important) step toward understanding the role of genetics in regulating biological processes. According to industry analyst, Dr. Kevin Davies:

Mining the human genome is a massive computational problem, but nothing compared to the daunting problems posed by proteomics—the total characterization of the identities, structures, complexes, networks and locations of all the proteins in the body. Understanding the properties of a single protein is hard enough. It takes a couple of months for a Cray T3[11] to simulate the folding of an average protein in [the lab]; the natural process takes mere microseconds.[12]

Not only were proteins more complex than DNA (genes had four bases while proteins were made from 20 amino acids), the number of proteins in the human body was estimated at more than one million, as many as 30 times the number of genes. As well, although DNA remained relatively stable throughout the human body, each cell expressed different proteins that interacted with each other in different ways. Moreover, protein expression changed with time, as aging, diet, stress and other external factors took their toll.

To characterize the sheer magnitude of the difference between genomics and proteomics, when Celera and the U.S. government completed the sequencing of the human genome in 2001, proteomics researchers at various sites around the world were still struggling to identify the proteome of a single strain of yeast (an organism that contained only a fraction of the number of genes contained in the human genome). "The mouse genome is more than 99 per cent the same as the human genome," explained Henderson. "But genomics doesn't matter because only four per cent of the proteins expressed from those genes mimic humans, and everything about disease depends on the expression of proteins."

Leading Companies in
Genomics and Proteomics Research

Beyond university and government laboratories, which tended not to commercialize their discoveries, the number of entrants into the field of proteomic research services was limited.

A lack of technological expertise and/or capital tended to act as barriers to entry.

Some of the more well-known companies were Celera Genomics, Large Scale Biology, MDS Proteomics, Oxford GlycoSciences, Millennium Pharmaceuticals and GeneProt. The business models for each of these were based upon lucrative royalty arrangements with partial payments upon initiation and potentially large payments upon the successful development of new drugs. All were in the process of becoming drug companies to some degree.

Millennium Pharmaceuticals had essentially become a drug development company, while Large Scale Biology and Celera were still at an early stage of the process. For each of these companies, initial commercial deals were either collaborations or based on the payment of royalties. These collaborations were few in number and large in scale. For example, approximately 80 per cent of Large Scale Biology's revenue was derived from a single collaboration with Dow AgroSciences (a division of Dow Chemical). Likewise, GeneProt derived most of its revenue from collaboration with Novartis.

After seeing meteoric valuations in 1999 and 2000, shares for the entire sector plunged in 2001 as investors pulled away from small loss-making technology companies. Oxford GlycoSciences (OGS) was the first company to enter the field of proteomics on a large scale, raising $230 million from stock offerings in 1999 and 2000.

With its primary focus being drug discovery, OGS had already amassed a large database of patented biomarkers. The company planned to release its first drug in early 2003, a compound used to treat a rare illness known as Gaucher Disease.[13] Eventually, OGS hoped that additional discoveries would allow it to compete with leading pharmaceutical firms.[14] In the first half of 2002, Oxford GlycoSciences reported a loss of $31 million on $9.3 million in revenues. The company's market value plunged from more than $4.5 billion in March 2000 to just over $138 million in 2002, even though the company had more than $240 million in cash and no appreciable debt.[15]

Toronto-based MDS Proteomics, another important player in the proteomics field, posted a loss of $35 million on revenues of $2 million for 2001. The company said that its main challenge was "the building of relationships with potential pharma and biotech partners"[16] in its quest "to become a world-leading proteomics drug-discovery business."[17]

Large Scale Biology of New Jersey was nearly bankrupt after its contract with Dow Agro-Sciences, which accounted for more than 80 per cent of the company's revenues, ended in August 2001. The company posted average annual losses of more than $23 million from 1999 to 2001, and saw its stock price decline by more than 97 per cent between August 2000 and June 2002. In the future, the company hoped to be able generate revenue from contract research and licensing agreements.[18]

Other companies did not fare much better. Millennium Pharmaceuticals' stock was down more than 90 per cent after posting losses of nearly $200 million in 2001. Celera Genomics, which moved away from genetic sequencing after completing the Human Genome Project, was down more than 93 per cent on a loss of more than $40 million for the same period. A spokesperson for Celera Genomics commented:

We believe that Celera remains the most promising company to discover and develop pharmaceuticals and diagnostics from an understanding of disease through molecular biology.[19]

Investors were skeptical that a research laboratory could compete with large pharmaceutical companies. Celera founder Craig Venter shared that opinion. Shortly after resigning as CEO, he reflected on his own situation. "I made a million dollars the hard way. I started with a billion dollars and worked my way down!"[20]

GeneProt described itself as "a global industrial-scale proteomics company" involved "in the discovery and development of new therapeutic proteins, protein drug targets and protein biomarkers." The privately held company used technology licensed by OGS and housed the world's largest commercial supercomputer at its facilities in Geneva, Switzerland. The company's partners included several leading biotechnology and pharmaceutical firms, including Novartis.[21]

Few companies developing proteomics technology were interested in providing outsourcing services to large pharmaceutical and biotechnology companies. Instead, most believed that the identification of potential drug targets was worth far more in terms of future royalties than could be gained by selling testing services or technology.

Two companies that did provide research and testing services on a fee-for-service basis or through contracts were Genomic Solutions and Proteomic Research Services, both based in Michigan. Proteomic Research Services was a relatively new company with a small staff and little instrumentation. Genomic Solutions, a company that designed and manufactured genomic and proteomic instrumentation, had been around longer, but services were minor component of the company's overall business, accounting for approximately eight per cent of revenues ($1.2 million in 2001).

THE JOINT VENTURE PROPOSAL

The PMC Acquisition

In February 2001, Cambridge Labs purchased Premier Medical Corporation (PMC) for $52 million, making it the company's largest acquisition to date.[22] Based in Amherst, Massachusetts, PMC was an international contract research organization that provided pre-clinical drug discovery and development services to the biopharmaceutical industry. Services included safety, efficacy and quality control testing for early stage pharmaceutical products. Reflecting on the acquisition, one PMC scientist noted:

> We had been bought and sold a number of times before by organizations that didn't know what we did. Cambridge certainly knew what we did. They had a really good brand name and that made it a good fit for us because it got us through the door with important clients.

Cambridge has very disciplined business practices. That was probably the biggest organizational adjustment for us. They brought a higher level of discipline and a higher level of expectation than the companies we were with before.

Even while the integration of PMC was still a work in progress, three senior PMC scientists, Jim York, John Post and Peter Kingston, began evaluating proteomics companies and technologies that they believed could provide important growth potential for their business. They concluded that Canterbury Proteomics Limited of Australia provided the best fit with their existing business and began talks with CPL management about ways that they could work together. After several discussions, CPL proposed that Cambridge Labs invest in a new U.S.-based joint venture to conduct high throughput proteomic analysis in order to identify drug targets that could lead to important new discoveries.

Canterbury Proteomics Limited: Company Background

CPL was founded in 1999 by a group of scientists from Monash University in Australia, under the direction of biologist Dr. Lewis Edwards. In the 1980s, Edwards was involved in a biotechnology company that attempted to produce biological agents that could be used to treat parasitic infections. When the venture failed, Edwards joined Monash University as director of the Center for Biochemical Analysis. Established in 1992 with funding from the Australian government, the center's goal was to develop improved instruments for the analysis of proteins. Clark Wilson, a PhD student at the center, soon began investigating proteomics as a counterpart to genomics. Specifically, proteomics referred to the study of "the complete set of proteins encoded in a genome."[23] Edwards commented on the significance of that event:

> When Clark Wilson presented his work at a conference in Italy in the fall of 1994, our intention was to draw attention to the need to focus on proteins as

the functional molecules of biology. We did this at a time when much of the scientific world's attention was focusing on genomics. Of course, developers of drugs had always been interested in proteins as they are the major targets for new drugs.

In 1997, the center submitted a proposal to the Australian government for approximately $44 million to expand the center. When the proposal was rejected, Edwards became concerned about his ability to retain skilled researchers at the center. Ultimately, his solution was to separate from the university and establish CPL as a privately-funded proteomics company. Initially five other scientists from the center joined Edwards, including Clark Wilson. The company later grew to more than 70 scientists and staff members, the majority of whom were PhDs.

After receiving a government grant for new technology start-ups and initial venture capital funding, CPL successfully solicited its first research contract from Dow AgroSciences.[24] At the time, Dow was eager to capitalize on improved agricultural products through genetic modification. Monsanto and others had already created crops that resisted disease, parasites and herbicides. However, Dow pulled out of the venture in 2001 on growing public opposition to genetically modified food.[25] The company then turned its attention to proteomics, improving on its existing technology to create a fully integrated protein analyser (see Exhibit 5).

The Proteomics Analyser was used to identify and analyse proteins as they are expressed from DNA. CPL partnered with several other companies, including IBM and Japan Biotech Corporation (JBC) to provide a complete product. IBM provided the information technology platform needed to store biological information in very large databases and compute the interrelationships between various protein components. Over a period of five years, proteomics research was expected to generate 1,000 times the data generated from genomics.[26] JBC was responsible for constructing much of the analyser system from specifications provided by CPL. The analyser would sell for as much as $8 million for a complete unit. Canterbury Proteomics held more than 20 technology and process patents for components of the system, some of which were believed to provide the company with distinct competitive advantages (see Exhibit 6).

The Proposal

The senior PMC scientists, York, Post and Kingston, had been discussing the technology with CPL. They proposed to Henderson that if Cambridge Labs were to invest $5 million for a 20 per cent share of a new U.S.-based proteomics venture, CPL would contribute the technology and expertise needed to bring products (i.e., biomarkers) to market. In return, Cambridge Labs would provide capital, industrial knowledge and client relationships. Henderson, who was by no means an expert in the field of proteomics, had to rely on the expertise of his scientists. However, he wondered whether the company was ready to enter into a joint venture so soon after the PMC acquisition.

"You know that every $1 million in earnings equals one cent in earnings per share (EPS)," he explained.

If we end up writing off the goodwill on this investment, it will cost us five cents a share, and that is probably equivalent to about $1 billion in market capitalization, because I'll miss the numbers by five cents. For a company our size in this market, investing $5 million is very risky. Having said that, I rely on you guys to tell me if this is the right technology for us. Is this the best technology?

Without hesitation, York responded:

Absolutely! We have looked at other companies, such as BioRad, but frankly they are not very innovative. I may be wrong, but I think the folks at CPL have the best long-term vision of where this field is headed.

Kingston added:

I don't know about their business or their management abilities, but their technology is superb,

Product news
received on 5 June 2002
from Canterbury Proteomics Ltd.

Next generation proteomics platform

Combination of separation technology, robotics, mass spectrometry and enterprise level computing delivers "comprehensive outcomes" through its ability to decipher proteomic complexity

Canterbury Proteomics has announced the release of the Proteomics Analyser, an integrated comprehensive solution designed to accelerate proteomics research and the discovery of new drugs to treat diseases such as cancer, infectious diseases and others.

The analyser brings together niche sample preparation and analytical technologies with enterprise level computing and extensive training and support programmes to offer an end-to-end solution for proteomics research.

Clark Wilson, executive vice president of bioinformatics, said: "We have created the analyser from the ground up for proteomics, combining the latest proteomics technology into one seamless platform. The combination of separation technology, robotics, mass spectrometry and enterprise level computing is unique to the analyser, which delivers comprehensive outcomes through its ability to decipher proteomic complexity."

Alliances with key partners such as IBM, Japan Biotech, Millipore, Sigma-Aldrich, and ThermoFinnigan enabled Canterbury Proteomics to accelerate the development of the Protein Analyser.

Lewis Edwards, CEO, Canterbury Proteomics said "The analyser will revolutionise and accelerate research in the pharmaceutical and biotechnology sectors, through its broad application in the discovery of diagnostic and prognostic markers, and an ability to identify and validate drug targets.

"Our technology has been developed by practitioners of proteomics, specifically for proteome research, and has been rigorously tested in our in-house projects in cystic fibrosis, cancer, infectious diseases and aging.

"Our ability to test our approaches in demanding in-house discovery programmes sets us apart from other vendors of proteomic technology," he said.

The Proteomics Analyser includes patented technology for protein separation, analysis and informatics, which together delivers faster, more reproducible results.

This empowers researchers to focus on their discovery outcomes while the analyser produces data and assembles it into useful biological information.

The Proteomics Analyser is integrated via a sophisticated informatics package that controls laboratory instrumentation and centralises all research outcomes into an IBM DB2 database software hosted on IBM eServer pSeries systems.

The software provides sophisticated analysis tools that allow information and projects to be shared between sites.

Mike Svinte, vice president of worldwide business development for IBM Life Sciences said: "Canterbury Proteomics has delivered a powerful solution for rapidly deciphering complex protein data. The Proteomics Analyser brings together leading edge technologies, including an information technology infrastructure based on IBM eServer and DB2 data management systems, that will support proteomic research today and scale to meet future requirements."

Exhibit 5   Canterbury Proteomics Press Release

Electrophoresis

- Electrophoresis Apparatus Method (pending)
- Cassette for Electrophoresis (pending)
- Increased Solubilisation of Hydrophobic Proteins (pending)
- Improved Gel for Electrophoresis (pending)
- Immobilized Enzyme Reactor
- US patent 5,834,272 and Italian patent MI95A0113
- CPL has agreed to purchase the above patents from a consultant
- Multi-Compartment Electrophoresis (pending)
- Improved Electrolyser (pending)
- Coated Hydropholic Membranes for Electrophoresis Applications (pending)
- Electrophoretic Apparatus (pending)
- Electrophoresis Apparatus Incorporating Multi-Channel Power Supply (pending)
- Electrophoresis System (pending)
- Electrophoresis Platform (pending)

Image Analysis

- Imaging Means for Excision Apparatus (pending)
- Analyzing Spots in a 2-D Array (pending)
- Method for Locating the Edge of an Object (pending)
- Methods for Excising Spots from a Gel Under White Light (pending)
- Method for Locating the Coordinates of an Object on a Flat Bed Scanner or the Like (pending)

Protein Processing

- Liquid Handling Means for Excision Apparatus (pending)
- CPL and Japan Biotech are joint owners/applicants
- Sample Collection and Preparation Apparatus (pending)
- CPL and Japan Biotech are joint owners

Bioinformatics

- Method and System for Picking Peaks for Mass Spectra (pending)
- Annotation of Genome Sequences (pending)

Exhibit 6   Patents and Patent Applications Related to the Proteomics Analyser System

absolutely superb. And their people are unsurpassed intellectually. In terms of integrated systems, CPL's technology is the best. What we don't want is to buy instruments from vendors that we have to piece together ourselves.

York rejoined:

My only concern is that CPL is a small entrepreneurial company. They are ambitious, but I am not sure that they have the business discipline to deliver a sophisticated system on the scale that we need. On the other hand, I am more confident knowing that they have strong partnerships with companies like IBM and Japan Biotech.

Henderson agreed that Cambridge Labs should meet with CPL to evaluate the opportunity for a joint venture. He first presented the plan to the board of directors, which gave its approval to begin negotiations. Two weeks later Edwards and some of his colleagues met with Henderson and the PMC team.

The Meeting

Edwards began with a presentation about CPL, its technology and the analyser platform. He explained:

Our primary goal is to be a discovery company which develops new diagnostics and drug targets. We have a team of highly skilled problem-solvers and we expect to be amongst the first proteomics companies to provide valuable and interesting outcomes. Many of the best-selling drugs either act by targeting proteins or are proteins themselves. In addition, many molecular markers of disease, which are also the basis of diagnostics, are proteins. The analyzer will automate much of the process of identifying potential targets. This will have major implications for pharmaceutical research and development.

Although the system was currently only able to process a few samples per hour, Edwards believed that it could be improved to a rate of 1,000/hour (the minimum effective rate needed for drug discovery) within a year. He continued:

Imagine the potential. This is an emerging technology that will result in lucrative deals for early entrants. For example, early entrants in the field of high throughput combinatorial chemistry and high throughput screening struck attractive intellectual property positions and royalty arrangements. The same is true for genomics companies like Celera and Millennium. If we sell a marker to a pharmaceutical company that eventually results in a drug worth $1 billion in revenues, we stand to gain $100 million in royalties. If you are willing to invest in our technology, eventually we think we can give you $50 million a year in royalties.

Henderson was concerned about how Cambridge's clients would react to the idea of paying royalties:

Drug companies are already seeing their margins eroded by generic competition for many blockbuster drugs. They can ill afford to give away their intellectual property and downstream revenue.

He was interested in the technology however. He explained:

Most of our clients have begun their own proteomic programs and would probably be interested in outsourcing much of the routine lab work. But it's really proteomic fee-for-service analysis that we are interested in providing to pharmaceutical and biotech clients. They would be the ones looking at new targets. I think it could help them with their early screening, but it's really the service, as opposed to the product, that we're interested in.

Henderson knew that most pharmaceutical companies had already announced proteomics programs in one form or other, and that the total proteomics market was estimated to be more than $2 billion in 2002, growing to $6 billion in 2005. Laboratory services had the potential to eventually win as much as 20 per cent of that business.

Henderson adjourned the meeting for lunch, giving both sides an opportunity to consider and discuss the morning's issues amongst themselves. Shortly afterward, he confided in his team that he didn't think the two companies were compatible:

I really have a hard time understanding Edwards. Forgive me for saying this, but he is too much of an academic. This is a university spin-off company. That doesn't necessarily make them great businessmen. Are they going to meet deadlines? They have a great concept in theory, but as they are talking about all this cutting-edge technology, all I can think about is deadlines and deliverables.

Expertise Versus Capital

After lunch, the two sides reconvened. Henderson began:

One of my big concerns is whether you will be around to support this venture. You're not a public company, so I can't see you're financial records. It doesn't seem like you have raised any capital. If I put $5 million into this venture, what happens if you go away next year?

Edwards was sure that CPL could raise the capital they would need. "We are going to raise $15 million from one investor, and possibly another $5 million from another."

Henderson asked, "Have you raised any money recently?"

Edwards replied, "Well, not yet. This is a tough market to raise capital in. However, we have some very strong partners in IBM and Japan Biotech. They wouldn't have partnered with us if they didn't believe in our long-term potential."

Anne Chifley, head of Discovery Programs for CPL, interrupted the conversation to suggesting that CPL's business model had the best long-term potential. She explained:

If we discover biomarkers through this joint venture, that is IP (Intellectual Property). It is *our* biologists, *our* scientists coupled with pharmaceutical companies and other partners who are discovering these biomarkers. We believe that pharmaceutical companies will want to partner with us because this is not an easy field to get into. It is a very difficult space to work in and you really have to understand what you're doing. The timing to capitalize on proteomics is extremely ripe right now.

Henderson was unconvinced. He countered:

Pfizer has 5,000 scientists searching for targets, while the joint venture would initially only have five. Cambridge Labs has never sought to earn royalties in any of its businesses and I doubt that we would be willing to diverge from our business model.

My biggest concern, however, is whether this will really work, because if it doesn't I'll miss my quarter. How is this going to impact my financial statements, if it doesn't work?

"So what if you miss the quarter," Edwards retorted. "This will work; it is just a matter of time."

Henderson explained:

You don't understand, I have to show a 20 per cent margin in the first quarter. No place in the world is like the U.S. with our focus on quarter to quarter results. Unfortunately, in American business the focus is on what this will do to my financial statements right now, not three years from now.

Edwards was adamant. "That's so short-sighted. It's going to work. Either you're in or you're out."

Henderson explained that much more had to be done before a decision could be made. For one, Cambridge Labs had to be sure that the technology did not infringe on any existing patents. Within 10 days, CPL had to prove that it owned the patent rights for the Proteomics Analyser system.

"We won't get sued. And if we do, we'll stop," they replied.

Being a lawyer, Henderson knew all too well the pitfalls that CPL's approach implied. The United States was a much more litigious country than Australia, and any patent infringement damages under American law could prove costly.

After the meeting, Henderson asked his team for alternatives.

Post suggested, "We could go ahead with the joint venture, but until their technology is proven to work, I don't see any reason to pay goodwill on the IP."

Kingston responded:

We could buy a Proteomics Analyser system for between $8 and $10 million and do it ourselves. However, there are several problems with that approach. First, we don't know if the system will actually work. We also will probably not be able to get fee-for-service exclusivity if we go that route. And finally, we don't have the same level of expertise in proteomics that they have.

York sat back in his chair with a facetious look on his face. "Or we could buy their company!"

"I *hate* that idea!" exclaimed Henderson. Everyone laughed.

Although he still had doubts in the back of his mind, Henderson was comforted by CPL's strong external partnerships. Therefore, at the next board of directors meeting he sought approval to enter into a joint venture with CPL under the following conditions:

1. The joint venture would provide proteomics testing and analysis on a fee for service basis to pharmaceutical and biotechnology clients.

2. Cambridge Labs would purchase 80 per cent of the shares for $4 million and CPL would purchase 20 per cent for $1 million.

3. The joint venture would be prohibited from pursuing drug discovery and development, but CPL could still pursue drug discovery outside of the joint venture.

4. The joint venture would have exclusive world-wide rights (with the exception of Japan where CPL already had assigned rights to its Japanese partner) to any proteomics services using CPL technology.

5. CPL would have the right to sell their systems to pharmaceutical companies that wanted to do their own, in-house proteomics services. However, these services could not be offered by the purchaser to other customers or spun off into a stand-alone company to provide services for a fee.

The Offer

Later that month Henderson again met with the CPL team to present his offer. Prior to the meeting, Kingston expressed concern.

I don't know how Edwards is going to react to our proposal, but I know that most companies would probably drop it and walk away.

Nevertheless, Henderson felt strongly that both parties brought equally valuable resources to the deal. Therefore, the equity stake of each partner should reflect its financial contribution.

When Kingston presented the terms of the deal to CPL, they were stunned. Did Cambridge Labs not value the technology, patents, and unique expertise that it would bring to the joint venture? Not only did Canterbury Proteomics own the intellectual property and patents that were the basis for the venture, it had the technical expertise that would allow Cambridge Labs to access this emerging scientific field. In addition, CPL brought valuable partners, such as IBM and Japan Biotech. One employee of Japan Biotech had even won a Nobel Prize for his work on protein analysis. With its assembled expertise, finding valuable drug targets would only be a matter time.
Kingston explained:

Proteomics Analyser is a new and unproven technology. Cambridge, because of its brand, has

access to a lot of customers that, frankly, you will have a hard time getting through the door with. These relationships, along with our reputation as a premier quality service provider, have created a powerful brand image in the industry.

Edwards was incredulous:

Our scientific staff alone, along with the Proteomics Analyser technology platform could potentially find several important drug targets. This will be worth hundreds of millions of dollars in royalty fees to be shared between the partners. By the third year of the venture the two companies will likely be sharing millions of dollars in revenue. Royalties clearly offer the greatest long-term payoff.

To prove Edwards' point, the CPL team produced a spreadsheet showing annual projected earnings from royalties.
Henderson conceded:

I don't doubt your projections, but we don't want to charge our customers royalties. We want to say to anybody that is interested in this technology, "Come and get it. Just pay us X number of dollars per sample." With more and more samples, we can drive the cost per sample down.
On the other hand, if you go off and do a deal with somebody and take a royalty, typically those people are going to say, "Well, you're not going to be able to do for somebody else what you did for us. We're paying you five per cent of the drug revenue, so you can't do the same for our competitors."
Beyond that, charging royalties is inconsistent with Cambridge's reputation in the pre-clinical industry. We don't take intellectual property positions with customers.

Finally, Henderson raised the issue of providing options to the PMC scientists who would manage the joint venture. They also wanted the right to spin off the joint venture through an IPO that would also grant them founders' shares. "These people will be critical to the joint venture," Henderson explained. "If they were to leave, the joint venture would be finished."
At first, the CPL team did not seem to understand what Henderson was saying. By Australian standards, the management team would be earning

very lucrative salaries. Now they wanted shares in the company! For Edwards, this was the final straw. He suggested that if Cambridge Labs could not present more reasonable terms, CPL would have no choice but to look for another partner.

Henderson replied:

Try raising $5 million in venture capital in the current market. I think you will find it very difficult. It is a very tough environment for people to write big checks.

NOTES

1. "Midsize Biotech Firms Take Hit, Many Struggling to Raise Cash," *Boston Globe*, June 10, 2002.
2. Alan Greenspan used the term "irrational exuberance" to refer to stock market valuations that were not supported by economic performance. From a speech given at the Annual Dinner and Francis Boyer Lecture of The American Enterprise Institute for Public Policy Research, Washington, D.C., December 5, 1996.
3. All monies in US$ unless otherwise specified.
4. In early 2000, the failure of prominent Internet companies, such as E-toys and Value America, caused many investors to reevaluate the market. As bearish sentiment began to take hold, the technology shares entered into an extended downward spiral. In March 2000, the technology laden Nasdaq exchange peaked at 5,000. By year's end, approximately half of that index's value had been erased.
5. Research and development (R&D) expenditures were approximately $500,000 in 1999, $1 million in 2000 and $2 million in 2001.
6. "Research Cost for New Drugs Said to Soar," *The New York Times*, December 1, 2001.
7. Biomarkers were commonly interpreted to be different from drug targets. While biomarkers and drug targets were often the same, usually biomarkers were surrogate measures of the **impact** of dysfunction generated by disease, condition or treatment. Treatments directed at the target can use biomarkers to assess their impact, efficacy, treatment scenarios, etc.
8. The genetic code of a human being comprised more than 200 times the data in a New York City phone book.
9. One example was the $45 million National Science Foundation-funded Terascale Computing

System in Pittsburg, Pennsylvania. Completed in 2001, the system was roughly the size of a basketball court, used 14 miles of interconnect cable, seven miles of copper cable and a mile of fiber-optic cable for data handling. It consumed 664 kilowatts of power (equivalent to 500 homes) and produced heat equivalent to burning 169 pounds of coal an hour. It was cooled by 900 gallons of circulating water per minute and 12 30-ton air-handling units (equivalent to 375 room air conditioners).
10. For more information on supercomputers and their role in Life Sciences, see *Note on Supercomputing*, Northeastern University Case Series No. 9B03E004, Ivey Publishing, 2003.
11. The Cray T3 was ranked 15 among the 500 most powerful computers in the world in 2001.
12. "Bio-IT: When Two Worlds Collide," *Bio-IT World*, March 2002.
13. "From Proteins to Profits," *Business Week*, December 26, 2002.
14. "The thing is: CAT/OGS," *Independent on Sunday*, January 26, 2003.
15. "From Proteins to Profits," *Business Week*, December 26, 2002.
16. "MDS Reports Fourth Quarter Fiscal 2002 Results," *PRNewswire*, December 12, 2002.
17. "Science Firm MDS Eyes Drug Discovery," *Montreal Gazette*, April 1, 2002.
18. Source: Large Scale Biology SEC filings.
19. "Genome Pioneer Celera Lays Off 132," *The Washington Times*, June 12, 2002.
20. "A Bubble Punctured by Realism," *The Financial Times*, November 11, 2002.
21. "GeneProt Licenses OGS' Automated Proteomics Patents," *Oxford GlycoSciences Press Release*, February 8, 2002.
22. The PMC acquisition added $75 million to revenues, which was nearly double any previous Cambridge acquisition.
23. "Prime Time for Proteomics," *Bio-IT World*, March 2002.
24. Initial funding included a $2 million grant from the Australian government and $10.2 million from private investors in exchange for 10 per cent of CPL's equity.
25. For a complete discussion of the issue of genetically modified food, see Ivey cases *Monsanto Europe (A) & (B)*, Ivey #9B02A007 and 9B02A008, 2002.
26. "Venture Capital the Cool-headed Way," *The Financial Times*, June 21, 2001.

FISHERY PRODUCTS INTERNATIONAL LTD.—A NEW CHALLENGE[1]

Prepared by Tammi L. Hynes and W. Glenn Rowe

Copyright © 2001, Ivey Management Services

Version: (B) 2004-01-12

BACKGROUND

It was early September 2000, and Chief Executive Officer (CEO) Vic Young was reflecting on the past few months. Since 1984, Young had led Fishery Products International Ltd. (FPI) through a host of challenges, ranging from the fishery crisis in the early 1990s to a recent hostile takeover bid by three united competitors. Though the bid was rejected, Young recognized that another takeover attempt was very possible and wondered if he could convince shareholders to remain confident in FPI's management team. FPI had experienced one of its best performances in more than a decade, with a projected annual earnings target of net income in excess of Cdn$0.75 per share. This compared with Cdn$0.51 per share in 1999. In late August, Young traveled to New Zealand to explore opportunities to give FPI a more international flavor in the fish-marketing business (see Appendix E for more details).

HISTORY

From its beginnings in the Atlantic Canadian fishery, FPI had grown into an international seafood company, producing and selling a complete range of seafood products around the world. Publicly traded and among the largest seafood companies in North America, FPI was headquartered in St. John's, Newfoundland, Canada. From its offices in Canada, FPI managed the operations of its subsidiaries in the United States, the United Kingdom and Germany.

The fishing industry has a long history in Atlantic Canada, dating back to the 1500s. By the early 1980s, however, over-fishing, over-capitalization (i.e., an excess of production

plants), and a recessionary economy led to a collapse of fish stocks and a fishery crisis. Several fishing companies had gone under or were near bankruptcy, and the federal and provincial governments stepped in to restructure the industry. In the mid-1980s, Fishery Products Ltd., the Lake Group Ltd., John Penney and Sons Ltd. and other seafood company assets were amalgamated into Fishery Products International Ltd. Through a cash infusion and conversion of debt to equity, the federal government gained 63 per cent of the new company; the Newfoundland government, 26 per cent; and a bank, 11 per cent.

For three years, Fishery Products International Ltd. operated as a crown corporation, until being privatized in 1987, after a profitable 1986. The firm was restructured and in an attempt to preserve local interests and prevent private control of a government-funded company, the provincial government passed the Fishery Products International Limited Act, limiting FPI's share ownership to 15 per cent of the voting, common shares, a restriction mirrored in the company's bylaws. According to the Act, a single shareholder could not own more than 15 per cent of the shares of the parent company FPI Ltd. and could not combine resources to acquire control of FPI.

In the late 1980s and early 1990s, FPI faced ongoing struggles. The whole industry was weakened by declining cod stocks, worker demands for wage increases and a high Canadian dollar that hampered exports. FPI was already operating below capacity when the federal government severely reduced cod total quotas to 132,000 tonnes on July 2, 1992. On September 6, 1993, the federal government and the North Atlantic Fisheries Organization[2] (NAFO) imposed a moratorium on flatfish species (e.g., American plaice, yellowtail, flounder) on the Grand Banks and further quota reductions in other groundfish stocks, including cod, a traditional key species.

Over time, FPI responded to these resource issues by sourcing fish internationally (including fish from Alaska and South America), by adding more value to its cod-based products and by moving away from cod and into other types of seafood, such as shrimp. The 1989 purchase of Clouston Foods Canada Ltd., a Montreal seafood brokerage, was an example of this shift in strategy, as was the company's 1992 purchase of Halifax-based National Sea Products' U.S. food service operation to use as a shrimp plant.

INDUSTRY OVERVIEW

As a global commodity, seafood was sourced, processed, sold and consumed worldwide. The market was competitive, with buyers at all levels demanding high quality and service along with competitive prices. Processors purchased raw material (fish) from seafood harvesters and developed the primary product into basic or value-added packaged seafood products. These processors typically distributed and marketed the products to wholesale and/or retail buyers in established markets around the world. Typically, firms were vertically integrated, procuring some supply from company-owned vessels, processing in company-owned plants and distributing and marketing through in-house representatives positioned in strategic markets. Generally, margins

remained higher with the fish harvesters on one end and retail chains and restaurants at the other end; processors, whose margins were typically less, were required to be highly efficient.

In 1998, Japan and the United States were the top seafood importers. Most of Canada's fish products were exported to the United States, where consumers spent approximately Cdn$50 billion per year on fish and shellfish products, followed by Japan, then the United Kingdom. Export information is detailed in Exhibit 1.

Seafood companies encountered competition both in procuring raw materials and in marketing end-products. In Canada there were nearly 150 companies that varied widely in size, sales volume and product delivery. None of Newfoundland's 16 seafood companies had a disproportionate share of the market for raw material and all competed with local and foreign processors.

Competition among different Newfoundland producers is particularly painful in this market. Because the market is somewhat fixed in size, when there is severe competition over price, all sellers have to lower their price, but they get virtually no return in terms of increased volume sales. Instead, each seller is simply undercutting other sellers, all fighting for the same customers.

Presentation to Howard Noseworthy,
Selector/Arbitrator for the 2000 Shrimp Fishery

Capital costs for startup were high, and a processing licence had to be obtained from the

Origin / Destination	January 1998	January 1999	January 2000
Canada to United States	649	807	1,106
Canada to All Countries	1,480	1,603	2,052
Canada to All Countries—shrimp, scallops, crab, filleted groundfish only	909	964	1,215

Exhibit 1   The Value of Canadian Fish Exports (in Cdn$ Millions)

Source: "Trade Data Online," Industry Canada, 2000, retrieved at www.strategis.ic.gc.ca, June 26, 2000.

provincial government. The provincial government was inclusive in trying to give these licences to as many communities as possible. New processors might have had difficulty obtaining raw material, as harvesters had established relationships with or financial ties to existing processors.

PROCUREMENT AND PRICING ISSUES

A critical issue in the seafood industry was resource sustainability. Significant over-fishing in many parts of the world had caused serious depletions of certain species stocks, threatening the viability of both harvesters and fish processors who relied on those stocks. In countries such as New Zealand, industry and government had collaborated to jointly manage fish resources and ensure a sustainable resource base. In Canada, the Department of Fisheries and Oceans (DFO) established fish quotas through the "total allowable catch" (TAC) while provincial and territorial governments issued processing licences. It was evident that DFO usually worked with the provinces and territories to sustainably manage fishery resources and balance quotas with processing capacity.

In most countries, raw material was purchased through free markets, auctions and direct sales. Newfoundland legislation, in an attempt to protect harvesters, required joint processor and harvester negotiation of minimum prices paid to harvesters for raw material. Unique to Newfoundland, this negotiation between processors, through the Fisheries Association of Newfoundland and Labrador (FANL), and harvesters, through the Newfoundland Fishermen, Food and Allied Workers' Union (FFAW), had occasionally delayed the fishing season and caused lost revenue for harvesters and processors alike. Beginning in 1998, both parties agreed to a task-force-recommended final offer selection process; in the event an agreement could not be reached, an arbitrator would determine a minimum price. In June 1999, an arbitrator was required to establish capelin prices and to establish and renegotiate shrimp prices in August 1999 and March 2000.

Market and economic conditions ultimately drive the market price of raw material. Driven by supply and demand, global market prices drive what processors will pay for raw material or processed product. For example, in the United Kingdom (where 46 per cent of worldwide cooked and peeled shrimp is consumed), shrimp prices declined between 1996 and 2000. In addition, foreign exchange rate fluctuations, oil price increases and even natural disasters can affect the cost of raw material. Protective economic barriers, such as tariffs, add costs and reduce margins and, therefore, influence the prices producers will pay to harvesters. Fluctuations in the Canadian dollar versus the U.S. dollar also affect prices foreign buyers are willing to pay to Canadian processors, though in recent years, the Canadian-U.S. dollar exchange rate has strengthened seafood exports, adding flexibility to the prices that processors are willing to pay for fish.

Seasonal variations in yields and the level of buying competition also affect prices. During summer months, shrimp yields decline as they become softer and harder to peel, effectively raising raw-material-per-pound or finished-product costs. Icelandic and Greenland companies were competing with FPI for Newfoundland shrimp supply, and this higher competition helped to raise shrimp prices. To avoid losing relationships with fishermen for species such as crab, processors invested Cdn$110 million in Newfoundland shrimp processing facilities.

While the negotiated prices were "minimums," a shift in market prices might cause individual processors and harvesters to negotiate pricing arrangements above this minimum. The effects of competition, economic conditions and other market volatilities made it virtually impossible to accurately predict annual raw material costs from year to year.

INDUSTRY CONSOLIDATION

Industry mergers and consolidations increased as companies attempted to leverage the benefits of technology and the Internet. The fishing industry was highly competitive, and industry margins were historically tight. Consequently, firms were looking to merge with or acquire other seafood companies. In mid-1999, a New Zealand firm, SIF Ltd., participated in several mergers and acquisitions, notably a merger with a major Icelandic seafood player, Iceland Seafood International. In late 1999, NEOS Seafoods Inc. (NEOS), a newly formed consortium of three companies from Newfoundland, Nova Scotia and Iceland, attempted an unsuccessful takeover bid for FPI Limited, which would have created a significant global industry player and U.S. supplier. On May 6, 2000, Icelandic Freezing Plants Corporation (IFPC) Plc., one of the companies that attempted the takeover, purchased 14.6 per cent of FPI's shares, citing an interest in FPI's U.S. market presence. The FPI Act ownership restrictions prohibited an individual shareowner from owning more than 15 per cent of FPI's outstanding common voting shares, and shareholders could not act together to acquire FPI. IFPC had also bought five per cent of each of High Liner Foods in Nova Scotia and Pescanova S.A. in Spain. To gain a stronger foothold in Europe's frozen flatfish market in the United Kingdom, IFPC purchased Árnes Europe, a subsidiary of the Icelandic fish and processing firm Árnes. Canadian firm High Liner Foods diversified its holdings into non-seafood products by acquiring Italian Village, a pasta products operation.

Business-to-business commerce on the Internet was generating substantial interest as companies could bring buyers and sellers together and automate transactions. In 2000, FPI, with eight players in the seafood market, announced the formation of "SeafoodAlliance.com." The participating companies hoped the "vertical portal" would help reduce transaction and processing costs in the seafood industry and enhance the development of individual e-commerce strategies. In addition to Sanford Limited, Scandsea and Young's Bluecrest Seafood Limited, which joined in July 2000, the group included Pacific Seafood Group, American Seafoods Inc., SIF Group, Pacific Trawlers/ Crystal Seafoods Inc., Clearwater Fine Foods Inc., Coldwater Seafoods (a subsidiary of IFPC), the Barry Group of Companies, High Liner Foods Inc. and FPI. These major seafood competitors operated globally and were headquartered in Canada, the United States, Iceland and New Zealand.

COMPETITION

Seafood Products

In addition to raw material competition, FPI faced direct product competition from other seafood products and seafood brands. Significant competitors were established companies offering full product lines of groundfish and shellfish and serving many or all levels of the food service industry, including food service, industrial and retail. Alternatively, some served many segments but also targeted niche markets. Branding was important, and seafood companies generally distributed and marketed their own recognized brands. All maintained rigorous quality standards, frequently citing their adherence to the Hazard Analysis Critical Control Point (HACCP) systems. Originally developed by the Pillsbury Company to provide safe food for American astronauts, the HACCP systems integrated inspecting food production at different levels of processing (rather than simply at the end product) and were designed to improve quality output.

Because many seafood competitors were privately held, availability of comparative financial information was limited. Several of FPI's competitors were involved in the e-commerce alliance: U.S.-based American Seafoods Group (ASG), Frionor (an ASG Company), Pacific Seafood Group and the Canadian-based firms Clearwater and the Barry Group. These firms offered complete lines of seafood products that included primary-processed and valued-added products. Value-added products included primary-processed seafood products that had been further processed through the addition of non-seafood products such as batter, stuffings and sauces. Frionor ("Frozen of the North"), an established Norwegian-based firm owned by privately held American Seafoods Group, produced frozen fish fillets, as well as value-added products (from pollock and other groundfish), such as Tortilla Crunch, marketed under the brand name, Ocean Cuts & Crunch.

Publicly held competitors included High Liner Foods Inc., Sanford Limited, SIF Limited,

and Icelandic Freezing Plants Corporation (IFPC) Plc (see Exhibit 2). The Sanford group was vertically integrated, both harvesting and processing a wide range of seafood products with its primary fillet products coming from whitefish species, such as hoki. New Zealand's

Firm[1]	FPI Ltd.	High Liner Foods Inc.	Sanford Limited	SIF Limited	IFPC Plc.
Headquartered	Canada	Canada	New Zealand	Iceland	Iceland
Revenue	708,911	302,392	265,555	675,982	760,125
Net Income	10,026	(4,067)	40,740	850	(3,731)
Total Assets	314,412	219,901	297,979	436,903	381,425
Current Ratio	3.32	1.68	1.25	1.14	1.14
Cost of Goods Sold/Revenue	0.89	0.74	Not Published	0.89	0.87
ROE (After Taxes)	6.14%	(0.06)%	18.4%	0.01%	(6.28)%
ROE (Before Taxes)	9.00%	(0.05)%	22.0%	N/A[2]	N/A[3]
Earnings per Share	0.66	(0.56)	0.41	0.03	(0.12)
Ownership/ Shareholders	Maximum of 15% of shares per shareholder	No restrictions (2 shareholders own in aggregate over 50%)[4]	2547 shareholders; no maximum evident (1 shareholder has 37%)	1964 shareholders; maximum of 10% of shares/ shareholder	N/A
Subsidiaries & Associates	4	3	18	23	6
Number of Employees	3,000	1,500	1,300[5]	1,700	1,300

Exhibit 2   FPI Competitors

Note:
All figures in Canadian dollars with Sanford, SIF and IFPC foreign exchange conversions using nominal rate as of January 1, 2000. With the exception of Notes 4 and 5, all data are from corporate Web sites. Web sites are: www.fpil.com; www.high linerfoods.com; www.sanford.co.nz; www.sif.is; www.icelandic.is.

1. All figures shown are on a consolidated basis for 1999.
2. SIF experienced an operating loss; i.e., net income before financial items was Cdn$1,916, but SIF was able to show net income due primarily to the gain on asset sales and income tax carry-forwards.
3. Write-offs, e.g., sale of Russian operations.
4. C. Milton, corporate secretary and treasurer, High Liner Foods Inc., e-mail communication, July 26, 2000.
5. E. Barratt, director, Sanford Ltd., e-mail communication, July 25, 2000.

largest aquaculture company, Sanford, exported primarily to Europe (31 per cent of sales) followed by North and South America (23 per cent). The company credited success in the U.S. market to its consistent quality and supply.

Headquartered in Iceland and with 10 subsidiaries, IFPC Plc., a global, vertically integrated firm, offered more than 40 species primarily harvested near Iceland. Primary customers included large supermarkets, distributors, wholesalers, and restaurants and food processors in Europe, United States and Asia. Committed to customer-centered product development, the company sold whole frozen fish, fillets and fillet portions, shellfish and a wide variety of convenience products.

Canadian-based High Liner Foods Inc. (formerly National Sea Products) was the largest Atlantic Canadian supplier of fresh groundfish to the U.S. market. It processed and marketed seafood and frozen pasta products under High Liner® and other brands and was strongly positioned in the retail frozen seafood market. The company operated in Newfoundland, Ontario and the United States and employed 1,500 people. Like FPI, it was vertically integrated, harvesting about 11,000 tonnes of seafood each year from Nova Scotia to Labrador. Though the company's processing facilities, featuring flow line technology, operated at about 41 per cent capacity, High Liner procured most of its raw material internationally.

Non-seafood Products

Non-seafood products that were typical alternatives to seafood also affected seafood consumption. In 1999, the per capita consumption of value-added seafood dropped from 1998, due to competition from lower-priced poultry and pasta. Rising seafood costs were partially passed on to the end-consumer, making seafood products less competitive with their substitute products, poultry and pasta. Rising costs led FPI to increase prices in 1998 and 1999, though it managed to minimize the price increases and maintain market position.

Despite price increases, worldwide per capita consumption of seafood products continued to grow, indicating seafood was becoming a dietary choice. In addition to being low in fat, cholesterol and calories, seafood was high in protein, easily digested and provided an excellent source of polyunsaturated fats and omega-3 fatty acids (believed to actively combat cholesterol buildup and reduce the risk of heart disease). As well, with an increase of disposable incomes worldwide, consumers had greater purchasing ability for more expensive seafood products. In Europe, there was concern that changes to the European Community's Common Agricultural Policy would reduce livestock production costs and lower the price of poultry and pork, making seafood exports to Europe less competitive.

FPI LTD.

Products and Marketing

To compete in its key markets, FPI maintained sales offices in Canada (St. John's, Montreal, Toronto, Calgary and Vancouver), the United States (Danvers, Massachusetts and Seattle, Washington), Reading, England and Cuxhavin, Germany and a brokerage and distribution network throughout North America and Europe (see Exhibit 3). Integrated information systems connected employees around the world (e.g., sales staff could log on to the company's intranet site to gather product nutritional and ingredient information).

FPI produced and marketed primary- and secondary-processed seafood products, including cold-water shrimp, snow crab, sea scallops, cod, flounder, sole, redfish, pollock, Greenland halibut, haddock and capelin. It also marketed and earned commission income on black tiger and warm-water farmed shrimp, king crab, farmed scallops, North Atlantic lobster, salmon and sea bass, sourcing these products from North America, Southeast Asia, South America and Europe. FPI was also the exclusive distributor of crab products from Atlantic Queen Seafood,

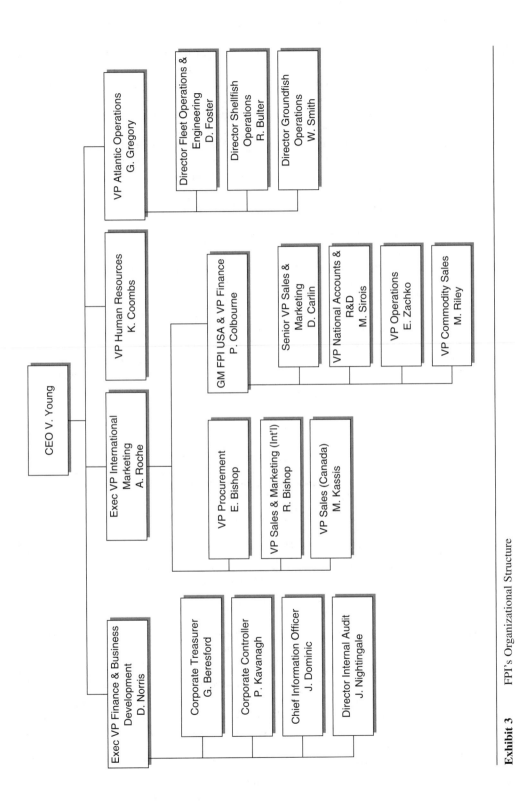

Exhibit 3   FPI's Organizational Structure

Source: P. Kavanagh, "Personal Communication and E-mail Communication," May–August 2000.

33

based in Atlantic Canada and Quebec. Exhibit 4 details FPI's product range.

FPI sold primarily to wholesale and food-service markets, including family restaurants, airline caterers, warehouse clubs and major grocery chains. It was the leading supplier of seafood to the North American foodservice market and Canada's private label retail sector (e.g., President's Choice), and was a leading supplier in marketing cold-water shrimp and snow crab in Europe, North America and Asia. With three-quarters of its value-added groundfish and shrimp products going to the North American foodservice market (mainly in the United States), the remaining 25 per cent was bought by the retail and club store industry sectors in the United States, Canada and Switzerland. In 2000, Switzerland was the only tariff-free European country for Canadian seafood exports.

FPI had been regularly recognized by industry associations and independent trade associations for its sales and marketing excellence. In 1999, FPI received several supplier awards from North America's largest independent foodservice distributor, several national restaurant chains and North America's largest retail chain, U.S.-based supermarket grocery retailer Kroger Company. The company's product innovation was maintained by full-time food scientists and food technologists.

FPI had developed a strong reputation for quality and brand leadership through new primary products, such as FPI ice shrimp and the reintroduced FPI flounder. Customers requested FPI by name, reflecting a commitment to brand loyalty. To fully incorporate customers' needs into product design, FPI's development staff would often act as an "extension" of the customer menu development department, combining efforts to generate new process concepts and value-added products, such as Italian Style Mussels and Thaw'n Eat Seafood Medley. Such value-added products typically generated more than 15 per cent of sales.

A challenge for all large seafood companies was that large customers, such as McDonald's, Price Club and Red Lobster demanded top quality and excellent service and competitive pricing.

Brand	Products	Producer
FPI (e.g., FPI Ice Shrimp, Thaw 'n Eat Seafood Medley)	North American groundfish (flounder, redfish, cod) and shellfish (cold-water shrimp, crab, scallops)	FPI
Mirabel (e.g., Catch of the Day family of shellfish)	Premium, specialty products; easy to serve and versatile.	FPI
Luxury, Atlantic Queen and Classic	3 "quality lines of shellfish" from Atlantic Queen: snow crab, rock crab, Atlantic crab	Atlantic Queen Seafoods
Clear Springs Idaho Rainbow Trout	Rainbow trout	Clear Springs
Freshwater Fish	Whitefish fillets, white fish, pickerel fillets, dressed lake trout, northern pike fillets, dressed tullibee	Freshwater Fish Marketing Corporation
Acadian Supreme	Atlantic lobster—boiled and tinned meat	Acadian Fisherman's Co-op
Hillman	Oysters	Hillman Oyster Co.

Exhibit 4   FPI's Product Range

Source: www.fpil.com/Canada/brand.htm, May 15, 2000.

While customers tended to be flexible regarding price (if they were assured of a stable, quality supply), there was a price point beyond which buyers would switch either to other seafood companies, to other seafood products or to substitute products, such as chicken and pork.

OPERATIONS

FPI harvested, procured, produced and marketed seafood through three operations: primary processing, value-added processing and seafood trading. Primary processing included sourcing and processing groundfish (such as cod, flounder, and turbot) and shellfish (such as cold-water shrimp, snow crab and sea scallops) into either ready-to-market products or further value-added products. All primary processing was done in Atlantic Canada through nine processing plants. One issue for FPI was how to use its extra capacity. For example, could the batter currently being used on fish be effectively used on other products, such as chicken, and be produced in one of the state-of-the-art plants that operated only part of the year?

Value-added or secondary processing involved sourcing, processing and marketing groundfish, shrimp and other shellfish. In other words, FPI increased the value of the primary-processed products by adding non-seafood ingredients such as batter, stuffings and sauces. FPI's value-added processing plant in Burin, Newfoundland, served its Canadian market while its plant in Danvers, Massachusetts, served the U.S. market. The company's seafood trading business involved brokering internationally sourced seafood products: warm-water shrimp, representing about 60 per cent of seafood trading sales in 1999; and king crab, lobster, scallops, salmon, sea bass, cold-water shrimp and other shellfish and groundfish accounting for, at most, eight per cent of trading sales in 1999. A challenge for FPI's operations was to increase the current level of integration between the operations group, which was cost-driven and the marketing group, which was revenue-driven. Through greater integration,

plants that were treated as cost centers might be able to operate as profit-driven centers. In 2000, the plants appeared to be given little, if any, information on the revenue-generating effect of what they produced.

QUALITY ASSURANCE

FPI's strong reputation for quality seafood products was the result of quality assurance practices and processing facilities that continually met or exceeded the regulatory requirements of the Canadian Food Inspection Agency (CFIA). In addition, FPI was periodically audited by the CFIA, the U.S. Food and Drug Administration, the U.S. Department of Commerce and, of course, its customers. FPI's quality management programs were based on the principles of HACCP. Many importers, such as U.S. companies, accepted seafood products only from foreign suppliers using an HACCP system.

PROCUREMENT

In addition to using 12 groundfish vessels, five sea scallop vessels and one shrimp vessel to harvest seafood species off Newfoundland and Nova Scotia and purchasing raw material from more than 3,000 independent Newfoundland fishers, FPI procured more than 25 seafood species in over 30 countries. Vertically integrated, FPI could reduce volatility in raw material costs and secure a certain volume of supply; however, environmental or natural conditions were beyond its control. In the past, ice conditions off the coast of Newfoundland and Labrador had delayed the fishery season. Furthermore, quotas restricted FPI's catch. As in many industrialized countries, Canada's fisheries were managed under a quota system, where quota licences provided harvesters with a "quasi-property right" to harvest certain quantities of fish. Processing licences were also required for each species. Since the government relaxed a freeze on crab processing licenses in 1996, the number of licences had increased from 19 to 36, all owned by 16 different companies. Although a company purchased a licence, it could choose not to use it if supply was not available or if processing was not economically viable.

Primary-processed shellfish had become an increasingly important business for FPI. Cold-water shrimp resources off Newfoundland were the world's largest, and the DFO controlled the total allowable catch (TAC) of cold-water shrimp. Since 1995, the TAC for shrimp off the northeast coast of Newfoundland and southern Labrador had increased by 166 per cent to 108,300 tonnes. This was divided between the inshore (small vessel) and offshore fisheries, with the inshore harvesters' quota having increased from 3,500 tonnes in 1996 to 47,400 tonnes in 1999. The Newfoundland government required that all of the inshore catch be processed ("cooked and peeled") in the province.

FPI obtained cold-water shrimp from two main sources: purchases from independent inshore harvesters and frozen-at-sea landings from its fishing vessel, the Newfoundland Otter. FPI was Newfoundland's largest cold-water shrimp processing company. Its 1999 supply was 16,100 tonnes, of which the NF Otter harvested 4,700 tonnes; more than 80 per cent was produced in "shell-on market-ready form" for European and Asian customers while the remainder was processed at two FPI plants. In 2000, FPI's total supply of shrimp was expected to be nearly 18,000 tonnes. By offering competitive prices and service, FPI purchased 9,300 tonnes of snow crab in 1999. While the TAC for snow crab had increased by 95 per cent since 1995, quotas were expected to decrease in 2000, due to recommendations based on scientific data. FPI's main competitive region for snow crab was Alaska, and market prices were expected to remain constant.

Meanwhile, sea scallops were sourced off Nova Scotia using five offshore vessels. In 1999, FPI was awarded 17 per cent of the 5,350 TAC. Due to an increase in sea scallop resources, FPI's quota was expected to increase by 20 per cent, and market prices were expected to drop in the United States, Canada and Europe.

Groundfish, including cod, greysole and yellowtail flounder, came from FPI's offshore groundfish fleet and independent inshore fishers. The government had slowly increased cod quotas since the early 1990s, but some scientists indicated that stocks were not rebuilding and recommended quota reductions.

TEAMWORK AND INNOVATION

FPI employed 3,400 people worldwide, with 3,000 in Atlantic Canada. The company credited its successes to employee commitment and teamwork, particularly through challenging industry times. The company had co-packing arrangements in shrimp processing plants in Thailand, Ecuador, Indonesia and Mexico; at fish processing facilities in Norway and Chile; and at aquaculture farms and secondary-processing plants in China. The company had sales offices the United States, Europe and Canada. There was low turnover among staff and executive management, reflecting FPI's commitment to employees. During an attempted takeover bid in November 1999, the company regularly advertised in local newspapers to publicly praise employees' work and dedication. In 1997, FPI appointed its first female plant manager, Angela Bugden, at its scallop harvesting operation in Riverport, Nova Scotia. Bugden was also responsible for the five scallop trawlers and the refit yard for the trawlers. Since 1997, FPI had also invested in teamwork training for the plant management teams at its two state-of-the-art shrimp plants in partnership with the Centre for Management Development at Memorial University of Newfoundland. FPI had to contend with the close relationships among members of the plant management team, plant employees and the fishers who supplied the plants. Such interpersonal relationships negated the sharing of sensitive cost information with outsiders, in turn, preventing the information from being used in subsequent negotiations between FPI and the employees' unions and between FPI and the fishers' association.

Trawler workers, plant workers and fishers were unionized through the Fishermen, Food and Allied Workers (FFAW) or the Canadian Auto Workers (CAW). The company enjoyed a positive relationship with its employees and the communities in which it operated as well as with union representatives; this relationship was particularly evident during the takeover bid, largely due to Young, whose negotiating abilities extended beyond his company's doors. As a special mediator for a 1994 labor dispute between Newfoundland teachers and the provincial government, Young was credited with preventing a bitter strike.

FPI also remained committed to sustainable resource management. Its environmental monitoring committee's operational practices ensured regulatory compliance and sound environmental policies. As well, the company had partnered with the Marine Institute at Memorial University of Newfoundland to research and develop leading and sustainable harvesting processes, and with Memorial University to research oceanography and fish conservation. FPI had also worked with the DFO to gather scientific resource data for more accurate allocation of quotas. In 1999, the company pioneered the use of groundfish seining technology, reducing unwanted by-catches and unwanted contact with the ocean floor.

INNOVATION AND ENVIRONMENTAL AWARENESS

FPI believed in "quality, honesty, teamwork and innovation" and continually invested in its primary- and secondary-processing operations to remain competitive, having invested more than Cdn$65 million since 1995. Spending Cdn$11 million to convert a groundfish plant and Cdn$6 million for new flow line processing technology in its largest primary-processing facility, FPI had two state-of-the-art shrimp plants and a world-class primary-processing facility. It had made significant investments in new technologies such as automated weighing, packaging and freezing technologies that had improved efficiency in its two value-added plants. These investments were considered vital to remaining competitive and meeting customers' changing needs.

PERFORMANCE

In the early 1990s, the company struggled through severe industry supply shortages and recorded provisions of Cdn$65 million and Cdn$20 million in 1992 and 1993 respectively. With the exception of losses in 1995 (due to lower groundfish and scallop quotas, a drop in crab prices, and poor U.S. and Mexico market conditions), profitability had slowly improved. From 1995 to 2000, operating and net margins remained relatively stable, and income per share had slowly climbed (see Exhibit 5). Despite a special charge of nearly Cdn$1 million related to the takeover bid, the company recorded a 1999 profit of Cdn$10 million (Appendix A), and, for the first time in 11 years, paid shareholders a dividend.

	1999	1998	1997	1996	1995
Weighted net income per share	0.66	0.55	0.51	0.37	−0.20
Operating margin	11.16%	10.19%	9.66%	9.30%	8.29%
Net margin	1.41%	1.24%	1.21%	.92%	−.51%

Exhibit 5   Net Income Per Share, Operating Margins, and Profit Margins 1995 to 1999

Source: FPI Ltd. (1994–1999) Annual Reports.

In the next few years, FPI had shifted its focus from sales to margin growth, and these higher margins led to a Cdn$9 million increase in gross profit, and a gross margin increase of nearly one per cent. Both Canadian and U.S. earnings have generally trended up. There was a significant drop in U.S. sales in 1998 when FPI focused on margins rather than sales volume, as warm-water-traded shrimp margins were relatively low and extremely volatile.

Canadian domestic sales grew 19 per cent from 1995 to 2000, reflecting increased crab quotas and production. Over the same period, U.S. domestic sales rose less than 2.5 per cent, attributed to intense competition from lower-priced poultry and pasta products. See Exhibit 6 for sales information segmented by line of business and dating back to 1996, when the company began capturing and publicizing this data. An increase in both the value-added and primary-processing lines reflected stable groundfish sales and a significant growth in shellfish sales, which had more than doubled since 1996. Sales of primary seafood products such as cold-water shrimp, snow crab and sea scallops increased

more than 23 per cent to Cdn$217 million in 1999. Primary groundfish sales also increased more than Cdn$8 million in 1999, mostly because more groundfish was sourced domestically than internationally. Commission sales on shellfish declined by nearly eight per cent over the four-year period.

Financial ratios were generally comparable with industry averages or slightly below industry averages, with debt and liquidity levels remaining strong (Appendix B and Exhibit 7). Like other local seafood companies, FPI financed independent harvesters and secured these by mortgages over vessels. Credit risk was minimized as FPI's 10 major customers contributed less than 30 per cent to sales, and no single customer contributed more than six per cent. In 1999, the majority of FPI's combined sales were denominated in U.S. dollars, exposing the company to the impact of the weaker Canadian dollar. FPI maintained natural hedges through operating, costing and borrowing in U.S. dollars as well as through foreign exchange hedging practices. FPI remained firm, stating that "Fishery Products International is

		1999		1998		1997		1996	
Primary Processing		%		%		%		%	
	Groundfish	$69,883	9.9	61,667	9.0	58,170	8.6	64,949	9.8
	Shellfish	142,078	20.0	105,375	15.5	72,619	10.7	68,098	10.2
	Other	5,145	0.7	9,102	1.3	8,664	1.3	11,119	1.7
		217,056	30.6	176,144	25.8	139,453	20.6	144,166	21.7
Value-added Processing									
	Groundfish	170,822	24.1	160,019	23.5	147,088	21.8	135,862	20.4
	Shellfish	53,641	7.6	58,487	8.6	57,724	8.5	47,844	7.2
		224,463	31.7	218,506	32.1	204,812	30.3	183,706	27.6
Seafood Trading									
	Shellfish	200,728	28.3	210,623	30.9	260,851	38.6	236,871	35.6
	Other	66,664	9.4	76,290	11.2	70,828	10.5	99,884	15.0
		267,392	37.7	286,913	42.1	331,679	49.1	336,755	50.6
Total Sales		$708,911	100.0	681,563	100.00	675,944	100.00	664,627	100.00

Exhibit 6   Segmented Sales Information (In Cdn$000s)

Source: Data from FPI Annual Financial Statements, 1996–1999.

Ratio	FPI (%)	Fish and Seafoods Industry (%)	Prepared Fish or Frozen Fish and Seafoods Industry (%)
Gross Margin	10.69%	17.30%	11.00%
Profit Before Taxes[2]	1.99%	2.60%	1.80%
Current Ratio	2.32%	1.30%	—
ROA Before Taxes	4.49%	5.30%	4.10%
ROE Before Taxes	8.65%	—	21.70%

Exhibit 7   Comparative FPI and Industry Financial Ratios[1]

Source: Statistics taken from "Manufacturing—Prepared Fresh or Frozen Fish and Seafoods; Wholesale—Fish and Seafoods," Robert Morris and Associates (RMA) Guide, 1999.

1. Canada, the United States and Mexico have adopted the North American Industry Classification System (NAICS) for industry product classifications; however, historical financial data is available only under SIC/ISC codes. SIC codes 5146 (Fish and Seafoods) and 2092 (Prepared Fresh or Frozen Fish & Seafoods) compare with FPI's NAICS code, 31170.

2. Data are for companies with US$25 million and over in revenue.

committed to maximizing long-term shareholder value."

Over all, share prices had declined since the company's initial public offering in April 1987, ranging from Cdn$5 to Cdn$7 from 1995 to 2000, with the exception of a price increase during late 1999 because of the hostile takeover bid by NEOS. Daily trading volume was comparatively low, ranging from approximately 61 to 1,500 trades versus 20,000 to 200,000 for Nortel; however, this did not appear to influence share price. Although EPS has increased each year since 1996 from Cdn$0.37 in 1996 to Cdn$0.66 in 1999, the Total Return Index Values chart (see Exhibit 8) demonstrates that FPI has not afforded shareholders the same return as other food processing companies or the equities market.

Stern Stewart offers an alternative method of corporate valuation through "market value added" or MVA. The greater a company's MVA, the higher its ranking versus other firms across industries. Nortel Networks Corporation has maintained strong and consistent rankings and created value for its investors while FPI has not

(see Exhibit 9 and Appendix C). Additionally, both FPI's and High Liner's rankings have dropped since 1989. However, as can be seen in Appendix C, costs of funds for both firms have decreased significantly since the early 1990s.

Ownership

The Takeover Bid

On November 5, 1999, FPI announced it was the target of an unsolicited takeover bid. NEOS offered Cdn$9 per share to acquire 100 per cent of FPI's 16 million outstanding shares. This bid was subject to the provincial government and FPI's shareholders approving removal of the 15 per cent ownership restriction. CEO Vic Young promptly responded that the offer was below book value of Cdn$10.75 and "extremely low." He pointed out that the FPI Act required any successful bid on FPI to have approval from FPI's shareholders and the provincial government to lift this restriction. The 15 per cent shareholder restriction was known as a "poison pill" and made a significant equity purchase of FPI impossible.

Quarterly Share Price (March, June, Sept., Dec.)

Source: Data taken from the TSE Review, Toronto Stock Exchange, 1987 to 2000, July 20, 2000.

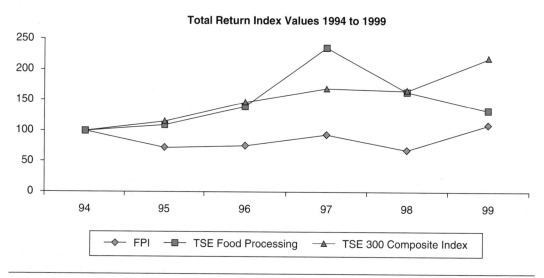

Total Return Index Values 1994 to 1999

Exhibit 8   Quarterly Share Price 1987 to 2000

Source: BMO Investorline 2000b, bmoinvestorline.com/QuotesCharts, July 5, 2000.

Having set the 15 per cent ownership cap during FPI's conversion from a crown to a public corporation in 1987, the government stated it would not lift this restriction unless the takeover group could show how it could add value to Newfoundland's economy versus FPI's shareholders, in particular. The government indicated it would consider lifting the restriction, given a "deal specific" acquisition or merger opportunity that was, in FPI's point of

MVA Ranking	1998	1997	1989	MVA 1998	EVA 1998	Operating–Capital year end	Return on Operating Capital	Cost of Capital
Nortel Networks	1	1	6	23,369,461	156,402	30,306,396	12.3	11.7
FPI Ltd.	251	270	189	−133,365	−8,967	361,549	4.3	6.9
High Liner Foods	202	253	85	−26,933	255	281,468	7.0	6.8

Exhibit 9   Comparative MVA Data for Nortel, FPI and High Liner Foods

Source: Richard Grizzetti, e-mail communication and www.sternstewart.com, July 2, July 28, 2000.

view, in the best interest of both its shareholders and the province.

During November and December 1999, FPI and NEOS appealed to shareholders, the public and other stakeholders. To alleviate employee concern, FPI ran ads in Newfoundland newspapers praising employees' commitment. NEOS ran its own ads highlighting its intention for the new private company. The two unions and several municipalities opposed the takeover and urged the government to maintain the ownership cap. Both the FFAW and CAW cited a positive labor relations climate at FPI as a primary reason for objecting to NEOS's bid, expressed concern about a concentration of fish-buying power and questioned NEOS's promises. FPI also began exploring other options, including an alternative bid from a "friendly partner." A few weeks after the initial bid, the government announced it would not remove the ownership restriction, and NEOS withdrew its offer.

FPI later stated that the two arguments against removing the restriction—concentration of fish-buying power and negative community response—were no longer relevant. It supported lifting the restriction in order to develop international alliances and partnerships, which otherwise could not be accomplished. FPI also felt there were enough dual-level government restrictions, making ownership restrictions unnecessary. If FPI could not grow through international partnerships, it might become unable to compete with larger firms.

Institutional Ownership

Canadian fishing companies were subject to foreign ownership restrictions and required majority-ownership by Canadian interests; U.S. companies faced similar foreign ownership restrictions. Unlike FPI, some competitor seafood companies were majority-owned by one or two investors. As well, institutional investors were the primary investors in many seafood companies. For example, ASG was controlled by an investment firm, one shareholder owned 37 per cent of Sanford Ltd. and two corporate investors owned the majority of High Liner's shares.

Occasionally, institutional owners had exerted pressure on a company's board when they disagreed with board decisions (e.g., in 1999, investors questioned an executive compensation scheme at Canadian pulp and paper firm, Repap Inc.) As of December 31, 1999, two-thirds of FPI's shares, including mutual funds and pension funds, were controlled by institutional investors who had the potential to exert pressure on the board. During the takeover attempt, institutional investors holding more than 50 per cent of FPI's shares requested FPI hold a timely meeting to evaluate NEOS's proposal. Many also lobbied the government to remove ownership restrictions.

An interesting issue for Young and his senior management team was that this share ownership had dramatically changed by July 2000. Sanford still owned 14.7 per cent, Hamblin Watsa owned 14.6 per cent and the Ontario Municipal Employees Retirement Fund still owned 11 per cent. Two new major shareholders were IFPC (an Icelandic seafood company) and Clearwater (a Canadian seafood company), both partners with the Barry Group in the unsuccessful takeover bid in November 1999.

LEADERSHIP AND GOVERNANCE

In 1984, Young became chairman and CEO of Fishery Products International. He was not expected to retire any time soon; however, it was not immediately evident who might replace Young or whether that person would possess Young's ability to build a strong culture and team commitment.

As chairman, CEO and president, Young was the only management member on FPI's board of directors. The chairperson of the human resources committee functioned as the lead director, overseeing the relationship between the board and senior management. At each meeting, the board held discussions without the CEO in attendance. It was not unusual for senior management to attend board meetings to present business information.

Board membership was fairly stable with a good mix of long-term members and newer members. Of the 11 unrelated members of the board, seven were from Newfoundland, three

were from Ontario and one was from New Brunswick. Two new directors were elected to the board in 1999. Appendix D presents a detailed summary of the current board.

The Future

Young believed FPI needed to focus on growing shareholder value. To do this, he believed in motivating employees to embrace the concept of growing shareholder value and "energizing" them to "make it happen."

FPI was focused on growing its EPS and restoring shareholder value by using key traditional groundfish, value-added and seafood trading operations, along with increasing shellfish operations. Young also hoped to grow through international alliances, mergers and acquisitions. The question now facing Young: how exactly should FPI increase shareholder value?

NOTES

1. This case has been written on the basis of published sources only. Consequently, the interpretation and perspectives presented in this case are not necessarily those of Fishery Products international Ltd. or any of its employees.

2. Founded in 1979, NAFO comprises 18 countries including Canada, United States, the European Union, Cuba, Korea, Denmark, France (St. Pierre and Miquelon), the Russian Federation, Iceland and Norway. Its goal is to guide management and to conserve fishery resources in the northwest Atlantic within the 200-mile limit (NAFO Convention). A map of this area is available at www.nafo.ca/imap/map.

APPENDIX A: FISHERY PRODUCTS INTERNATIONAL LTD.,
CONSOLIDATED FINANCIAL DATA (FOR YEARS ENDING DECEMBER 31) (IN CDN$000S)

	1999	1998	1997	1996	1995
Sales	$ 708,911	681,563	675,945	664,598	643,009
COGS	633,124	614,467	613,617	606,473	593,096
Gross Profit	75,787	67,096	62,328	58,125	49,913
Commission Income	3,327	2,382	2,968	3,665	3,394
Operating Income	79,114	69,478	65,296	61,790	53,307
Administration and Marketing	45,456	42,152	39,963	39,865	39,711
Depreciation and Amortization	9,883	8,967	8,656	7,872	8,484
Profit sharing	1,541	1,088	1,063	840	
Interest	7,146	7,467	5,890	5,669	8,242
	64,026	59,674	55,572	54,246	56,437
Operating Income before undernoted	**15,088**	**9,804**	**9,724**	**7,544**	**(3,130)**
Exchange Gain					
Gain (loss) on disposal of PP&E				21	438
Equity in loss of joint venture					
Unusual item(s)	(965)				
Net income before taxes	**$14,123**	**9,804**	**9,724**	**7,565**	**(2,692)**
Income taxes	$4,097	1,378	1,531	1,455	587
Net Income	**$10,026**	**8,426**	**8,193**	**6,110**	**(3,279)**
Weighted net income per share	0.66	0.55	0.51	0.37	(0.20)
Gross Margin	10.69%	9.84%	9.22%	8.75%	7.76%
Operating margin	11.16%	10.19%	9.66%	9.30%	8.29%
Net margin	1.41%	1.24%	1.21%	0.92%	−0.51%

Source: 1995 to 1999 Annual Reports.

APPENDIX B: FISHERY PRODUCTS INTERNATIONAL LTD.,
CONSOLIDATED BALANCE SHEET AT DECEMBER 31, 1999 (IN CDN$000S)

Assets	
Current Assets	
Cash	$916
Accounts Receivable	80,664
Inventories	119,471
Prepaids	5,637
Total Current Assets	206,688
Property Plant and Equipment	93,677
Other Assets	14,057
Total Assets	**314,402**
Liabilities and Shareholders' Equity	
Current Liabilities	
Bank Indebtedness	43,124
Accounts payable & accrued liabilities	37,252
CP LTD	8,351
Total CL	88,727
LTD	62,323
	151,050
Shareholder's Equity	
Share Capital	48,044
Contributed Surplus	75,083
Retained earnings	41,535
Foreign Currency Translation Adj.	(1,310)
Total Equity	163,352
Total Liabilities and Shareholders' Equity	**$314,402**

Appendix C: 2000 Stern Stewart MVA Ranking Information, Fishery Products International Ltd. and High Liner Foods (in Cdn$000s)

MVA	1999	1998	1997	1996	1995
FPI Ltd	(98,526)	(130,317)	(93,338)	(105,870)	(103,387)
High Liner Foods	(70,809)	(18,434)	(24,250)	(38,591)	(45,074)
Stock Market Value					
FPI Ltd	245,220	229,117	249,901	195,309	191,083
High Liner Foods	177,205	254,894	173,552	157,001	154,602
Operating Capital Year-End					
FPI Ltd	342,830	358,502	337,630	296,198	289,010
High Liner Foods	240,540	272,969	191,235	195,321	197,870
EVA					
FPI Ltd	(5,465)	(8,745)	(9,455)	(16,262)	(30,764)
High Liner Foods	(20,456)	499	(2,932)	(7,842)	(8,388)
Return On Operating Capital (r)					
FPI Ltd	4.9%	4.3%	4.5%	3.7%	0.5%
High Liner Foods	−1.0%	7.2%	6.1%	3.9%	4.1%
Cost of Capital (C*)					
FPI Ltd	6.5%	6.9%	7.7%	9.3%	11.5%
High Liner Foods	6.5%	7.0%	7.6%	7.9%	8.4%

Source: Richard Grizzetti, e-mail communication, www.sternstewart.com, July 2 and 28, 2000.

APPENDIX D: FISHERY PRODUCTS INTERNATIONAL LTD., BOARD OF DIRECTORS

James C. Ballie	1992 – present	Partner, Tory, Tory, DesLauriers & Binnington, Toronto, ON
R. William Blake, PhD	1999 – present	Dean, Faculty of Business Administration, Memorial University of Newfoundland, St. John's, NF
Bruce C. Galloway	1999 – present	Company Director, Oakville, ON
Janet C. Gardiner	1987 – present	Treasurer, Chester Dawe, Ltd., St. John's, NF
Michael F. Harrington	1998 – present	Senior Partner, Stewart McKelvey Stirling Scales, St. John's, NF
Albert F. Hickman	1984 – present	President, Hickman Motors Ltd., St. John's, NF
Thomas E. Kierans	1990 – present	Chairman & CEO, Canadian Institute for Advanced Research, Toronto, ON
Rev. Desmond T. McGrath	1987 – present	Education Officer, Fish, Food & Allied Workers, St. John's, NF
Frances M. Nichols, FCA	1991 – present	Chartered Accountant, Grand Falls-Windsor, NF
Elizabeth Parr-Johnston, PhD	1994 – present	President & Vice-Chancellor, University of New Brunswick, Fredericton, NB
Vincent G. Withers	1995 – present	Company Director, St. John's, NF
Victor L. Young	1984 – present	Chairman & CEO, Fishery Products International Ltd., St. John's, NF

Committees of the Board of Directors		
Audit	**Growth & Diversification**	**Human Resources**
Vincent G. Withers (Chair)	James C. Baillie (Chair)	Albert F. Hickman (Chair)
Janet C. Gardiner	R. William Blake, PhD	James C. Baillie
Michael F. Harrington	Bruce C. Galloway	R. William Blake, PhD
Alfred F. Hickman	Thomas E. Kierans	Bruce C. Galloway
Rev. Desmond T. McGrath	Elizabeth Parr-Johnston, PhD	Michael F. Harrington
Frances M. Nichols, FCA	Vincent G. Withers	Thomas E. Kierans

APPENDIX E: A NEWSPAPER INTERVIEW WITH
VIC YOUNG, THE TELEGRAM—AUGUST 26, 2000

Fishery: FPI Boss looking for business in New Zealand

Young seeks more international flavour: Telegram Correspondent

Fishery Products International (FPI) chairman and CEO Vic Young will travel to New Zealand next week to explore opportunities that he hopes will give FPI a more international flavour in the fish-marketing business.

Young said the full week of discussions will include talks with several New Zealand seafood companies, including Sanford Ltd., which owns 14.7 per cent of FPI.

He said he will be exploring opportunities associated with the potential for FPI to market New Zealand products in North America and for New Zealand companies to market FPI products in New Zealand and Australia.

Co-operation

He said the issue of international co-operation in the fishing industry is becoming increasingly important as the battle with the chicken, beef, pork and turkey industries intensifies.

Recently, FPI and a consortium of 12 international seafood companies announced the formation of Seafood Alliance.com.

Members of the alliance have agreed to investigate industry-wide opportunities arising out of the Internet and business electronic commerce.

The total sales of the companies in the alliance is US$5 billion.

The list of major shareholders of FPI has undergone significant change in the last several months. There are now five shareholders that own approximately 64 per cent of the outstanding shares in FPI.

These major shareholders include: Sanford; Hamblin Watsa (a Canadian investment firm) at 14.5 per cent; IFPC (an Icelandic seafood company) at 14.6 per cent and Omers (a Canadian retirement fund) at 11 per cent.

In addition, Clearwater Fine Foods, a Canadian seafood company, owns approximately nine per cent. Clearwater and IFPC were partners in an unsuccessful FPI takeover bid that was launched in November last year.

FPI is experiencing one of its best performances in more than a decade this year.

In its recently released second-quarter report, the company indicated its annual earnings target for 2000 was net income in excess of 75 cents per share, compared with 51 cents per share earned in 1999.

"If achieved, this would represent FPI's best performance on a fully-taxed basis in over a decade," said Young.

The company has indicated it will continue to pursue potential mergers, acquisitions, international alliances and other growth opportunities.

He said that one of the things he will be exploring while in New Zealand is the use of New Zealand hoki (whitefish) as raw material in value-added products in North America.

He said he will also be looking at the potential for technological and personnel exchanges in the areas of harvesting and fish processing.

NonStop Yacht, S.L.

*Prepared by Ken Mark and Jordan Mitchell
under the supervision of Professor Charlene Nicholls-Nixon*

          Version: (A) 2004-06-22

INTRODUCTION

On February 17, 2003, Paul Metcalf, founder of NonStop Yacht S.L. (NSY), wondered how best to pursue growth for his startup. NSY provided a central, one-stop Internet e-commerce Web site to service the mega-yacht[1] industry. Metcalf's business concept was to provide captains and crew with information and the ability to shop online for any parts or services related to the functioning of their vessel: from finding a light bulb, to selecting a new satellite system, to arranging a photographer in the Cayman Islands.

Based in Barcelona, Spain, NSY grew rapidly, achieving sales of US$200,000[2] in its first year of operation. But second-year sales were below Metcalf's expectations and the two-year-old NSY had yet to post break-even results. With cash becoming an issue and investors reluctant to provide further capital, Metcalf felt it was time to revisit whether he had chosen the most appropriate business model to capture value from the NSY concept. He was keenly aware that he had to make a decision quickly. There would be no margin for error.

THE RECREATIONAL MEGA-YACHT INDUSTRY

A mega-yacht was loosely defined as any yacht greater than 45 metres in length. Owning mega-yachts was a hobby of the immensely wealthy. Despite the global recession, the yachting world was still growing rapidly because "yacht owners were typically high net-worth individuals and corporations with cash to burn."[3] In 2003, there were approximately 5,000 mega-yachts in the world, ranging in cost from an average of $10 million to $50 million and higher. The industry included another 5,000 superyachts[4] in its boat count.

Examples of mega-yachts included the following, rated by Power and Motoryacht as the top two mega-yachts in 2002:[5]

- The Savarona: 124 metres in length, featuring a Turkish bath with 300-ton marble fountains and basins that are more than 200 years old, 39 bathrooms, 17 bedrooms and an exquisite gold and marble balustrade.[6]

- The Alexander: 121 metres in length, launched in 1976 and owned by Greek real estate billionaire John Latsis. The mega-yacht was in the headlines in 2000 when Prince Charles of Britain and his lover, Camilla Parker Bowles, were photographed cruising in it.

Economic activity in the mega-yacht industry was estimated at $1,035 million worldwide, of which new builds accounted for $383 million. The maintenance, refit and repair business sectors accounted for the other $652 million. (At any time, there were about 1,600 mega-yachts docked for service.) In September 2002, consultants estimated that demand in the worldwide market would continue to increase by six per cent per year and even more in the near-term outlook.[7]

Ports of Call

There were a few key ports of call for mega-yachts: South Florida, Majorca, the French Riviera, and St. Maarten. The impact of mega-yachts was not to be underestimated: South Florida alone claimed that mega-yachts were a significant portion of the $9-billion per annum recreational marine industry.[8] Frank Herhold, executive director of the Marine Industries Association of South Florida, a trade group with about 800 members, stated:

> Mega-yachts are a very fragile, mobile community. About 900 mega-yachts visit South Florida each year, and 800 of them stay. They spend about $500,000 per visit.[9]

Various economic impacts included purchases of goods and services, as well as maintenance, repairs, refittings and docking fees (between $7 to $10 per foot per day) billed by local marinas and boatyards. In South Florida, the recreational marine industry directly employed an estimated 39,000 people and generated indirect employment for another 109,000.[10]

To attract visitors and support the community, South Florida also held the Fort Lauderdale Boat Show, displaying $1.6 billion of boats, mega-yachts and accessories to thousands of visitors. The show's average $500-million annual impact was welcomed by the city.[11]

Customers

Americans purchased 45 per cent of all superyachts and mega-yachts, up from 10 per cent to 12 per cent a decade ago.[12] Customers bought mega-yachts and superyachts in the same way they bought other large-ticket items. Within their network of contacts and friends, they located yacht brokerages that could equip them with the most impressive yacht they could afford.

Mega-yacht owners typically spent six to 10 weeks a year onboard their yacht, frequently entertaining guests' with the key but subtle aim of putting their immense wealth on display during this short period of time. Typically, no expense was spared to provide the highest levels of comfort and luxury for guests—fresh, premium food was cooked by chefs, crews were fully staffed, and the mega-yacht had to be in pristine condition at all times. A typical mega-yacht would have six crew members, including a captain, mate, chief engineer, cook, stewardess

and deck hand. In extreme cases, the mega-yacht had 90 to 100 full-time crew.

When not in use by the owner, mega-yachts were often made available for charter. During this three-to-four-month time period, the yacht owner turned over the care of the vessel to the chartering party and the yacht management service. The level of luxury depended on the amount the party was willing to spend.

For the rest of the year, the mega-yacht was moored in port, in dry storage or in dock for repairs. The generally accepted industry rule was that operating expenses accounted for 10 per cent of the yacht's value per year. Of this amount, a quarter was due to spare parts, consumables and upgrades. The other three-quarters covered fuel, food, communication costs, docking fees, crew payroll and repair and refit yard fees. Every four to five years, a mega-yacht required a major refit costing up to 20 per cent of the yacht's value.

Yacht Builders

At any time, there were about two dozen specialty yacht builders in the world constructing mega-yachts. Mega-yachts took between one and three years to build. In 2002, 56 per cent of new mega-yachts were built in Europe, 35 per cent in the United States, and the remainder were built in Asia and South Africa. In 2002, industry observers calculated that yacht builders were completing 482 mega-yachts for 2003, a 4.7 per cent drop from the previous year.[13] Although yacht builders focused on construction, related services could add substantially to their bottom line. Rybovich Spencer, a West Palm Beach, Florida-based full-service shipyard and shipbuilder, said its service and dockage business, consisting of repairs and refits for over 80 mega-yachts, brought in an additional $5 million in sales during a six-month period between 2001 and 2002.[14] Yacht builders invested between $2 million to $15 million to upgrade current facilities to serve mega-yachts.[15]

The growth in the industry had led to a proliferation in the number of yacht builders, and in 2002, signs of consolidation appeared. Palmer Johnson Inc., a shipbuilder and refitter based in

Sturgeon Bay, Wisconsin, announced its intentions to focus on the mega-yacht industry with its acquisition of two Fort Lauderdale marine companies specializing in supplying parts, equipment and fuel to the yachting sector.[16]

Yacht Management Companies

There were dozens of yacht management companies providing such services as parts procurement, crew hiring and management, co-ordination of yacht maintenance, and organizing charters. As an example of a service provided, organizing charters helped mega-yacht owners recoup some of the investment in their vessel: rental rates ranged from $50,000 per week to $584,000 per week for the 325-foot Christina O, a yacht for up to 36 people that once belonged to the late Aristotle Onassis. These costs did not include tips, food, alcohol and fuel (which could add another 20 per cent to 40 per cent to costs).[17] The fees for dockage in the Mediterranean could range from $1,000 to $2,000 per night. The yacht management company's commission, included in the total amount, would be between 10 per cent to 20 per cent.

Consolidation in this industry was also starting to take place, as transnational players began moving into the lucrative U.S. market. In 2002, the Rodriguez Group, a French yachting services company, purchased Fort Lauderdale-based Bob Saxon Associates Inc., a yacht management and charter company with 27 employees.[18]

THE PARTS PROCUREMENT PROCESS

Given the nature of conspicuous consumption in the mega-yacht industry, most mega-yachts were filled with specially made and expensive parts (see Exhibit 1). There were three main categories of boat parts:

1. *Spare parts*—typically more urgent than anything else, this category referred to parts that had unexpectedly broken down. Examples included: a replacement pump for the head (toilet), a new hydraulic seal for the steering system, a non-standard valve in the sewage system or a new electronics board for the unit that closes the curtains in the owner's stateroom.

2. *Consumables and stock spares*—this category included parts that were less urgent but necessary to have in the case of a breakdown or replacement. Examples included: oil and fuel filters, light bulbs, pump seals, electronic switches, crockery (pots and pans) for the galley (kitchen), charts and tools.

3. *Upgrades and refits*—this category included a range of products from fire and safety to the entertainment or communication systems.

Because the range of products required by mega-yachts was so great, suppliers were located around the world. The majority of the suppliers were located in the United Kingdom, Germany, Holland, France, United States, Australia, Scandinavia and Japan. As the industry continued to mature, more standardization and consolidation of suppliers was expected to occur.

There were four main suppliers to mega-yachts:

- Commercial/Industrial—engines, laundry, kitchen and electrical system suppliers
- Consumer Products—entertainment systems, fixtures in bathrooms, furniture, etc.
- Small Yacht Products—rope handling equipment, navigation equipment, electronic system suppliers
- Dedicated Suppliers—small number of manufacturers that catered to the mega-yacht market

The thousands of parts and equipment manufacturers sold their wares through exclusive distributors. Analysts indicated that Germany had a 26 per cent share of the market, followed by the United Kingdom and the Netherlands each with an 18 per cent share, the United States with 14 per cent, Norway with nine per cent, France with six per cent and Finland three per cent.[19]

Owners rarely ever dealt with the purchasing of boat parts or servicing, leaving these duties to the crew (40 per cent of the time) and yacht repair and refit specialists (60 per cent of the time). The crew dealt with ongoing or emergency

The scope of supply included any parts for the following systems aboard a mega-yacht or superyacht:

- Main Engines
- Propulsion Units
- Generators
- Air Conditioning
- Refrigeration
- Water Makers
- Shorepower Conversion Units
- Sewage Systems
- Stabilization Systems
- Bow Thrusters
- Fuel Purification
- Oil Purification
- Fresh Water System
- Hot Water System
- Communication Systems
- Navigation Electronics

- Compressed Air Systems
- Entertainment Systems
- Fire Fighting Equipment
- Safety Equipment
- Hydraulics
- Sails and Rigging
- Kitchen Equipment
- Cranes
- Tenders
- Jet-skis
- Diving Equipment
- Anchor Handling Equipment
- Alarm Systems
- Charts
- Helicopters
- Other Sea Craft

Exhibit 1   Parts Requirements for Mega-Yachts

repairs while yacht repair and refit specialists handled regularly scheduled maintenance. The crew had several ways to deal with parts procurement: They could leave the task to the yacht management company; they could rely on a purchasing agent; or they could approach parts distributors (see Exhibit 2).

Yacht management companies and purchasing agents would locate the products from their database or collection of catalogues. They would then order the part, look after the paperwork and have the part shipped to their warehouse or directly to the yacht. Typically, they would add a percentage fee, ranging between five per cent to 10 per cent of the cost of the part. For important customers, the purchasing agent would have the clout to negotiate a cheaper price than the yacht owner would receive by dealing directly with the manufacturer. Parts could also be obtained through local yacht agents. Like purchasing agents, local yacht agents (who typically also managed many other sideline businesses), generally had local knowledge of their port, any local suppliers and local import laws. The yacht agent

would add a small percentage to the cost of the product or service.

Alternatively, crews could pursue parts procurement independently. This approach usually involved a lengthy investigation period where they would have to track down products and product information through contacts, magazines, catalogues and the Internet. In some cases, crews were able to contact the distributor or manufacturer directly and arrange to have the product shipped to the yacht. Although contacting parts suppliers was not simple (there were thousands of suppliers), extra commissions for intermediaries would not have to be paid.

Crews could also locate and purchase boat parts by directly contacting yacht builders and/or repair and refit yards. Yacht builders would typically specialize in parts they used to equip the vessels they were building. Repair and refit yards did not always have a wide contact base of suppliers and would add 10 per cent to 15 per cent onto the cost of the product or service. Their businesses were based on charging for the labor component of the refit or repair. In most major ports, there would be

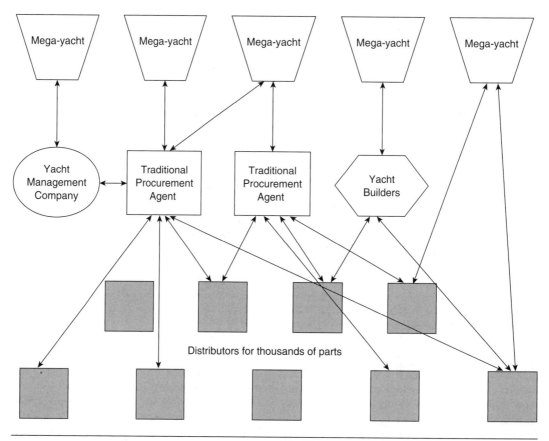

Exhibit 2   Traditional Parts Procurement Process

one or two major refit yards. For example, the predominant refit yards in Spain included MB 92 in Barcelona and Izar in Cartagena.

THE NSY VALUE PROPOSITION

Because mega-yachts were transient sea craft that sailed frequently from port to port, supplies and equipment were often needed on a last-minute basis. Locating the right spare or replacement part was often a frustrating endeavor for mega-yacht crews; there were literally thousands of manufacturers worldwide, each making

non-standard boat parts. Attempting to describe the boat part while connected to procurement agents on satellite telephone was not the ideal solution. Often, agents themselves had to resort to haphazard guessing to correctly identify the item requested. To compound the problem, most parts suppliers did not have their catalogues online; the catalogues were often in paper form and updated annually.

Metcalf believed that his company's e-commerce Web site had an advantage over traditional methods of procurement. While connected to the Internet, mega-yacht crews could browse the catalogues of a variety of suppliers on the NSY site. Instantaneous access to current product information would virtually eliminate many of the problems crews commonly associated with parts procurement, including: how to find and contact the manufacturer and local distributor, describing the part, ensuring appropriate measurements (metric versus imperial), managing time zone differences, dealing with communication problems, locating—sending and receiving agents, managing customs clearance and arranging payment.

Metcalf explained why he chose to operate NSY as an e-commerce site:

> I thought the Internet was the best method of delivery to a customer base that was located all over the world and constantly moving. The fit was perfect! I felt the problem of parts procurement could be better addressed using the Internet. The biggest problem in getting boat parts was getting the right information about the product. So, I figured if I could have an Internet site and an up-to-date catalogue on CD that gave the information *and* delivered the product, it would be better than the current method of finding the parts yourself or by using an agent who is serving dozens of other customers. My plan was to have a huge catalogue of everybody's catalogue. A person from the boat would order a part and say, "Okay, I'm in this place," and the product would be dropped shipped from the supplier in that area. (see Exhibit 3).

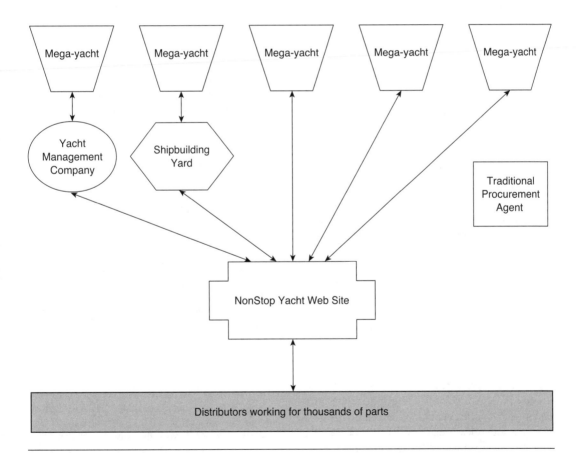

Exhibit 3   NonStop Yacht Facilitates Parts Procurement

Metcalf believed that NSY's competitive advantage would be its database and network of suppliers, the ability to ship anywhere in the world from Barcelona, the flexibility of its cost structure and the transparency of billing. Taken together, the benefits provided a compelling value proposition to the crew of super-yachts and mega-yachts, which included:

1. Up-to-date catalogue on CD, allowing the crew to browse and shop off-line then upload the order by fax, e-mail or through the Internet (the hard-copy catalogue of National Marine had some parts not available for the past six years);

2. Automatic accounting for the captain or yacht management company;

3. Password-protected expenditure levels for captain, mate or engineer;

4. Automatic receipt copies, invoice copies and VAT[20] receipts;

5. Links into maintenance scheduling software if used on the yacht;

6. Easy reordering of parts or groups of parts;

7. Intelligent add-on sales with instant access to view the available options;

8. Product pictures and part diagrams; and

9. No time zone issues.

With the NonStopYacht.com Web site, Metcalf aimed to become the Web-based purchasing agent of choice to crew members and yacht management companies. NSY's continually updated Web site could be instantly accessed by customers, with orders placed online or by telephone.

NSY's Business Model

Initially, Metcalf had envisioned building NSY as a virtual corporation. The Web site would be NSY's only interface with the customer. Supplies would be procured from a growing network of vendors that agreed to post their merchandise with NSY and then have NSY arrange the shipping directly to the customer.

NSY's revenues were generated from dealer margins that were earned when merchandise was sold through the Web site. Suppliers were not required to pay listing fees. The business model worked as follows: NSY would utilize the supplier's country-specific distributor to ship product to customers. In the process, it would earn dealer margins on the wholesale prices of these products. NSY aimed to charge end-customers prices similar to those offered by local dealers. In the rare case that the supplier did not have a distributor, NSY would arrange for the part to be shipped directly to the customer. In these situations, NSY would earn both distributor margins and dealer margins.

Metcalf and his team worked feverishly for months, making over 900 supplier contacts around the world with a combined product offering that included over 20,000 branded items. The process of getting all of the suppliers and their products had been an arduous task. Metcalf recalled:

We basically rang up all the suppliers, told them about the idea and many of them said "great." The biggest challenge was convincing them of our main objective, which was *not* selling *against* their distributors. Once we convinced them that the customer would order from us, then we would go through their designated distributor in that country.

At the same time as agreements were being signed with a critical mass of suppliers, the Web site was developed. Then, attention turned to building traffic on the site:

When we finished the basic structure of the Web site, we sent out passwords to various mega-yachts and got their feedback on what they liked and didn't like about the site. The site was ugly because I designed it initially. We had three people working on the back end, and before its final release, I hired someone who improved the look and consistency of the appearance.

We opened the Web site to resounding silence in June 2001. We had visitors but not many purchasers. We got the phone calls: "My boss was on your site and he would like to order this." The Web site did not work the way I wanted it to as an e-commerce site. However, it did provide parts information to crews.

Since initial sales had been much slower than Metcalf had anticipated, he decided to move from a hidden office to a publicly accessible area. As soon as he had created a face for NSY to deal directly with customers, sales started to pick up. The business model quickly evolved from an Internet-based venture to a hybrid "bricks and mortar" enterprise:

> What we were finding was that customers were looking on the Web site to find the information; then we'd get a call saying, "Yes, we saw this boat part on your Web site and would like to order it." The decision to move from a strictly e-commerce company to dealing directly with the customer was quite simple, really. We were located upstairs in a non-public area and were trying to operate it as a strictly e-commerce business. But we kept on getting calls. We decided to move downstairs, and put in a free Internet access terminal for the crew to use. That helped out immensely. Once we saw that the e-commerce solution alone wouldn't work, we developed a face to the crews of the mega-yachts. Crews are able to come in, use our Internet, ask us about products and do the order either over the phone, by fax or in person. The site is updated, but it's in hibernation, since most of our sales are generated through the office.

Metcalf and the investors decided to open up the second NSY office in Palma Mallorca, Spain, in October 2002. Metcalf believed Palma to be a vital hub of activity for superyachts and mega-yachts and was confident that the new office was a natural extension of the Barcelona location.

The accessibility to information within the mega-yacht industry made it possible for Metcalf to obtain the names and lengths of the yachts, the major equipment being installed, the yard where the yacht was built and the present captain's name. The only information that was not available was details relating to the owner. NSY advertised in three publications that were frequently referenced and read by captains and crews: Professional Yachtman's Association News, The Yacht Report, and Showboats. Another important advertising method was the attendance of Metcalf and his team at the major boat shows in Europe and the United States.

THE NSY TEAM

In February 2003, the NSY management team was composed of Metcalf as chief executive officer (CEO) and president, Stephanie McKay as commercial manager and Sam Jones as marketing and sales specialist. Contract employees such as Robert Franks performed computing or administrative tasks. Each individual brought a unique and complementary set of skills and experience to NSY.

Metcalf had spent six years in computer sales in his native United Kingdom before pursuing a career in the sailing world in 1993. He worked first as a sailing instructor in Greece, and then went to work on a variety of small- and medium-sized yachts, ranging in size from 12 metres to 52 metres. During this time, Metcalf's travels took him throughout the Caribbean, North America and the Mediterranean. The experience gave Metcalf a wide base of yachting knowledge including electrical, plumbing, engine rooms and general maintenance. It also gave him valuable contacts with owners, captains and engineers within the industry. Metcalf was 30 years old when he began writing the NSY business plan in October 1999. He received his initial seed capital from Riva y Garcia on June 16, 2000 (see Exhibit 4).

In 2003, McKay had worked at NSY for two years. She was responsible for the establishment of many of the relationships with suppliers due to her savvy negotiation skills and ability to speak three languages. Her prior experience had been based in emergency assistance with a leading insurance company, working in both the United Kingdom and France. Being with NSY from the beginning, McKay wrote an entire manual of procedures and established strong ties with yacht refit yards in the Mediterranean.

Jones had worked for NSY for nine months. During this time, he had managed to increase the walk-in traffic and the direct-to-yacht business through his personable selling approach to

By February 2003, there had been three rounds of investment in NonStop Yacht:

Round	Investor	Date	Amount (US$)
1	Riva y Garcia + Barcelona EMPREN	06/16/2000	180,000
2	Riva y Garcia + Barcelona EMPREN	12/16/2000	180,000
3*	Riva y Garcia + Barcelona EMPREN	04/01/2001	51,085
TOTAL			411,085

*The third joint small round of financing was in the form of a loan with the plan that the investment would be returned in cash or equity, with valuation based on performance against target.

Riva y Garcia

Riva y Garcia was an investment banking boutique with offices in Barcelona and Madrid. Its primary focus was on corporate finance for Catalonian and Spanish companies as well as the operation of three institutional investment funds, one of which was WebCapital, the fund that invested in NonStop Yacht.

Sebastian Waldburg, director private equity from Riva y Garcia, commented on why he gave Metcalf the funding:

He [Metcalf] had worked in the sector and had detected a serious need. He wanted to use the Internet as a tool to fill a gap. We thought it was a good approach and an interesting sector. It's a small sector worth a lot of money. You don't have to talk to a million customers.

VC firms invest in the person. Paul has the experience and knowledge in the industry. He has a strong capacity in being flexible in terms of where the business will take him.

On his expectations of NonStop Yacht's financial commitment, Walburg said:

The financial model we had built showed us a 34 per cent return. This year I want to see them break even. That would be sales of 70,000 Euros a month. And I don't mean an average of 70,000 a month. Every month, at least 70, which would cover their fixed costs. By next year, I want to see a 50 per cent to 80 per cent growth rate in sales.

Barcelona EMPREN

Barcelona Empren was an organization focused on providing start-up and seed capital to companies in telecommunications, biotech, engineering and software companies. Its shareholders included pre-eminent leaders in Spain from the following sectors: public institutions (27.5 per cent), telecom (22.5 per cent), banks (35 per cent), industrial sector (10 per cent) and public utilities (five per cent).

Emilio Gómez I. Janer, analyst with Barcelona Empren, commented on giving funding to NSY:

He's an innovator in the yachting industry, he has an excellent niche in the marketplace and Paul and his team are experts in the sector. He knows what the problem in the industry is and he has the knowledge and experience to make it successful.

On his expectations of financial results, Gómez commented:

Originally, we had planned a 30 per cent IRR.[1] I wanted to see $500,000 in sales in 2002 and $1 million in 2003.

Exhibit 4   Financing of NonStop Yacht

1. Internal Rate of Return.

the 30 to 40 mega-yachts sailing into Barcelona each year. In October 2002, he was placed in charge of the new Palma office. The team used the services of Robert Franks, an experienced U.K. computer programmer based in Barcelona, for any issues with the Web site and for the integration and set-up of any new technologies relevant to NSY.

COMPETITOR REACTION

Metcalf believed that NSY's key competitors would be the major traditional procurement agents, yacht builders or parts-related Web sites, but none of these parties took visible action following the launch of NonStopYacht.com in June 2001.

Very little information was publicly available about the companies that acted as purchasing agents in the mega-yacht industry. Many of these firms were private companies or one-person operations with closely guarded lists of clientele. Worldwide, Metcalf believed there were three major traditional procurement agents:

• *National Marine*, Florida, United States— This competitor was the largest purchasing agent in the world with annual sales of approximately $10 million, employing 35 people. Its focus was almost entirely U.S.-based and was not well known in Europe. National Marine published a 1,000-page catalogue annually and sold parts to mega-yachts and superyachts throughout the world.

• *Alex Spares*, United Kingdom—The operation began in 1972 and was comprised of one principal and one assistant. Annual sales were estimated at approximately $1 million. Spare's competitive advantage was his experience of over 30 years in the industry and his extensive personal network of contacts, including many mega-yacht captains and crews.

• *Versillias Supplies,* Viareggio, Italy—The operation relied mostly on dealings with Mediterranean mega-yachts and suppliers. Their sales were approximately $1 million.

In addition to these "majors," there were approximately another 200 small local yacht agents located around the world that did not specialize in locating and sourcing local parts and services for yachts in their locale. Rather, they acted as the "person on the ground" to arrange everything from getting fresh flowers to renting a limousine for the boat's owner. According to Metcalf, none of these small enterprises had the clout or worldwide name recognition of National Marine, Alex Spares or Versillias.

By February 2003, there was some industry speculation about the possibility of strategic alliances between NSY and its major competitors, specifically National Marine, Alex Spares and Palmer Johnson.

Emerging Competitors: Vertically Integrated Yacht Builders?

Two major yacht builders had started to incorporate a completely vertical operation including building, selling, chartering, servicing, refitting and ordering parts for the mega-yachts. Frequently, these parts were required for the building projects in which the yard was involved.

Palmer Johnson Inc.

Started in 1918, this was one of the world's preeminent builders, involved in yacht repair and support services of sailboats, superyachts and mega-yachts. With over $300 million in sales, Palmer Johnson usually built 40 yachts per year. Their subsidiaries included companies that built production, semi-custom and custom luxury yachts; operated brokerage yacht sales across the United States, United Kingdom, France and Singapore; refitted, repaired and painted mega-yachts; and operated a global logistical support unit serving mega-yachts worldwide. Being one of the biggest yacht builders, refit yards and brokerages in the world, Metcalf believed Palmer Johnson had a good reputation and significant clout with suppliers. In 2002, Palmer Johnson was expected to seek growth through expanding the service side of their enterprise.

Lurssen

Located in Bremen, Germany, Lurssen had a long history in ship building dating back to 1875, with many of the world's firsts in yachting, including the invention of the first motor boat in 1886. Lurssen was another of the world's major yacht builders with sales of approximately $150 million. A highly diversified company, they were involved in the production, servicing and logistical support of mega-yachts as well as Naval vessels. They typically built 30 mega-yachts per year. Their competitive advantage was similar to Palmer Johnson's in their worldwide reputation, history and clout with suppliers.

The Failed Alliance Between
Palmer Johnson and Lurssen

Palmer Johnson and Lurssen had tried to form a strategic alliance in the mid-1990s, but it had failed due to differences in business objectives. Both companies were yacht builders, which meant they were competing for the same superyacht and mega-yacht contracts. As well, their repair and refit yards were not complementary and both companies found it challenging to agree upon an efficient way to procure and sell boat parts. Last, management from both companies was unable to reconcile the U.S. German management styles.

METCALF'S OPTIONS

In 2003, Metcalf was experiencing substantial pressure to raise NSY's performance to meet investor expectations. Moreover, he was also personally motivated to see a payoff for the exhausting schedule he had been keeping since launching the venture two and half years earlier. So far, the results had been disappointing. Metcalf's original plan for growth called for sales of $10 million and profits of $1.97 million by the end of the 2003 fiscal year (see Exhibit 5). In the first full year of operation, NSY generated sales of $200,000, which was consistent with Metcalf's business plan. However, in 2002, the sales were $300,000, or 11 per cent of the original business plan. NSY was just cash flow positive.

Metcalf was now wondering whether he should revisit the NSY business model. He believed there were three alternative business models that had the potential to improve the company's performance. Metcalf's quandary was deciding how to choose from among these options.

	Year 1	Year 2	Year 3	Year 4	Year 5
Sales	214,720	2,654,484	10,698,465	13,908,004	18,080,406
Sales Growth %		1136%	303%	30%	30%
Profit	(414,188)	317,189	1,973,416	2,648,157	3,537,727
Profit Growth %		−176.6%	522.2%	34.2%	33.6%
# of Yachts	1,600	1,712	1,832	1,960	2,097
"Total Mega-yacht Market Size (millions)"	160.0	171.2	183.2	196.0	209.7
Growth %	7%	7%	7%	7%	7%
NSY Market Share	0.13%	1.55%	5.84%	7.10%	8.62%

Exhibit 5   Original Financial Projections for NonStop Yacht

Option #1: Signing an Agreement With Palmer Johnson or National Marine

Metcalf felt there were trade-offs associated with entering into a strategic alliance with Palmer Johnson or National Marine:

> The problem is, if we sign an agreement with National or Palmer Johnson to become their European arm, we become a third party. We have to stop dealing direct with the crew of the mega-yachts.
>
> Signing the agreement with National or Palmer would give us high volume and low margin. We would charge them a fixed cost of 5,000 to 6,000 Euros a month and add an additional five per cent margin. The advantage of the mixture of dealing with agents and direct to the mega-yachts is higher margin . . . an average of about 25 per cent versus the current 15 per cent. The problem is slow growth.

The decision was not based purely on sales or gross margin dollars as Metcalf was confident that, by signing the agreement, his sales would reach $3 million immediately, with potential for 50 per cent growth in the second year, 30 per cent in the third, tapering down to 10 per cent growth per year in subsequent years.

To accommodate the increased volume, Metcalf would have to contract two extra administrative people at $20,000 a year plus 25 per cent in employee tax. In the second year, he would likely add another person. Metcalf could gain savings of approximately $10,000 per year on his rent by moving into an office without public access. New computers and additional office furniture, which were treated as expenses, would require an additional outlay of $2,000 per terminal, including telephone and Internet hook-up. With this option, NSY would likely experience a five per cent increase in expenses each year. The main investment would be the increased accounts receivables, estimated to represent approximately 20 days. NSY typically paid its bills in 15 days and did not carry any inventory.

Option #2: Growth Through Repair and Refit Yards and Dealing Direct to Yachts—a "Hybrid" Option

Metcalf felt there was a great opportunity to service the yacht refit yards, local yacht agents and yacht management services, while trying to deal directly with the mega-yachts at the same time. But there were two potential problems with this approach. First, if NSY contracted with a refit yard, the company might have to cease dealing directly with the yachts in order to avoid conflict of interest. Second, NSY could lose its name recognition with the end consumer if it relied upon yacht refit yards, agents or management services to generate sales. Metcalf expected a margin of five per cent to 15 per cent when dealing with a third party and a margin of 25 per cent when dealing directly with the yachts, making a blended margin of approximately 20 per cent.

With this growth option, Metcalf believed he could generate sales of more than $2 million in three years, with a growth rate of 15 per cent for each subsequent year. NSY could accommodate this type of growth with its current team in Barcelona, although Metcalf expected that each additional bricks-and-mortar office would require another two employees at $20,000 per person. It was probable that, in addition to the Palma office, two more offices would be required in Antibes, France, and Monaco.

The start-up for each new office was estimated to be $10,000, plus $2,000 per employee for the computer and office equipment. The yearly amount of telephone, consumables and miscellaneous expense was estimated at $20,000 per office. Metcalf expected that NSY would require an average increase in travel expense of $5,000 per office. The rent and related expenses for a small office per year in major ports in the Mediterranean was estimated to be about $2,000 per month. Since NSY expensed its computers and office equipment, the only working capital requirement would be an increase in accounts receivable.

Option #3: Organic Growth Through Opening Multiple Locations

Metcalf felt that the recently opened Palma office would generate more walk-in traffic and would continue to present a company "face" to the crew of the mega-yachts. Metcalf further believed that yacht crews would be more apt to deal with NSY if they constantly saw a shop in each major destination. Thus, an alternative business model was to expand by continuing to open locations in key ports around the world. Sebastian Waldburg, from Riva y Garcia, commented on the viability of expanding with a bricks-and-mortar approach:

> Yes, NSY is a relatively low-budget operation. If they replicate the small offices, say in Antibes or Monaco, and before they open up their office, if they can arrange to be the back-office for yacht refit yards and yacht management services, they could cover their fixed costs of running it. They could likely charge the yacht management services or the refit yard a fixed monthly fee with variable charges for purchases.
>
> It's important to have the local touch and the local being-in-touch. With a little office, they can give constant and consistent quality and service.

Emilio Gómez I. Janer from Barcelona Empren commented:

> I'm the biggest proponent of this approach. Yes, I believe it's necessary to have brick-and-mortar presence in each port. You need to have close proximity to where the sales happen.

Without actively pursuing the yacht refit yards and yacht management services, Metcalf felt that he could achieve sales of $500,000 with the Barcelona and Palma office. With two additional offices (each costing $15,000 to set up and $75,000 to run per annum), he felt that he could reach $1.5 million in annual sales five years from now.

NOTES

1. Defined as yachts over 45 metres in length.

2. All dollar amounts in U.S. dollars unless otherwise stated.

3. Christopher Dinsmore, "Yard Gets Off To Quick Start," *The Virginian-Pilot*, February 6, 2002.

4. Superyachts were defined as being between 25 to 45 metres in length and costing in the million-dollar range.

5. Michael Field, "Booming Super-Yacht Industry Getting Even More Extravagant," *Agence France-Presse*, June 28, 2002.

6. A ramp.

7. "United Kingdom Report Says Superyacht Boom is 'Only The Beginning'," *Advanced Materials and Composite News*, September 7, 2002. (Note: The report uses the words "superyacht" and "mega-yacht" interchangeably.)

8. Joseph Mann, "Sturgeon Bay, Wis.-Based Marine Firm Focuses on Mega-yachts," *Fort Lauderdale Sun-Sentinel*, June 4, 2002.

9. Joseph Mann, "Fort Lauderdale, Fla.-Area Summit Seeks to Buoy Recreational Marine Industry," *Fort Lauderdale Sun-Sentinel*, October 18, 2002.

10. Ibid.

11. Linda Rawls, "Buoyant Nautical Market Welcomes Lauderdale Show," *The Palm Beach Post*, November 1, 2002.

12. Angus MacSwan, "Rich Sail Through Troubled Times on Superyachts," *Reuters News*, November 3, 2002.

13. Dale K. DuPont, "Fort Lauderdale, Fla.-Based Magazine Says Mega-yacht Orders Are Down," *Miami Herald*, October 23, 2002.

14. Joseph Mann, "West Palm Beach, Fla.-based Boatyard, Boatbuilder, Logs Strong Sales Period," *Fort Lauderdale Sun-Sentinel*, May 31, 2002.

15. Joseph Mann, "Fort Lauderdale, Fla.-Shipyard Gets Upgrades," *Fort Lauderdale Sun-Sentinel*, November 2, 2002.

16. Joseph Mann, "Sturgeon Bay, Wis.-Based Marine Firm Focuses on Mega-yachts," *Fort Lauderdale Sun-Sentinel*, June 4, 2002.

17. Dirk Wittenborn, "Chartered Waters," *Independent On Sunday*, June 2, 2002.

18. Joseph Mann, "Fort Lauderdale, Fla.-based Yacht Services Company Sold," *Fort Lauderdale Sun-Sentinel*, July 4, 2002.

19. "United Kingdom Report Says Superyacht Boom is 'Only The Beginning'," *Advanced Materials and Composite News*, September 7, 2002. (Note: The report uses the words "superyacht" and "mega-yacht" interchangeably.)

20. Value Added Tax (European).

STRATEGIC DIRECTION AT QUACK.COM (A)

Prepared by Benji Shomair under the supervision of Professors Kenneth G. Hardy and Amy Hillman

Version: (A) 2002-02-27

> Quack.com is out to break the mold of Internet access and make it simple for consumers to find information they need, whenever and wherever they are, in the most intuitive manner possible—by speaking.
>
> Alex Quilici, president
> and co-founder of Quack.com

It was June 2000, and Quack.com (Quack) was in dire straits. An early entrant in the public voice portal market, Quack was quickly running out of money. Quack's management team had just returned from a road show to obtain a second round of venture financing but had been unsuccessful. To aggravate this issue, over the past month Quack's two major competitors each had received $50 million[1] in funding. At the current burn rate (expenses per month), Quack could survive for only three more months on its existing bridge financing. Alex Quilici, president and co-founder of Quack.com, sat in Quack's Silicon Valley offices scribbling doodles on a piece of paper as he weighed his options.

THE COMPANY

Quack was founded in 1998 on the premise of "providing customers quick and ubiquitous access to the benefits of the Web" and the vehicle for this access was the telephone. With constant access to telephones anywhere in North America, Quilici thought that the phone presented the perfect entry point for the Web.

> Telephone penetration in this country is 99.9 per cent. The computer rate isn't anywhere near that.
>
> Joe Racanelli of Bid.com,
> an early investor in Quack.com

What Quack envisioned was an application of voice recognition technology that would allow customers to use the Web simply by speaking. A user would call a phone number and be connected to Quack's computer. Then the user would make a request such as, "What is the weather in San Francisco?" Quack's computers would then use voice recognition technology to understand the question, input the question into a search engine (using the entire Web or an internal database) and find the answer. Voice software applications would then read the answer back to the user. The goal for Quack was to support any type of activity supported by the Internet such as information retrieval, e-commerce, communication and personal information management, and use the telephone as the interface (Exhibit 1).

The original business plan intended for revenues to be derived from multiple sources. Advertising and sponsorship of the public voice portal, commissions from sales purchased through the voice portals, development fees for creating third-party voice portals and a licensing fee for the Quack software suite were all planned as revenue streams. Advertising, sponsorship and commissions were the major projected revenue streams for Quack.

Quack was founded by Alex Quilici, former professor of electrical engineering at the University of Hawaii, and by Steve Woods and Jeromy Carriere, former members of the Carnegie Mellon University's Software Engineering Institute. Quack's management team had extensive background in world-class artificial intelligence research, software research, prototyping and product development.

After beginning product development, Quack's software architects had realized that

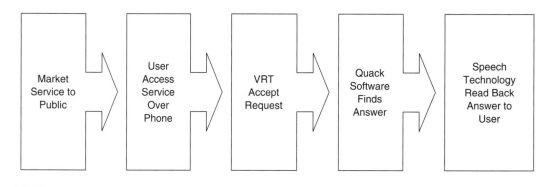

Exhibit 1   Quack Value Chain

VRT= Voice Recognition Technology

coding software for each individual site and service would be too time-consuming. Instead, the Quack development team designed and built a comprehensive tools-based architecture that was built on SpeechWorks voice recognition technology. It would automatically generate voice applications from existing Web sites.

The Quack Voice Architecture comprised three main components (tools). *QuackCollect* generated Web agents that automatically collected information from existing Web sites and brought it into the Quack system for delivery to a user through a voice application. *QuackFusion* aligned different data formats such as html, xml and wav into a single voice application. *QuackContext* provided an interface with SpeechWorks technology to manage call sessions and other aspects such as caller profiles, personalization and targeted advertising.

The architecture would support services in three major applications: public voice portals for consumers, private voice portals for telecom companies and voice-enabled enterprise applications for businesses.

VOICE PORTALS

Why do we have a dial tone?

The dial tone originally served as an indicator of being connected to the telephone network. In reality, the dial tone was an internal technology. The earliest phones connected customers to a live operator who was eventually replaced by automatic switching and the dial tone. This switch to automation was driven by cost issues. In 2000, many felt the next evolution of the dial tone would be back to its "live operator" roots through voice portals.

The vision was to have users greeted by a computer instead of a dial tone. Voice activated dialing could be used rather than tone dialing. Selected cell phones already offered this ability, but this feature was built into the cell phone hardware rather than into the telecommunication hardware. With a voice portal, voice activated dialing could be delivered to any phone in the world.

The possibilities for this technology were impressive. For example, voice portals could become the "gatekeepers" to customers. If a person wanted to order a taxi, the user could simply say "taxi" into the phone and be connected with the "preferred" taxi partner of the voice portal.

The estimates of the future size of the market suggested a large opportunity. The Kelsey Group predicted that by 2005, speech portals would gross more than $5 billion. Infrastructure expenditures in this area were expected to reach $6 billion by 2005. These sales would be driven by the estimated 128 million people worldwide

	2000	2001	2002	2003	2004	2005
Total Speech Users	16	22	32	48	96	128
Speech Portal Users	2	5	11	18	28	45
Speech Portal Shoppers	0	1	3	8	12	18

Source: The Kelsey Group 2000

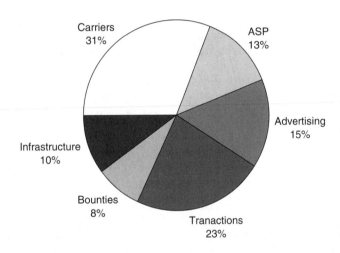

Speech Portal Revenue Analysis (2005)

Carriers 31%
ASP 13%
Advertising 15%
Tranactions 23%
Bounties 8%
Infrastructure 10%

Exhibit 2   Market Predictions, Speech Portals: North America Usage Forecast (in millions)

Source: The Kelsey Group 2000

(45 million Americans) who would be registered to get information through voice portals (see Exhibit 2).

There were three main types of voice portals: public voice portals for consumers, private voice portals for telecom companies and voice enabled enterprise applications for businesses. *Public voice portals* mimicked their online siblings by offering a variety of services to the general public. Audio e-mail, weather reports, sports scores, traffic reports and restaurant guides were all offered through voice access. Ads were placed intermittently through the service. Some voice portals charged subscription fees for access, while others were supported by sales of advertising.

Private voice portals were targeted for sale to telecommunications companies. Both cell phone or landline carriers were very interested in voice portals. Because they both currently "owned" the dial tone, these companies were assumed to be very interested in extracting more revenue from their asset (the dial tone). When picking up a phone, rather than having to dial a phone number, users could be greeted by a voice portal that would house voice mail, address books and would offer all the services of a public voice portal. For wireless carriers, a voice portal was especially attractive because wireless carriers charged by the amount of time used and a voice portal could increase the number of minutes used.

Enterprise applications of voice portals could provide customer service, reduce costs and generate new revenue streams for many businesses. The Goldman Sachs 2000 Mobile Internet report indicated that there would be significant opportunity as corporations looked to support increasingly mobile workforces and leverage the mobile Internet as a new sales channel. Many large volume and repetitive transactions (e.g., stock trading) had already been automated through touchtone dialing on the Internet, yielding huge cost savings.

Voice interfaces could be the next step to allow for the automation of even more services. For example, Ford and GM had identified that consumers make a large portion of their cell phone calls from their vehicles and consumers want to be connected to services such as driving directions. By June 2000, GM had launched OnStar, a button on the dashboard of GM cars that connected drivers to audio driving services. As of 2000, live agents answered OnStar calls, but automated voice solutions could reduce car makers' call centre costs and allow for location-specific services. In the travel industry, 24-hour access to flight information, ticket purchase or traffic updates could all meet customer needs. Voice automated services would make these services available without the high cost of call centres. Furthermore, pure Internet companies could use voice interfaces to extend their brand and services into the offline world. For example, Yahoo by Phone would allow non-Web users access to Yahoo's services.

QUACK'S POSITION

Quack was founded to focus on the public voice portal markets. Quilici and the management group envisioned bringing the utility and convenience of voice portals to customers everywhere.

On March 31, 2000, Quack's services were first offered to the public. Launched in the Minneapolis/St. Paul twin city area, Quack was the first public voice portal in the world. Quack operated a toll-free number (1 800 73 QUACK) for its customers and used the service as a testing ground for its technology. With the success of the pilot project, on April 10, 2000, Quack quickly followed by offering the first nationwide (U.S.) voice portal, thus beating its competitors by mere hours.

As of April 10, 2000, Quack's voice portal offered nationwide weather, news, traffic, sports, stock and movie information. Quack also allowed users to personalize the voice portal. A user could visit the Quack Web site and create a free "account" with their own preferences. The user could then access the Quack voice portal and use their account name to automatically receive predetermined stocks, weather or other information.

Quack's major competitor, Tellme Networks, launched its nationwide voice portal on April 10, 2000, the same day. Tellme's voice portal offered nationwide personalized restaurant, movie, airline, stock, news, sports, weather and traffic information. Tellme offered one added service named "phone booth." After calling the toll-free Tellme access number, users were allowed free two-minute calls to anywhere in the United States. In an early trial of the Tellme service, users had to first sign up for the service on the Internet. Quack's portal did not have this sign-up restriction, making its service accessible to the entire offline population of the United States.

Financial Position

Like many of its peers, by June 2000, Quack had yet to turn a profit. Moreover, it had produced no revenue (see Exhibit 3). The company was burning funds at a rate of $600,000 per month. Voice portals had four types of costs: customer acquisition, infrastructure, telephony and development costs, of which customer acquisition costs were by far the largest. Customer acquisition costs were predominantly sales and

---

BALANCE SHEET (1999)

Assets

Current assets

Cash and cash equivalents	$12,538
Short term investments in marketable securities	—
Accounts receivable	815,000
Prepaid expenses	—
Total current assets	827,538

Property and equipment	
Computer and equipment	2,500,000
Furniture and fixtures	50,000
Leasehold improvements	60,000
	2,610,000
less: accumulated depreciation	390,000
Net property and equipment	2,220,000
Total	3,047,538

Liabilities and Shareholder's Equity

Current liabilities

Accounts payable	20,000
Accrued expenses and other current liabilities	137,000
Deferred revenue	—
Total current liabilities	157,000

Shareholders Equity

Convertible Preferred stock, $0.001 par value; none and 7,750,072 shares authorized; none and 7,738,072 issued and outstanding	8,000
Additional paid in capital	9,076,000
Accumulated deficit	(6,193,462)
Total shareholders equity and liabilities	$3,047,538

Net revenues	$—
Cost of revenues	—
Gross profit	—

Operating expenses:

Sales and marketing (Customer acquisition)	3,156,000
Telephony expenses	1,656,000
Product development	1,272,000
General and administration	708,000
Amortization of computing infrastructure	390,000
Total operating expenses	7,182,000
Income (loss) from operations	(7,182,000)
Investment income	—
Income before tax	(7,182,000)
Provision for taxes	—
Net income (loss)	(7,182,000)
Net loss per share	(0.32)
Shares used in computing net loss per share	$22,541,000

Exhibit 3   Income Statement (1999)

marketing expenses. This involved business development and publicizing the public voice portal. Quack employed two sales people selling advertising and two business development people selling partnerships. The company defined an acquired customer as a customer who registered with Quack for personalized voice portal services. This service was free to customers but allowed Quack to charge a premium to sponsors for more targeted advertising.

As of June 2000, 20,000 visitors had come to the voice portal during the first two months and 200 of them had registered for personalized voice portal services.

In June 2000, Quack was in need of further funding to continue operations. The founders of the firm went on a road show to promote their company to all the major venture capitalists in Silicon Valley. Leading venture capitalists such as Sequoia Capital, Media Technology Ventures, Softbank, Atlas Ventures and Draper Fisher Jurvetson were all unreceptive to the deal. This was worrisome for Quack for two reasons: first, the company was running out of money with only three month's of cash reserves left; and second, two of Quack's major competitors had just closed funding deals for over $50 million dollars each.

With a user population parallel to that of its biggest competitor (Tellme Networks) Quack was currently tied for the market leadership in voice portals. However, after the first few months of running the Quack voice portal, the business-to-consumer (B2C) model for voice portals seemed to be showing signs of weakness. Quack's management believed that the failure of its road show could be related to its B2C focus.

The stock market already had reflected disappointment in Internet business models. On June 1, 2000, Nasdaq index shares closed at $87.375 per share, down from a high of $221.625 per share on March 17, 2000. Leading Internet bulls, such as Goldman Sach's Chief Investment Strategist Abby Joseph Cohen, were tempering their earlier optimism about Internet stocks. Government agencies were even beginning to scrutinize the new economy companies—most notably, an antitrust ruling against Microsoft's monopolistic activities. The B2C sector was being hit hardest; online retail pioneers such as Cdnow.com and Peapod admitted they would have to fold if they couldn't raise more funding.

It was also becoming apparent that, based on existing revenue models, the cost structure for voice portals was too steep to be profitable. Falling advertising rates lowered Quack's estimated revenue per customers. This increased the numbers of customers needed for Quack to break even. The new projected number of customers required for Quack to break even was considered unrealistic by management (it required a highly optimistic 90 per cent+ penetration of target market in the United States). Moreover, it was predicted that advertising rates would continue to fall. Quack had to lower its costs (beginning with the largest cost, customer acquisition) or find new revenue streams.

Quack's executives examined new revenue models for voice portals such as subscription fees, but Quack's competition was already offering voice portal services free of charge. Another suggestion was to find a company with an existing subscription-based revenue stream that might want to add to its product offering by including Quack's voice portal for an additional fee. In this scenario, Quack could sell or lease its portal technology to businesses, so that businesses could differentiate their product or service in the marketplace.

Quack began to look more closely at a business-to-business strategy. Discussions began with various businesses and enterprises interested in voice applications. On May 22, 2000, the first major business deal was struck between Quack and Lycos. Lycos, a Web media company and Internet portal, licensed Quack's technology to offer its Web content over the phone. It was the first of the major Internet portals to move into the voice portal market.

But Quack's management was still unsure about which strategic direction was most appropriate. Both B2B and B2C strategies were under way. The company was founded with the goal of delivering a voice portal to the masses.

The technology and development teams were motivated and driven to produce a *consumer* portal. Although it might be the path to profitability, B2B was not nearly as appealing as a consumer business to Quack's staff. Quack's technology development team, in particular, was motivated to develop a public portal. A strategy shift to emphasize the B2B market might be interpreted by the technology development team as "selling out." The technology developers were the key asset of the company and would be almost impossible to replace in the short term. The fiercely competitive environment had made development engineers for voice portals highly in demand.

MARKET CONDITIONS

The marketplace for voice portals in mid-2000 appeared turbulent and unstructured. Because the market was still in its infancy, the industry's boundaries were still undefined. Many players from very different industries were clashing for dominance in the voice portal space. Major players included the pure voice portals, Internet portal/new economy media companies, telecom carriers and the speech recognition companies.

Voice Portals

Tellme Networks

Tellme Networks (Tellme) offered services similar to Quack's at 1800 555 TELL. First to market alongside Quack, as of June 2000, Tellme's service required online registration. By July 2000, this was expected to change after Tellme completed its systems testing. In June 2000, Tellme was tied with Quack for dominance of the public voice portal market.

Tellme had impressive financial backing; Benchmark Capital, Kleiner Perkins Caufield & Byers and The Barksdale Group were all early investors in the firm. These were leading and well-known venture capital firms in the United States. The company had been started by expatriates of Microsoft and Netscape. Parts of both the Internet Explorer and Netscape Navigator design teams came together in the creation of Tellme. The high-profile management team and financiers of the company gave Tellme a prominent position in the media. Moreover, Tellme undertook an aggressive branding campaign, making it the best-known brand in voice portals as of 2000.

Tellme was also the best funded of the voice portals. With $188 million in venture funding, Tellme's "war chest" scared many competitors in the industry. In May 2000, for example, Tellme raised another $50 million (at an estimated valuation of $600 million) from AT&T. The investment was in the form of telephone access and minutes, essentially erasing Tellme's telephony costs for the next 10 years. Although still focused on its public voice portal, this funding deal indicated Tellme's receptiveness to working with telecom companies. It also gave credibility to the voice portal business.

BeVocal Inc.

BeVocal Inc. offered products and services for the voice application market. It ran a free consumer voice portal (1800 4B VOCAL), offered private label work for telecom companies and enabled existing Web sites with voice features. Although trailing Quack in the consumer voice portal area, BeVocal had more experience in selling voice technology to businesses. In May 2000, BeVocal also raised $45 million from Mayfield fund, U.S. Venture Partners, Technology Crossover Ventures and Trans Cosmos USA. For descriptions of other voice portals see Exhibit 4.

Internet Portal/ New Economy Media Companies

Lycos

Founded in 1995, Lycos was a leading Web media company and owner of the Lycos Network, one of the most-visited hubs on the Internet, reaching nearly one out of every two U.S. Web users. The Lycos Network was composed of Lycos.com, Tripod, WhoWhere, Angelfire, MailCity, HotBot, HotWired, Wired

Company	Service	Fees	Customers
Audiopoint Fairfax, Va. www.myaudiopoint.com	Launched a consumer voice portal in April. Also offers voice-access technology and hosting services to telecom, Internet and media companies.	The consumer service is free. Audiopoint charges setup and monthly fees; shares transaction revenue.	Won't disclose the number of customers for consumer voice portal or for private-label and hosting.
BeVocal Santa Clara, Calif. www.bevocal.com	Launched a consumer voice portal in June. Also offers voice-access hosting to Web sites and other companies.	Consumer service is free. Charges setup fees for hosting, monthly fees for server capacity and transaction fees.	In pilot tests with unnamed wireless carriers, retailers, financial services and travel companies.
HeyAnita Los Angeles www.heyanita.com	Expects to launch a consumer voice portal this fall. Offers an ASP option, hosting and licensing voice technology to telecoms and others.	Voice hosting includes one-time setup fee and 7 to 12 cents per minute; licensing includes fees per line or port.	Has partnerships with Korea Telecom and SK Telecom to create consumer voice portals in Korea.
InternetSpeech San Jose, Calif. www.internetspeech.com	Its NetEcho consumer voice portal lets callers hear info, listen to any Web site or check Web-based e-mail. Recently launched technology for dot-coms to voice-enable their Web sites.	Plans to charge consumers $29.95 a month for approximately six hours of use; software licenses include an undisclosed one-time fee and royalties.	It's testing its consumer voice portal with 200 customers; also negotiating with several unnamed Fortune 500 companies.
Talk2.com Salt Lake City www.talk2.com	Built technology slated to launch in the fall for companies to provide phone-based voice access to info on a corporate intranet, including e-mail and other data behind a firewall. Is developing private-label voice portals for wireless carriers.	Prices not yet determined.	Talk2 is testing its enterprise services with several unnamed corporate customers and three wireless carriers.
Tellme Networks Mountain View, Calif. www.tellme.com	Launched a consumer voice portal in late July with news, sports, restaurant lists and more, from content providers such as CNN, ESPN and InfoUSA. Also offers open-source based voice-access development services.	The consumer service is free. Tellme charges business customers per-minute or per-line usage fees, and will eventually collect transaction fees.	Handled more than 1.5 million calls to its consumer voice portal since starting tests in April. First business customer is Zagat.
TelSurf Networks Westlake Village, Calif. www.888telsurf.com	Expected to launch a consumer voice portal. Will also private-label the portal to wireless carriers, ISPs, portals and others.	The company's consumer voice portal will be free with ads, or 6 cents a minute without; prices for TelSurf's private-label voice portal haven't been set.	TelSurf is testing its private-label voice portal with undisclosed customers in the U.S. and Latin America.

Exhibit 4   Competition

Source: www.thestandard.com

News, Webmonkey, Suck.com, Sonique, Quote, Gamesville and Lycos Zone. Lycos, Inc. was a global Internet leader with a major presence throughout the United States, Europe, Asia and Latin America.

On May 22, 2000, through an agreement with Quack, Lycos became the first Internet portal to offer voice services. The agreement gave much-needed exposure to Quack and its services, but was rumored to be financially unattractive. It was believed that Quack had accepted a "standard Internet deal." Quack received a percentage of advertising revenue and a fee based on the usage of the voice portal. In this scenario, Quack assumed all the cost risk.

Yahoo

Yahoo was a global Internet media company that offered a branded network of comprehensive information, communication and shopping services to millions of users daily. The first online navigational guide to the Web, www.yahoo.com was a leading guide in terms of traffic, advertising, household and business user reach, and was one of the most recognized brands associated with the Internet.

Yahoo did not offer any voice or phone access services. However, Yahoo's strong brand, large user base and skill at packaging and running a consumer portal might be leveraged for profit in the voice portal market. Moreover, with a market capitalization of $70.95 billion in June 2000, Yahoo had the financial resources to enter new markets.

AOL

AOL America Online was a world leader in interactive services, Web brands, Internet technologies and electronic commerce services. The company operated two worldwide Internet services (America Online and Compuserve) several leading Internet brands including ICQ, AOL Instant Messenger and Digital City, the Netscape Netcenter and AOL.com portals, and Netscape Communicator and Navigator browsers. After merging with the Time Warner media company in June 2000, extensive content and cable properties were added to its portfolio.

In the voice portal space, AOL ran AOL MoviePhone, the nation's largest movie listing guide and ticketing service. MoviePhone was operated through touch pad entries but was rumoured to be investigating voice technologies to reduce costs and increase functionality. Moreover, as the largest subscription fee-based Internet service providers, AOL presented an attractive and valuable user base for the voice portal market. AOL was also financially powerful. With a share price of $53.75 per share and market capitalization of $238.7 billion, AOL also had the financial resources to enter new markets.

Speech Recognition Technology Companies

Speechworks International, Inc.

Speechworks International, Inc. was a leading provider of over-the-telephone automated speech recognition solutions (products and services). Speechworks provided the voice recognition "back-end" software for the Quack technology.

Speechworks' focused on businesses that were aiming to harness the value of voice recognition technology. Speechworks built custom solutions for businesses that were generally focused on one application. This was different from Quack's voice solution which was a multi-application platform that dealt with the higher complexity of tasks at the same time. Quack did not compete with Speechworks or its competitors.

Speechworks had built the voice applications for E*trade, Amtrak, Apple Computer, MapQuest.com, United Airlines, MCI WorldCom and Nortel Networks.

Nuance Communications Inc.

Nuance Communications Inc. developed, marketed and supported a voice interface software platform that made the information and services of enterprises, telecommunications networks and the Internet accessible from any telephone.

The software platform consisted of software servers that ran on industry-standard hardware and performed speech recognition, natural language understanding and voice authentication. Nuance was Speechworks' major competitor and provided the back-end technology to both BeVocal and Tellme.

Nuance also focused on selling to businesses. Its technology enabled the voice applications of Charles Schwab & Co., Fidelity Investments, American Airlines, Sears and telecommunications carriers such as British Telecommunications.

Both speech recognition companies had strong core competencies in voice recognition technology. In the B2B voice portal industry, they were dominant players but neither was expected to enter the consumer voice portal industry. Although Nuance and Speechworks offered a different product and service from Quack, these companies' long list of blue chip clients might make entrance to the B2B voice portal market more difficult.

Telecommunication Carriers

AT&T Corporation

AT&T Corporation provided voice, data and video communications services to large and small businesses, consumers and government entities. AT&T and its subsidiaries provided domestic and international long distance, regional, local and wireless communications services, cable television and Internet communications services. AT&T also provided billing, directory and calling card services to support its communications business. AT&T's primary lines of business were business services, consumer services, broadband services and wireless services.

AT&T had already showed an interest in voice portals when it invested $50 million in Tellme Networks. The investment was made in the form of an undisclosed amount of telecom access and minutes. It was also rumored that AT&T would give Tellme control of directory assistance on its networks. This would give unparalleled exposure to Tellme's voice portal. Every caller looking for directory assistance would reach the Tellme portal.

Verizon Communications

Verizon Communications, the newly created name for the June 30, 2000, merger between Bell Atlantic and GTE, was one of the world's leading providers of communications services. With 95 million access lines and 25 million wireless customers, Verizon companies were the largest providers of wireline and wireless communications in the United States. Verizon's global presence extended to 40 countries in the Americas, Europe, Asia and the Pacific.

Among the largest telecom carriers, Verizon did not offer voice portal services. However, with 120 million customers in the United States, Verizon was an attractive potential customer who could greatly leverage voice portal technology across its user base.

Over all, analysts were unsure who would dominate this emerging marketplace. Although Quack had been first to market, Tellme had such strong media and financial backing that no clear market leader existed. Moreover, the existing Internet portals had such strong brands and large user bases that their entrance into the market could destroy the fledgling voice portals. Aggravating this confusion were the telecom carriers, who could lock out both the Internet and pure voice portals from the market if they chose to switch the dial tone of all phones to their own private voice portals. And finally, many people believed that there did not necessarily need to be one winner in the voice portal market. Mergers, acquisitions or alliances could take place changing the competitive landscape and further complicate a prediction of market leadership.

JUNE 2000

In June 2000, Quack executives faced many major decisions that could reshape the company and dictate the future of the firm. Without another round of financing, Quack's current burn rate would allow the company to survive just three more months.

The company was still grappling with the issue of a B2C or B2B focus. A new revenue model would need to be found for the consumer portal . . . and selling voice portals to businesses would be a difficult shift. Quack had limited experience selling to businesses. The company had been founded to deliver voice portals to consumers, but Quack executives now wondered whether or not public voice portals could ever be profitable.

Tied to this strategic issue was the issue of financing. As soon as a strategic direction was chosen, additional funding would be needed to keep Quack alive. Concerned after Quack's unsuccessful search for second round financing, the original Canadian investors in Quack had found an alternative offer in Canada. Led by Caisse de Depot, the largest labor-sponsored fund in Canada, a group of Canadian investors had offered a second round of financing to Quack at a low valuation with a high dilution of shares.

News of Quack's financial worries spread across Silicon Valley. Tellme approached Quack executives to gauge the company's receptiveness to being acquired. Although not a formal offer, Tellme was theorizing that there would be a similar acquisition situation as the WebMD merger with Healtheon. They believed that there was not room for two players in the public voice portal market, but perhaps there was room for one well-funded company. Quack's management now had another financing option. However, Tellme was still focused on the consumer portal market and Quack's management could not foresee this business being profitable. Thus, Quack executives thought that merging with Tellme would not create a new revenue model to make the concept more sustainable.

The proposed merger would be paid for mostly with Tellme stock issued to Quack's current management and investors. Tellme's shares were not publicly traded, and a lock-up period would exist during which Quack's management and investors would not be able to sell their stock. Quack's investors would have to wait to sell their shares in Tellme. For this reason, the sustained profitability of a merged Tellme/Quack was a concern for Quack management.

Alex Quilici slumped into his chair as he considered his decisions. Perhaps he had other options. Alliances or mergers with other companies that could lower Quack's costs or create new revenue streams might be more attractive than the Tellme offer. There was also the option of continuing operations without funding. Whether operating in the B2B space, B2C space or both, if one venture deal was being offered, new offers would be available in the future. This assumed that Quack continued its leadership and innovation in its market. These funding offers would also presumably be at a higher valuation and lower dilution than the Caisse de Depot deal.

In the interim, there were alternative financing options to extend the life of the company. One example was a phenomenon developed in California called "Silicon Valley Financing." Although computer companies scrutinized small personal computer purchases, multimillion-dollar purchases would be given to companies on credit. This credit allowed companies three months to pay. After running out of funding, Quack could continue to purchase all of its needed hardware without paying for three months. Many "cash strapped" technology companies used this tactic. Although a short-term solution, an extra three months of operations could be financed this way. However, would an extra three months really solve Quack's problems?

NOTE

1. All funds are in U.S. currency.

PHARMA TECHNOLOGIES INC.

*Prepared by John Herbert under the supervision
of Professors Charlene Nicholls-Nixon and Rod White*

                    Version: (A) 2004-09-21

In February 1999, the corporate offices of Pharma Technologies Inc. (PTI) were housed in the biosciences complex at a major medical research University in Canada. In spite of the cramped conditions, the excitement at the fledgling company was palpable. PTI had recently obtained a patent for a revolutionary approach to the treatment of sexual dysfunction. This technology would form the basis for a new oral therapy to treat male erectile dysfunction (MED). Drs. Mitchell Abram, Justin Hall and Jeffrey Blair, the University scientists responsible for the discovery, believed their approach would equal or surpass Pfizer's widely acclaimed Viagra™ as the preferred treatment for this condition.

Blair Glickman, who had joined the company in June 1998 as president, shared their conviction and saw great potential to leverage their proprietary technology into other new businesses:

> We are consumed right now by short-term milestones, but when I think of what PTI will be in the future, I don't want us to be defined narrowly as a company focused on the sexual dysfunction market. I hope that PTI will be in a position to apply its knowledge of peripheral vascular disorders to other areas, like congestive heart failure, renal failure, and even male pattern baldness. I envision PTI as establishing a series of comprehensive partnering agreements around our platform technologies.

Although everyone in the company was enthused about the future potential, they were also fully aware of the pressures for day-to-day results. The $2 million representing the first tranche of PTI's financing would run out in about nine months. In order to access the second tranche of $3 million, Glickman and his team had to ensure that the company achieved the rigorous technical and business milestones set out by its investors.

The path of progress was both slow and winding. While PTI had obtained a "method of use" patent giving it exclusive rights to use Factor X for the treatment of sexual dysfunction, it did not actually own any of these compounds. Therefore, a critical technical milestone for PTI was to complete the technologically sophisticated and time-consuming studies associated with screening various compounds for use in PTI's oral therapy. On the business side, this also meant negotiating an agreement with the owner of the compound for subsequent co-development of the product. The PTI management team felt that there would be considerable interest in their technology. The combination of PTI's method of use patent with the right compound could result in a drug capable of generating sales in the billions of dollars.

Glickman faced a short window of opportunity: competing technologies were already in existence and new alternatives were under development, most by major pharmaceutical firms. PTI needed to make substantive progress while the sexual dysfunction market was still attractive and before all of their existing capital was depleted. In addition, the company had a variety of other exciting technologies that were in various stages of the patent application process. The question facing Glickman was how to proceed and which issues should receive highest priority.

THE CONDITION OF SEXUAL DYSFUNCTION

Sexual dysfunction is the inability or unwillingness to engage in sexual intercourse. In men, this condition is easily diagnosed as male erectile dysfunction (MED), the clinical inability to obtain and hold an erection sufficient for intercourse.

In addition to being strongly related to age, sexual dysfunction in men was also associated with the patient's physiological/organic, neurogenic and psychogenic condition. Physiological or organic conditions such as hypertension, diabetes and excess cigarette/alcohol consumption were the most common causes of MED. Neurogenic conditions such as multiple sclerosis and spinal cord injuries were also related to MED. Finally, the cause could be psychogenic in nature due to stress, anxiety or conflict.

In October 1998, it was estimated by Cowen & Company, a privately held research firm, that there were approximately 10 million to 20 million MED suffers in the United States. Female sexual disorders (FSD) were more complex and more difficult to diagnose. However, the FSD market was believed to be equal in size.

In February 1999, the Journal of the American Medical Association published a report on "Sexual Dysfunction in the United States." The report cited studies' indicating that sexual dysfunction was highly prevalent, ranging from 10 per cent to 52 per cent of men and 25 per cent to 63 per cent of women. The report also cited prior studies, which had showed that 34.8 per cent of men aged 40 to 70 years suffered from moderate to complete erectile dysfunction. The National Institutes of Health Consensus Panel described erectile dysfunction as an important public health problem.

THE MARKET FOR
TREATMENT OF SEXUAL DYSFUNCTION

The market for treatment of sexual dysfunction was believed to hold considerable potential. Cowen and Company's 1998 report on the outlook for therapeutic categories suggested that the worldwide MED market was valued in excess of $1 billion in 1998, with approximately five per cent to eight per cent of the roughly 55 million sufferers undergoing treatment. This market was

forecast to grow to almost $8 billion by 2002. It was believed that this growth in the MED market would occur as the number of sufferers grew to 80 million and as the percentage seeking treatment increased to over 20 per cent due to more efficacious and convenient treatments as well as social acceptance.

The MED market was traditionally dominated by injectable and topical therapies. This changed in 1998 with the entry of Pfizer's Viagra™, the first breakthrough medication in the oral market. At $10 per pill, and prescriptions ranging from 10 to 50 pills, Viagra™ captured 36,000 prescriptions in the first week it was on the market.

According to Cowen and Company, oral therapies would grow to represent an estimated 90 per cent of the MED market. This method of therapy, useful in mild to moderate cases of MED, was usually administered first regardless of the severity of the MED due to its ease of use. It was expected that oral therapies would continue to dominate in the future with an estimated market share of 93 per cent by 2002.

The report also observed that more invasive treatments for MED, such as injectable and topical therapies, had lost market share to oral therapy and represented only nine per cent of the MED market in 1998. These therapies were projected to continue being used only in the more severe cases of sexual dysfunction and were expected to retain approximately six per cent of the MED market in 2002.

Finally, the market for implants and surgery was estimated at only one per cent and was not expected to change, since this form of therapy was reserved for patients with no other treatment options.

COMPETITION IN THE
MARKET FOR ORAL THERAPIES

Cowen & Company's report, "Therapeutic Categories Outlook," predicted an increasingly competitive market for oral therapies. In 1998, Pfizer's Viagra™ was the sole player in the oral MED market capturing sales of $850 million.

Viagra™, a drug initially developed to treat hypertension, was projected to continue to dominate even as new competitors entered the oral market. It was expected to capture at least 75 per cent of a much larger oral MED market in 2002, producing sales of over $5 billion.

It was anticipated that Schering-Plough/ Zonagen would enter the oral market in 1999 with a product called Vasomax™, which was administered sublingually. This product worked differently than Viagra™ using a compound called phentolamine to enhance blood flow in the penis. Vasomax™ was in the late stages of phase III clinical testing. Although it appeared to be less effective than Viagra™, Vasomax™ had fewer side effects. As a result, it was predicted that Vasomax™ could capture approximately 15 per cent of the oral market by 2002.

Takeda Abbott Pharmaceuticals' (TAP) also had a product in Phase III of clinical testing. TAP's product, based on a compound called apomorphine$_{SL}$, was expected to enter the market in 2000. This method of treatment worked in the central nervous system, but had not yet been proven to be as effective as Viagra™. TAP's apomorphine$_{SL}$-based product was predicted to capture approximately 11 per cent of the oral market by 2002.

The Cowen report observed that several other companies, such as Merck and Bristol Myers Squibb, also had oral products with compositions similar to Viagra™ in Phases I and II of clinical testing. These competitors were expected to enter the MED market within three to four years.

THE REGULATORY APPROVAL PROCESS

Prior to marketing a drug for the treatment of disease, such as MED, companies were required to obtain approval from each of the countries in which they planned to release the drug. In the United States, approval was granted by the Food and Drug Administration (FDA). In Canada, the process was governed by the Health Protection Branch of the Department of Health. Because of the difference in market size, approval in the United States was critical to the commercial success of PTI's oral therapy for MED.

The first step in receiving regulatory approval in the United States involved pre-clinical testing of the drug's compounds first *in vitro* (in cell cultures) and then *in vivo* (in live animals hosts) to assess the toxicological and pharmacokinetic properties of the compound. Once this stage of testing was completed, the company would file with the FDA for Investigational New Drug (IND) status. This approval would give the company clearance to proceed with clinical testing on humans; a three-phase process, which can take several years and cost in excess of a $100 million to complete. After a drug completes all three phases of clinical trials, it is granted New Drug Approval (NDA) by the FDA. At this point, the company can begin manufacturing and marketing the drug.

Generally speaking, it can take as many as 10 years and cost as much as US$500 million for a compound to move through the development process from patenting to NDA approval. Only five in 5,000 compounds that enter pre-clinical testing are approved for human testing. Of those, only one in five is approved for sale. Because of the long time frame for regulatory approval, patents (which are usually granted at the beginning of the development process and have a 20-year life span) often have only a few years of protection remaining by the time the drug is actually made commercially available.

The long lead times for drug development, coupled with the comparatively short life span of patent protection following FDA approval, places considerable pressures on firms engaged in drug development to expedite the development process.

COMPANY BACKGROUND

In February of 1999, PTI occupied approximately 1,200 square feet of space, comprised of a single administrative office, a research lab and an office/lab combined space. PTI employed a total of four people: Terri Vaughn, executive assistant; Blair Glickman, president; Dr. Jeffrey Blair, vice-president operations/business development; Jake Randall (manager—research programs). PTI also paid, on a contract basis, for the services provided by John Ross, the company's part-time chief executive officer (CEO), and Drs. Hall and Abram, the principal scientists and founders of PTI. Hall served as the company's vice-president of clinical affairs, while Abram acted as vice-president of research and development (R&D).

Drs. Hall and Abram had been involved in a creative research partnership long before they formed Pharma Technologies Inc. Both men held faculty appointments. In his role as Professor of Urology and member of the Human Sexuality Group at a major Canadian hospital, Dr. Hall was involved in more than 20 Phase II, III and IV clinical trials involving disease states related to sexual dysfunction and reproduction. Dr. Abram held a full professorship in cardiovascular pharmacology. Both Abram and Hall had published over 70 peer-reviewed papers or book chapters each. They had also been recipients of numerous research grants and career merit awards.

Hall and Abram, who had worked together in other research and development projects for the treatment of MED, had an idea for a product based on a very novel technology. They took their concept to a major pharmaceutical firm, but it did not go forward. So they kept their concept "secret" and continued developing the technology independently. The thesis work of Dr. Jeffrey Blair, a PhD student of Mike Abram, provided the basis for the initial technology platform around which Pharma Technologies Inc. was formed. Blair received his PhD in 1997 in cardiovascular pharmacology and had received research traineeship awards from organizations such as: the Heart and Stroke Foundation of Canada, the Canadian Hypertension Society and Pfizer/Medical Research Council of Canada.

In early 1996, Drs. Blair, Hall and Abram began working with the University's incubator facility to obtain patent protection for their technology. It was through this facility that they met Glickman. Glickman, who was working as vice-president of commercial development, had been involved in the formation, financing and growth of a number of technology-based start-up ventures. His expertise included business development, patenting and licensing.

Blair, Hall and Abram were anxious to proceed with the development of their oral therapy for MED, but they needed a business infrastructure. With the help of Glickman and others at the incubator, PTI was formed in March 1997. Hall commented that, although the three founders were reluctant to accept venture capital financing, they were anxious to proceed. So in exchange for an option on future equity, they obtained $250,000 in seed capital from a venture fund specializing in medical research.

During the period between early 1996 and late 1997, the incubator filed a total of six patent applications, based on PTI's technology, with the U.S. Patent and Trademark Office (USPTO) of the U.S. Department of Commerce. The University, the registered assignee of these patents, subsequently granted PTI an exclusive worldwide license to use the technologies.

In November 1998, PTI obtained seed capital to proceed with technology development from two well-known Canadian venture capital (VC) funds. Together, they provided funding of $5 million in two tranches: $2 million at the time of signing; $3 million upon satisfactory completion of technical milestones and the signing of a partnership agreement with a pharmaceutical company for co-development of the technology.

Credibility with the financial and business community was an issue for PTI. At age 36, Glickman had considerable experience in the high-technology arena, but lacked the "gray hairs" expected by prospective commercial partners and investors. For this reason, the board appointed John Ross as part time CEO in November 1998. Ross was a well-known and well-respected figure in the Canadian biotechnology industry. He had served as CEO of a major Canadian biotechnology company and prior to that, held an executive position at a multi-national pharmaceutical firm.

Prior to the second tranche of financing described above, approximately two-thirds of PTI's common shares were held by the four principals, Abram, Hall, Blair and Glickman. The University incubator, the PTI Trust and the initial outside investor held the remaining one-third common shares. The subsequent two VC investors held convertible preferred shares in equal proportions.

The board of directors was composed of five members: Ross; Glickman; Dr. Hall and one representative each from company's major investors. John Malcom, the president of the incubator, Hall and Blair also attended the company's board meetings. Blair kept the minutes.

PLANS FOR TECHNOLOGY DEVELOPMENT

PTI's product development programs were based upon a significant portfolio of intellectual property. In the area of sexual dysfunction PTI had established two strategic product development programs, PTI Oral Therapy and PTI Local Therapy, each targeting a distinct segment of the MED market. In addition, the company had a number of interesting research initiatives at earlier stages of technical development.

PTI Oral Therapy

While PTI was actively pursuing a variety of initiatives, oral therapy represented the company's most promising technology and was clearly the immediate focus of attention. As described below, the PTI technology differed from Pfizer's Viagra™ product in several important ways, which the PTI management team believed would provide the basis for a competitive advantage.

The Underlying Technology

Male Erectile Dysfunction (MED), the clinical inability to obtain and hold an erection sufficient for intercourse, occurs when blood vessels to the penis become constricted, thereby preventing the level of blood flow required to achieve an erection. Scientists had believed for years that these blood vessels became constricted in men, over time, due to reduced levels of nitric oxide, a molecule that is released by the blood vessels and causes them to remain open.

Pfizer's Viagra™ was the first therapy to attempt to solve this problem and had been very well accepted in the marketplace. Viagra™ worked through the use of a phosphodiesterase (PDE) inhibitor, which prevented the breakdown of nitric oxide, thereby keeping the required blood vessels open. Research by scientists at PTI had revealed that the breakdown of nitric oxide in these patients was only the symptom and not the real problem causing MED.

Nitric oxide is expressed by endothelial cells into the smooth muscle cells of the blood vessels in the penis. PTI scientists discovered an inverse relationship between levels of nitric oxide and the amount of Factor X, a small protein released from the lining of the blood vessels. As the amount of Factor X is increased, levels of nitric oxide decrease, causing the smooth muscle cells to contract, thereby constricting the vasculature and substantially blocking blood flow to the penis. PTI scientists believed that the solution to the underlying problem of MED would be to reduce the levels of Factor X expressed into the smooth muscle, as opposed to increasing the local levels of nitric oxide. This approach would offer three distinct advantages over the market leader Viagra™.

First, while Viagra™ increased the level of nitric oxide throughout the body, the PTI method decreased the levels of Factor X only where it was over expressed in the penis, thereby reducing the likelihood of side effects (known or unknown) in patients. Second, because Viagra™ operated by manipulating the levels of nitric oxide in the body, it could not be taken by patients using nitrate therapy to manage cardiovascular disease. In contrast, because the PTI method did not affect nitric oxide levels, it would provide a safe alternative for these patients. Finally, because the PTI method addressed the underlying physiology of MED, it had the potential to prevent the progression of sexual dysfunction rather than just temporarily treating the symptoms.

Although the oral therapy was being developed initially as an acute treatment, PTI scientists believed that ongoing research would demonstrate its use as a chronic treatment which, when administered in at-risk patient populations, could prevent the onset or progression of sexual dysfunction and effectively reverse the disease process.

In April 1998, the University received U.S. patent approval for the use of Factor X in applications related to the treatment of sexual dysfunction. In turn, the University gave PTI the exclusive worldwide license for the technology. The company was still waiting for approval of a worldwide Patent Cooperation Treaty. This was the first step in the process for patent approval in approximately 90 other countries. Companies typically narrowed this field to a smaller subset of countries (approximately 18) in which they then pursued the lengthy and expensive process of obtaining full patent protection.

Development Milestones for the Oral Therapy

The development of a product using the PTI method of treatment required the identification of a compound to antagonize the action of Factor X. A research scientist at a Europen pharmaceutical company first discovered the scientific potential of 'Factor X' for this purpose in 1983. Researchers at the company produced the first usable compound as a result of their search for alternative therapies for cardiovascular disease. By 1999, at least 10 major pharmaceutical firms were pursuing clinical testing of Factor X for treatment of a variety of illnesses, such as congestive heart failure, hypertension and acute renal failure. While PTI's method of use patent gave the company exclusive rights to pursue the development of a treatment for sexual dysfunction by manipulating Factor X levels, PTI did not possess a Factor X compound.

The management team at PTI believed that they could greatly shorten the development timeline for their oral therapy and reduce the associated costs by partnering with a firm that possessed a Factor X compound. Firms with Factor X had taken these compounds through various stages of pre-clinical

testing, to assess their toxicological and pharmacokinetic properties. This testing provided valuable information about how long the compound would remain in the body after it was administered, the efficacy of the compound at different dosage levels, etc. PTI scientists believed that they would face less of a hurdle in taking their product through the regulatory approval process if they could access a compound that had already successfully passed the first one or two stages of clinical testing in the treatment of a different disease.

Therefore, rather than developing an Factor X compound internally, PTI's strategy was to approach these firms to determine if their molecules had potential for use in the treatment of sexual dysfunction. Subsequently, the company formed non-binding materials transfer agreements with five of these firms, involving a total of 16 different compounds. There was no financial consideration associated with the signing of these agreements.

Following the signing of the agreements, PTI initiated a rigorous three-step screening process, involving the use of laboratory rats, to assess the efficacy of the various Factor X in the treatment of sexual dysfunction. The screening process served as a "funnel" for evaluating the compounds: All of the compounds would be evaluated at Step 1, but their performance in that stage of screening would determine whether or not they proceeded to Step 2. Similarly, only a subset of the compounds that passed the hurdles in Step 2 would move on to Step 3. PTI planned to rank the compounds based on the results of the first two steps. The third step would be conducted after a partnership agreement had been signed with the owner of one of the top-ranked compounds.

Solid scientific results were critical, since PTI would rely upon the data from these experiments to prove to any prospective partners that its method of treatment would be effective.

Development Timeline

PTI's investors required the completion of five milestone activities as a condition to releasing the second tranche of financing: 1. Completion of pre-clinical efficacy studies on a target list of compounds. 2. Identification of two potential lead development candidate compounds. 3. Communicate results of pre-clinical studies to compound owners. 4. Finalize the selection of a lead development candidate compound. 5. Negotiate a collaborative agreement for the development of the lead compound candidate. PTI had allocated $360,000 of its operating budget to the achievement of these business milestones.

The PTI management team expected to make progress across several of the milestones simultaneously. For example, the company's projections called for the completion of the screening process and the ranking of the compounds by April 1999. During this time, the PTI management team would also be assessing the attractiveness of each of the potential partners from a business perspective and seeking to identify a champion for the project within each firm. Over the next four months, they would conduct initial meetings with the proposed partners to disclose the screening results and to discuss collaboration. An additional four months would be needed to negotiate an agreement, with finalization of the partnership agreement targeted for November 1999. Once the partnership was formed, the PTI management team believed that an oral product could be on the market within two to three years.

While the oral therapy was the primary focus of PTI's business development efforts, the company was also pursuing a program for local therapy and developing a novel delivery device. Both of these initiatives were also believed to have significant potential.

PTI Local Therapy

The local therapy involved the development of an injectable and/or topical product that enabled the administration of two compounds that had already been approved and were available on the market. The injectables currently available on the market used a high level of a drug called Factor Y, which caused pain and discomfort in patients. PTI's local therapy program represented advancement over the current products by combining Factor Y with a second therapeutic agent that reduced pain and improved efficacy.

PTI had the following milestones in the local therapy program over the next 11 months:

- Select a supplier of components.
- Fix components of the final product.
- Obtain IND approval to conduct clinical trials.
- Find a manufacturing partner for assembly, packaging and sterilization as well as a distribution partner.

PTI had reserved $215,000 of its operating budget for the completion of these milestones during the next year. Subsequently, Glickman planned to form a collaborative agreement with a partner in order to complete a one-year Phase II study. He expected that PTI would be required to contribute approximately $1 million toward the cost of this study.

In early 1999, PTI received notice that the examiner for the patent pertaining to the local therapy had raised several broad concerns/objections that would need to be addressed before the company could proceed with product development. Glickman was confident that the issues raised by the examiner could be resolved fairly quickly.

Delivery Device

Creams and suppositories had been poorly received in the MED market due to low efficacy and lack of comfort. PTI was working to develop a drug delivery device that did not involve a cream or suppository. This device could eventually be licensed for therapies beyond sexual dysfunction.

PTI had the following milestones for the project over the next 14 months:

- Identify formulation to be used.
- Contract out development of a prototype.

Of the PTI operating budget, $472,000 had been allocated for the completion of these milestones. This would be followed by five months of manufacturing trials and IND approval for clinical studies in collaboration with a partner. PTI expected to be required to contribute an additional $50,000.

Other Research Initiatives

In addition to PTI's oral and local therapy programs, the company was also pursuing a number of other research initiatives. PTI scientists had discovered a method of identifying a vascular condition that would help aid in the diagnosis of MED and FSD. A provisional patent had been filed with the U.S. FDA in May 1998. PTI was also investigating other novel methods for the diagnosis and treatment of MED and FSD. The company intended to file a provisional patent application for this technology with the FDA in the summer of 1998. Finally, PTI had been experimenting with a technology that could be used in the treatment of vascular conditions, such as premature aging of the skin.

PRESENT SITUATION AT PTI

Although PTI had sufficient capital for the next few months, Glickman knew that the company's cash requirements were accelerating and that there was significant pressure to achieve results in order to access the next tranche of financing from their investors.

Glickman projected that the first tranche of $2 million would be exhausted by November 1999. At present, PTI's burn rate for its baseline operation was around $50,000 per month. This covered payroll, consulting fees, administration and overhead expenses. Over the next few months though, the company needed additional cash to pay for contract research associated with the continued development of the oral therapy product. Specifically, PTI was committed to expenditures in the neighborhood of $360,000 over the next six months to advance the milestones on this project. There was an additional liability of $200,000 for research being performed off-site to advance specified milestones contained in their most recent financing agreement.

In order to access the second payment of $3 million, Glickman needed to have a commitment from a corporate partner. PTI's main challenge was to complete its screening process so

that it would be possible to identify a suitable partnership candidate. Timing was critical. A partnership agreement had to be reached and results obtained before competing therapies entered the market, before the company's money ran out, and before PTI's patent was challenged.

Achieving Key Scientific Milestones

In late January 1999, Jake Randall, a PhD candidate in pharmacology, had been hired as the manager of research programs. By February, Randall had completed Step 1 of the screening process on 12 of the 16 compounds. Two compounds had failed to make it through Step 1 and 10 compounds had been advanced to Step 2. While it was taking longer than anticipated to test the molecules, Randall's mandate was clear: he had to finish the screening of the Factor X compounds by April so that the company would be in a position to complete negotiations for co-development of the product by the November deadline.

Forming a Partnership Agreement for Co-development of the Oral Therapy

One of the key issues surrounding partner selection was whether PTI should proceed with technology development vis-à-vis out-licensing or in-licensing. Integrated pharmcos would be more likely to push PTI to out-license its technology, while smaller firms would be more willing to allow PTI to in-license their technology.

Under an out-licensing agreement, the target firm would obtain a license for PTI's oral therapy technology. The responsibility for the clinical research program would reside with the partner firm, with the possibility that a portion of it would be contracted back to PTI. From Glickman's perspective, this was less appealing because it meant that PTI would be giving up control and revenue-generating potential. However, partnering with an established and integrated pharmaceutical company offered the potential for PTI to leverage its chance of future success by obtaining support to launch all of its research initiatives, rather than being restricted to only two or three.

Under an in-licensing agreement, the target firm would grant PTI a license to use its Factor X compound as the basis for developing an oral therapy. PTI's scientists would perform the research required to take the product through completion of Phase II clinical trials. The final stages of clinical testing, production, distribution and marketing would then be licensed to a third party. All three partners would then share in the proceeds from the sale of the end-product.

There was also the possibility of a collaborative agreement between PTI and a small pharmco to jointly take the product through Phase II clinical testing. The advantage to this approach was that PTI could retain some control over the development process, although to a lesser extent than would be possible with an in-licensing agreement. The final stages of clinical testing and commercialization would either be turned back to the partner or licensed to a third party for completion.

The resources and capabilities to be offered by a partner varied considerably across the firms being considered by PTI, depending on their size and commitment to the sexual dysfunction market. To the extent that the target firm did not have an established position in the market, Glickman and his colleagues would have to work harder to persuade the firm of the huge market potential for their oral therapy. Moreover, they would have to be able to demonstrate the benefit of partnering with PTI, in terms of the reduced costs of product development (PTI had already done the pre-clinical research) and the shorter time frame for regulatory approval associated with using a proven Factor X compound.

The size and resource position of potential partners would also affect the ability of the end-product to achieve market penetration. Hall noted:

It is more than the compound that matters. It's all about timing. We are concerned about our oral therapy being the only drug in its class; the only treatment operating on the principle of Factor X reduction. In contrast, there will be three drugs in the same class as Viagra™. I am concerned that if our product is the only one in its class, it will not get noticed. A single drug could also be out-marketed by Viagra™. We need a top 20 company in order to make sure that our product can compete effectively. Alternatively, there is space for more than one Factor X drug to compete. Another thing we could do is arrange non-exclusive licenses to avoid being the only one in our class.

Blair saw the decision differently. He was concerned that the search for a large, established player would lengthen the time frame for product development:

In a large company, it takes a long time to figure out whom you have to talk to; find the right people with decision-making authority. You need to be assured of proper diligence and movement, or your deal will get lost. It might make sense to look at an intermediate company to co-develop the technology, rather than going right away to a multinational company.

ALPES S.A.: A JOINT VENTURE PROPOSAL (A)

Prepared by David T.A. Wesley under the supervision of Professors Henry W. Lane and Dennis Shaughnessy

As Dennis Shaughnessy, senior vice-president (VP) for Corporate Development and general counsel for Charles River Laboratories (CRL), prepared his presentation to the company's board of directors,[1] he wondered how the board would react to his request to invest up to $2 million in a

Mexican joint venture (JV) to create a state-of-the-art specific pathogen-free (SPF) egg farm.

Shaughnessy believed that the production and pre-incubation of SPF eggs for international agricultural vaccine companies in Mexico represented a long-term growth opportunity for CRL. The proposed joint venture with ALPES, a family-owned company that provided animal health products and services, would allow both companies to more aggressively exploit this opportunity and offered attractive financial returns for both partners.

Shaughnessy knew that to win over the board, he would also need to win over the support of company chief executive officer (CEO) Jim Foster. Without it, the JV would never come to fruition. But Foster viewed the proposed joint venture as a potential distraction for Specific Antigen-Free Avian Services (SPAFAS) as it continued to expand rapidly in the United States. He also worried about the risks of investing in a country like Mexico, with an unstable currency and an uncertain market. He was especially concerned about the plan to partner with a small, family-owned company that was not making a new investment of their own, but rather relying solely on CRL's capital to fund the project. Finally, after nearly 50 years in business, CRL had never successfully conducted business in Mexico.

CHARLES RIVER LABORATORIES

Founded in 1947 by Henry Foster, Charles River Laboratories was the global market leader in the commercial production and supply of laboratory animal models for use in discovery research and the development and testing of new pharmaceuticals. Foster took his company public in 1968, raising $3 million. In 1981, Foster sold the company to Bausch and Lomb (B&L) for $110 million.

Henry Foster continued as CEO under B&L until his son Jim succeeded him in 1992. Jim Foster was eager to expand the company but, at the time, B&L had been experiencing its own challenges, and was reluctant to invest the needed capital. Nevertheless, Charles River

Laboratories remained one of B&L's most profitable divisions, at times contributing more than 10 per cent of B&L's corporate net income.

The company's strategic growth objective was to grow its existing businesses by between 12 per cent and 15 per cent annually and its entire business by 20 per cent. This plan left a "strategic growth gap" of five per cent to eight per cent each year. Charles River Laboratories then pursued technology platform acquisitions, joint ventures, technology licensing and strategic partnerships to fill the gap.

Charles River Laboratories served customers in more than 15 countries worldwide. These were primarily large pharmaceutical companies that, together with biotechnology firms, accounted more than 75 per cent of Charles River Laboratories' sales. The remaining customers included animal health, medical device and diagnostic companies, as well as hospitals, academic institutions and government agencies. As a result of its leadership position in the industry, CRL had not lost any of its 20 largest customers in more than 10 years. The company's largest customer accounted for less than three per cent of total revenues.

Specific Antigen-Free Eggs and Avian Services

CRL's entry into avian services traced its beginning to Shaughnessy's visit to Merck's New Jersey headquarters to discuss the pharmaceutical company's use of CRL animal models. Over lunch, one Merck executive offhandedly remarked that they had to do something about "that old chicken farm."

Shaughnessy was puzzled. "Why on earth does Merck own a chicken farm?" he asked.

"Well, we have been developing poultry species to help us better understand genetics," replied the Merck executive.

Now, of course, we're doing our genetic work in mice, but we still have these chicken farms. Currently, we're using the farms to produce SPF eggs that we use to make those few human vaccines left that haven't converted over to newer technology for their production, and what remains of our agricultural vaccine operations.

Contaminated poultry posed a serious risk to human health. The U.S. Department of Agriculture estimated that such bacteria caused more than four million illnesses and up to 3,000 deaths each year.[2] For that reason, poultry had to be vaccinated against pathogens that were harmful to humans, including salmonella and campylobacter.

Material for vaccines used to inoculate poultry was produced when a target virus was injected into fertilized eggs. As the eggs matured, they became natural bioreactors in which isolated pathogens expanded geometrically. Specific pathogen-free eggs were raised in controlled environments that were free from common bacteria, viruses and other contaminants. These "biosecure" environments[3] were important for the production of poultry vaccines, since contaminated chicken eggs often contained antibodies that killed the target virus. Contaminated eggs also posed the risk of introducing unwanted pathogens into the vaccine.

Shaughnessy was intrigued. He wondered aloud, "Well, we raise lots of mice as you know. Maybe we would be good at raising chickens." "Then why don't you buy it?" replied one Merck executive, who had for some time been seeking a buyer for SPAFAS. Shaughnessy agreed to meet with the head of SPAFAS to further discuss the matter.

Charles River Laboratories eventually agreed to acquire SPAFAS from Merck for $6 million in cash, an amount roughly equal to the business's annual revenues. During the due diligence process, Shaughnessy learned that some human vaccines were still produced in eggs.

Companies that produced influenza vaccines alone consumed more than 100 million eggs annually, although nearly all of these were not SPF eggs, but rather standard farm-grade eggs.[4] Shaughnessy recalled:

When we bought SPAFAS, our grand scheme was the conversion of production of inactivated human vaccines like flu vaccine, from commercial eggs to SPF eggs. That will dramatically increase demand for SPF eggs, and the business will grow dynamically.

Convincing human vaccine producers to switch to SPF eggs proved to be a Herculean task. At a cost of pennies per egg, farm-grade eggs were significantly cheaper than SPF eggs, which could cost as much as a dollar per egg. Shaughnessy quickly realized that convincing CRL's traditional vaccine customers would be more difficult and time consuming than first imagined. In the meantime, opportunities for growth were limited to agricultural applications, principally avian vaccines sold to the integrated poultry companies. As a consequence, potential marketing synergies between SPAFAS and Charles River Laboratories were less than anticipated. With projected annual poultry industry growth set at a lethargic three per cent, Shaughnessy wondered if SPAFAS could hope to achieve CRL's aggressive growth objectives.

One consolation was that demand for SPF eggs had exceeded available supply by between five per cent and 10 per cent worldwide. Accordingly, in fewer than four years following the acquisition, SPAFAS more than doubled its annual revenues while improving its operating margin to nearly 20 per cent. In order to support this growth, CRL continuously invested capital in expanding domestic SPF egg production capacity. Recently, the board of directors had approved a significant capital investment in SPAFAS for increased production in the United States. Meanwhile, the company's two main competitors failed to respond to rising demand by adding new capacity of their own, allowing SPAFAS to continue to increase its market share.

Based on recent projections, SPAFAS was expected to attain revenues of $25 million within the next two to three years. However, projections of this kind were based on growth within the existing business, and did not account for opportunities to expand internationally. In Shaughnessy's estimation, accessing international markets could further improve revenues to as much as $50 million within four to five years.

SPAFAS International

y ser-
30 per
ent in
)unted
oultry
:luded
uch as

npany
a and
breed
on at a
;ement
name,
rs who
rds of
hough
: to be
e seen
. facil-
ie cost
ded to
nchise
'AFAS

...ccine producers
... eggs, Shaughnessy hoped to grow the company through the purchase of SPAFAS franchises in Brazil, Mexico and India from their current owners. Once purchased, SPAFAS could integrate its worldwide operations and consolidate the revenues.

Since franchisees were typically large poultry integrators,[6] the value of the SPF egg business was relatively small (typically less than five per cent of revenues). Furthermore, agricultural companies appeared less suited to manage a biotech operation and rarely devoted the funds needed to make SPF operations internationally competitive. In their current state, Shaughnessy thought the owners of these companies would be eager to sell the franchises in order to concentrate on their core poultry businesses— provided they were offered a fair price.

Shaughnessy was surprised by the Brazilian franchisee's reaction, which was one of distrust. Instead of selling the franchise, the Brazilian franchisee eventually decided to sever ties with SPAFAS and continue the operation independently. The Indian reaction was far less acrimonious, but still failed to result in an agreement, although India remained a SPAFAS franchisee.

ALPES

Finally, Shaughnessy turned his attention to the Mexican franchisee, ALPES S.A.[7] Founded in 1974 as a member of the IDISA group of companies, ALPES was the sole producer of SPF eggs in Mexico. The company was owned by the Romero family, which also owned a large poultry operation known as Grupo Romero.

In the early 1950s, Socorro Romero[8] established a medium-sized poultry farm in the high desert of Tehuacán, east of Mexico City. Shortly afterward, she was joined by one of her two brothers. Together they created the venture that would eventually be known as Grupo Romero.

Grupo Romero was officially founded in 1963 by Socorro Romero to produce boiler chickens for the Mexican market. In the early 1970s, Socorro asked her brother Miguel,[9] who had recently completed a Ph.D. in chemistry at Harvard University and had begun working for a U.S.-owned company in Mexico City, to help improve the company's feed formulation. The idea was to reduce the company's dependence on third-party suppliers. Nutrition was the most expensive variable cost item in poultry farming, and by vertically integrating feed production, Grupo Romero could both reduce costs and increase reliability.

Realizing that a wider need existed for animal health services, Miguel Romero decided to start his own company, which later became known as Grupo IDISA. IDISA soon began offering services throughout Mexico and Latin America.

Although by this time poultry vaccines could be purchased from various international animal health firms, no one provided vaccines that were specifically suited to Latin American farmers. In 1972, Miguel Romero contacted poultry vaccine researchers at Cornell University in Ithaca, New York, who agreed to coordinate a vaccine development project with the Universidad Nacional Autónoma de México (UNAM). After several contaminations at the Mexico City research site, however, both parties agreed to abandon the project.

Refusing to admit defeat, Miguel Romero decided to continue the research on his own. In 1974, he founded ALPES as the SPF egg subsidiary of IDISA (see Exhibit 1). He turned to SPAFAS, which at the time was a relatively small family business in Connecticut, for technical assistance. SPAFAS sold ALPES breeding stock and provided technical advice on creating a biosecure environment within which SPF chickens could be raised. All knowledge transfer and technical support was provided informally through a "handshake" agreement between the two family-owned companies.

Alejandro Romero described the early business affiliation between ALPES and SPAFAS as an "open relationship" in which both parties benefited from the honest exchange and sharing of information and product innovations.[10] Finally, ALPES became the exclusive Mexican distributor for imported SPAFAS eggs and embryos.

By 1978, ALPES had its own well-established production facilities. As a result of the readily available supply of SPF eggs and embryos, international vaccine manufacturers began to establish operations in Mexico.

All forms of cooperation between ALPES and SPAFAS were conducted through informal "handshake" agreements between the original owners. Although Merck maintained this arrangement when it acquired SPAFAS in 1986, the Romero family was wary of the new management, with whom it had no relationship. The Romeros sought to formalize a deal, eventually establishing ALPES as a franchise of SPAFAS, with exclusivity within Mexico and Central America.

Alejandro Romero joined Grupo IDISA in 1989 after completing his master's degree in chemical engineering at the University of British Columbia in Canada.[11] Knowing that IDISA could not depend on his father's leadership forever, he pushed for structural changes such as a professional management staff and the use of

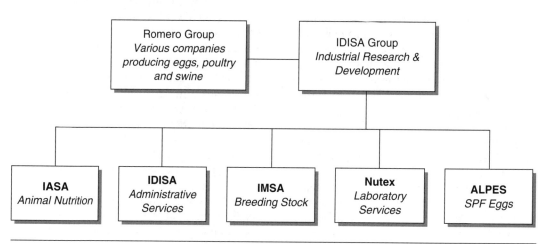

Exhibit 1 IDISA Group of Companies

Source: Company files.

external auditors and consultants. When Miguel Romero passed away in 1997, Alejandro became CEO and chairman of Grupo IDISA.

IDISA had annual revenues of approximately $2.9 million compared to Grupo Romero revenues of approximately $200 million. The board of directors included Alejandro Romero's mother, aunt and sister, a veterinarian with a master's degree from Cornell University.

To comply with Mexican law, the company held formal board meetings once a year (ALPES Mission and Organizational Vision Statements are provided in Exhibit 2).

Market Conditions

In 1994, the North American Free Trade Agreement (NAFTA) came into effect, facilitating

---

DEFINITION and MISSION

IDISA, which stands for Vital Research and Development and Animal Health,[1] is a world-class group of companies dedicated to providing optimal solutions to the needs of the health, farming and industrial sectors, through differentiated products and services, based on research and development.

AIM

To unite material, financial and technological resources and, through human intervention, to transform them into goods and services that generate wealth, in a wider sense, as a combined set of economic and social benefits for workers and investors.

VISION

We envision IDISA as a group of companies:

1. with a high level of synergy derived through integration;
2. that leads the domestic market in each of its specialized functions, while increasing its international market presence;
3. offering vital solutions that meet the needs of its clients, while providing products and services that optimize the relationship between costs and benefits;
4. generating leading edge, innovative and differentiated technologies, products and services;
5. committed to the continuous improvement and quality of its products and services;
6. that consolidates existing business and develops new lines of business;
7. committed to satisfying its shareholders with an optimal return on investment, to suppliers with fair treatment and to the communities in which it operates through the generation of employment and environmental responsibility;
8. that motivates and rewards employee achievements and performance, permits and encourages their personal development, and offers opportunities for growth and advancement consistent with their capacity and career path; and
9. with an institutional structure that is flexible and facilitates decision making in an adaptable, efficient and effective manner.

Exhibit 2   Organization of Group IDISA

Source: Company files.

1. As translated from the Spanish acronym for Investigación y Desarrollo Integral y Salud Animal.

the free flow of goods and services, which resulted in a number of changes that had a direct impact on ALPES. Fearing increased competition from imports, Alejandro Romero sought to mitigate the effect by establishing exclusivity contracts with suppliers, customers and potential competitors.

While some business left Mexico as feared, the overall effect of NAFTA proved positive. Vaccine producers increased production in Mexico, from which they supplied the United States and Canada, while competition from imports failed to materialize. ALPES hastily doubled its production to meet rising demand.

ALPES was the major supplier of SPF eggs to Mexico's two largest animal vaccine producers, InterVet and Anchor. Netherlands-based InterVet was one of the world's largest poultry vaccine manufacturers with more than $1 billion in revenues and operations in 55 countries. InterVet purchased approximately 80 per cent of the SPF eggs produced by ALPES. Anchor, the Mexican subsidiary of Boehringer Ingelheim of Germany, accounted for most of ALPES' remaining sales. Both companies had recently invested several million dollars in new plants near Mexico City to meet growing demand for animal vaccines in Europe and Asia.[12] InterVet projected a doubling of its need for SPF eggs to four million units within one year. Eventually, changes in European and Asian vaccine regulations could result in a further increase in overall demand for SPF eggs in Mexico to more than 10 million units per year. To meet this growing demand, both InterVet and Anchor had begun importing SPF eggs from the United States, primarily from SPAFAS.

European countries had very strict quality standards that had to be met before vaccines could be imported. For ALPES, meeting those standards proved particularly challenging.[13] Not only did the company need to improve its facilities to meet international standards, but rising levels of poultry production in the surrounding area had significantly increased the likelihood of contamination. One ALPES customer produced a large lot of vaccine before contaminants were discovered. When the entire lot had to be recalled, the customer's reputation suffered.

Capital Investment Needs

On his first visit to Charles River Laboratories, Alejandro Romero met Jim Foster, Dennis Shaughnessy and several other senior managers for the first time. His task was to present the ALPES business case and discuss opportunities in Mexico under NAFTA. Specifically, the head of InterVet in Mexico, who was both a long-time friend and customer of the Romeros, had been pressing Alejandro Romero to expand production in order to meet InterVet's growing demand for SPF eggs. Both agreed that any new facility would need to have considerably greater production capacity as well as superior sanitary standards, including sealed and quarantined animal housing, a laboratory and service buildings, where eggs could be pre-incubated prior to being shipped to customers. IDISA was unwilling to invest these funds itself because of "high borrowing costs in Mexico" and the "relatively small contribution to the total returns of Grupo Romero." Romero hoped that Foster would agree to either loan ALPES the money needed to expand its facilities, or make a minority equity investment that would still leave control of the business in the hands of the Romeros.

Loaning ALPES the funds was dismissed outright. As a growth-oriented firm, Charles River Laboratories was simply not in the business of lending money. The idea of becoming a minority shareholder was also looked upon unfavorably as it would limit participation in the business and prevent CRL from fully consolidating the company's revenues in its income statement.

Shaughnessy explained that CRL was primarily interested in acquisitions. If the Romeros would be willing to sell ALPES outright, CRL would certainly be interested. He also expressed concern about the real rates of return for the existing business under its current management, which had been between negative 25 per cent and negative 28 per cent for each of the last three years.

Romero explained that the poor rates of return had been a consequence of unforeseen contaminations, which had both reduced revenues and increased costs.[14] A new facility would greatly reduce the risk of contamination. Shaughnessy and Foster appeared skeptical that new facilities alone would reduce the contamination risk, given that strict compliance with biosecurity principles had not been part of the ALPES work environment.

Ultimately, ALPES was not for sale, explained Romero. "We want to continue this business," he added. "Especially now, we see great opportunities that we want to take part in." His bottom line position was that if CRL were unwilling to invest in ALPES, IDISA would seek other investors.

The company had already entertained the option of partnering with SPAFAS's primary competitor, Lohmann-Tierzucht International of Germany. Lohmann-Tierzucht was the SPF eggs subsidiary of the PHW Group, a large international animal health company with more than 30 subsidiaries worldwide, including SPAFAS's primary competitor in the United States. Shortly after CRL acquired SPAFAS, the Romeros began discussions with Lohmann-Tierzucht in order to ensure an uninterrupted supply of breed stock. More recently, ALPES began using Lohmann genetic lines in its SPF egg production.

As a compromise between the two positions, Alejandro Romero suggested that both parties consider a joint venture. If Charles River Laboratories contributed the funds needed for a new facility, IDISA would contribute buildings, land and other assets currently owned by ALPES (see Exhibit 3). Both parties agreed to consider the matter.

CURRENT ASSETS	
Cash And Cash Equivalents	56,703
Accounts Receivable	282,628
Inventory	92,613
Birds	390,674
TOTAL CURRENT ASSETS	**822,618**
PROPERTY PLANT AND EQUIPMENT	112,003
OTHER ASSETS	16,249
TOTAL ASSETS	**950,870**
LIABILITIES AND STOCKHOLDERS' EQUITY	
CURRENT LIABILITIES	
Trade Accounts Payable	92,397
TOTAL CURRENT LIABILITIES	**92,397**
LIABILITIES	
Income Taxes Payable	8,346
Accrued Liabilities	88,912
TOTAL ACCRUED LIABILITIES	**97,258**
SHAREHOLDERS' EQUITY	
Capital Stock	541,681
Retained Earnings	1,040,207
Revaluation Deficit	(1,025,286)
Accumulated Income	204,613
TOTAL STOCKHOLDERS' EQUITY	**761,215**
TOTAL LIABILITIES AND STOCKHOLDERS' EQUITY	**950,870**

Exhibit 3   Aves Libres de Patógenos Específicos, SA Balance Sheet (in US$)

Source: Company files.

Alejandro Romero returned to Mexico to discuss the joint venture opportunity with family members. The one concern that was raised was the effect a joint venture would have on the decision-making process of the company, from a family-oriented process to one that was more institutional. Even so, everyone recognized that the change was necessary if ALPES and IDISA, and even Grupo Romero, were to continue to mature into world-class international companies. Alejandro Romero called Shaughnessy to express his family's willingness to enter into formal negotiations.

First Encounters With Mexico

Shaughnessy made three visits to Mexico, each time accompanied by one or two senior managers from SPAFAS, before presenting his findings to CRL's management and board of directors. The first was an official meeting with members of the Romero family, which, outside of Alejandro Romero's visit to the United States earlier in the year, was the first of its kind between the Romeros and anyone from Charles River Laboratories.

Several weeks later, Shaughnessy made a second trip that included a tour of ALPES's facilities in Tehuacán. As he left Mexico City, he was unprepared for the isolation and poverty that he would encounter in the Mexican countryside, both of which left a strong and lasting impression upon him. And while Grupo IDISA's headquarters was a modern facility in the center of Tehuacán, a maquiladora[15] city with more than 300,000 inhabitants, the company's poultry farms appeared to him to be below standards.

On his third visit, Shaughnessy had dinner at the Romero estate in Tehuacán. He recalled:

We had a six-hour Mexican dinner with the entire Romero family, and we talked about books, education, philosophy and all the things that people think about when they reflect on their lives, family and society. Out of that came the stories of who they are. For example, before that visit, I didn't know that they had already been in negotiations with Merck for a long time to do some sort

of joint venture. And I didn't know that Alejandro's father had been a federal deputy in Mexico and had been instrumental in several campaigns to clean up government corruption.

The Romeros seemed to be very high-quality people, as did their siblings and other family members. We discussed what it is like to be a prominent and successful Mexican. That carried over to their views on business. These were clearly business people with great personal integrity and commitment, the type of people that could be the foundation for a strong business partnership.

Those views seemed a stark contrast to what Shaughnessy was accustomed to in the United States, where quarterly earnings targets often appeared to drive company strategy. Alejandro Romero explained:

For us as a company, success comes from three factors. One is hard work, another is people, and the other is honesty or trust. You have to have those factors in hand and then profit comes as a consequence. Profit is really not a final objective. It is a consequence of doing things right and doing the right things.

After these visits, Shaughnessy became less concerned about the potential impact of the rural poverty surrounding the ALPES operations. He also became convinced of the integrity and competence of his Mexican counterparts.

Before returning to the United States, Shaughnessy notified the Romeros that he would recommend the joint venture to the Charles River Laboratories board of directors. He warned them however that neither the board of directors nor the CEO had the same level of knowledge of the Romeros family and its businesses. Without that first-hand knowledge, their support might not be easily won.

THE JOINT VENTURE PROPOSAL

Shaughnessy presented the following terms of the joint venture to the Charles River Laboratories board of directors:

SPAFAS would invest $2 million in cash into a new joint venture company to be located near Mexico City, in exchange for 50 per cent of its equity. Our partner, ALPES, would contribute its existing SPF and commercial egg (for vaccines) assets to the joint venture company for its 50 per cent equity interest. Profits would be shared equally.

The $2 million cash investment would be used to increase the SPF egg production capacity of the joint venture ($1.5 million), establish a pre-incubation facility ($250,000), and compensate ALPES for associated goodwill and management services ($250,000).

The existing ALPES business, which would be contributed to the joint venture, represents nearly $2 million in sales and an estimated 15 per cent operating margin. The $2 million in-kind contribution value assessed to this business, when considered in the acquisition context, reflects favorable purchase price multiples in the range of 1 × Revenues and 6 × EBIT.

As shown below in the Financial Summary, the joint venture will produce $3 million in sales next year, more than doubling by year four, with operating margins forecast to be in excess of 30 per cent (see Exhibit 4).

	Year 1	Year 2	Year 3	Year 4	Year 5	Total
Sales	2,941,028	4,916,477	5,837,466	6,686,183	7,562,987	27,944,141
Cost	2,097,306	2,951,721	3,347,327	3,712,698	4,093,262	16,202,314
Cost germ egg	288,830	617,171	781,550	932,897	1,088,253	3,708,701
Gross margin	554,892	1,347,585	1,708,589	2,040,588	2,381,472	8,033,126
Packaging, Shipping, Delivery	243,475	292,622	307,253	322,616	338,747	1,504,713
Distribution margin	311,417	1,054,963	1,401,336	1,717,972	2,042,725	6,528,413
G&A	225,455	271,805	285,395	299,665	314,646	1,396,966
Total Cost before tax and finance	2,855,066	4,133,319	4,721,525	5,267,876	5,834,908	22,812,694
Finance Cost	709	745	782	821	962	4,019
Operating Income	85,253	782,413	1,115,159	1,417,486	1,727,117	5,127,428
Tax	4,175	5,495	5,770	6,058	6,361	27,859
Total Cost	2,859,950	4,139,559	4,728,077	5,274,755	5,842,231	22,844,572
Operating Net Income	81,078	776,918	1,109,389	1,411,428	1,720,756	5,099,569
Assumptions						
Unit price/egg ALPES I[1]	$0.54	$0.57	$0.60	$0.63	$0.66	
Unit price/embryo ALPES I	$0.68	$0.71	$0.75	$0.79	$0.83	
Unit price/egg ALPES II[2]	$0.11	$0.12	$0.12	$0.13	$0.13	
Unit price/embryo ALPES II	$0.16	$0.17	$0.18	$0.19	$0.19	
Inflation	5.00%	5.00%	5.00%	5.00%	5.00%	
Exchange Rate	$7.50	$7.50	$7.50	$7.50	$7.50	

Exhibit 4   Pro Forma Income Statement (Proposed Joint Venture) (in US$)   *(Continued)*

	Year 1	Year 2	Year 3	Year 4	Year 5	Total
Cost germ egg ALPES I	$0.10	$0.10	$0.11	$0.11	$0.12	
Prod Cost/Egg ALPES I (OLD FARM)	$0.38	$0.40	$0.42	$0.44	$0.46	
Prod Cost/Embryo ALPES I (NEW FARM)	$0.49	$0.45	$0.47	$0.49	$0.52	
Prod Cost/Egg ALPES II	$0.09	$0.10	$0.10	$0.11	$0.11	
Prod Cost/Embryo ALPES II	$0.16	$0.16	$0.17	$0.18	$0.19	
# Egg sold (ALPES I)	1,732,398	1,732,398	1,732,398	1,732,398	1,732,398	
# Embryo sold (NEW FARM)	1,038,465	3,632,946	4,683,974	5,525,636	6,301,817	
# Egg ALPES II sold	2,952,630	2,952,630	2,952,630	2,962,630	2,952,630	
# Embryo ALPES II sold	6,091,089	5,947,948	5,308,544	4,737,875	4,228,554	
# Total house	5	10	11	12	12	
# Years depreciation building	20	20	20	20	20	
# Years depreciation equipment	7	7	7	7	7	
# Years depreciation vehicles	5	5	5	5	5	

Exhibit 4 (Continued)

Source: Company files.

1. ALPES I eggs were SPF eggs used primarily in the production of live vaccines (flocks tested negative for 28 avian pathogens).

2. ALPES II eggs were clean, commercial fertile eggs used for the production of inactivated vaccines (flocks tested negative for eight pathogens).

Market opportunities notwithstanding, several board members raised objections. First, some were concerned by the complex organizational structure of Grupo IDISA, which consisted of five legally independent companies that were all owned by the same family. Others were equally concerned with the large number of inter-company transactions between ALPES, IDISA and other Romero companies. And finally, some of the directors were concerned about the lack of transparency of a company that only held board meetings once a year and did not appear to have strategic plans, operating budgets, meeting minutes or other formal corporate documents that are routine for U.S. public companies. Some members of the board wondered if they could make an informed decision about a business that they knew so little about.

Some members of the board were especially concerned about media reports that often portrayed Mexico as a country plagued with endemic corruption and economic instability. The directors from Bausch and Lomb recalled an earlier "unpleasant experience" with a Mexican optics distributor who had defrauded the company. Both the CEO and the board of directors wanted assurances that the Romeros could be trusted and that the joint venture would serve the strategic interests of Charles River Laboratories, not just those of ALPES and Grupo IDISA.

NOTES

1. Charles River was a wholly owned subsidiary of Bausch & Lomb (B&L). As a result, its board was largely controlled by senior management of B&L.

2. Caroline Smith DeWaal, "Playing Chicken: The Human Cost of Inadequate Regulation of the Poultry Industry," Center for Science in the Public Interest, Washington, D.C., March 1996.

3. Biosecurity involved unique animal housing with pressure-filtered air. The integrity of these facilities was maintained through decontamination and control procedures for both animals and humans to prevent the entry of unwanted pathogens.

4. "Dirty" eggs contained pathogens that could be harmful to other poultry. Many experts believed that human beings were immune to poultry diseases. However, in 1997, Hong Kong experienced the first known cases of avian flu in human beings. Since then, avian flu outbreaks in humans have been reported in Europe, the United States and Asia. More recently, scientists have linked the Spanish Flu of 1918 that claimed up to 50 million lives to avian flu, "1918 Killer Flu Secrets Revealed," BBC News UK Edition, February 5, 2004.

5. Breed stock eggs were used to restock hatcheries with hens that had specific genetic profiles. While the eggs were more expensive, the number needed to restock hatcheries was relatively small.

6. A poultry integrator carries out different aspects of poultry production through its various farms and related businesses. These include growing, breeding, care, transport, processing and marketing of eggs, boiler chickens and other end-use poultry products.

7. ALPES (Aves libres de patógenos específicos) was a Spanish acronym equivalent to SPAFAS.

8. Aunt of Alejandro Romero, CEO of ALPES.

9. Alejandro Romero's father.

10. For example, some innovations in building design and construction, such as the use of cement rather than wood, were later adopted by SPAFAS as more effective in the prevention and elimination of potentially harmful contaminants.

11. Alejandro Romero also held degrees in engineering and business administration (MBA) from Mexican universities.

12. More than two-thirds of Mexico's vaccine production was exported.

13. Poultry vaccines made from "dirty" eggs were permitted in Mexico and Central America, but they were strictly prohibited in the United States, Europe and Japan.

14. ALPES had to decontaminate the farm and restock its facilities several times in the past three years.

15. Known officially as the in-bond industry, maquiladoras were export-oriented factories that operated under special trade rules established by the Mexican government. International companies often established maquiladora factories in order to produce lower cost goods destined for the U.S. market. Under NAFTA, most products manufactured in Mexico could enter the U.S. free of duties.

2

Selecting the Right Partner

In Brief

It should come as no surprise that appropriate partner selection is a strong determinant of how successful an alliance will ultimately be. Inexperienced companies should exercise patience and discipline during the selection phase and resist the temptation to "do a deal" as quickly as possible.

Key factors to consider during the selection process are the overall strategic fit between the partners, the complementarities of each organization's strengths, weaknesses and operational practices, the sustainability of the relationship, consideration of how partner cultures may clash or complement one another, the degree of commitment to the partnership, and, finally, the personal chemistry between both companies' management.

Throughout the partner selection phase, it is highly recommended that objective tools or methods be used that will facilitate the most impartial assessment of partner candidates. To conduct due diligence with rose-colored glasses may prove detrimental in the long run.

A long with unfocused strategic objectives, poor partner selection ranks high among the reasons for alliance failure. Partner selection is an area where taking shortcuts comes back to haunt companies later.

It invariably takes longer than anticipated to find the right partner. Regardless of whether a company proactively searches for a partner based on its identified needs or it is approached by another company, it is important to commit the time and resources to thoroughly analyze the potential opportunity. Depending on the scope and complexity of the alliance, it may take several months or even a couple of years to complete the deal.

Furthermore, in many cases, there is likely to be more than one right partner. Hence, it is important to invest the time to determine which potential partner is best positioned to meet a company's strategic needs. Small companies looking for alliance partners are often tempted to look for shortcuts as they find themselves facing time and financial pressures. They may succumb to the temptation to partner with any company that expresses a willingness to partner, whether or not it meets their strategic needs. Invariably, this move is a mistake. Being willing isn't sufficient—a partner *must* fit a company's strategic needs.[1]

Small companies can also be overwhelmed in the face of overtures from a large company to form a partnership. The reputation and image of the large company or the excitement of being approached by a major corporation can often cause the small company to neglect the necessary partner evaluation or to ignore its own strategic objectives. Whether a company is looking for a partner or is reacting to an overture, the same level of due diligence is required.

Establish Criteria—First

Once the partnering objectives discussed in the introductory text of Chapter 1 have been established, managers should decide how many partners to approach. The search process starts by formalizing partner profile screening criteria, developing a list of prospects, ranking the list against the criteria, and then focusing on a manageable number of the best prospects.

The partner selection criteria matrix in Figure 2.1 is similar to the gap analysis but now affords a closer assessment of the optimal synergies between an organization and a partner. The matrix can be used to help create a profile of the ideal partner. This needs to be done *before identifying any companies.*

Identifying Prospective Partners

Existing distributors, suppliers, and customers with whom a company already has a good relationship are often a good place to start when identifying potential partners. Prior familiarity with a potential partner has its pluses and minuses. On the plus side, the potential partners may be well known, and there may even be a preexisting relationship and level of trust that can facilitate the formation of the new venture. At the same time, however, familiarity can promote complacency. The result may be the failure to explore new approaches and more productive relationships because of the ease of dealing with familiar prospects.

Beyond immediate business relationships, some of the best sources to use for generating a list of potential partners are the following:

- Business networks
- Industry associations
- Domestic and foreign venture capital groups
- Trading houses
- Investment bankers
- Business reporters and editors in the target territory
- Business directories and partnering databases
- Foreign investment promotion agencies

Use this matrix to help you create a profile of the ideal partner.
Create this criteria *before you identify any companies.*

From your gap analysis, list **partner competencies** sought. (e.g., Customer base, IP, infrastructure, etc.)	1. 2. 3.

What are the characteristics of a partner that would find our **core competencies** desirables?	1. 2. 3.

What is the **ideal size and structure** of a partner (e.g., European presence, central organization, $100M revenues)	1. 2. 3.

What are some **key relationships** we would like the partner to bring to the table? (e.g., Tier 1 customers, suppliers)	1. 2. 3.

What other factors are of crucial importance to our partner selection? (e.g., track record)	1. 2. 3.

Figure 2.1   Partner Selection Criteria

- Foreign trade offices (e.g., JETRO)
- Regional and municipal economic development authorities
- Government embassies and consulates abroad

Venture capital firms can be a particularly useful source. These firms may have prospective partners in their portfolios, might be willing to participate financially in the partnership, or could have incubators or networks that can be leveraged.

The explosion of partnership interest in recent years is reflected in exponentially increasing information sources and databases on partnering opportunities. Governments at all levels, as well as leading industry associations and consulting firms, are increasingly active in profiling companies interested in partnerships.

CONDUCT PARTNER DUE DILIGENCE

The first rule in partner due diligence is one cannot do too much of it. Making partnership decisions based on a superficial determination of similarities or apparent compatibility can be a fatal mistake. Research has clearly demonstrated that successful alliance builders develop an intimate knowledge of a potential partner's management culture, previous alliance experience, and strategic objectives.[2]

Implementation must be kept in mind during the evaluation of potential partners. Ultimately, the right partner is one who has the resources required to create the strategic value a company is seeking and who is similar enough in terms of organization and outlook to make the arrangement work. Partners therefore should be evaluated in terms of their strategic, cultural, and operational fit.[3]

STRATEGIC FIT

In evaluating strategic fit, managers should be searching for a partner who has complementary assets and capabilities. This partner should help fill the strategic gap identified in the introductory text of Chapter 1 and not simply offer redundant capabilities. Having identical strategic assets is not a good basis for a partnership because the possibility of competitive conflict can be high over the long term. Companies should bring complementary differences to the venture for it to create real value.

Managers should also take into account *the balance of need between the partners.* Alliances between strong and weak companies seldom work because excessive dependency can seriously affect the power balance and the evolution of the relationship. In principle, the partners should be similar in strategic strength, although they may be quite different in other ways.[4]

The nature and durability of the strategic fit is also a critical consideration. It is important that the long-term objectives of the partners are not in conflict and that the intended benefits can be sustained. The combined capabilities of the partners should achieve a sustainable competitive advantage for both partners. A good strategic fit exists where the short-term alliance value serves each partner's long-term strategic ambition equally well. Ambitions are often more predictive of alliance evolution than the starting points.[5] The failure of a partner to recognize and understand the ambitions of the other can often lead to tension in the alliance or, worse, the creation of a new competitor.

Strategic fit should also consider *how the potential partner is positioned in terms of strategic networks.* In high-tech industries, where almost all companies are linked to others by means of a network of cooperative agreements, partner selection at the level of individual players or alliances may overlook the strategic benefits that broader alliance networks can provide. Depending on whether the partner is an industry leader or follower, the partner may be a source of competitive advantage alongside the traditional company-based competencies that the individual partner brings.

Strategic Fit

Pricedex Software Inc. is a developer of a world-class product, part, and pricing information management platform particularly suited to integrating all sources of product information in manufacturing environments. While Pricedex has concentrated on the North American market, its solution is global; hence, the small Ontario-based company recognized the importance of establishing alliances to facilitate global expansion. Pricedex wanted to pilot a partner program with a company of similar size, culture, and reputation to ensure strong compatibility. The company purposefully avoided partnering with a large consulting firm for its first alliance because of the risk of "getting lost" in a larger firm's broader priorities. At the same time, it sought a partner that had sufficient resources to locally support the solution. In July 2003, Pricedex formed an alliance with Xcellerate IT, an Australian solutions provider. Xcellerate IT served similar manufacturing customers and would therefore require minimal training and education while potentially expanding into new vertical markets. In addition, Xcellerate IT was small enough that Pricedex was ensured that sufficient commitment and priority would be given to the relationship.

Finally, many believe that a good strategic fit is *likely to involve partners of similar size.* Cooperation between large and small firms adds some significant problems to achieving strategic alignment. Research indicates that substantial size differences can erect a barrier to successful collaborative activity.[6] There are, however, ways to overcome some barriers, which will be outlined in the later section on implementation. Small firms contemplating an alliance with a larger partner should look for one with a good collaborative history and one with experience in dealing with small firms. History does repeat itself, and if a firm is serious about alliances, it will place a premium on maintaining an excellent reputation as a fair and reliable partner.

THE PARTNER'S AGENDA

While it may be extremely difficult to get at some of the hidden agendas that potential partners bring to the table, it is important to try to develop an insight into the real reason why a partner wants the alliance. Collaboration can be just another competitive tactic. A Bain & Co. study suggests that 90% of all alliance negotiations fail to terminate in an agreement.[7] This high rate is partially due to some firms entering discussions purely to gain competitive intelligence about a technology, specific vendors or customers, and so on and have no serious intent to complete negotiations.

In some instances, alliances proceed but for entirely different reasons. Large firms have, on occasion, entered into partnerships with smaller firms simply to hedge bets and were not truly committed to the alliance. There are numerous examples of small companies signing away marketing rights to corporations that just sat on their product innovation. In other instances, partnerships have been entered into for preemptive reasons, such as immobilizing or preventing a partner from entering into a deal with another firm. Detailed homework can frequently predict and thereby prevent such unhappy outcomes.

A good technique to use for understanding a potential partner's agenda is to empathize, role-play, and brainstorm among a team. This will help one understand what benefits the partner wants to derive from the partnership and recognize whether those benefits will be at the company's expense.

Given the proliferation of alliances in recent years, it is also likely that the potential partner may be engaged in numerous other relationships. The assessment should involve an evaluation of the potential partner's other alliances. In many cases, access to this broader network can be very advantageous. In others, it can be threatening. Managers should determine, for example, whether the prospective partner is allied with any of their company's competitors and whether it is in an area in which their company is vulnerable. If so, they should ensure very early in the game that there are appropriate mechanisms in place to mitigate any risk such as preventing shared

Partner's Agenda

Ottawa-based Corel Corporation is best known for its flagship vector drawing product, CorelDRAW, and in 1995 was enjoying undisputed market leadership in the PC-based illustration software market. That year, the company discovered Xara Ltd., a small software company in the United Kingdom. This company had developed an impressive product that could potentially threaten CorelDRAW's dominance if it expanded beyond its existing U.K. customer base. In a preemptive move, Corel negotiated exclusive licensing rights for the Xara technology, enticing Xara with its instant access to global distribution and strength of the Corel brand. Once in its control, however, Corel's development and marketing activities continued to emphasize CorelDRAW, and market penetration of the Xara product stalled. It was many years before Xara Ltd. could regain control of the technology. It finally relaunched a much improved Xara X in May 2004.

proprietary data from leaking to competitors. Managers should also understand whether the other alliances limit the prospects of expanding their relationship in the future. If the broader alliance context presents too much risk, it may be prudent to walk away.

Next to proper due diligence, the best way to deal with hidden agendas and uncertainties is giving the partnership a clear focus and visible boundaries in terms of duration and scope—and, most of all, deal with a partner who has a good "alliance" reputation.

CULTURAL FIT

Culture involves a set of shared values and beliefs throughout an organization that drive consistent behavior and thought. It can affect business logic, competitive behavior, time orientation, and decision making. How two prospective partners' cultures might coexist becomes a critical indicator of the alliance's potential for success, particularly when the alliance requires frequent and close interaction.

Cultural fit directly affects the ability of partners to work together to meet their common objectives. It is often ignored in partner evaluations despite the fact that culture clashes between partners have been identified as a key reason for alliances to fail. All too frequently, executives focus on examining the hard facts, such as the financial and technical aspects of the partnership, and ignore the nonquantitative human factors. This is unfortunate, as KPMG found that soft or relationship problems were the cause of 70% of alliance failures.[8] Another study expands on this point and stresses the importance of minimizing as much as possible organizational dissimilarity. Where foreign parent companies are involved, the study recommends the joint venture to emulate the foreign parent's organizational climate because dissimilarity of organizational climate is far more crucial than even differences in national culture.[9]

Unlike strategic fit, where nonredundant qualities are desired, strong cultural fit looks for similarities. The more cultural similarities that exist between partners, the less chance there is of undue misunderstanding and tension between the partners that leads to mistrust.

The cultural evaluation index in Figure 2.2, adapted from an index used by Canadian forestry company Abitibi-Price, is a useful method of gaining objective insight into the potential partners' cultural fit.[10] Individual members of the potential partners should score their organization on the cultural dimensions shown. (For additional insight, have each partner score the other partner as well to reveal any differing perceptions.) Individual member scores are aggregated and compared with the other partner's aggregated score. The extent to which cultural dimensions are similar or different between the companies will signal the degree of cultural fit that exists.

When dealing with a foreign partner, the definition of cultural fit expands since there are numerous political, economic, legal, and cultural factors related to the specific market that need to be carefully assessed before a deal is signed. These include the following:

- The attitude of the foreign country toward foreign investment, its treatment of intellectual property, and its political stability
- Potential risk of expropriation
- The relationship between the potential partner and the host government or domestic political groups
- Local currency stability
- Restrictions on capital repatriation and remittances

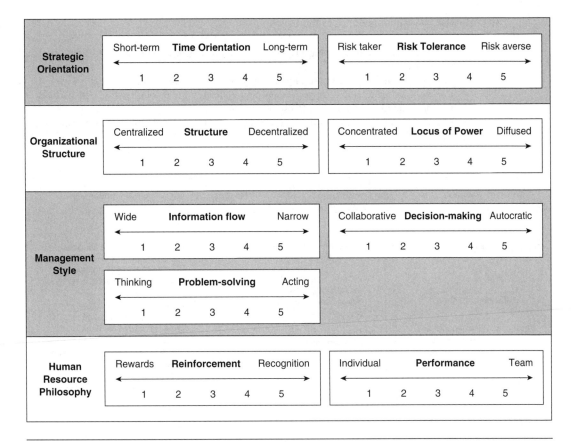

Figure 2.2   Cultural Evaluation Index

Source: M. L. Marks and H. Mirvis, *Joining Forces* (San Francisco: Jossey-Bass, 1998), 65–6.

- The bureaucratic and regulatory environment
- Prevalence of corruption
- Labor unrest
- Corporate and family relations of partner firms

Key insights can be gained by visiting a country's trade commissioner's office or similar foreign trade office for additional information on doing business with specific foreign countries.

ASSESS THE OPERATIONAL FIT

A company's culture is reflected throughout the organization's operational practices, including its management and organizational structure, decision-making practices, and employment policies.

In particular, managers need to do the following:

- Pay close attention to the company's established policies and commitment to alliances at an operational level
- Look for whether measures are in place such as dealing with channel conflict
- Determine whether employee performance measures reinforce collaboration with partners or whether individual employee interests will be in conflict
- Ensure that financial/accounting practices are compatible and that there is sufficient financial capacity to support the needs of the alliance

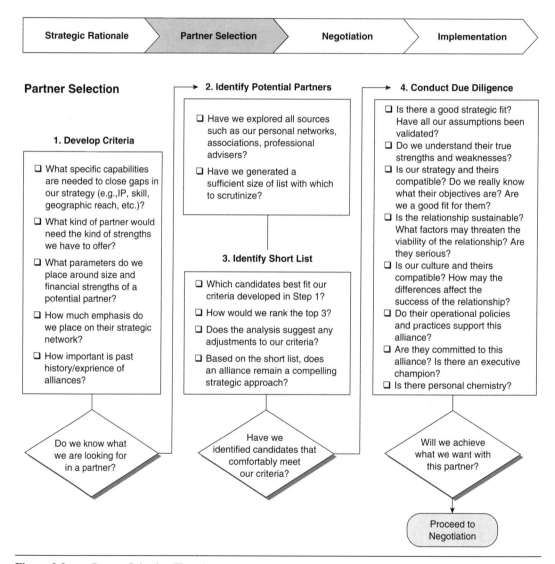

Figure 2.3   Partner Selection Flowchart

Next, they should consider what the nature and sources of external influences will be on their partner. If the partner is a subsidiary, it is important to determine how much autonomy it has from the parent company. Similarly, managers should make note of any key customers or shareholders who may exert disproportionate influence or whether dividend and reinvestment strategies support the objectives of the alliance.

Finally, managers need to assess the company's alliance track record. A 1998 Booz Allen study found that financial results improved dramatically as a company gained alliance experience. Companies experienced in alliances were found to earn twice the return on investment in alliances of inexperienced companies.[11] The study also found that the degree of improvement varied from one industry to another. For example, in telecommunications, it found as much as a fourfold increase as experience increased. Where experience may be lacking, alliance champions should be clearly identified that have sufficient influence within the organization to effectively advocate on behalf of the alliance.

THE PERSONAL DIMENSION

Alliances are cemented at the level of individuals. Despite all of the research done on potential partners, in the end, managers are likely to find that the greatest challenges come from the people and the relationships involved. It is the people on either side that will make or break the partnership. Good personal chemistry and mutual respect between key decision makers and operations people are therefore an important ingredient for success. Are they "our kind of people"? While there are no hard-and-fast rules for determining personal chemistry, it is extremely important to try to get a good sense of the people with whom managers could be working. One way is to check with previous partners. Another is to conduct face-to-face due diligence with an array of managers from the potential partners. One CEO, for example, took this one step further by frequently going fishing with senior executives from potential partners to get a sense of their character and compatibility. Time spent getting to know the key people in the potential partner's firm to see how both teams relate to each other is time well invested.

CASES

Ben & Jerry's—Japan

The CEO of Ben & Jerry's Homemade, Inc. needed to give sales and profits a serious boost; despite the company's excellent brand equity, it was losing market share and struggling to make a profit. The company's product was on store shelves in all U.S. states, but efforts to enter foreign markets had only been haphazard, with non-U.S. sales accounting for just 3% of total sales. The CEO needed to focus serious attention on entering the world's second largest ice cream market, Japan. An objective of Ben & Jerry's was to use the excess manufacturing capacity it had in the United States, and it found that exporting ice cream from Vermont to Japan was feasible from a logistics and cost perspective. The company identified two leading partnering options. One was to give a Japanese convenience store chain exclusive rights to the product for a limited time. The other was to give long-term rights for all sales of the product in Japan to a Japanese American who would build the brand. For the company to enter Japan in time for the upcoming summer season, it would have to be through one of these two partnering arrangements.

Assignment Questions

1. Should Ben & Jerry's commit to entering the Japanese market the following summer?

2. If Ben & Jerry's were to enter the Japanese market the following summer, should it do so with Mr. Yamada or with Seven-Eleven? Why?

Larson in Nigeria (Revised)

The vice president of international operations must decide whether to continue to operate or abandon the company's Nigerian joint venture. Although the expatriate general manager of the Nigerian operation has delivered a very pessimistic report, Larson's own hunch was to stay in that country. Maintaining the operation was complicated by problems in staffing, complying with a promise to increase the share of local ownership, a joint venture partner with divergent views, and increasing costs of doing business in Nigeria. If Larson decides to maintain the existing operation, the issues of increasing local equity participation (i.e., coping with indigenization) and staffing problems (especially in terms of the joint venture general manager) have to be addressed.

Assignment Questions

1. What are the three major issues (in order) confronting David Larson?

2. How would you recommend that each be handled?

Privatizing Poland's Telecom Industry: Opportunities and Challenges in the New Economy and E-Business

As it entered the 21st century, the Polish government faced the dilemma of how to develop an optimal telecom structure and related services. For decades, the government owned and operated a national telecom monopoly, but in the late 1990s, it gradually allowed the entry of some competitors, many of whom brought new technologies. The government had undertaken a major privatization program, and it faced the question of whether, and how, it should privatize; yet privatization would have to be accompanied by ongoing regulation to ensure that managerial decisions were made in the interests of the nation, as a whole. This challenge of continual government intervention could reduce the attractiveness of acquiring the government-owned agency, despite its market dominance. Students will have the opportunity to analyze the telecommunications industry in Poland; determine the technological changes that will affect the future of telecommunications throughout the world and the Polish telecom industry; examine the current regulatory environment in the Polish telecommunication market; evaluate the current state of, and the opportunities in, e-business in Poland and the rest of Europe; and develop a comprehensive action plan for a joint venture partner.

Assignment Questions

1. Analyze the telecommunications industry in Poland today. What are the technological changes that will likely affect the future of telecommunications throughout the world? How relevant are these changes to the Polish telecom industry?

2. Examine the current regulatory environment in the Polish telecommunications market. How will the future of Poland's membership in the European Union (EU) influence the regulatory position of the government? Is there a way to still influence the authorities after Poland becomes an EU member?

3. Evaluate the current state of, and the opportunities in, e-business in Poland and the rest of Europe. What are the major stumbling blocks to faster growth and adoption of electronic business? What are the opportunities?

4. Assess the Telekomunikacja Polsak SA (TPSA) position in the market. How likely is it to succeed in the future? How good an investment is the company to France Telecom?

5. Develop a comprehensive action plan for France Telecom to succeed in the joint venture with TPSA. Evaluate the most serious problems that the French will likely encounter.

6. Evaluate the opportunities for foreign investors in the Polish telecom industry and in e-business.

Prosoft Systems Canada (A)

Prosoft Systems Canada is a major competitor in the enterprise software business. The company is planning to bid on a large contract with the city of Winnipeg. Prosoft is considering bidding on the project in a partnership with a major systems integrator, but the company has just been approached by two other partners about including them in their bidding process. Prosoft must decide whether to bid independently or in one or more alliances. The complexity of forming and managing alliances in the enterprise software business is explored. The supplement Prosoft Systems (B), product 9B03A003, poses the issue of developing an alliance policy for guiding similar decisions.

Assignment Questions

1. What are the unique characteristics of (1) the enterprise software industry and (2) the public sector as a customer for enterprise software?

2. Who are the key stakeholders in this process, and what are their sources of power?

3. What criteria does Armstrong need to consider when selecting an integration partner? Prioritize the criteria and justify your prioritization.

Cameron Auto Parts (A)—Revised

This case is about a small U.S. auto parts producer trying to diversify his way out of dependence on the Big Three. Having signed a license agreement in the United Kingdom, the company now faces an opportunity to establish a joint venture in France for the EU. However, the prospect upsets the U.K. licensee, who is clearly doing very well. The case ends with the company, run off its feet in North America, trying to decide whether to enter Europe via licensing, joint venture, or direct investment.

Assignment Questions

1. Should Cameron have licensed McTaggart or continued to export?

2. Was McTaggart a good choice for licensee?

3. Was the royalty rate reasonable?

NOTES

1. For a discussion of the partnering challenges facing small firms, see James W. Botkin and Jana B. Matthews, *Winning Combinations: The Coming Wave of Entrepreneurial Partnerships Between Large and Small Companies* (New York: John Wiley, 1992), 116–7.

2. J. R. Harbison and P. Pekar, *Smart Alliances: A Practical Guide to Repeatable Success* (San Francisco: Jossey-Bass, 1998), 49.

3. For a discussion of fit, see J. Child. and D. Faulkner, *Strategies of Cooperation: Managing Alliances and Joint Ventures* (New York: Oxford University Press, 1988), 92–9.

4. Ibid., 95.

5. Y. Doz and G. Hamel, *Alliance Advantage: The Art of Creating Value Through Partnering* (Boston: Harvard Business School Press, 1998), 114.

6. See Y. Doz, "Technology Partnerships Between Larger and Smaller Firms: Some Critical Issues," *International Studies of Management and Organization* 17 (1998): 31–57; M. Kelly, J.-L. Schaan, and H. Joncas, "Collaboration Between Technology Entrepreneurs and Large Corporations: Key Design and Management Issues," *Journal of Small Business Strategy* 11 (2000): 60–76; and K. R. Harrigan, "Strategic Alliances and Partner Asymmetries," in *Cooperative Strategies in International Business,* edited by F. Contractor and P. Lorange (Lexington, MA: D.C. Heath), 205–26.

7. See D. K. Rigby and R. W. T. Buchanan, "Putting More Strategy in Strategic Alliances," *Boards and Directors,* Winter 1994, 14–9.

8. G. Kok and L. Wildeman, "Crafting Strategic Alliances: Building Effective Relationships," KPMG Report, 1998.

9. Carl F. Fey and Paul Beamish, "Organizational Climate Similarity and Performance: International Joint Ventures in Russia," *Organization Studies* 22, no. 5 (2001): 853–82.

10. M. L. Marks and H. Mirvis, *Joining Forces* (San Francisco: Jossey-Bass, 1998), 65–6.

11. Harbison and Pekar, *Smart Alliances,* 34–5.

BEN & JERRY'S—JAPAN

Prepared by James M. Hagen

Copyright ©1999, Ivey Management Services   Version: (A) 2001-10-31

On an autumn evening in Tokyo in 1997, Perry Odak, Angelo Pezzani, Bruce Bowman and Riv Hight gratefully accepted the hot steaming oshibori towels that their kimono-bedecked waitress quietly offered. After a full day of meetings with Masahiko Iida and his lieutenants at the Seven-Eleven Japan headquarters, the men from Ben & Jerry's welcomed the chance to refresh their hands and faces before turning to the business at hand. It had been just over nine months since Odak had committed to resolving the conundrum of whether to introduce Ben & Jerry's ice cream to the Japan market and, if so, how. The next morning would be their last chance to hammer out the details for a market entry through Seven-Eleven's 7,000 stores in Japan or to give the go-ahead to Ken Yamada, a prospective licensee who would manage the Japan market for Ben & Jerry's. Any delay in reaching a decision would mean missing the summer 1998 ice cream season, but with Japan's economy continuing to contract, perhaps passing on the Japan market would not be a bad idea.

Perry Odak was just entering his eleventh month as CEO of the famous ice cream company named for its offbeat founders. He knew that the Seven-Eleven deal could represent a sudden boost in the company's flagging sales of the past several years. He also knew that a company with the tremendous brand recognition Ben & Jerry's enjoyed needed to approach new market opportunities from a strategic, not an opportunistic, perspective. Since meeting Masahiko Iida, the president of Seven-Eleven Japan just 10 months earlier, Odak was anxious to resolve the question of whether entering the huge Japan market via Seven-Eleven was the right move or not.

BEN & JERRY'S
BACKGROUND: 1978 TO 1997

1978 to 1994: Growth from Renovated Gas Station to $160 Million in Sales[1]

Brooklyn school mates Ben Cohen and Jerry Greenfield started their ice cream company in a defunct gas station in Burlington, Vermont in 1978, when both were in their mid 20s. The combination of their anti-corporate style, the high fat content of their ice cream, the addition of chunky ingredients and catchy flavor names like "Cherry Garcia" found a following. In addition to selling by the scoop, they began selling pints over the counter and the business grew. With the help of less visible team members, Jeff Furman and Fred (Chico) Lager, the founders took the company public to Vermont stockholders in 1984, later registering with the Securities and Exchange Commission (SEC) for nationwide sale of stock. The company name was Ben & Jerry's Homemade, Inc. and it began trading over the counter with the symbol, BJICA.

Stockholder meetings were outdoor festivals where standard attire included cut-offs and tie

dyed T-shirts and where Cohen was liable to call the meeting to order in song. In addition to being a fun company, Cohen and Greenfield determined that it would be a socially responsible company, known for its caring capitalism. Highlighting its community roots, Ben & Jerry's would only buy its cream from Vermont dairies. In the case of one of its early nut flavors, "Rain Forest Crunch," the nuts would be sourced from tribal co-operatives in South American rain forests where nut harvesting would offer a renewable alternative to strip cutting the land for wood products, and where the co-op members would hopefully get an uncommonly large share of the proceeds. As another part of its objective of "caring capitalism," Ben & Jerry's gave 7.5 per cent of pretax profits to social causes like Healing Our Mother Earth, which protected community members from local health risks, and Center for Better Living, which assisted the homeless.

The product Cohen and Greenfield were selling was exceptionally rich (at least 12 per cent butterfat, compared with about six to 10 per cent for most ice creams). It was also very dense, which was achieved by a low overrun (low ratio of air to ice cream in the finished product). This richness and density qualified it as a superpremium ice cream. Haagen-Dazs (founded in New Jersey in 1961) was the only major competitor in the superpremium market. While Haagen-Dazs promoted a sophisticated image, Ben & Jerry's promoted a funky, caring image.

As Ben & Jerry's began to expand distribution throughout the Northeast, it found increasing difficulty obtaining shelf space in supermarkets. Charging Haagen-Dazs with unfairly pressuring distributors to keep Ben & Jerry's off their trucks, Greenfield drove to Minneapolis and gained national press coverage by picketing in front of the headquarters building of food giant Pillsbury which had earlier acquired Haagen-Dazs. His homemade sign read "What is the Doughboy afraid of?," a reference to Pillsbury's mascot and to the company's apparent efforts against the underdog ice cream makers from Vermont. This David versus Goliath campaign earned Ben & Jerry's national publicity and, when combined with some high powered legal action, it gave them freer access to grocery store freezer compartments.

A policy was in place that the highest paid employee would not be paid more than seven times what the lowest paid worker earned. Part of the anti-corporate culture of the company was a policy which allowed each employee to make up his or her own title. The person who might otherwise have been called the public relations manager took the title "the Info Queen." Cohen and Greenfield took turns running the company. Whether despite, or because of, these and other unusual policies, the company continued to grow (see Exhibit 1). In 1985 the company bought a second production plant, this one in nearby Springfield, Vermont. A third plant was later built in St. Albans, Vermont. By the late 1980s, Ben & Jerry's ice cream had become available in every state of the union.

1994 to 1997:
Responding to Fallen Profits

By 1994, sales exceeded $150 million, distribution had extended beyond the U.S. borders and the company had over 600 employees. The future was not encouraging, though, with 1994 actually bringing in a loss. While Ben & Jerry's unquestionably held the second largest market share (at 34 per cent compared to Haagen-Dazs' 44 per cent) of the American superpremium market, the company had started to lose market share. Net income had also suffered badly since reaching a high in of $7.2 million in 1993 (Exhibit 2). While Cohen was most often the company's CEO, much of the company's growth occurred while Chico Lager was either general manager or CEO between 1982 and 1990. Ben was particularly engaged in efforts to further the cause of social justice by such activities as attending meetings of similarly-minded CEOs from around the world. Board member Chuck Lacy had taken a turn at the helm, but he lacked aspirations for a career as

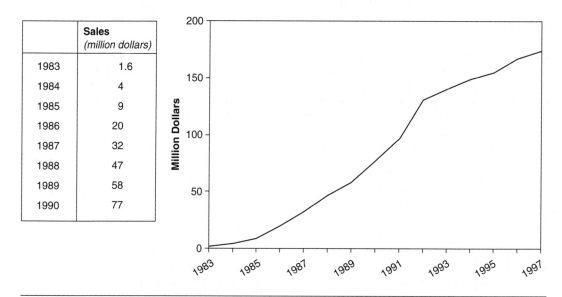

	Sales (million dollars)
1983	1.6
1984	4
1985	9
1986	20
1987	32
1988	47
1989	58
1990	77

Exhibit 1   Ben & Jerry's Annual Sales

Source: Ben & Jerry's Annual Reports

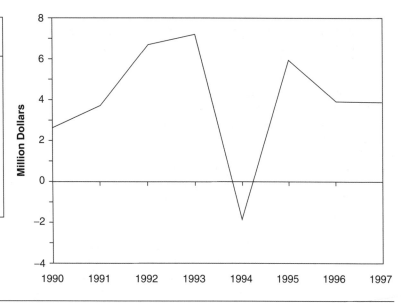

	Net Income (million dollars)
1990	2.6
1991	3.73
1992	6.67
1993	7.2
1994	−1.86
1995	5.94
1996	3.92
1997	3.89

Exhibit 2   Ben & Jerry's Net Income

Source: Ben & Jerry's Annual Reports

a CEO, just as the company's namesakes did. The slowdown in growth and retreat in market share comprised a threat to the company's survival and to the continuation of its actions and contributions for social responsibility.

The company had never had a professional CEO and it had avoided commercial advertising, relying for publicity on press coverage of its founders' antics and social interest causes. This approach was apparently losing its effectiveness and the company could no longer feature an underdog image in its appeals for customer support. Relaxing the rule on executive compensation, the company launched a highly publicized search for a CEO, inviting would-be CEOs to submit a 100-word essay explaining why they would like the job. In 1996, Bob Holland, a former consultant with McKinsey & Co., took the presidency, bringing a small cadre of fellow consultants with him. All of Holland's highly schooled management sensibilities were put to the test as he took over a company that had lacked effective management in recent years, commencing employment for a board of directors that was suspicious of traditional corporate culture. By this time, Cohen, Greenfield and Furman still had considerable influence over the company, controlling about 45 per cent of the shares. This permitted them, as a practical matter, to elect all members of the board of directors and thereby effectively control the policies and management of the firm. Holland's relationship with the board didn't work and eighteen months later he was out, the company's decline had not been reversed and morale among the employees was at a low.

While the board was willing to pay a corporate scale salary to its CEO, it was unwilling to let go of the company's tradition of donating 7.5 per cent of before tax profits to not-for-profit social causes. A spirit of socially responsible business management would need to continue, as that was still the company's stock in trade as much as the ice cream was. With this, as well as the need to survive, in mind, the board hired

Perry Odak at the recommendation of one of its members at a base salary of $300,000, with a start date in January 1997.

While Odak had grown up on a dairy farm in upstate New York, it was not this dairy background that landed him the job as CEO of Ben & Jerry's. His experience at turning around troubled companies was far more important. Odak was recruited away from a consultancy assignment at U.S. Repeating Arms Company, which he had been instrumental in turning around from its decline into red ink. This followed diverse experiences ranging from senior vice president of worldwide operations of Armour-Dial, Inc. to president of Atari Consumer Products, along with numerous consultancies and entrepreneurial activities that included the start-up team and management of Jovan, a fragrance and cosmetic company. A professional manager who thrived on challenges and abhorred mere maintenance of a company,

Odak had entered the business world with a degree in agricultural economics from Cornell University topped with graduate coursework in business.

THE MARKET FOR SUPERPREMIUM ICE CREAM

Ice cream is noted as far back as the days of Alexander the Great, though it was first commercially manufactured in the United States in 1851. By 1997, almost 10 per cent of U.S. milk production went into ice cream, a $3.34 billion market. The ice cream brands that dominated American supermarket freezer cases are given in Exhibit 3 and Exhibit 4. National (as opposed to regional) branding of dairy products, including ice cream, was a recent phenomenon. Dreyer's (owned in part by the Swiss food giant, Nestle,

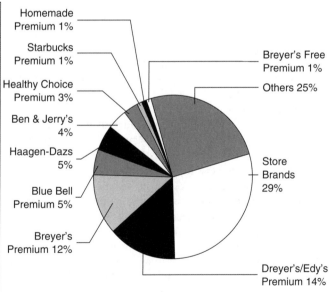

	Sales (million dollars)
ALL BRANDS	3.34
Store Brands	1.00
Dreyer's/Edy's Premium	0.46
Breyer's Premium	0.40
BlueBell Premium	0.17
Haagen-Dazs	0.15
Ben & Jerry's	**0.12**
Healthy Choice Premium	0.10
Starbucks Premium	0.03
Homemade Premium	0.02
Breyer's Free Premium	0.02

Exhibit 3   Top U.S. Ice Cream Brands, 1996 to 1997

Source: Ben & Jerry's

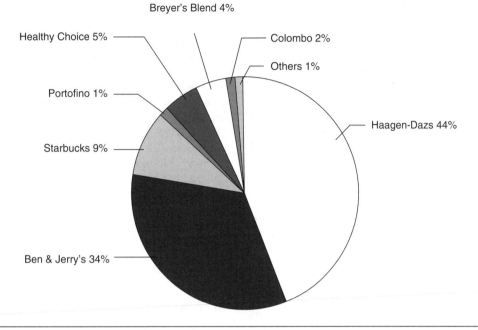

Exhibit 4   Share of Superpremium Ice Cream Brands, U.S. Market

Source: Ben & Jerry's

and branded Edy's on the East Coast) was the biggest brand at 13.9 per cent of the U.S. market, in terms of value. The next biggest was Breyer's, a unit of the Dutch-English firm, Unilever, at 12 per cent. Blue Bell (from Texas) was fourth biggest at 5.2 per cent, and Haagen-Dazs (owned by the U.K. beverage and food company then known as Grand Metropolitan) was at 4.6 per cent. Ben & Jerry's came in at about 3.6 per cent of the market. Healthy Choice Premium ice cream (owned by the agribusiness and consumer food firm ConAgra) was close behind with 3.2 per cent. Starbucks (one of Dreyer's brands) had 1.0 per cent. The biggest share of the market (some 30.2 per cent) came from the retailers' private label products and a number of economy brands (with which Ben & Jerry's did not regard itself to be competing) made up the balance.

There are considerable economies of scale in ice cream production, so despite the advantages of having dispersed production in order to reduce costs of transporting the frozen finished product or the highly perishable cream, milk and egg yolks that are principle raw ingredients, each major manufacturer generally had only a few plants to serve vast markets. Market leader, Haagen-Dazs, had just two plants in the United States, while Ben & Jerry's had three. Even with relatively few plants, Ben & Jerry's was operating at only about half of plant capacity in 1997.

While the Ben & Jerry's brand had the country's fifth highest share of the ice cream market (in terms of value), it still accounted for only a small 3.6 per cent of the market. Ben & Jerry's, though, measured its competitive strength not in general ice cream sales (including many store brands and economy ice creams), but rather in sales of superpremium (high fat content) ice cream. The market for this product was much less fragmented, with Haagen-Dazs getting 44 per cent and Ben & Jerry's getting 34 per cent of the $361 million of supermarket (excluding convenience store and food service) sales measured and monitored by scanner data. If the two companies' frozen yogurts and sorbets were included, their market shares would be 36 per cent for Ben & Jerry's and 42 per cent for Haagen-Dazs. Both companies specialized in superpremium products, with additional sales being derived from sorbets, frozen yogurts and novelties. Haagen-Dazs had really pioneered the category back in 1961 when Reuben Mattus in New Jersey founded the company. The company was later acquired by the giant food company, Pillsbury, which in turn was bought in 1989 by the U.K. liquor and food giant, Grand Metropolitan.

Both Ben & Jerry's and Haagen-Dazs had achieved national distribution, primarily selling their product in supermarkets and convenience stores. Ben & Jerry's had 163 scoop shops, compared to 230 Haagen-Dazs shops. Dairy Queen (with 5,790 shops worldwide) and Baskin Robbins dominated the scoop shop business, though their products were not superpremium. Prices for Ben & Jerry's and Haagen-Dazs would range from $2.89 to $3.15 per pint, often more than twice as expensive as conventional (high overrun/lower butterfat) ice cream and premium brands. Starbucks and Portofino ice creams were other much smaller contenders in the United States with their "premium plus" products, characterized by a butterfat content slightly under that of the superpremium category.

Statistical evidence indicated that ice cream consumption increased with income and education. Starting in the mid 1990s, though, sales growth started to fall off and Ben & Jerry's experienced a decline in profits, even suffering a loss in 1994. Haagen-Dazs and Ben & Jerry's product sales were very widely available across the entire U.S. market and it was clear that future growth would have to come from new products or from new (non-U.S.) markets. More troubling was that Ben & Jerry's was beginning to lose market share in both the total ice cream market and, more importantly, the superpremium market.

BEN & JERRY'S INTERNATIONAL SALES

Ben & Jerry's was intentionally slow to embrace foreign markets. Cohen was opposed to growth for growth's sake, so the company's few adventures overseas were limited to opportunistic arrangements that came along, primarily with friends of the founders. Meanwhile Haagen-Dazs had no such hesitation. By 1997, it was in 28 countries with 850 dipping shops around the world. Its non-U.S. sales were about $700 million, compared to about $400 million of domestic sales. Ben & Jerry's, on the other hand, had foreign sales of just $6 million, with total sales of $174 million. In terms of non-U.S. superpremium ice cream sales, Haagen-Dazs and Ben & Jerry's were still the leading brands, but Haagen-Dazs was trouncing Ben & Jerry's.

Canada

Ben & Jerry's first foreign entry was in Canada in 1986, when the company gave a Canadian firm all Canadian rights for the manufacture and sale of ice cream through a licensing agreement. While about one-third of the product was exported from the United States, high Canadian tariffs (15.5 per cent) and particularly quotas (only 347 tons annually) made export impractical. In 1992 Ben & Jerry's repurchased the Canadian license and as of 1997 there were just four scoop shops in Quebec. The Canadian dairy industry remained highly protective even after enactment of the North American Free Trade Agreement.

Israel

Avi Zinger, a friend of Cohen's, was given a license, including manufacturing rights, for the Israel market in 1988. His 1997 sales totalled about $5 million, but the only revenue accruing to Ben & Jerry's Homemade, Inc. would be licensing income and this amount was negligible. To assure quality coming from the plant in Yavne, Israel, Zinger and his staff received training at the Waterbury factory. As of fall 1997, there were 14

Ben & Jerry's scoop shops in Israel, with the shops selling such items as gifts, baked goods and beverages, in addition to the ice cream. Zinger also sold Ben & Jerry's products through supermarkets, hotels, delis and restaurants.

Russia

The company entered into its first foreign joint venture in 1990 by establishing the firm Iceverk in the Russian republic of Karelia, which is Vermont's sister state. This grew out of Cohen's travel to Karelia as part of a sister state delegation in 1988. A goal of the joint venture effort was to promote understanding and communication between the peoples of these two countries. The joint venture agreement specified the following division of ownership shares: Ben & Jerry's—50 per cent; the Intercentre cooperative—27 per cent; Petro Bank—20 per cent; and Pioneer Palace (a facility similar to a YMCA, that provided the location)—three per cent. Half of any profits would stay with the Iceverk and the balance would be divided among the partners. Ben & Jerry's contributed equipment and know-how to the venture, while the local partners provided the facilities for the factory and for two scoop shops. After considerable, mostly bureaucratic, delays, the shops opened in July 1992. By 1993, there were three scoop shops and about 100 employees. Iceverk opened several more scoop shops and the venture began to sell pints in supermarkets locally, as well as in Moscow. Ben & Jerry's hired James Flynn to put his University of New Hampshire marketing degree to good use by serving as marketing rep in Moscow. Sales improved as food service customers increasingly bought the product. In 1996, Ben & Jerry's terminated the joint venture, giving its equity and equipment at no cost to its joint venture partners. A retrospective view of that decision is that the company felt that the management time needed to keep the partnership going was too demanding, given the perceived potential. Iceverk no longer uses the Ben & Jerry's name, though it does continue to make ice cream in Petrozavodsk, Karelia's capital.

United Kingdom

In 1994 there was much discussion at Ben & Jerry's headquarters in Burlington about whether the company was ready to strategically (rather than just opportunistically) move into international markets. Susan Renaud recalled the consensus being that no, they were not, but just three months later the company shipped a container of product to Sainsbury, an upscale supermarket chain in the United Kingdom. Cohen had met a Sainsbury executive at a meeting of the Social Venture Network and the executive had encouraged him to ship over some product. This launch was made with no idea of what the pricing would be, nor any knowledge of what kind of packaging and ingredients were acceptable in that market. The company was shipping a 473 ml package, while the standard was 500 ml. With its foot in the door, the company thought it best to try other outlets in England, as well. It tried out one distributor, which had agreed to donate one per cent of its Ben & Jerry's turnover to charity. Sales did not materialize and another distributor was tried, this time without the charity constraint. The product had a distinctive market position, with one radio commentator alleged to have said, "If Haagen-Dazs is the ice cream you have after sex, Ben & Jerry's is the ice cream you have instead of sex." By 1997, U.K. sales totalled $4 million.

France

In 1995, the company entered France with great ambivalence. CEO Holland was all for entering the French market and the company sent off a container of product to Auchan, a major retailer Cohen was introduced to through Social Venture Network ties. As global protests grew over French nuclear testing, though, there were discussions in the company about withdrawing from the French market or vocally protesting against the French government. With this internal disagreement concerning the French market, there was no marketing plan, no promotional support and no attempt to address French labelling laws. The company hired a French public relations firm, noted for its alternative media and social mission work, and separately contracted with a sales and distribution company. But there was no plan and nobody from Ben & Jerry's to coordinate the French effort. In 1997, sales in France were just over $1 million.

Benelux

Ben & Jerry's entry into the Benelux market was also without strategic planning. In this case, a wealthy individual who had admired the company's social mission asked to open scoop shops, with partial ownership by the Human Rights Watch. By 1997, there were three scoop shops in Holland. Sales totalled a mere $287,000, but there was the prospect of using the product reputation from the scoop shops to launch super-market and convenience store sales.

In short, Ben & Jerry's fell into several foreign markets opportunistically, but without the consensus of the board and without the necessary headquarters staff to put together any kind of comprehensive plan. As the company had never developed a conventional marketing plan in the United States, it lacked the managerial skill to put together a marketing campaign for entering the foreign markets.

As a result, by 1997, Ben & Jerry's international sales totalled just three per cent of total sales. While the company had nearly caught up with Haagen-Dazs in U.S. market share, Haagen-Dazs was light years ahead in the non-U.S. markets. With declining profits and domestic market share at Ben & Jerry's, it was beginning to seem time to give serious attention to international market opportunities.

FOCUS ON MARKET
OPPORTUNITIES IN JAPAN

Background on the Market for Superpremium Ice Cream in Japan

In the 1994 to 1996 period when Ben & Jerry's was having its first taste of a hired professional

CEO (Bob Holland), it struggled with the prospects of strategically targeting a foreign market and developing a marketing plan for its fledgling overseas operations. In particular, the company made inquiries about opportunities in Japan, the second largest ice cream market in the world, with annual sales of approximately $4.5 billion (Exhibit 5). While the market was big, it was also daunting. Japan was known to have a highly complex distribution system driven by manufacturers, its barriers to foreign products were high and the distance for shipping a frozen product was immense. Ben & Jerry's would be a late entrant, more than 10 years behind Haagen-Dazs in gaining a foothold in the market. In addition, there were at least six Japanese ice cream manufacturers selling a superpremium product. A major Japanese frozen desserts company, Morinaga Seika, had made proposals to Ben & Jerry's on two different occasions in 1995. In both cases the proposals were rejected. In January 1996, Morinaga actually conducted focus groups to evaluate Ben & Jerry's products. It was beginning to seem appropriate to taking a closer look at the Morinaga proposals and other options.

Despite the challenges of entering Japan, that market had several compelling features. It was arguably the most affluent country in the world, Japanese consumers were known for demanding high quality products with great varieties of styles and flavors (which practically defined Ben & Jerry's) and it seemed that the dietary shift toward more animal products was still underway. By 1994, Japan's 42 kilogram annual per capita consumption of milk was less than half that (103 kg) of the United States, and cheese consumption was about one-tenth that of the United States. Commercial dairy sales had really only taken off after World War II, when school lunch programs were initiated with milk as a regular component. Incomes in Japan increased dramatically from the 1950s to the 1980s so that animal-based food products and home refrigerators were affordable to a large number of people.

Though Haagen-Dazs' financial figures were not published by its parent, Grand Metropolitan, market intelligence suggested that the ice cream

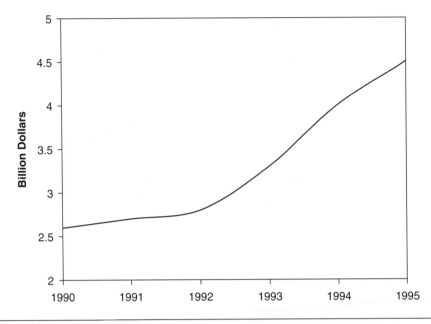

Exhibit 5   Japan Ice Cream Market Size

Source: Ben & Jerry's

maker had Japanese sales of about $300 million, with Japan providing the highest margins of any of its markets. Haagen-Dazs had managed to capture nearly half the superpremium market in Japan. It entered the market as an imported product and later began production in Japan at a plant owned jointly by Haagen-Dazs, Sentry and Takanashi Milk Products. About 25 per cent of Haagen-Dazs' sales there appeared to be from scoop shops. In addition to gaining visibility through scoop shops, Haagen-Dazs operated a fleet of ice cream parlor buses, with upper deck cafe tables, at exhibitions and other public gatherings. On the one hand, Haagen-Dazs would be a formidable competitor that would likely guard its market share. On the other hand, there would be no apparent need for Ben & Jerry's to teach the local market about superpremium ice cream. The market seemed to welcome imported ice cream and expectations of falling tariffs on dairy products suggested new opportunities for ice

cream imports from abroad. Haagen-Dazs' flavors were generally the same as U.S. flavors, with some modifications, such as reduced sweetness. While prices were attractive in Japan, about $6 per pint, it was unclear how much of that would go into the pockets of the manufacturer versus various distributors.

In contemplating an entry in the Japan market, it was hard to avoid thinking about the case of Borden Japan. Borden introduced a premium ice cream to the market in 1971 through a joint venture with Meiji Milk. The product was highly successful and Borden was leader of the category. In 1991, the Borden-Meiji alliance came to an end and Borden had extreme difficulty gaining effective distribution. Borden did not follow industry trends toward single serving cups of ice cream and it suffered greatly when distributors started lowering the price of the product, sending the signal to consumers that Borden was an inferior product. After sales had fallen by more than

	Brand	Size (ml)	Price (Yen)
Home Cup	Bleuge	950	950
Pint	H. Dazs	474	850
	Lotte	470	850
	Meiji	470	950
Personal Cup	H. Dazs	120	250
	Meiji	145	250

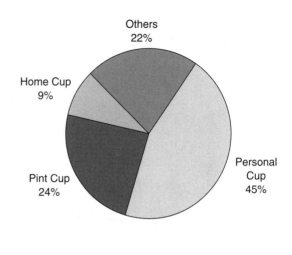

Exhibit 6   Japan Superpremium and Premium Sales by Package

Source: Fuji Keizai Co.

two-thirds in just two years, Borden withdrew from the Japan market. Desserts were uncommon in Japan, leaving ice cream primarily for the snack market. Thus, single serving (about 120 ml) cups became popular, accounting for about 45 per cent of sales (Exhibit 6) and ice cream came to be sold increasingly in convenience stores. By 1993, about a quarter of all ice cream sales were in convenience stores, compared to 29 per cent in supermarkets (Exhibit 7).

One concern at Ben & Jerry's was its size. With total worldwide sales of just over $150 million, it was very small in comparison to Haagen-Dazs, which had estimated sales of $300 million in Japan alone. At least five Japanese companies already in the superpremium market were larger than Ben & Jerry's, with leaders Glico, Morinaga, Meiji and Snow Brand all having total ice cream sales three to four times that of Ben & Jerry's and, in each case, ice cream was just part of their product line.

Cohen was not very enthusiastic about the sort of financial or managerial commitment that was apparently required to enter the Japan market and he couldn't see how entering that market fit

in with the company's social mission. Others on the board shared his attitude. Two immediate problems were that entering Japan would not be the result of any social mission (the concepts of social mission and corporate charity being very foreign in Japan) and the company's lack of international success suggested that it may already have been spread too thin in too many countries. Jerry Greenfield, however, was interested enough to visit Japan on a market research tour in early 1996. The purpose was to see just how Ben & Jerry's might gain distribution if the company were to enter the Japanese market. Valerie Brown of Ben & Jerry's fledgling marketing department accompanied Greenfield. Contacts for the visit came primarily from Valerie's classmates at Harvard Business School, from a consulting company and from the Japan External Trade Organization.

Alternative Strategies for a Ben & Jerry's Entry into Japan

In his visit to Japan, Greenfield was willing to consider entry into Japan through such

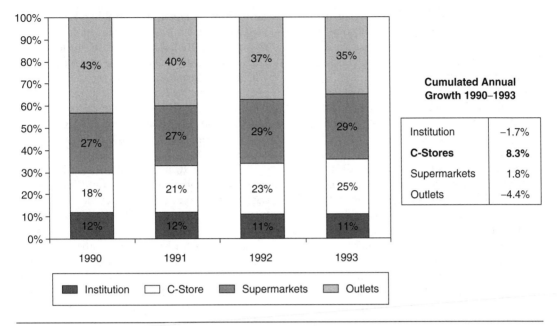

Cumulated Annual Growth 1990–1993	
Institution	–1.7%
C-Stores	**8.3%**
Supermarkets	1.8%
Outlets	–4.4%

Exhibit 7   Japan Ice Cream Market by Channel

Source: Ice Cream Data Book (Morinaga).

diverse distribution channels as Amway Japan, Domino's Pizza and department stores. One of his meetings was with the Japanese distributor of Dreyer's, the American company with partial ownership by the Swiss food giant Nestle. Dreyer's, not being perceived as a direct competitor, was Ben & Jerry's largest distributor in the United States. Dreyer's had licensed its trademark with a joint venture operation in Japan in 1990. Sales had since fallen and the joint venture seemed to have had difficulty with its biggest customer, Seven-Eleven Japan. The retailer's demands for just-in-time delivery required Dreyer's to maintain large inventories and the retailer demanded the right to rapidly drop flavors which did not meet sales expectations.

Another meeting was with a high level team of Seven-Eleven executives, including Masahiko Iida, the senior managing director, and Yasayuki Nakanishi, the merchandiser of the Foods Division. Iida expressed interest in selling Ben & Jerry's ice cream, suggesting that Ben & Jerry's could sell directly to Seven-Eleven, avoiding some of the distribution costs that are typical of the usual multi-layer distribution system in Japan. On the other hand, a major American beverage distributor in Japan warned that it would be the kiss of death to enter the market through some kind of exclusive arrangement with a huge convenience store chain like Seven-Eleven. The balance of power would be overwhelmingly in the retailer's favor.

Meiji Milk Products (with $447 million of ice cream sales), in combination with its importer, the giant Mitsubishi Trading Company, expressed interest in distributing Ben & Jerry's products. This team clearly had very strong distribution resources, including an exclusive supply contract for Tokyo Disneyland. One concern was that Meiji already had a superpremium brand called Aya. Despite Meiji's strong interest, though, this option had probably become a long shot on account of earlier protests by Ben & Jerry's leadership of deforestation practices by another division of Mitsubishi.

Other marketing possibilities that had surfaced in 1996 included an arrangement with the advertising agency that had charge of Japan Airlines' in-flight entertainment, as well as a chance to open a scoop shop at a highly visible new retail development about to be built at Tokyo Disneyland. If anything, the many options, focus groups and proposals made the decision about what to do with Japan even more difficult. The fact that the Ben & Jerry's board was divided on whether the company even had any business in a Japan launch discouraged further action.

By late 1996, Holland was following up discussions with a well-recommended Japanese-American who was available to oversee marketing and distribution of Ben & Jerry's products in Japan. Ken Yamada, a third generation Japanese American from Hawaii, had obtained the Domino's Pizza franchise for Japan. His compensation would be a margin on all sales in Japan. When Bob Holland's employment with Ben & Jerry's ended later in the year, he was still in discussion with Yamada, but he was still lacking the enthusiastic support of the board of directors for a possible entry into Japan.

A Fresh Look at the Japan Options

Perry Odak assumed leadership of Ben & Jerry's in January 1997, inheriting the file of reports on possible strategies for entering the Japan market. Neither the file nor institutional memory indicated much momentum leading toward any one of the Japan strategies. In being hired, however, Odak had the board's agreement that the company's sales (and especially profits) must grow and that non-U.S. markets were the most likely key to that growth.

In February 1997, Odak added a business-related detour to a scheduled trip to Thailand with his wife. He stopped by Tokyo for a courtesy call to Mr. Iida, the President of

Seven-Eleven Japan, a controlling parent company of 7-Eleven U.S.[2] This was to more or less make up for Ben & Jerry's inability to send a CEO to a January "summit" meeting in Dallas at which Mr. Iida and the head of the U.S. 7-Eleven operations had wished to meet face to face with the leaders of its major suppliers. 7-Eleven U.S. was, in fact, Ben & Jerry's biggest retail outlet and Ben & Jerry's was a major supplier to Seven-Eleven.

After about 10 minutes of pleasantries at this introductory meeting at the Seven-Eleven headquarters in Tokyo, Iida asked Odak point blank: "Is there anyone at Ben & Jerry's who can make a marketing decision? We'd like to sell your product, but don't know how to proceed or with whom." Rather taken aback at this surprisingly direct inquiry, Odak replied that he could indeed make a decision and he resolved to sort through the Japan options and get back to Iida in short order.

Back in Burlington, Odak installed Angelo Pezzani as the new international director for Ben & Jerry's Homemade. Odak had known Pezzani since 1982 when they both started work at Atari on the same day. Pezzani's position was then general consul of Atari Consumer Products Worldwide. Going over the options with Pezzani, it appeared that partnering with Yamada was still the strongest option for entering Japan, but the Seven-Eleven option had not yet been well developed for consideration. Yamada represented considerable strength with his Domino's success and with the fact that Domino's already offered ice cream cups as part of its delivery service in Japan. Possible drawbacks were his insistence on having exclusive rights to the entire Japan market, with full control of all branding and marketing efforts there.

Pezzani and Odak decided to continue negotiations with Yamada, keeping that option alive, and to simultaneously let Iida know that they wanted to explore options with Seven-Eleven. They requested an April meeting with Iida in Japan to move things along. The April meeting would include Mr. Nakanishi, the head of frozen ice desserts for Seven-Eleven Japan, and Bruce

Bowman, Ben & Jerry's head of operations. To work out ground arrangements for the meeting, Odak and Pezzani needed someone on the ground in Japan and they called on Rivington Hight, an American who had learned Japanese in the U.S. intelligence service, married a Japanese woman and had been living in Japan for much of the past 30 years. No stranger to Odak or Pezzani, Hight had also worked for Atari in 1982 as president of Atari Japan. Like Odak and Pezzani, he had held a variety of management positions and consultancies in the years since.

The April meeting in Japan was basically intended to lay the framework to begin hashing out the many details that would be involved if Ben & Jerry's were to enter the Japan market through Seven-Eleven. It was a chance for the critical players in each company to get together. Perry brought Pezzani, Bowman and Hight. Arriving at the Ito-Yokado/Seven-Eleven headquarters building at the foot of Tokyo Tower, the Ben & Jerry's team walked into a lobby full of sample-laden salespeople and manufacturers nervously awaiting their chance to put their products on the shelves of some 7,000 stores. The receptionist quickly identified Odak and company and immediately put VIP pins on their dark lapels, directing them to the VIP elevator that went straight to the executive suite on the 12th floor. A hostess there immediately guided the group across the plush white carpeting to a spacious meeting room, where they were served tea while awaiting Iida and Nakanishi. Odak arrived with more questions than answers, but he was determined that any product Ben & Jerry's might sell in Japan would be manufactured in Vermont, where the company had considerable excess capacity. Also, the costs of labor and raw dairy products were higher in Japan than the United States, so the 23.3 per cent tariff and cost of shipping seemed not to be prohibitive. As a result of the Uruguay Round of GATT, the tariff would be reduced to 21 per cent in the year 2000. The introductory meeting went well, but they had not yet addressed any of the difficult issues except to establish that it would be possible to export the product from Vermont to Japan.

Wrestling With the Details of the Seven-Eleven Option

Odak, Pezzani and Bowman had a full plate of issues to resolve. The first question was market. Iida had said he was interested in Ben & Jerry's product because it was something new to Japan and particularly unique with its chunks. Seven-Eleven had even tried to get a Japanese company to co-pack a chunky superpremium ice cream, but the Japanese packer was unsuccessful with its production processes. Research supporting a clear market for this novel product in Japan was scant, though it seemed unlikely that Seven-Eleven would commit shelf space to a product it had any doubt about and both Iida and Nakanishi certainly knew their market. A skeptical view of Seven-Eleven's interest in bringing Ben & Jerry's to Japan was that Seven-Eleven's combined U.S. and Japan operations would become so important to Ben & Jerry's (potentially accounting for a substantial portion of its sales) that Seven-Eleven could, in some fashion, control the ice cream maker. Even if that were not part of Seven-Eleven's motivation, it could be a concern.

While Ben & Jerry's management was leaning toward an entry into Japan, it was not a foregone conclusion. The entry would require a commitment of capital and managerial attention. As the product would be exported from the United States, there would be the risk of negative exchange rate movements that could make exports to Japan no longer feasible, thus making Ben & Jerry's financial picture less predictable. Commodity risk was also a serious concern in that the price of milk could rise in the United States, hurting Ben & Jerry's relative to competitors producing ice cream in Japan.

Assuming that an entry into the Japanese market was desirable, there were a number of apparent options for gaining distribution there, making it necessary to seriously consider the pros and cons of entering by way of Seven-Eleven. The most obvious pro was immediate placement in the freezer compartments of over 7,000 convenience stores in that country. In the early 1990s, the convenience store share of the ice cream market had increased and it appeared that these stores were now accounting for at least 40 per cent of superpremium ice cream sales in Japan. Equally positive was the fact that Seven-Eleven had taken advantage of its size and its state-of-the art logistics systems by buying product directly from suppliers, avoiding the several layers of middlemen that stood between most suppliers and Japanese retailers. These cost savings could make the product more affordable and/or allow a wider margin to protect against such risks as currency fluctuation.

On the negative side, if the product was introduced to the market through a convenience store and it was just one of many brands there, would it be able to build its own brand capital in Japan like Haagen-Dazs had? Would the product essentially become a store brand? Without brand capital it could be difficult to distribute the product beyond the Seven-Eleven chain. An alternative approach of setting up well located scoop shops, along with an effective marketing or publicity campaign, could give the product cache, resulting in consumer pull that could give Ben & Jerry's a price premium, as well as a range of marketing channels. Would committing to one huge retail chain be a case of putting too many eggs in one basket? A falling out between Ben & Jerry's and Seven-Eleven Japan could leave the ice cream maker with nothing in Japan. Even during discussions with Ben & Jerry's, the retailer was known to be terminating its supply agreement with the French ice cream manufacturer Rolland due to allegedly inadequate sales. Presumably Seven-Eleven could similarly cut off Ben & Jerry's at some future date.

While weighing the pros and cons of the business arrangement, there were also production issues which Ben & Jerry's had to consider. Nakanishi insisted the ice cream be packaged only in personal cups (120 ml) and not the 473 ml (one pint) size that Ben & Jerry's currently packed. The main argument for the small cups was that ice cream is seldom consumed as a family dessert in Japan, but rather is consumed as a snack item. A secondary argument was that,

for sanitation purposes, customers liked their own individual servings. Cake, for example, was generally served in restaurants with each slice individually wrapped. Nakanishi's insistence was despite the fact that Seven-Eleven stocked Haagen-Dazs and some of its local competitors in both sizes.

Bruce Bowman embraced the challenge of designing a production system that would accommodate small cups that the company had never packed before. It seemed that about $2 million of new equipment would be needed, though it could be installed in the existing buildings. The sizes of some of the chunks would have to be reduced in order for them to not overwhelm the small cups. Besides requiring these known adjustments to production operations, Seven-Eleven might be expected to request other product changes. Japanese buyers were known for being particularly demanding in their specifications.

Ben & Jerry's had long been shipping ice cream to the West Coast and to Europe in freezer containers. Shipments to Japan were feasible, though the Seven-Eleven approach to just-in-time inventory procedures would make delivery reliability especially key and, of course, costs would have to be minimized. Logistics research indicated it would likely take at least three weeks shipping time from the plant in Vermont (the St. Albans plant would be used if the Japan plan were implemented) to the warehouse in Japan. Because of the Japanese label needed in Japan, production would have to carefully meet the orders from Seven-Eleven. The product could not be shifted to another customer, nor could another customer's product be shifted to Japan.

A number of sticky points needed to be resolved. In addition to changing the package size, Seven-Eleven wanted to provide its own design for the package art and the design would definitely not include a photo of Ben and Jerry. Packaging had always been an important part of the Ben & Jerry's product. Funky lettering and the images of Ben and Jerry are part of what made the product unique. If Seven-Eleven were given control over the package art, what would that do to the benefits of developing a global branded product? Would consumers be confused about the placement of the product as they travelled? On the other hand, the carton designs had already been evolving somewhat and maybe a bit more evolution would satisfy Seven-Eleven. In fact, the earlier focus groups by Morinaga brought out the concern that it was too bad the "strange Ben & Jerry's packaging" had to detract from the good ice cream.

Ben & Jerry's sent a number of samples to consider and Nakanishi developed a short list that would be tested (if the deal went forward) in a couple dozen Seven-Eleven stores so that the top five flavors could be identified for the market entry. "Chunky Monkey" was near the top of Nakanishi's list, though the name absolutely had to change, he said. It turned out that only minor ingredient modifications would be needed to reduce the sweetness and to replace "vegetable gum" with "protein solids."

Through numerous communications and several meetings during the summer of 1997, a number of issues were discussed and resolved. For example, Seven-Eleven would acquire only a six-month exclusive right to Ben & Jerry's and even that would be only for the specific flavors being sold to Seven-Eleven. Because of its relatively small size and inability to cover a loss, Ben & Jerry's was asking for sale terms that would transfer title (and all risk) for the product at the plant gate. It also was asking for 12 weeks lead-time on any order to allow for sourcing of ingredients, as well as efficient production scheduling. It appeared that these requests would not be too burdensome for Seven-Eleven. The sensitive issue of price was intentionally left until late in the discussions. Haagen-Dazs was being sold for 250 yen per 120 ml cup and Seven-Eleven wanted to position Ben & Jerry's at a slightly lower price point. This would be problematic for Odak, who had recently increased the domestic price for Ben & Jerry's ice cream in part to support the product's position as equal or superior in quality to Haagen-Dazs.

A concern yet lurking in the boardroom in Burlington, Vermont was what would be the company's social mission in Japan. Since the early 1990s, the company had moved beyond using its profit to fund philanthropy. The new imperative was to make the workplace, community and world a better place through regular day-to-day operations. On the other hand, profits were still needed in order to even have day-to-day operations and a new market (such as Japan) could be the ticket to those profits. In the meantime, no particular social mission had emerged from the summer discussions of entering the Japan market.

The Approaching Deadline for a Summer 1998 Japan Launch

Odak and his staff had made steady progress narrowing and developing their Japan options during the summer of 1997. If they were to enter the Japan market for the summer 1998 season, though, they would have to commit to one plan or another no later than autumn 1997. Two distinct entry options had emerged.

The Yamada option was largely the same as it had been at the beginning of the year. His proposal was to have full control of marketing and sales for Ben & Jerry's in Japan. He would position the brand, devise and orchestrate the initial launch and take care of marketing and distribution well into the future. He would earn a royalty on all sales in the market. By giving Yamada full control of the Japan market, Ben & Jerry's would have instant expertise in an otherwise unfamiliar market, as well as relief from having to address the many issues involved in putting together an entry strategy and in ongoing market management. Yamada knew frozen foods and he had an entrepreneurial spirit and marketing savvy, evidenced by his success in launching and building up the Domino's pizza chain in Japan. Giving up control of a potentially major market, though, could not be taken lightly. Because Yamada would invest his time in fleshing out and executing a marketing plan only after reaching agreement with Ben & Jerry's, there was no specific plan available for consideration. Even if there were, Yamada would retain the rights to change it. For the near term, however, Yamada would expect to add selected flavors of Ben & Jerry's ice cream cups to the Domino's delivery menu, providing an opportunity to collect market data based on customer response.

The Seven-Eleven option would leave Ben & Jerry's in control of whatever market development it might want to pursue beyond supplying Seven-Eleven in Japan. While Seven-Eleven would provide an instant entry to the market, the company would not be in a position to help Ben & Jerry's develop other distribution channels in Japan. The retailer thought it could sell at least six cups per day at each store, which would be the minimum to justify continuing to stock Ben & Jerry's. Looking at the size of Seven-Eleven's ice cream freezer cases suggested that this would require approximately 10 per cent of Seven-Eleven's cup ice cream sales to be Ben & Jerry's products. Ben & Jerry's was as yet unknown in Japan and it did not have the budget for a marketing campaign there. Sales would have to rely primarily on promotional efforts by Seven-Eleven, but the company was making no specific commitment for such efforts.

Another option was increasingly compelling— that of holding off on any Japan entry. Japan's economy was continuing to languish, with increasing talk that it could be years before recovery. A financial crisis that had commenced with a devaluation of Thailand's currency in July 1997, seemed to be spreading across Asia. If the pending Asia crisis hit an already weakened Japanese economy, the economics of exporting ice cream from Vermont to Japan could become infeasible. Though the value of the yen had recently fallen to 125 yen to the dollar, Ben & Jerry's could still sell the product at the plant gate at an acceptable profit with room for both shipping expense and satisfactory margins for

Seven-Eleven and its franchisees. If the rate went as high as 160 yen to the dollar, then the price in Japan would have to be raised to a level that might seriously cut into demand, especially relative to Haagen-Dazs, which had manufacturing facilities in Japan.

It would be a long evening meal as Odak, Pezzani, Bowman and Hight gave their final thoughts to the decision before them. Not only had Odak promised Iida that he could make a decision, but Yamada needed an answer to his proposal as well. In any event, Ben & Jerry's had to proceed with one plan or another if it was going to have any Japanese sales in its 1998 income statement.

Notes

1. Monetary values are in U.S. dollars unless otherwise noted.

2. A brief explanation of the relationship between the Japan Seven-Eleven organization and the U.S. 7-Eleven organization is in order. 7-Eleven convenience stores originated in Texas in 1927 as a retail concept of Southland Corporation, which had been in the ice business. Southland began using the 7-Eleven banner in the 1950s because the stores would be open from 7 a.m. to 11 p.m. The business grew through company-owned and franchised stores. Southland gave a master franchise for Japan to the Ito Yokado Company, a large supermarket operator there, which in turn established Seven-Eleven Japan to conduct the 7-Eleven business in Japan through company-owned and franchised stores. In the 1980s, Southland was in financial distress and Ito Yokado, along with its subsidiary, Seven-Eleven Japan, bailed out Southland, acquiring a controlling interest in the company. In this light, Odak's dinner with Iida in Japan constituted a sort of executive summit between Ben & Jerry's and its largest customer.

LARSON IN NIGERIA (REVISED)

Revised by Professor Paul W. Beamish and
Harry Cheung (originally prepared by Professor I. A. Litvak)

   Version: (A) 2004-02-02

David Larson, vice-president of international operations for Larson Inc., was mulling over the decisions he was required to make regarding the company's Nigerian operation. He was disturbed by the negative tone of the report sent to him on January 4, 2004, by the chief executive officer (CEO) of the Nigerian affiliate, George Ridley (see Exhibit 1). Larson believed the future prospects for Nigeria were excellent and was concerned about what action he should take.

COMPANY BACKGROUND

Larson Inc. was a New York-based multinational corporation in the wire and cable business. Wholly-owned subsidiaries were located in Canada and the United Kingdom, while Mexico, Venezuela, Australia, and Nigeria were the sites of joint ventures. Other countries around the world were serviced through exports from the parent or one of its subsidiaries.

The parent company was established in 1925 by David Larson's grandfather. Ownership and management of the company remained in the hands of the Larson family and was highly centralized. The annual sales volume for the corporation worldwide approximated $936 million in 2003. Revenue was primarily generated from the sale of power, communication, construction and control cables.

Technical service was an important part of Larson Inc.'s product package; therefore, the company maintained a large force of engineers to consult with customers and occasionally supervise installation. As a consequence, licensing was really not a viable method of serving foreign markets.

BACKGROUND ON NIGERIA

Nigeria is located in the west-central part of the African continent. With 134 million people in 2003, it was the most populous country in Africa and the ninth most populous nation in the world. Population growth was estimated at 2.5 per cent annually. About 44 per cent of the population was under 15 years of age. A majority of the labor force in Nigeria worked in agriculture but there was a trend of more people moving to urban centres.

The gross domestic product in 2003 was about $55 billion. While per capita GDP was only about $433, on a purchasing power parity basis it was substantially higher at $900. GDP had grown from 1998 to 2003 at about two per cent to three per cent annually. This increase was fuelled in part by growth in agriculture and the export sales of Nigeria's oil reserves.

During the 1998 to 2003 period, Nigeria's annual inflation rate had ranged between 10 and 11.7 per cent. This high level had contributed to the change in the value of the naira from 85.3 to the U.S. dollar in 1998 to 129.8 to the U.S. dollar in 2003.

THE NIGERIAN OPERATION

Larson Inc. established a joint venture in Nigeria in 1994 with a local partner who held 25 per cent of the joint venture's equity. In 1999, Larson Inc. promised Nigerian authorities that the share of local ownership would be increased to 51 per cent within the next five to seven years. Such indigenization requests from developing country governments were quite common.

In response to the request from head office for a detailed overview of the Nigerian situation and its implications for Larson Inc., Ridley prepared the following report in December, 2003. It attempts to itemize the factors in the Nigerian environment that have contributed to the problems experienced by Larson's joint venture in Nigeria.

Repatriation of Capital

1. While the Nigerian Investment Promotions Commission (NIPC) has removed time constraints and ceilings on repatriation, the divesting firm still has to submit evidence of valuation. In most cases the valuation is unrealistically low. This has represented substantial real-capital asset losses to the overseas companies concerned.

Remittance

2. A problem regarding remittances has arisen as a result of the Nigerian Insurance Decree No. 59, under which cargoes due for import to Nigeria have to be insured with a Nigerian-registered insurance company. For cargoes imported without confirmed letters of credit, claims related to cargo loss and damage are paid in Nigeria; however, foreign exchange for remittance to pay the overseas suppliers is not being granted on the grounds that the goods have not arrived.

Problems Affecting Liquidity and Cash Flow

3. A number of problems have arisen during the last two years that are having a serious effect upon liquidity and cash flow, with the result that the local expenses can be met only by increasing bank borrowing, which is not only an additional cost but also becoming more difficult to obtain.
   a) Serious delays exist in obtaining payment from federal and state government departments for supplies and services provided, even in instances where payment terms are clearly written into the contract concerned. This is particularly true for state governments where payment of many accounts is 12 months or more in arrears. Even after payment, further delays and exchange-rate losses are experienced in obtaining foreign currency for the part that is remittable abroad. This deterioration in cash flow from government clients had, in turn, permeated through to the private clients.
   b) There is a requirement that a 100 per cent deposit be made on application for foreign currency to cover letters of credit.
   c) In order to clear the cargo as soon as possible and to avoid possible loss at the wharf, importers normally pay their customs duty before a ship arrives.
   d) Most company profits are taxed at a flat rate of 30 per cent. Firms operating in Nigeria must contend with a number of arbitrary levies and taxes, imposed mainly by state governments eager to augment their extremely thin revenue bases. The federal government attempted to put a halt to such practices by specifying which taxes all three (federal, state and local) tiers of government can collect, but it has not been entirely successful in enforcing compliance. Tax authorities are constantly trying to "trip up" companies in the course of inspections or audits, through their "interpretation" of the tax legislation. Consequently, net earnings after tax are insufficient to cover increased working capital requirements.

Incomes and Prices Policy Guidelines

4. Many of the guidelines issued by the Productivity, Prices and Incomes Board are of direct discouragement, as they make operations in Nigeria increasingly less attractive in comparison with other areas in the world. Although these guidelines were removed in 1987, increases for wage, salary, fees for professional services and auditing are still subject to final government approval.

Offshore Technical and Management Services

5. Restrictions on the reimbursement of expenses to the parent company for offshore management and technical services are a cause of great concern, since such services are costly to provide.

Exhibit 1   The Ridley Report

Professional Fees

6. The whole position regarding fees for professional services provided from overseas is most unsatisfactory. Not only are the federal government scales substantially lower than those in most other countries, but also the basis of the project cost applied in Nigeria is out of keeping with normally accepted international practice. The arbitrary restriction on the percentage of fees that may be remitted is a further disincentive to attracting professional services. Moreover, payment of professional fees in themselves produces cash flow problems exacerbated by long delays in payments and remittance approvals.

Royalties and Trademarks

7. The National Office of Technology Acquisition and Promotion (NOTAP) restricts the payment of royalties for the use of trademarks for a period of 10 years, which is out of keeping with the generally accepted international practice. This can be extended only under special cases. Limits for licensing and technical service fees are between one per cent to five per cent of net sales. Management fees are chargeable at two per cent to five per cent of a company's profit before tax (or one per cent to two per cent of net sales when no profits are anticipated during the early years). The maximum foreign share of consulting fees is five per cent. Such applications, however, are only granted for advanced technology projects for which indigenous technology is not available. Further, service agreements for such projects have to include a schedule of training for Nigerian personnel for eventual takeover and Nigerian professionals are required to be involved in the project from inception.

Quotas, Work Permits, and Entry Visas

8. It must be recognized that expatriate expertise is a very important element for this business, but expatriate staff is very costly. Unfortunately, at the present time there are a number of difficulties and frustrations, such as the arbitrary cuts in expatriate quotas, the delays in approving quota renewal, and in some cases, the refusal of entry visas and work permits for individuals required for work in Nigeria. Expatriate quotas are usually granted for two to three years subject to renewal.

Expatriate Staff

9. In general, the conditions of employment and life in Nigeria are regarded as unattractive when compared with conditions in many other countries competing for the same expertise. These differences are due to: the general deterioration in law and order; the restrictions on salary increase and home remittance; the difficulties in buying air tickets; the poor standard of health care; the unsatisfactory state of public utilities such as electricity, water, and telecommunications; the harassment from the police, airport authorities and other government officials; the general frustrations related to visas and work permits mentioned above. The situation has now reached a stage where not only is recruitment of suitably qualified, skilled experts becoming increasingly difficult, but we are also faced with resignations and refusals to renew contracts even by individuals who have worked and lived here for some years. Furthermore, the uncertainty over the length of time for which employment in Nigeria will be available (due to doubts whether the necessary expatriate quotas will continue to be available to the employer) is most unsettling to existing staff. This and the restriction of contracts to as little as two years are important factors in deterring the more highly qualified applicants from considering posts in Nigeria. These factors are resulting in a decline in the quality of expatriate staff it is possible to recruit.

Local Staff

10. Nigeria has one of the strongest national unions in Africa — the National Labor Congress (NLC). It is almost impossible to discipline a worker without attracting confrontation with the union. On certain occasions, some union members can be very militant. The union is also continuously attacking the employment of expatriates and trying to replace them with Nigerian staff.

Exhibit 1 (Continued)

11. Inadequate local technical training leads to low quality workers who tend to be lazy and not quality conscious.

12. The desirability of maintaining a tribal balance in the work force limits the options in recruiting the best workers.

13. Nigerian companies suffer heavily from pilferage, which normally accounts for two per cent of sales.

Public Utilities

14. The constant interruption in public utility services not only affects the morale of all employees but also has a very serious impact upon the operation of the business itself. Unless reasonable and continuing supplies of electricity, water, petroleum products and telecommunications can be assured, and the highway adequately maintained, the costs related to setting up and operating escalate.

Continuity of Operating Conditions

15. The general and growing feeling of uncertainty about the continuity of operating conditions is a matter of considerable concern. It would seem that this uncertainty is engendered by a whole range of matters related to: short notice changes (sometimes even retrospective) in legislation and regulations; imprecise definition of legislation and regulations, which leads to long periods of negotiation and uncertainty; delays between public announcement of measures and promulgation of how they are to be implemented; and sometimes inconsistent interpretation of legislation and regulations by Nigerian officials.

Government Officials

16. Foreign partners have to rely on their Nigerian counterpart to handle the government officials. But it is impossible to measure its performance nor to control its expense in these activities. In addition, carefully cultivated relationships with officials could disappear, as they are transferred frequently.

Bribery

17. Surrounding many of the problems previously listed is the pervasive practice of bribery, known locally as the *dash*. Without such a payment it is very difficult to complete business or government transactions with native Nigerians.

Exhibit 1 (Continued)

Sales revenue for the Nigerian firm totalled $45 million in 2003. Of this revenue, $39.4 million was realized in Nigeria, while $5.6 million was from exports. About 40 per cent of the firm's Nigerian sales ($16 million) were made to various enterprises and departments of the government of Nigeria. The company was making a reasonable profit of 10 per cent of revenue, but with a little bit of luck and increased efficiency, it was believed it could make a profit of 20 per cent.

The Nigerian operation had become less attractive for Larson Inc. in recent months.

Although it was widely believed that Nigeria would become one of the key economic players in Africa in the 2000s and that the demand for Larson's products would remain very strong there, doing business in Nigeria was becoming more costly. Furthermore, Larson Inc. had become increasingly unhappy with its local partner in Nigeria, a lawyer who was solely concerned with quick "paybacks" at the expense of reinvestment and long-term growth prospects.

David Larson recognized that having the right partner in a joint venture was of paramount importance. The company expected the partner or partners to be actively engaged in the business, "not business people interested in investing money alone." The partner was also expected to hold a substantial equity in the venture. In the early years of the joint venture, additional funding was often required and it was necessary for the foreign partner to be in a strong financial position.

The disillusionment of George Ridley, the Nigerian firm's chief executive officer (CEO), had been increasing since his early days in that position. He was an expatriate from the United Kingdom who, due to his background as a military officer, placed a high value upon order and control. The chaotic situation in Nigeria proved very trying for him. His problems were further complicated by his inability to attract good, local employees in Nigeria, while his best expatriate staff requested transfers to New York or Larson Inc.'s other foreign operations soon after their arrival in Nigeria. On a number of occasions, Ridley was prompted to suggest to head office that it reconsider its Nigerian commitment.

THE DECISION

David Larson reflected on the situation. He remained convinced that Larson Inc. should maintain its operations in Nigeria; however, he had to design a plan to increase local Nigerian equity in the venture to 51 per cent. Larson also wondered what should be done about Ridley. On the one hand, Ridley had been with the company for many years and knew the business intimately; on the other hand, Larson felt that Ridley's attitude was contributing to the poor morale in the Nigerian firm and wondered if Ridley had lost his sense of adaptability. Larson knew Ridley had to be replaced, but he was unsure about the timing and the method to use, since Ridley was only two years away from retirement.

Larson had to come to some conclusions fairly quickly. He had been requested to prepare an action plan for the Nigerian operation for consideration by the board of directors of Larson Inc. in a month's time. He thought he should start by identifying the key questions, whom he should contact, and how he should handle Ridley in the meantime.

PRIVATIZING POLAND'S TELECOM INDUSTRY: OPPORTUNITIES AND CHALLENGES IN THE NEW ECONOMY AND E-BUSINESS

Prepared by Marius Siwak under the supervision of Professor David Conklin

Version: (A) 2001-01-31

As it entered the 21st century, the Polish government faced the dilemma of how to develop an optimal telecom structure and related services. For decades, a government owned and operated telecom, TPSA, had held a monopoly, but in the late 1990s the Polish government gradually allowed the entry of some competitors, many of whom brought new technologies.[1] The government had undertaken a major privatization program throughout the economy, and it faced the question of whether and how it should privatize TPSA. Yet privatization would have to be accompanied by ongoing regulation in order to ensure that managerial decisions were made in the interests of the nation, as a whole. A number of comments by Izabela Moziek, a representative of TPSA, served to emphasize the concerns of the government.

The government will never release its grip on the company because we are strategically such an important part of the nation . . .

. . . We have several new development plans in place now to secure a leadership position in the future. Most of all, the Polish government has several military and other contracts with the company and it will always have an interest in preserving TPSA's well-being . . .

There is still a strong government presence in the day to day operations of the company.

This challenge of continual government intervention could reduce the attractiveness of acquiring TPSA, in spite of its market dominance. For potential foreign investors, a host of additional difficulties appeared to be so severe that perhaps the privatization bidding process should be ignored. Existing infrastructure was largely obsolete, and employees lacked the skills and motivation to transform TPSA into a modern, competitive entity. Meanwhile, alternative modes of entry into the telecom sector might be pursued, and some, like wireless and the Internet could threaten TPSA's future.

In the new era of e-business, would Poland be able to retain the economic momentum that its 1990s market reforms had created? A new investor could be very discouraged about the prospects for the "new economy" and e-business. The future success of the Polish economy as a whole would depend very much upon a transformation in Poland's telecom industry, but would this transformation occur soon? A special report on Poland in "Computer World Top 2000" emphasized:

> Another threat is looming on the horizon—the new model of the economy. The development of electronic business, which will most likely become an economic standard in the developed parts of the world, puts Poland in the dramatic pursuit after escaping leaders. Every Polish enterprise must take a long and hard look at itself once again and answer the question: "to which part of the chain of value creation does it want to belong?" How well Poland adopts e-business solutions will dictate whether it will belong to the part of the world that engages in costly production or the part that carries out lucrative distribution.

Poland's leaders had been shifting the nation successfully from communism to free enterprise, and analysts expected that they would continue along the path of transferring decision-making to the private sector. Many potential investors recognized the key role to be played by the telecom structure and e-business. Perhaps now was the time to achieve a "first mover advantage." The very low level of Poland's involvement in the new economy and e-business might be seen as an ideal business environment for developing market share and attaining extraordinary profits.

THE DEAL[2]

> The government wanted to ease TPSA into a competitive environment. The logic behind our decision was that the company had never operated in a competitive environment before and we were afraid that opening up the lucrative long distance segment of the market too quickly might bring the company down. First of all, TPSA is, strategically, an important part of our development policy. Second, the Ministry of Treasury planned to sell off part of the company to a strategic investor. If TPSA's earnings degenerated dramatically, simply no one would buy it. Besides those reasons, we wanted to create a much needed local infrastructure, given the low telephone penetration ratio in the country.
>
> Andrzej Plachecki,
> Director of Strategic Development—
> Ministry of Telecommunications.

In 1999, the Ministry of Communication issued an invitation to foreign telecom providers to participate in the sale of a 35 per cent stake in the national telecom carrier—TPSA. From a dozen of companies that expressed their interest, two bidders emerged: France Telecom and SBC Communication. In November, 1999, SBC withdrew from the negotiation process citing ambiguity of the Polish telecom market regulation as a main reason for its exit from negotiations. France Telecom remained the only interested party and in December, 1999, the Ministry of

Treasury rejected the French offer giving two main reasons for the rejection: too low a price (about US$2.5 billion), and planned employment cuts that were too drastic.

After this failed effort, the government considered selling its stake in TPSA through capital markets, but the potential price that the Ministry could attain would be lower than that from selling off a package to a strategic investor. Furthermore, the government rightly perceived the importance of the much needed business expertise which a strategic investor would bring to the organization. TPSA lacked experience in customer service and was far behind the cutting edge of the new economy and e-business. Therefore, for TPSA to survive in the long run, a strategic investor's influence seemed necessary.

Early in 2000 the Ministry of Treasury issued another invitation to telecoms around the world. This time two bidders emerged and remained till the end: France Telecom once again and Telecom Italia. On May 22, 2000, the government of Poland named France Telecom as a winner of the bidding process. Analysts estimated that France Telecom paid approximately US$5 billion for a 35 per cent stake in TPSA. France Telecom had an option to buy additional 16 per cent of the company, thus eventually achieving a controlling stake in the Polish national carrier.

Five billion dollars is not the only expenditure, however, that France Telecom would face in the near future. The next stage of negotiations would involve a so-called "Social Package." TPSA employees were represented by several labor unions. In order to restructure properly and to revive the company, the new investor would likely have to release a large number of people. Izabela Moziek was clear in regard to the employee profile: "Until recently, the hiring process has been based more on family and friends than on necessary skills."

A new collective agreement had to be negotiated with the unions prior to any major layoffs. In particular, the severance pay might turn out to be very expensive. It was estimated that in order to avoid problems with the unions, France Telecom would have to pay two full years of pay to each laid off employee. An average salary within TPSA was about US$500 per month, thus, if the company decided to lay off, say, 15 per cent of its workforce, it would cost at least an additional US$200 million to complete the restructure. Even such a generous package did not fully protect the company from a conflict with the unions, nor did it guarantee its acceptance. Bickering among unions could stall the process for months. Furthermore, France Telecom would have to invest additional billions of dollars if it wanted to transform TPSA into a modern telecom provider with broadband capacity.

The company generated over US$200 million a year in net profit.[3] But so far TPSA operated uncontested and no company other than TPSA even had a permit to build a true alternative infrastructure. In the years 2002/03 this situation would change. The entire Polish market would open up to competition without restrictions. Given that alternative networks existed, such as cable TV, or were in the planning stage, could the company sustain its profitability in the long run?

After 2003, what would stop an American telecom company or any major European telecom provider from entering the market, with superior financial resources and technical expertise, to establish modern broadband telecom services? Was the high price paid for the stake in TPSA well justified in light of technological changes reshaping the telecom industry? Was TPSA well positioned to become a modern telecom provider by the world standards?

FROM COMMUNISM TO CAPITALISM![4, 5]

With the legalization of Solidarity in 1989 and the ensuing democratization of the government, Poland emerged from the communist rule that had endured from the end of the World War II. From the ashes of a centrally planned economy, a decade after embarking on aggressive restructuring, Poland, by 2000, had become one of the most successful economies in Eastern Europe. Initially, investment may have appeared risky and uncertain. However, history demonstrates that the often-oppressed Poles are a resilient and adaptable people; perhaps an ideal site for economic reform and a platform into eastern European countries. Starting with no banking laws and no property rights, there were now more than two million entrepreneurs in such sectors as retail trade, construction, and light manufacturing. Private business now accounted for about 60 per cent of the GDP.

Except for a very minor increase in 1999, inflation and unemployment had steadily trended down. The economy had made consistent progress with annual real growth between five and seven per cent. In the 1990s, the Monetary Policy Council (MPC) enhanced its credibility with swift and decisive policies to manage economic crises. In 1997/98, when the economy appeared to be overheating, the MPC responded with a tightening of monetary policy. Poland did not escape the late 1990s financial crises of less developed countries entirely, as growth slowed to 1.5 per cent in 1Q99 but it rebounded to 4.9 per cent by 3Q99. Economic reform had become an ongoing process with the Polish government. In 1997 large scale privatization was initiated, resulting in restructuring of entire sectors of the economy. Privatized businesses typically demonstrated improved efficiencies very quickly. Despite these efforts, in 2000 the state still owned some 3,000 enterprises (125 with more than 500 employees) and still dominated many sectors. Government plans anticipated privatization of 70 per cent of the remaining businesses by 2001. All this progress had been achieved despite having nine different governments in ten years.

The foremost economic objective of Poland was ascension into the EU. As two-thirds of Poland's trade was with the EU a large degree of integration had already been achieved by 2000. The MPC was attempting to maintain the budget deficit at 2.5 per cent of GDP. With the minor crisis in 1999 it reached 3.5 per cent, but a budget law required a maximum of 2.75 per cent by 2000. The concern with these statistics was that many of the state owned enterprises were accumulating accounts payable by not remitting taxes and social security contributions. The EU

inflation target of zero to two per cent was beyond reach for Poland in the near term. The MPC preferred to set a realistic target: four per cent by 2003. This was a very practical approach as inflation declined from 800 per cent in 1989 to a rate of 7.7 per cent in 2000. Poland managed foreign currency exchange with a "crawling peg regime." The zloty was allowed to trade within a 15 per cent band either side of a centrally fixed rate that was depreciated at 0.3 per cent per month against a euro/dollar basket. This policy was changed in 1999, and the currency was allowed to flow freely in the market, without initially losing any value.

Poland's imports had recently substantially exceeded exports. Imports peaked in 1998 at 146 per cent of exports and were anticipated to decline gradually. Encouragingly, the bulk of the imports were in the category of investment goods. Despite the fiscal budget deficit and the current account deficit, Poland had increased its international reserves as a result of capital inflows. Foreign debt declined on a real basis and as a percentage of GDP. Poland's success in funding its expansionary policy was due to the high level of foreign direct investment (FDI). For the ten years ending 1998 FDI was US$30.7 billion, and it was forecast to be US$10.5 billion in 2000. Privatization was a significant element of these FDI inflows.

Poland recently embarked on a major restructuring of its social safety net, employment and tax laws. These latter reforms were essential to improve the effectiveness of public spending and to remove the ambiguity of hidden subsidies. The government had recognized the need to modernize infrastructure; specifically roads, airports, and seaports. Despite the fact that unemployment had steadily trended down, it remained the highest in eastern Europe with the natural rate of unemployment (NRU) estimated at 10 per cent. Poland reputedly had the most profligate welfare system in eastern Europe. Furthermore, the discouraged worker phenomenon was supplemented by hidden unemployment in rural areas, second wave baby boomers and the potential for nearly half of the work force to be

	1994	1998	2000E
Real GDP growth, %	5.30	4.80	5.50
GDP per capita, US$	2,407.00	3,872.00	4,190.00
Inflation, annual average %	33.30	11.70	7.70
Unemployment, annual average %	15.00	10.60	10.50
Current account balance, US$ million	(944.00)	(6,858.00)	(10,500.00)
Current account balance as % of GDP	(1.00)	(4.60)	(6.50)
Interest rate, short term, %		24.50	15.50
Foreign exchange rate, US$	2.27	3.48	4.15
Fiscal deficit/surplus as % of GDP		(2.50)	(2.50)

Exhibit 1   Polish Economic Statistics

women. Planned tax reforms were significant and positive; corporate tax reduction from 34 per cent to 22 per cent by 2004, personal tax reduction from a 20 per cent, 32 per cent, and 44 per cent three-tier structure to a two-tier structure of 18 per cent and 28 per cent by 2001. Increases in VAT and consumption taxes plus economic growth were expected to offset these reductions in tax revenue. Tax reform was a significant prerequisite of EU compliance. It was hoped that educational initiatives to eliminate the gap with the EU would help address the high NRU. These reforms would hopefully counteract rising tensions in the labor force.

However, many observers saw serious difficulties for the Polish economy. In a general survey in May 1999, the following comments suggested that all was not well.[6]

Most of the people who lived in Poland during the intervening years think about how much more change is needed, how unfair the transition from communism has been, how their safe, secure lives have been irretrievably upset, how much uncertainty lies ahead.

By most accounts, about a third of Poles felt better off than they did a decade before, a third thought they were in roughly the same position and a third believed themselves to be worse off.

Polish Finance Minister Leszek Balcerowicz was equally clear in his own mind about what should be done: "Our financial and economic strategy for the next 10 years focuses on the crucial issues of tax reform, public finance and privatization . . . Key to the economic strategy must be privatization of the state sector, which still controls some 40 per cent of the Polish economy."

Joining the EU would not be easy. Many Poles argued for special entry concessions, and negotiations over the terms and conditions for EU membership would involve internal conflicts. Unemployment among rural youth was very high and threatened social instability. Polish farmers struggled to survive with low agricultural prices, in the context of cheap food imports. Lurking in the background was a widespread set of concerns about the rapidly increasing foreign ownership of Polish land and industry.

THE TECHNOLOGICAL REVOLUTION
IN THE GLOBAL TELECOM INDUSTRY

In recent years, especially in the North American market, traditional plain telephone service had become a commodity. One of the loudest buzzwords in the new era of telecommunication in the 21st century was a "residential gateway" that promised to deliver an integrated set of telephony, internet connectivity, data transmission, home networking, and entertainment features through one box that connected to virtually everything. Such a prediction pointed to broadband as necessary for the telecommunications future. The pipes leading from the Internet to the living rooms of consumers, capable of carrying digital bits in torrents would enable households to download music and video from vast entertainment libraries, shop in real time, or make a video call to a distant relative.

The most substantial bottleneck in this telecom revolution was in the local loop, the last mile of infrastructure linking the system to each household or business. Hence the issue of capacity enhancement in the local loop became truly significant for each nation's twenty-first century competitiveness.

At this point in time, it was not clear how the constriction in the local loop could best be overcome. The cable industry covered only a portion of the population, and required huge capital outlays in order to provide optimal "broadband" access. For traditional telecoms, digital subscriber lines (DSL) offered more carrying capacity on existing copper wires, but deteriorated with distance, and signals interfered with each other if more than a limited number of customers were covered in each neighborhood. Wireless and satellite technologies were still in the early stages of development, and some technologies encountered weather difficulties and needed "line-of-sight" with customers. Likely, there would be a variety of solutions, each geared to certain market niches: urban versus rural, large business versus small- and medium-sized businesses, and an array of differing preferences among residential consumers. It was quite possible that the technologies that would be most successful had not yet been developed.

In the twenty-first century, telecommunications would become increasingly important for each nation, not just as a stand alone industry, but because of the role it played in increasing the efficiency of existing business and in creating new start-up enterprises throughout the economy. Poland's competitiveness as a nation would depend on the ability of the telecom infrastructure to support this array of new enhanced services, and Poland's productivity improvements, with increases in living standards, would depend on ongoing innovations in these enhanced telecom services. Affordability, quality and breadth of service had become critical components in determining the value of the telecom system to other businesses. Hence it was important for Poland to turn to a new set of policy and regulatory issues that would place an even greater emphasis on enhancing competition.

As the marginal cost of carriage tended towards zero, and as competition fostered huge investments in fibre optic cable, the DSL technologies, wireless networks, and telecom carriers in many countries were entering an era of commoditization of basic service provision. Future profits would rest on the ability of telecom companies to provide value-added services to their customers in the face of heightened Polish and global competition. These realities would change the structure of Poland's telecom industry.

In many countries, the Internet and all its associated technologies were creating a new economy and new industry structures. Its effects were well documented. But what was not as well known—except among technology visionaries, such as Bill Gates, Steve Case, and John Chambers—was the extent to which the convergence revolution would change the way all businesses and governments operated, thus enabling enormous productivity improvements. For this reason, the term e-enhanced services (electronically-enhanced) came to represent the various services and products that could be delivered over the telecommunications infrastructure. By no means an exhaustive list, the following were important sectors that would present profound regulatory challenges over the coming years:

1. E-Retail

2. E-Advertising

3. E-Banking and E-Financial Services

4. E-Entertainment

5. E-Pornography

6. E-Gambling

7. E-Medicine

In the context of major global telecom changes, the enhancement of domestic culture would become increasingly difficult. Many enhanced services dealt with the provision of content, and this relationship raised a series of issues in regard to how to enhance domestic involvement in this content. For instance, vertical integration in the telecommunications field was stretching into traditional content arenas that were previously the sole domain of broadcasters. Whether and how a government should regulate the Internet and its content had become a major issue for most countries. How could the government effectively promote domestic content on the Internet, particularly in light of international trade agreements that required increasingly open international competition?

Furthermore, throughout the world, the challenge for regulators was to entrench competition and innovation in an industry characterized by economies of scale and scope in service delivery, while protecting consumers and investors from fraud, misleading advertising, and certain other socially unacceptable behaviors. For example, if an entrepreneur set up a website to sell mutual funds, should the entrepreneur be subject to the same regulations as a broker at an investment firm? If so, were these regulations enforceable?

Many countries were finding that the traditional regulatory environment in each business sector had to be re-examined to determine its appropriateness in the new telecom era. However, the government's ability to regulate each of the sectors that used the telecom infrastructure would be severely constrained. In countries with radio and TV broadcasts sent over the telecommunications infrastructure and Internet commerce growing by leaps and bounds, a key question was whether over arching regulation of telecoms must be combined in some way with the separate regulation of each service provider that was using the telecom infrastructure. Telecom policy would then be seen as much broader in scope than it had been in the past, for it would include social policy and commercial regulation. Conversely, telecom policy, per se, could in turn become limited in scope, as social policy and commercial regulation determined the optimal telecom framework.

The number of people who had taken advantage of broadband services was still quite small in most countries, including Poland. The take-up rate was low because of high hardware prices and the lack of compelling new reason for consumers to step up their services. When traffic increased, images decayed. The problem was expected to ease as long distance telecom companies and Internet providers improved their networks and electronics. As the technical problems with broadband effectiveness disappeared, the new battle for a "residential gateway" could become intense.

The recent merger between AOL and Time Warner and its European equivalent between United Pan European Communications and SBS Broadcasting reflected the perception that those who controlled content and direct access to homes would be best poised to be the future leaders in the new era of telecommunication and e-business. However, which of the many existing technologies or transmission media were best positioned to become a standard for the future telecommunication services? In 2000 there were no clear leaders. The experts were widely divided over which technology was best suited to accommodate the rapid evolution of electronic business. Some pointed to DSL as a future standard of broadband, others name DTH (Direct To Home), cable, or wireless as the potential leader of broadband telecommunication services. Meanwhile, satellites might also come to play a role. Unfortunately, it seemed too early to tell which technology was likely to live on, and which was likely to fail.

POLAND'S REGULATORY ENVIRONMENT

The main regulatory body of telecom services was the Ministry of Communication. However, the Ministry of National Defense and Internal Affairs had a limited influence, as well as contracts with the TPSA regarding national security. Telecom services were considered to be of national strategic importance. A separate board—KKRiTV—was a regulatory body appointed by the government of Poland to regulate and control radio and television content. Although there was a trend toward creation of multimedia telecommunications including TV programming and radio transmission, there was no plan to merge the two regulatory organs. Furthermore, because of an extreme political segregation within Polish government such fusion seemed to be impossible, at least for the time being.

On November 23, 1990, the Polish government decided to de-monopolize its telecommunication market.[7] The government started selling off licenses for various services (these licenses were not subject to an automatic renewal). Separate licenses were sold for data transmission, telephony, Internet services, mobile telephony, and cable TV services. For example attaining a license for telephone services did not mean that the operator was free to provide a full range service offering. Additionally, cable providers were not allowed to provide voice services, and only one license was awarded for telephone services per small region in order not to create too intense competition for TPSA. Moreover, the telecom providers were not allowed to provide their services or build infrastructure across the regions, thus TPSA still held its monopoly in the highly lucrative long distance segment. There was no maximum connection or transfer price established by the Ministry, which left TPSA free to dictate any price for connection to its long-distance system.

The law was amended several times since 1990 to accommodate change in the telecom industry as well as to solve problems and disputes as they arose. For instance, Era GSM, a subsidiary of Elektrim, started providing long distance telephone calls via the Internet, at about one-third the price compared with TPSA. However, TPSA claimed to be cross subsidizing high cost rural telephony from its long distance profits, and so lobbied the government to prohibit Internet telephony. The Ministry of Telecommunication agreed with the TPSA position and threatened to pull out the license from Era. However, confronted with the company's appeals to other European governments, the Ministry backed off and eventually allowed Era's Internet telephony. Nevertheless, as Andrzej Plachecki emphasized, "Internet telephony has not really taken off despite all the savings that it has promised."

As of 2000 there was a new telecom law in the makings. The new act included sweeping changes. In 2003, when the new law would take effect, the market would open up to any firm that wanted to provide any telecom services upon getting an appropriate license. The licenses would be renewable, not subject to being reviewed, as before. A license would be sold based on the carrier's capability to provide a service. The Ministry of Communication would cease to exist and a small telecom regulatory entity would be formed under the Ministry of Transportation. However, the telecom services were still perceived to be of a strategic national importance. This fact combined with the government's desire to develop much needed telephone infrastructure in less developed regions of the country presented an opportunity for TPSA to influence the authorities in the future.

THE STATE OF THE TELECOMMUNICATIONS MARKET IN POLAND[8]

Telekomunikacja Polska S.A. (TPSA) was established in December, 1991, when the Polish Post, Telegraph, and Telephone Office, founded in 1928, was broken into separate entities. However, Telekomunikacja Polska S.A. remained wholly owned and operated by the government of Poland. From the very beginning of its existence, TPSA operated profitably and by 2000 was the most profitable organization in the country.[9] Until 1995, TPSA operated as a single telecommunication service provider without any competition. Only in 1995 did the Ministry of

Communication decide to deregulate the telecom market slightly in order to prepare Poland for the integration with the European Union and to prepare TPSA to operate in a competitive environment. Thus at the end of 1995, TPSA for the first time faced so called competition. However, TPSA still held an exclusive right to provide intercity as well as international phone services until 2002 and 2003, consecutively, and competed locally only with one company for innercity telephone services, with the exception of the Warsaw region where two competitors were allowed.

In the Polish market, broadband services were mainly geared towards data transmission. TPSA, and a few other companies, banks in particular, provided fast DSL services. Their networks, however, were still underdeveloped and their services extremely expensive.

The Telecom market in Poland could be characterized as extremely underdeveloped, with under 30 fixed lines per 100 inhabitants.[10] In comparison, developed European countries had about a 60/100 ratio. This low penetration indicator was even lower outside the major cities in Poland. For example, in more remote and less developed regions,[11] which represented about 40 per cent of the country, this percentage was 10 to 12 per cent or less. These regions had a much poorer and more dispersed population, which made the development process more expensive and unprofitable. TPSA held about 96 per cent of the fixed line telecom service market in Poland (nine million subscribers).[12]

Company Name	Services Provided	Number of Subscribers of Fixed Telephone Service	Number of Cellular Subscribers	Market Share in Mobile and Fixed Service Provision	Net Profit in US$ - Last Reported
1. TPSA	Fixed telephone Mobile Satellite Radio broadcasting Internet Data transmission	9 million	400 thousand	96% 17%	200 million
2. Netia SA	Fixed telephony Internet Data transmission	250 thousand	N/A	2%	(100.1 million)
3. Elektrim SA	Fixed telephony Internet Cable TV Mobile Data transmission	120 thousand	1.5 million	1% 51%	25 million
4. Polkomtel	Mobile Data transmission Internet		1.1 million	32%	40 million
5. UPC (WIZJA TV)	Cable TV DTH				N/A

Exhibit 2   Polish Telecommunications Providers—Overview

Netia S.A.

The second largest telecom provider was Netia S.A. The company was established in 1990 to exploit anticipated deregulation of the telecom market in the country. In 1998, Netia launched its IPO on NASDAQ. About 30 per cent of the company was held by Telia AB, a Swedish national carrier. Telia was also dynamically involved in the telecom market in the majority of the Baltic States. Telia had three mobile telephone systems and one cable TV subsidiary in Sweden. An additional 40 per cent of Netia S.A. was held by GE Capital, Motav (a cable system media company from Israel), Danker (a diversified telecom provider also from Israel), Goldman Sachs Capital Partners, and Shamrock Holdings Inc. (a private investment firm owned by R.E. Disney). Netia Telekom S.A. had serviced 458,251 lines and had 260,388 subscribers.[13] The corporation had a permit to provide fixed line telephone services in five major Polish cities and covered a territory inhabited by 33 per cent of the country's population. Aside from fixed telephony, Netia had three permits to provide internet services and one permit to provide data transmission using ISDN protocol.

Netia's infrastructure was based on modern fiber optic technology. Although no telephone operator other than TPSA had a license to provide intercity and international services, or even build intercity infrastructure, Netia already started to lay down fibre optic cables to connect its five local area networks in anticipation of further market deregulation. Once completed, such a network would finally create a truly alternative telecom service, free of dependency on TPSA's infrastructure. Also, given that Telia AB was a modern telephone company with extensive infrastructure in Northern, Central, and Eastern Europe, in 2003 when the Polish market would become fully opened to competition, the company would be able to provide international call services.

Elektrim S.A.

Elektrim S.A., with its subsidiary "Era," was the third largest telecom provider in Poland.

Vivendi Corporation was the majority shareholder with a 49 per cent stake in Elektrim. Vivendi also had a large stake in the two largest European pay TV companies: BskyB and Canal Plus. In addition to fixed line telephone services, Elektrim held a majority stake in Era GSM, a leading cellular telephone provider, as well as in Aster City, which was a cable TV operator with 240,000 subscribers[14] mainly in the Warsaw region. Through Aster City, Elektrim planned to provide full multimedia telecom services in the near future. This was the only company other than TPSA that could provide a full range of multimedia telecom services.

There were about 70 other local telecom service providers in Poland.[15] The great majority of them were small and undercapitalized, however, by 2000, one could observe a slow but steady consolidation trend among them.[16] It was safe to assume that once the full scale market deregulation became a reality, these small operators would either merge or be taken over, creating yet another full range telecom alternative to that of TPSA.

The Wireless Market

Mobile telephony appeared in Poland in 1991 with the establishment of PTK Centertel (owned by TPSA), although the network only began operating several years later. At the beginning, Centertel based its services on the analogue network. The analogue market was now saturated with 260,000 subscribers.[17] Digital networks began to dominate in 1997. At the end of 1996 two competitors were awarded licenses by the Ministry of Communication to provide cellular telephone services using the digital system GSM 900. Era GSM (owned by Elektrim) and GSM Plus (owned by Polkomtel) dominated the market.

The Ministry of Communication did not initially issue the same permit to use GSM 900 technology to Centertel to prevent TPSA from establishing yet another monopolistic position in the mobile telephone market. However, Centertel was given such a license in 1999, perhaps because its two competitors were firmly entrenched and perhaps to increase the value of the firm in light of the planned sale of a 35 per cent stake in TPSA to a strategic investor. At the end of 1999 the size of the mobile telephone market in Poland was estimated to be over three million subscribers, and it was growing at the rate of 25 per cent per annum.

Spectrum Allocation

Throughout the world, a major political issue concerned the question, how best to allocate spectrum for wireless operators. In the past, the Polish government had used an auction process. However, recent experiments with auctions in other countries had encountered serious problems. *The Economist* emphasized:

> The auction process was designed almost entirely by experts in game theory, one of the economics profession's most esoteric fields. . . .
> . . . Poorly designed auctions can make governments look foolish. For example, in 1990, New Zealand conducted a so-called second-price sealed-bid auction. Under this scheme, the highest bidder wins, but instead of paying its own bid price the winner pays the next-highest bid price. In New Zealand many bidders got spectrum rights for prices far below what they had offered. In one case, the top bid was NZ$100,000 (US$60,000) but the winner paid only NZ$6.

A large number of auction questions remained. Should winners be required to pay immediately, or should payments be spread over a certain time period? Would "the winner's curse" frequently mean that the winning bidder would have paid too much? Would license interdependencies be impeded by the bidding process that allocated each regional spectrum individually? Would some bidders simply not have the capability or qualifications to implement their plans? Should forfeiture penalties be incurred by bidders who failed to comply with certain commitments? Should there be reserve prices and minimum opening bids? Should there be a series of rounds in the bidding process in order for each bidder to arrive over time at an optimal bid?

As an alternative process for spectrum allocation, some governments used a comparative selection process in which public servants examined a wide variety of aspects of each applicant's proposal. Of particular importance to some governments was the concept of universal service, and each proposal could be evaluated on the degree to which it promised to serve high cost as well as low cost areas.

Alternative Telecom Infrastructures

There were other alternative potential telecom infrastructures. For instance, the Polish Railway Company ran its trains almost exclusively on electricity, and so the company had a very extensive electric cable network throughout Poland. Polish Hydro possessed similar infrastructure. There were several studies underway to adopt electric wire for data transmission. Although the necessary hardware and software were still very expensive and underdeveloped, the possibility existed that in the future this alternative medium could create effective competition for traditional telecom providers.

It was important to note the presence of a major broadband communication provider— United Pan-European Communication Company— in the Polish Market. UPC, headquartered in Amsterdam, was one of the most innovative broadband communication providers in Europe and owned and operated the largest broadband communication network on the continent. UPC provided cable TV, satellite services, telephony, high-speed internet access, and programming services in 18 countries across Europe and Israel. As of March 31, 2000, on an aggregate basis, UPC's systems passed approximately 11.5 million homes (over one million in Poland).

UPC was a consolidated subsidiary of Denver based United Global Com Inc. (NASDAQ: "UCOMA"), and Microsoft had an interest of approximately seven per cent in UPC.[18] The company had some of the most technologically advanced cable systems available anywhere in the world today. UPC owned a unique cable infrastructure backbone called AORTA (Always On Ready Time Architecture) which would eventually interconnect each of the UPC's local country operations. Long-term leasing arrangements for two dedicated high capacity fiber optic routes provided a transatlantic link for this AORTA backbone with the dynamic North American market. At this time in Poland, UPC owned and operated a cable TV provider—Wizja TV—satellite services, and Internet access. In 2003, there would be no obstacles for the company to provide a full range of telecom services of the highest quality, thus weakening the dominant role of TPSA in the Polish telecom industry.

TPSA Position in the Polish Market

On November 18, 1998, TPSA floated its shares on the Warsaw and London Stock Exchanges, and the company ceased to be wholly owned by Poland's State Treasury. Fifteen per cent of its shares were now in private hands. Additionally, 15 per cent of the company shares were distributed among its employees, leaving the State with a 70 per cent stake. Although the company had a new management structure composed mainly of professional managers, the president of TPSA, Pawel Rzepka, had been appointed by the government and represented "Unia Wolnosci," one of Poland's ruling political parties.

TPSA employed 72,800 people (12.7 per cent with a university degree)[19] and could be characterized as overstaffed. Work on the company's restructure was initiated in 1998, to prepare the organization for real competition in 2003, when the Polish telecom market would completely lose most restrictions. However, several strong labor unions existed within the company, making it extremely difficult to reduce multiple duplications within TPSA. Furthermore, many employees had been working for the company for a long time and their attitudes towards change remained questionable, making it difficult, despite management's effort, to create a modern, lean and flexible telecom provider out of TPSA.

Since 1991 the company had diversified its services into a multitude of different areas of telecommunication, but each had a very small number of customers concentrated in certain geographical areas. These included:[20]

Polpak

This was a public tele-info network commissioned in 1992 and used for data transmission. Polpak, in 1998, comprised 53 nodes covering the entire country and connected to 140 states worldwide. The network was particularly useful to small- and mid-size enterprises. Polpak also allowed for simultaneous data transmission between subscribers working with various protocols and speeds. The system was fully compatible with several international standards. The maximum speed at a subscriber's port was up to two Mbits/sec.

Polpak-T

This was a new, more modern network based on frame relay and ATM protocols. It was the only European network based fully on the ATM technology operating with a speed of up to 150 Mbits, allowing connections to networks in 220 countries. Polpak-T permitted the creation of virtual channels. In the next two years, the network was supposed to connect all major cities in Poland.

VSAT

VSAT was a satellite data transmission and telephone connection system, which used Eutelest. There was very limited information about the system.

Polkom 400

Available since 1996, Polkom was a modern, public electronic mail system based on the X.400 international standard.

ISDN

TPSA offered fast data transmission based on DSL-like technology. It was also involved in radio and television broadcasting, and land and marine radio communication. Also, TPSA was the largest internet provider in Poland. It allowed free of charge access to the net through its countrywide telephone number, however, the company charged on per minute basis for staying connected to phone lines. The charge varied depending on the day and the time of use, but a person extensively using the Internet (four to five hours per day) could expect to pay approximately US$150 per month, which in terms of an average Polish salary equaled roughly 25 per cent of monthly pay.

Centertel, a mobile telephone company, was another TPSA subsidiary, in which the company held a majority stake, however, Centertel did not have a monopoly in the mobile telephone market (currently the firm held only 19 per cent of the entire market)[21] and it competed with two dynamic enterprises—ERA GSM, owned by Polska Telefonia Cyfrowa, and GSM PLUS, owned by Polkomtel. The number of cell telephone subscribers at the end of 1999 exceeded three million people. As the numbers suggest, mobile services were emerging as a strong substitute for fixed telephony, especially because the cost of using cellular telephones was often comparable to or even lower than that of stationary phone service.

Nonetheless, the great majority of TPSA revenue came from the fixed line telephone market. The company held 96 per cent of this segment, which amounted to about nine million subscribers. Due mainly to limited competition and lack of price regulation from the government, the cost of any telephone call was extremely high for the average Pole. For instance, an international phone call was 81 per cent more expensive than that made from Canada, taking into account purchasing power parity. In real terms, an overseas call cost, on average, US$1.50 per minute.

In 1998, the company earned a profit of approximately US$200 million on $2.5 billion revenue.[22]

TPSA's plans for future developments included, among others, investment in Data Transmission systems, developing its cellular subsidiary, upgrading its obsolete infrastructure, and heavy investment in Internet services.

Although there were many question marks surrounding the company, TPSA held a leading position in every segment of the Polish telecom market. The company was strongly involved in Internet commerce, broadband, and wireless services, which had been named as a strategic objective in TPSA's several consecutive annual reports.

The Threat of Call-Back Service

In recent years, a new industry had been developing to take advantage of differentials in long distance telephone rates among countries. Customers throughout the world were provided with the U.S. telephone number of a call-back service. The user would telephone this number and then hang up after one or two rings and the call-back's computer would immediately call back the customer using a U.S. line. With this connection, the customer would be able to dial any number in any country using U.S. lines and being billed at U.S. rates. This process threatened to reduce the long distance business of carriers that were charging rates above the U.S. levels. By 2000, this process was being used largely by U.S. residents travelling abroad and by U.S. corporations with branches located in foreign countries. However, call-back corporations were looking eagerly to markets such as those of Poland where long distance rates were much higher than U.S. rates. Call-back corporations could hire local agents who would actively solicit the international telephone business of local residents and corporations.

Was There a Future for the Internet and E-Business in Poland?

The internet market in Poland was still in its infancy. The size of the market was estimated to be between US$50 million and US$55 million annually. Approximately 350 licensed ISPs serviced the industry. However, there were only a few companies with their own networks. TPSA and NASK (Science and Academic Computer Network) together controlled more than half of the internet market. TPSA currently operated international links to the United States and Canada and NASK operated a link to Sweden.

At this time, TPSA offered a country wide telephone number to access the Internet at the cost of a local telephone connection, which was approximately 10 cents per three minutes or five cents per three minutes after ten o'clock at night. TPSA modems and access numbers were always overloaded and the quality of an access was poor. For instance, the file transfer rate throughout the day equaled approximately 0.5 to 1.5 kbs. After ten at night, it was nearly impossible to gain an Internet access, as almost every Internet user went on line to take advantage of low night rates. Flat fee, unlimited Internet access existed, however, it cost about US$50 per month and there was a one time connection fee which equaled US$250. In general, relatively problem free Internet access existed between midnight and six o'clock in the morning.

There seemed to be an urgent need for more ISPs as well as better infrastructure. Unfortunately, TPSA was not forthcoming to offer special arrangements for ISPs using TPSA's infrastructure, and it was often being accused of monopolistic practices by blocking the possibility for other internet providers.[23]

NASK, with its Internet partner Netia SA, provided similar services. Their service was slightly cheaper and more easily accessible. However, Netia, with fewer than 300,000 phone subscribers, offered its services to a rather limited number.

Internet was also becoming available through cable TV providers such as Wizja (owned by UPC) and Aster City (owned by Elektrim). Although the quality of service was quite good and the price significantly lower when compared to that offered by TPSA, cable modems were still very expensive (US$300 which represents approximately 80 per cent of a good monthly salary in Poland). Overall, without more providers with their own bone infrastructure, Internet services in Poland would lag behind those of Western European and North American countries.

E-business was almost non-existent in Poland. Even though there were more than 300 web sites offering products and services, their average turnover amounted to only US$12,500 per year. Most users quoted lack of trust in an online payment security system as a reason for not shopping on the internet. Fraud seemed to be quite widespread in everyday life and the lack of an efficient legal system to deal with the problem would likely remain a major stumbling block to e-business evolution in Poland.

The attitude towards shopping in general was quite different from that in North America. It was strongly embedded in the Polish culture to shop in person with the possibility to touch and see the products. Catalogue sales did not exist in the past, and so there was no tradition to shop this way either.[24] Furthermore, for e-business to develop properly, an efficient payment system had to exist. Only six per cent of Poland's population had a credit card. The great majority of cardholders did not use them because of the interest charges and widespread fraud involving credit cards.

In addition, only 35 per cent of the country's population had a bank account and almost everyone preferred to pay cash for products and services.[25] Moreover, the banking system in Poland was insufficient to support online transactions. Previously the Polish government planned to sell off a majority of its banking holdings. However, the government decided not to proceed with bank privatization because it was perceived that allowing foreign capital into the Polish banking system would somehow threaten national interest and security. The logic behind the decision was not very clear, especially because the major stakeholders in the largest Polish banks were insurance companies which were being sold to foreign investors. Instead, the government decided to sell its stake in the banks to Polish investors through the Warsaw Stock Exchange in order to preserve national ownership.

Another obstacle to a wider acceptance of e-business, especially business-to-business (B2B) was, of course, poor access to the Internet. First of all, an average Pole had to spend his or her two monthly salaries to buy a non brand computer. Only about six per cent of Poles had a computer at home. Second, Internet access was extremely expensive. Only 14 per cent of Poland's population was online, and of these, 80 per cent accessed the Internet from work. The average age of an internet user in Poland was about 25 years of age.

Interest in Internet banking was limited to the young and wealthy generation. A recent survey showed that two-thirds of Poles never heard of home banking and 80 per cent of them did not want it.

B2B accounted for more than half of e-business transactions in Poland.[26] Multinational companies were the main users. Mid-size and smaller businesses simply could not afford the necessary hardware or usage fee to participate in this sector. As of 2000, about 70 per cent of Polish companies did not have any plans to participate in any form of electronic business. The entire European e-business market lagged behind that of North America. Perhaps the difference stemmed from the social attitude towards shopping, perhaps it was tied to the economic performance of the region, or perhaps the obstacle was the poor telecom infrastructure when compared to that of North America.

However, the current situation could change in the European's favor. The third generation of cellular technology, UMTS, which was well developed, could overcome the problem with an inadequate fixed infrastructure.[27] The UMTS protocol, which would be fully introduced in 2003, was capable of transferring data at speeds of up to 2 Mbps. With such a transfer rate, full multimedia content could be easily handled by service providers. Furthermore, unlike in North America where wireless companies used different standards, this protocol was likely to become widely accepted across the European continent. Also, the introduction of the Euro, which was going to eliminate the need for currency exchange, was

likely to increase e-business volume. Even by 2000 the majority of credit cards allowed charges expressed in Euro. And, upon joining the EU, which still remained questionable, any border tariffs would cease, thereby boosting Internet shopping on the continent.

In Eastern Europe, Poland included, cellular telephony seemed to be the most dynamic segment of the telecom market. The prices of wireless services were almost identical to those of fixed telecom providers. International phone calls made from the cellular phone were slightly cheaper than those made through TPSA. The service was quite reliable and the handsets were often given away in exchange for signing a one year lease. Moreover, the volume of purchased computers was growing at approximately 25 per cent a year despite the low average personal income.[28] In addition, as the inflation in the country decreased and as the new, more efficient legal system was put into place, analysts predicted wider acceptance of credit cards. Furthermore, the size of Poland's population was quite large (40 million people). It was predicted that by 2003 about 25 per cent of the population would have direct access to the Internet, which represented about 10 million potential e-customers.

There was another important aspect of the future of e-business in Poland. The country had a large number of software engineers and information technology specialists. Unfortunately, there was also a mass exodus of qualified personnel as Polish companies simply could not compete in salary terms with the Western European and North American firms. However, the government of Poland recognized the problem and was anxiously trying to address it.[29] But until those changes became a reality, people in Poland would probably remain fascinated by the Internet, but shop elsewhere.

THE WAY AHEAD?

The Polish government had decided to privatize TPSA and to introduce more competition in the telecom market, but at the same time it wished to maintain control over many aspects of this vital sector. France Telecom, as well as others, wished to purchase a controlling interest in TPSA, but the price required by the government seemed to be excessively high. The TPSA infrastructure might be obsolete in the context of rapid technological change, and the employee skills and attitudes might be an increasingly severe burden.

In a nation that was shifting dramatically from communism to free enterprise, there might be a vast array of new entrepreneurial opportunities in e-business. Future EU membership and traditional linkages with other formerly communist nations could make Poland a gateway between western and eastern Europe. However, as Poland entered the 21st century the new economy and e-business had scarcely made an appearance. Necessary improvements in the telecom infrastructure remained in the future. For all the stakeholders and potential stakeholders in Poland's telecom industry, the way ahead seemed quite confusing.

NOTES

1. See the TPSA website at: http://www.tpsa/pl/english/index.html

2. Note: TPSA financial information is presented in Appendix 1.

3. Annual Report, TPSA-1998.

4. This section was written by Rick Ironside, Clive MacKay, Connie Martin and Maureen O'Brien.

5. Note Exhibit 1—Polish Economic Statistics.

6. The New Poland, *Time Magazine*, May 3, 1999.

7. Studia nad integracja Europejska, Telekomunikacja, Warszawa, 1997.

8. See Exhibit 2—Polish Telecommunications Providers—Overview.

9. Studia nad integracja Europejska, Telekomunikacja, Warszawa, 1997.

10. The Polish Electronic and Telecommunication Industry, PIAZ 1999.

11. Studia nad integracja Europejska, Telekomunikacja, Warszawa, 1997.

12. The Polish Electronic and Telecommunication Industry, PIAZ 1999.

13. Projekt Emisyjny Akcji Netia Holdings, Warsaw 2000.

14. Projekt Emisyjny Akcji Netia Holdings, Warsaw 2000.

15. Studia nad integracja Europejska, Telekomunikacja, Warszawa, 1997.

16. Ministry of Communication, Interview, May 2000.

17. The Polish Electronic and Telecommunication Industry, PIAZ 1999.

18. Annual Report, UPC 1999.

19. Annual Report, TPSA 1998.

20. Annual Report, TPSA 1998.

21. The Polish Electronic and Telecommunication Industry, PIAZ 1999.

22. Annual Report, TPSA 1998.

23. Studia nad integracja Europejska, Telekomunikacja, Warszawa, 1997.

24. Computer World Polska, Top 2000, Polski Rynek Informatyczny i Telekomunikacyjny, May 2000.

25. Ibid.

26. The Polish Electronic and Telecommunication Industry, PIAZ 1999.

27. Computer World Polska, Top 2000, Polski Rynek Informatyczny i Telekomunikacyjny, May 2000.

28. Computer World Polska, Top 2000, Polski Rynek Informatyczny i Telekomunikacyjny, May 2000.

29. Nowa Trybuna Opolska, May 2000-06-20.

APPENDIX A: TELEKOMUNIKACJA POLSKA
CONSOLIDATED BALANCE SHEETS AS AT 31 DECEMBER 1999 AND 1998

		31 December	
Translation of the report originally issued in Polish			
	Note	1999	1998
		(in PLN millions)	
ASSETS			
Current assets			
Cash and cash equivalents	6	783	3,642
Marketable securities	26(d)	16	—
Receivables	7	2,651	2,162
Current income taxes		313	258
Inventories	8	150	205
Current assets		3,913	6,267
Fixed assets			
Property, plant and equipment	9	21,555	17,230
Intangible assets	10	950	475
Investments	11	152	217
Fixed assets		22,657	17,922
Non-current receivables		2	1
Assets		26,572	24,190
LIABILITIES AND SHAREHOLDERS' EQUITY			
Current liabilities			
Loans and other borrowings	12	721	3,329
Accrued expenses and other payables	13	3,801	2,849
Provisions	24(e)	90	—
Deferred income	14	195	224
Current liabilities		4,807	6,402
Non-current liabilities			
Loans and other borrowings	12	10,337	7,209
Accrued expenses and other payables	13	490	329
Deferred income	14	271	264
Deferred income taxes	15	288	576
Non-current liabilities		11,386	8,378
Minority interest	16	270	274
Shareholders' equity	17		
Common stock		4,200	4,200
Share premium		832	832
Revaluation reserve		2,332	2,332
Retained earnings		2,745	1,772
Shareholders' equity		10,109	9,136
Liabilities and shareholders' equity		26,572	24,190

(Continued)

(Continued)

	Note	12 months ended 31 December	
		1999	1998
		(in PLN millions)	
Revenues	18	**13,160**	**10,887**
Employee related expenses		(3,048)	(2,723)
Depreciation and amortisation		(2,357)	(1,891)
Payments to other operators		(1,383)	(1,037)
Purchased services		(1,910)	(1,673)
Goods purchased for resale		(382)	(314)
Other operating expenses, net		(1,240)	(965)
Operating expenses		**(10,320)**	**(8,603)**
Operating profit		**2,840**	**2,284**
Interest and other charges, net	19	(1,345)	(883)
Profit before income tax		**1,495**	**1,401**
Income tax	15	(572)	(654)
Minority interest	16	106	27
Net income before obligatory dividend		**1,029**	**774**
Obligatory dividend	20	—	(160)
Retained income		**1,029**	**614**
Earnings per share (in PLN):			
Net income before obligatory dividend		0.74	0.55
Obligatory dividend		—	(0.11)
Retained income per share		0.74	0.44
Weighted average common stock outstanding (millions)		1,400	1,400

Source: Annual Report, TPSA 1999

Prosoft Systems Canada (A)

Prepared by Eliza O'Neil under the supervision of Professor Terry Deutscher

Version: (A) 2004-01-05

In mid-July 2001, Rob Armstrong, the public sector account executive (AE) for the Western Region of Toronto-based Prosoft Canada, had been thinking over the firm's latest opportunity to make a software sale in the municipal market. Delta Management Solutions (DMS), one of the company's global implementation partners and its preferred partner in the municipal/cities industry, had approached Prosoft with a bid opportunity with the City of Winnipeg. Armstrong's decision was not whether or not Prosoft should participate in the City of Winnipeg bid, but instead how many bids the company should submit, with which implementation partners, and how the bid development teams should be configured.

Prosoft first entered the municipal government sector in 1999, forming a preferred partnership with DMS, who had been in the space since 1993. Prosoft recognized that gaining a foothold in municipal government could lead to other 'public' opportunities, such as education, health care and utilities. Armstrong knew that each public sector bid increased insight into the municipal market—the decision drivers, the requirements and the degree to which the standard Prosoft product would have to be configured for this customer segment. As well, his past experience with other municipalities such as

York Region and the cities of Brampton, Waterloo, Hamilton and Sudbury, told him that the Prosoft DMS product would be a good fit with Winnipeg's needs (see Exhibit 1).

John Ford, chief financial officer (CFO) for the City of Waterloo, said of his experience with the City of Waterloo's DMS/Prosoft project:

[The] Government Advantage™ approach has proven its worth at the City of Waterloo. It has enabled us to more effectively manage our resources and enhance our reporting and communications, while still being affordable for an organization of our size.[1]

Clients	Size (Employees)	Modules	Timeline	Modifications
York Region	3,000	GL, AP, PO, AR, BI	6 months	Minor
		Base HR, Payroll	10 months	Minor
City of Brampton	2,100	GL, AP, PO	5 months	Minor
		Base HR, Payroll	8 months	Customized Time Entry
The City of Waterloo	700	GL, PO, IC, AR, BI, T&L	3.5 months	Interfaces only
		PC, AM	4 months	Interfaces only
The City of Hamilton	10,000	Road map to 8 — Prosoft Version 8 upgrade strategy	4 weeks	In progress
Greater Grand Sudbury	2,000	GL, AP, PO, AR, BI, PR, Inv, Employee Portal	5 months	In progress
		Base HR, Payroll	8 months	In progress

Legend:

HR	Basic Human Resources	PO	Purchasing
GL	General Ledger	BI	Business Intelligence
AP	Accounts Payable	IC	Inventory
AR	Accounts Receivable	AM	Activity Management
		PC	Product Costing
		T&L	Time and Labor

Exhibit 1 DMS/Prosoft Historical Municipal Clients

Source: Company files.

In general, municipalities' software decisions were driven by five key characteristics: budgetary constraints—a "do more with less" philosophy; increased constituent demand for a single point of contact with the municipal government; a system that was flexible and adaptable—due to increased municipal downloading, amalgamation and reorganization; a program that incorporated performance measurement; and a software package that could replace and integrate the information of inflexible legacy systems. The combined Prosoft DMS offering addressed many of these buying criteria by bundling consulting services and software, offering fixed fees and structuring integrations that could be rapidly implemented and required minimal product modifications.

THE COMPANY

While the Canadian division was not established until 1991, the origins of the Prosoft date back to 1987, when the company's two founders, Dan Difrangia and Kevin Marks, built a human resources application. This application was unique in that it was the first to be built on a client-server platform instead of a traditional mainframe. This change in technology increased accessibility and availability of real-time information for the end-user. As the Prosoft Web site explained, the company was "putting more power into the hands of users."

After they established Prosoft as a human resources management software (HRMS) company, the two founders expanded their vision to include software applications for other functional areas such as finance, customer and supplier management. The firm's goal was to be a leader in the field of enterprise software solutions by creating applications that empowered the user, were adaptable in a changing marketplace and were supported by superior customer service. These goals were echoed at a functional level as the pair recognized that their software packages must also be easily configured to the customers' environment, rapidly implementable and scalable. To meet their customer service

goals, Prosoft developed application support, ongoing education and consulting services that facilitated the desired speed, quality and ultimate success of implementation.

As Prosoft continued to advance its technology (by moving into Internet-based applications) and aggressively pursued new market opportunities, the company founders also recognized that their key revenue driver was software licences. Given the invasive nature of enterprise software implementations, Prosoft had found that upon completion of a successful software implementation, the customer would be hesitant to change software vendors for future upgrades or additional functionality. Successful configuration of the base product to meet the customer's needs created satisfaction and, thus, ongoing revenue streams.

Like its American parent, Prosoft Canada was considered a key player in the enterprise software industry in Canada. As a subsidiary, Prosoft Canada benefited from the deep pockets, experience and resources of its much larger American parent, while maintaining the flexibility to modify products to the design requirements of the Canadian market place, and to negotiate its own alliance partnerships.

Similar to other software companies, Prosoft was a quarterly driven company. As with any firm, missing established sales and revenue targets resulted in significant market reaction. Over the past 10 years, Prosoft had seen its stock price fluctuate between lows of $1.59 per share in 1993 and highs of $59 per share in 1998. For this reason, accurately predicting the outcome of the sales cycle and establishing stable revenue flows was crucial. In general, Prosoft's sales cycles could last anywhere from three months to four years.

During its first 10 years in Canada, Prosoft had focused on penetrating large and medium-sized companies. Over this time, many Prosoft customers had expanded their use of Prosoft applications to other functional areas within their organizations. These product expansions resulted in ongoing revenue in the form of software licences, upgrades and associated implementations; however, it was critical for future growth that Prosoft Canada continue to open new markets and expand current ones. Reflecting this focus, the company's Canadian sales organization was composed of highly trained teams in which individuals specialized by industry, geography and product.

Prosoft Product Lines

In general, the company handled four major product areas, known as 'pillars': customer, supplier, human resources and financial management.

Customer Management

The customer relationship management (CRM) application facilitated better customer management through the creation of a central, real-time repository of customer account information that could be accessed by authorized areas of the organization, such as sales, finance or customer service. The market segment for this application consisted of organizations that were highly dependent on customer service and on information sharing within the sales function and within the rest of the company. For example, a customer service representative (CSR) working in a call centre could update a customer on the status of their account, i.e., if the customer had purchased a number of items, the CSR could advise the customer on the number of items that had been shipped, delays and reason for the delays, the financial balance of their account. Similarly, a sales representative in the field could review their customers' account histories, the rate at which they were using the product, and estimate their future needs. Each piece of information was dependent on external departments, e.g., accounting, operations, distribution, etc., for inputting transaction information.

Supplier Management

The supplier management software (supply chain management—SCM) application allowed sharing of a common view of the customer among different players in the supply chain. It improved efficiency and accuracy, thereby reducing transaction costs for each member of the supply chain.

The market segment for this application consisted of industries that were highly dependent on the performance of those before or after them in the supply chain, e.g., computer and component manufacturers or courier companies.

Human Resources Management

The human resource management software (HRMS) application created a central repository of real-time employee information that was accessible to many different functional areas within the organization, allowing for more holistic and efficient decision-making. The market segment for this application consisted of large organizations with complex human resources, e.g., call centres and banks.

Financial Management

The financial management software application (FMS), similar to the applications above, created a central repository of real-time customer and supplier account information. Employees in numerous departments could provide their customers with real-time account status information, and managers could base their analysis and decision-making on the most recent information. The market segment for this application was broad, as most companies needed to integrate financial information; however, this ability to review customer accounts was especially important for organizations with large customer service and sales organizations.

Beyond application development, Prosoft also provided consulting and educational services that complemented their product offering. With over 3,000 consultants worldwide, Prosoft consulting services provided application needs assessment, project planning and implementation. Prosoft sold its consulting services under the value proposition that customers derived greater benefit when their software purchases were paired with consulting services because this enabled them to achieve rapid deployment and accelerated knowledge transfer. Customers could also take advantage of customer education services in the form of Prosoft University and hosting services.

As a market leader, Prosoft continued to advance technology and introduce products that met the customers' growing need for information at their fingertips, anywhere, any time. In the company's business model, once the substantial research and development investment for new products was covered, sales and marketing costs were the major expenses related to software. It was not uncommon for hundreds of thousands of dollars to be spent on the development of a client proposal.

THE INDUSTRY

Through the late 1990s, the enterprise application industry experienced unprecedented growth as companies embraced the concept of efficient data. Despite this growth, it was a commonly held view that while most companies within the industry focused on single applications (for example, CBL Systems with CRM), few had achieved a 360-degree view of the customer or fully integrated solutions. It was estimated that even the most mature markets were less than 50 per cent penetrated. Because of the lengthy and costly development cycle, the primary challenge for the industry players was to develop software and customers in the vertical segments that were forecasted to represent substantial future opportunities. As well, ongoing software enhancements and new product developments were critical to the maintenance of market position and expansion of established verticals.

The industry players were divided into three forms: 1) software development, 2) integration, and 3) hardware or platform. The division of these roles blurred as the industry matured. The resulting hybrid organizations consisted of software vendors, such as Prosoft, with their own consulting/implementation teams; consulting companies with proprietary software; or partnerships between a software provider and a consultancy. This is not to say that a software provider with its own consulting services, such as Prosoft, would not partner with an outside consultancy. These global, national or industry-level partnerships were formed on the basis of shared interests, for example, revenue targets, industry capabilities, individual corporate relationships (between the client and the consultancy or software vendor, or between the vendor and the consultancy), or initial lead development. In the case of Prosoft Canada, the company's consulting services were involved in 30 per cent to 40 per cent of projects as either the prime or subcontracted integrator. In general, consulting services were lucrative, generating two to three times the revenue of the software and delivering gross margins that averaged 45 per cent (see Exhibit 2).

THE BID PROCESS

New business leads could be developed in a number of ways:

- A regional sales person identified a client need;
- An RFP (request for proposal) or RFQ (request for quotation) was sent out by companies intending to purchase software solutions;
- A consulting firm, hired by a customer to assess its software requirements, recommended a provider (usually through the above RFP process);
- A number of software providers volunteered to assess the software needs of an individual organization and develop an overarching technology strategy and proposal; or
- In the case of government or public service, tenders, RFPS and RFQS were posted to a government contracts site, usually in conjunction with a preliminary scope of work statement and bid open/close dates.

Each bid, whether an RFP or a lead developed by the regional sales force, represented a significant investment. According to Mark Derraugh, regional director for the western region of Prosoft Canada, the bid process typically took from three to five months from start to finish and cost hundreds of thousands of dollars. In the public sector, the regulated requirements for the bid process meant that the bid cycle was substantially longer. Over time, Prosoft had refined its bid process and had subsequently developed specific process steps and associated functions (see Exhibit 3).

	1998	1999	2000	2001
Revenues				
Licence fees	664,277	339,676	496,115	645,421
Services	810,491	1,061,838	1,118,079	1,325,119
Development and other services		27,632	122,279	102,713
	1,474,768	1,429,146	1,736,473	2,073,253
Costs and Expenses				
Cost of licence fees	44,418	42,578	38,901	61,323
Cost of services	465,670	564,404	606,334	698,329
Cost of development services		25,107	111,053	93,124
Sales and marketing	407,023	391,572	447,952	513,928
Product development	237,970	297,212	320,512	298,998
General and Administrative	73,828	97,387	108,103	155,567
	1,228,909	1,418,260	1,632,855	1,821,269
Recurring operating income	245,859	10,886	103,618	251,984
Other income, net	20,778	21,335	36,375	37,603
Provision for income taxes	(102,495)	(11,184)	(48,298)	(98,021)
Net Income	164,142	21,037	91,695	191,566
Basic earnings per share	0.66	0.08	0.33	0.64
Diluted earnings per share	0.58	0.08	0.30	0.59
Shares used in basic calculations	249,807	263,914	279,672	297,999
Shares used in diluted calculations	281,059	272,128	302,916	323,625

Exhibit 2   Consolidated Pro Forma Income Statements (Unaudited) for years ending December 31 (in US$000)

Source: Company files.

First, each individual opportunity was assessed by the account executive and the regional director for fit with the Prosoft product, immediate investment requirements, short-term and long-term revenues and strategic fit. At this time, the potential integration partner or partners were identified and approached.

Second, if the opportunity assessment was positive, Prosoft approached the client with an preliminary overview of the benefit that a Prosoft system could provide to the client organization. Upon approval by the client, a small proposal team was developed to research or 'discover' the current capabilities, systems, and infrastructure of the potential client. This step was carried out with the co-operation of the client, so bidding vendors had direct access to accurate client information. The discovery phase also allowed the vendors to develop important relationships with the clients. Due to the invasiveness of the discovery process, the client usually limited the number of vendors to three or four teams that were allowed to participate in on-site research.[2]

Third, the demonstration phase allowed vendors to show the customer how their product could meet the software and system needs (identified during the discovery phase) better than competing products. Configuration requirements were outlined in terms of a potential project plan and associated timeline, resource requirements, scope and cost. For Prosoft, project profitability was closely linked to its ability to minimize software modification (configuration) and speed and accuracy of implementation. For these reasons, it

Sales Process

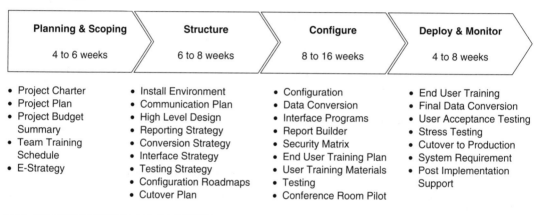

Opportunity Assessment Timeline varies depending on initiative owner, i.e., Prosoft or customer RFP	Discovery 2 to10 weeks	Proposal & Demonstration 4 to 8 weeks	Vendor Selection 2 to 4 weeks
• Evaluation of bid opportunity with regard to: • Fit with software • Strategic importance of customer • Cost/Benefit	• Assessment of client requirements via exploration of current environment – including existing systems, resources, and future needs	• Vendor demonstrations of software capabilities and functionality • Presentation of proposed project timelines, resource requirements, and cost	• Selection of software vendor and implementation partner

Methodology

Planning & Scoping 4 to 6 weeks	Structure 6 to 8 weeks	Configure 8 to 16 weeks	Deploy & Monitor 4 to 8 weeks
• Project Charter • Project Plan • Project Budget Summary • Team Training Schedule • E-Strategy	• Install Environment • Communication Plan • High Level Design • Reporting Strategy • Conversion Strategy • Interface Strategy • Testing Strategy • Configuration Roadmaps • Cutover Plan	• Configuration • Data Conversion • Interface Programs • Report Builder • Security Matrix • End User Training Plan • User Training Materials • Testing • Conference Room Pilot	• End User Training • Final Data Conversion • User Acceptance Testing • Stress Testing • Cutover to Production • System Requirement • Post Implementation Support

Exhibit 3   Government Advantage™ Sales Process and Methodology

Source: Company files.

was critical that the basic product should already meet the majority of a client's requirements. While the capabilities and functionality of the software was the primary driver of vendor decisions, the selection of an implementation partner was also significant. The implementation partner would be responsible for overarching project management, ensuring that the current project fit with the long-term information technology (IT) goals of the company, and facilitating the change management required during software integration.

Fourth, after the demonstration of the software product, the customer chose a vendor/integration partner combination and a version of the presented software solutions from the pool of competing vendors.

Once a vendor/integration partner pair was selected, the actual project planning and scoping began. While the discovery phase of the project generated estimates of required tasks, resources, budget and timelines, all of this needed to be confirmed while project teams were formed and initiated to the project. On average, this phase took four to six weeks.

The actual structure of the project took place after the project teams were in place. The teams developed a more detailed, high-level plan of how the software would be installed, for example, the conversion strategy for the movement of data from legacy to current systems, the testing strategy and the cutover plan. On average, this phase lasted six to eight weeks.

The configuration phase was usually the longest phase of the project, depending on the required modifications and the state of the client environment. On average, this phase lasted eight to 16 weeks. During this phase, the project team configured the out-of-the-box product, converted the client data from the legacy systems into the software solution, developed and conducted training, and tested the finalized system.

In the final phase of the project, lasting on average four to eight weeks, the end-users were trained on the product, final data conversion and stress and acceptance testing were completed, the system went live and was cut over to production, and the project team moved into a role of postimplementation support.

See Exhibit 3 for a more detailed overview of the DMS Prosoft Government Advantage™ sales and implementation processes. Since the DMS Prosoft partnership's formation in 1999, it had completed several major municipal software implementations (see Exhibit 1). While Prosoft was the segment leader for software provision, DMS was the lead integrator, closely followed by Praxus Consulting Services (Praxus). The increasing number of software producers with integration capabilities posed a growing and significant threat in the rapidly growing market. Other segment leaders included AC Consulting (integration only), International Business Solutions (IBS) (primarily integration—software to a lesser extent), Vision Systems (software and integration), and Enterprise Application Software (EAS) (software and integration).

The complexity of the sales/partnering process ultimately resulted in an equally complex sales incentive structure. Each sales representative's compensation plan was weighted towards the sale of software licences or towards the sale of services; however, in the majority of sales situations, both software and services were being sold. In Armstrong's case, his incentives favored the sale of software licences. Service

sales were also included as part of his overall compensation system, at a rate of two per cent. The commission was large enough to encourage promoting Prosoft's consulting services when it made sense to do so, but did not penalize the sales person unduly when it did not.

THE MUNICIPAL GOVERNMENT MARKET

In 2001, the enterprise software market for the public sector was a relatively unexploited market for Prosoft. Statistics Canada suggested that of the 914 municipalities and 13 provincial and territorial governments in Canada, the majority had annual IT budgets and departments dedicated to the advancement of the underlying IT infrastructure of the communities.

The Decision Process

The decision process for the public sector was highly driven by the desire to: a) achieve value for constituents, and b) create a transparent selection process that would mitigate the risk of being accused of impropriety.

Most government contracts (tenders, RFPs and RFQs) were posted to the sponsoring municipality's or provincial government's Web site. These public tenders contained basic information about the scope of the work required and the bid process. Interested vendors had to obtain the full scope of work and RFP/RFQ information in person from the city hall and they usually paid a fee for the privilege to bid. Bids were evaluated by appointed committees within the government as to their ability to meet functional requirements and price. The decision process for a municipal bid typically took longer than for that of a comparable industry bid, due to the number of stakeholders and the political implications for the decision-makers.

Once the working committee made a decision, it would recommend a vendor to the city council, at which time the merits of the decision were open for debate by the entire council. The vendor was ultimately selected by a vote by city council. It was important for vendors not to

	Prosoft Systems	Vision Systems	EAS	CBL Systems
Pure Internet	✓	⊘	⊘	✓
End-to-end Bus. Process	✓	✓	✓	⊘
Integrated Analytics	✓	⊘	⊘	⊘
E-commerce	✓	✓	✓	✓
Web Look & Feel	✓	⊘	⊘	⊘
Global	✓	✓	✓	✓
Scalable & Reliable	✓	✓	✓	✓
Easy to Use	✓	⊘	⊘	⊘
Best in Class Functionality	✓	⊘	⊘	✓
Integration	✓	✓	✓	✓
Open	✓	⊘	⊘	⊘

Exhibit 4   Competitive Comparison

Source: Company files.

underestimate the importance of the political nature of this decision process. The desire to publicly demonstrate progress and results, and the public appetite for a particular topic could considerably help or hinder the funding and progress of any public sector project.

According to analyst reports, the average initial software sale value to a city was $654,000, but this number could easily be tripled once licence revenue and integration service fees were added in.[3]

Competition

The Canadian enterprise software industry was dominated by international firms with financial, technical and marketing resources greater than or equal to Prosoft. In Canada, Prosoft's primary competitors were CBL Systems (CRM only), Vision Systems and EAS. Each of the competitors had product offerings in specific areas, i.e., CRM, ERP or SCM, collaborated with alliance partners, supported different technology platforms and had varying levels of competence in each area of software (see Exhibit 4).

While 'preferred' relationships existed between integrators and software providers, the reality was that customer preference, existing business and personal relationships, and relative position within an industry determined the bid strategies of the players.

Ultimately, Prosoft felt that its major advantage in an increasingly maturing industry was its product and its continuous innovation. In addition, Prosoft was actively developing its alliance strategy with the goal of creating more meaningful (potentially contractual) relationships. Although Prosoft Canada had not yet developed formal analysis of the strengths and weaknesses of potential partners, there were discussions about doing so in an effort to develop a more formalized alliance/bid process.

THE SITUATION: THE CITY OF WINNIPEG BID

In the case of the City of Winnipeg, contract bids were posted to the city's Web site. The city

Chief Information Officer and

- Develop of recommend City policy and approve administrative directives
- Act as the senior specialist and decision-maker on IT issues
- Develop IT Strategic Plan and ensure progress towards goals
- Ensure efficient and effective IT services
- Continuously enhance performance of IT

IT Executive Committee

- Review and advise CIO on IT Strategic Plan
- Provide advice to the CIO in terms of opportunities, risks, policies, directives, standards and overal IT effectiveness
- Ensure high level of coordination of IT initiatives

IT Committee

IT Working Groups

- IT Requirements Review
- Technology Standards
- Vendor Reviews
- Proposed Solutions

- Identify areas where collective efforts are in the Council's best interest
- Coordinate, collaborate and leverage efforts to ensure efficient use of IT resources
- Identify emerging trends, technology and industry standards and recommend City policies, directives and standards
- Ensure timely progress toward strategic goals and continuously enhance the performance of IT
- Make recommendations to the CIO and Executive IT committee

Exhibit 5   City of Winnipeg: Governance Process

Source: City of Winnipeg: *IT Strategic Plan*

planned to follow a formal process of: (1) RFP; (2) proposal submissions; (3) reviews and subsequent recommendations by IT working groups, IT committees, the chief information officer and the IT executive committee; and (4) deciding by vote of the entire council. Exhibit 5 portrays the governance process and the associated roles and responsibilities within it.

The City of Winnipeg's overarching IT strategy, complete with vision, principles (with supporting pillars) and specific goals, was defined in its 'IT Strategic Plan.' This report specified the requirements, discussed the five principles and four key goals of the IT plan, and identified the decision criteria against which bids would be examined. The vision of "creating innovative

information technology solutions in support of civic services" gave rise to four specific goals, namely:

1. To enhance citizen and employee access to information and services;

2. To integrate and streamline resource management systems;

3. To improve the capture of information to create knowledge; and

4. To enhance work management capabilities.

Each of these objectives, and the principles associated with them, was discussed at length (summarized in Exhibit 6) in the IT plan.

The City of Winnipeg's municipal corporate information technology budget adopted in 2002 was $18,073,000, to be spent over six years.[4] Of this budget, 81 per cent or $14,680,175 could potentially be tied to functionality incorporated in the DMS/Prosoft system. The breakout was as follows: enterprise resource planning System (ERP)—$2,736,000; city clerks (office automation and electronic records management)—$1,260,000; communications network infrastructure—$1,007,000, network computing initiatives—$1,260,000; e-government—$8,455,000.[5]

In the discovery phase of the bid process, Prosoft learned that IBS would be bidding with J Edison as their software partner. J Edison was a mid-market player that the Prosoft team had previously encountered, but the depth of Prosoft's competitive knowledge of J Edison was limited to four or five manufacturing sector bids.

As Prosoft proceeded with the discovery phase of the project, the company also learned that the municipality had expressed a strong interest in using Praxus Consulting Services (Praxus), the consulting arm of the leading global accounting firm, as the software integrator. Praxus had yet to select a software partner, but was an alliance partner with whom Prosoft had worked successfully on a many integration projects. This presented an interesting challenge and opportunity for Prosoft. Should it pursue an alliance with Praxus? It was not without precedent, especially in public sector bids, for Prosoft to work on additional bids with different integrators. However, it was a costly approach, as Prosoft had to resource various independent bid teams, with firewalls between them in order to protect the confidentiality of its competing partners. Also, selection of an alternative integration partner could potentially have an impact on Prosoft's 'preferred vendor' relationship with DMS in this industry. If the DMS/Prosoft shared revenue targets were missed because of alternative vendor selection, it could cause tension in the relationship between the two companies.

As the proposal and demonstration phases came to completion, IBS and J Edison were eliminated and the City of Winnipeg distinctly expressed a preference for the Prosoft system.

Reacting to the information, a member of IBS Canada senior sales management team contacted Andy Aicklen, general manager of Prosoft Canada, in order to explore the possibility of an IBS/Prosoft alliance on this deal.

Because the DMS team was working jointly with Prosoft on the bid, they also were aware of the client preferences and the fact that other integration partners were approaching Prosoft. As the tension escalated, Aicklen received phone calls from DMS seeking assurance that if additional bids were developed, Aicklen would ensure 'fair treatment' of the DMS bid and ensure appropriate firewalls were in place so competitive information regarding DMS's approach to the bid would not be compromised. Armstrong assured Aicklen that he would be ready on July 22 to outline his strategy and partnering recommendations for the purposes of this transaction.

Alternative Strategies

Armstrong knew that while Prosoft's decision about partnering would be made as a team, Aicklen would be looking to him for his recommendation and analysis. At this point, he felt that he had enough information to make a decision on what to do with the City of Winnipeg bid. As Armstrong saw it, he had four main choices (and multiple options based on various combinations of the choices outlined below):

1. Go with DMS exclusively

Continue to develop the City of Winnipeg bid with DMS, forgoing the potential partnerships with Praxus and IBS. The objective would be to leverage the strength of the DMS/Prosoft's market leading 'Government Advantage™' offering and also to strengthen the partnership with DMS in the public sector. DMS had also suggested that it may have an additional software partner that could provide a 'plug and play' application, compatible with Prosoft's application, which would ensure that the DMS/Prosoft bid exceeded the bid technical specifications. As Armstrong pondered this, a colleague stuck his head into the office to give him an update on the City of Kingston bid—DMS had won over Praxus.

Serve Citizens

Goal

- Enhance citizen and employee access to information and services

Measurement

- Increased and integrated channels of access to information services
  - Provide citizens and government services with multiple integrated access channels to service (e.g., Internet, front counter, call centres)
  - Increase applications and information on Internet and intranet, including a common look and feel

Support Business Requirements

Goal

- Improve the capture of information to create knowledge

Measurement

- Increased number of shared applications and databases to combine and analyse information
  - Find and capitalize on opportunities by co-ordinating plans and initiatives across the organization
  - Develop a process in advance of the capital budget for issues of shared significance

Integrate at Every Opportunity

Goal

- Integrate and streamline resource and management systems

Measurement

- Reduction in the number of duplicate systems and databases
  - Provide systems to help manage anticipated change in the city's workforce
  - Reduce the number of diverse computer applications and duplicate functionality and require a large number of interfaces
  - Provide employee and managerial self-service

Invest Strategically

Goal

- Enhance work management capabilities

Measurement

- Increase the number of city services using shared work management tools/systems
  - Support investment decisions with sound business cases
  - Support and participate in the optimization of collective interests and being prepared to sub-optimize solutions in some areas, as appropriate
  - Facilitate, promote and encourage reuse

Work Together

- Ensure that priority-setting is well understood
- Commit to cross-departmental partnerships
- Supporting informal service arrangements and clusters as well as formal service agreements
- Assign lead departments on solutions where rapid delivery is required and fully shared cross-developmental planning is not expedient

---

Exhibit 6   City of Winnipeg: Goals, Measurement and Specific Characteristics Associated With
Information Technology Principles and Pillars

Source: City of Winnipeg, *IT Strategic Plan*

2. Develop a bid with Praxus Consulting Services

Develop a primary (that is, stopping bid development with DMS) or secondary proposal (also continue with DMS) with Praxus, thereby virtually ensuring the win of the bid with the City of Winnipeg. The major risk of not partnering with the remaining potential integration partners was that either Praxus or IBS might potentially develop a strong bid with a competitor. On the other hand, each subsequent bid not only added additional costs, but required the creation of firewalls between the working teams at Prosoft and the expenditure of management time in reassuring the alliance partners that bid information was not being shared among Prosoft resources on the different teams. However, each additional bid also increased the probability of Prosoft being selected as the software vendor.

3. Develop a bid with IBS

Develop a primary or secondary proposal with IBS. The objective would be to build this initial partnership with IBS into future alliances, leveraging brand recognition of the IBS name.

4. Develop an independent bid that uses Prosoft Consulting as the integrator

The objective would be to maximize Prosoft's revenue on this bid and establish Prosoft Consulting as a viable integrator in the municipal market. However, Armstrong knew that he would face concern that failure to leverage the already established relationships with potential alliance partners would allow them to partner with alternative vendors and shrink the market for Prosoft.

Armstrong's analysis would take a lifetime view of the customer and the value of potential alliance partnerships. He also noted that the revenue generated by each alternative was similar; however, it varied with the incremental cost of each additional bid and had different strategic implications with each integration partner. In starting to think about the required analysis he typed some high level categories and figures into a spreadsheet (see Exhibit 7).

Using the assumptions from Exhibit 7, Armstrong estimated the Net Present Value of a customer, assuming a discount rate of 12 per cent (see Exhibit 8).

City of Winnipeg Sale Value[1]		1,687,376
Cost[2]		73,102
	Total	1,614,274
Average License Revenue[2]		506,655
Cost[2]		48,139
	Total[3]	458,516
Services Value[2]		1,040,218
Cost[2]		548,188
	Total	492,030
Maintenance Fee[4]		337,475

Exhibit 7   Lifetime Value of a Customer: Variables and Assumptions for NPV (US$)

Source: Company files and industry reports

1. Total value of bid, $14,680,175 is converted in USD (at 1.45) and spread over 6 years
2. Calculation based on total license (services) revenue (cost) x % of total customers that are new # number of new customers
3. License revenue included in sale revenue
4. 20% of software sale (based on industry average)

Years	1	2	3	4	5	6	7	8	9	10
Initial Sale[2]	1,614,274	1,614,274	1,614,274	1,614,274	1,614,274	1,614,274				
Upgrade[1]					532,710				807,137	
Service[1]					162,370				162,370	
Maintenance	337,475	337,475	337,475	337,475	337,475	337,475	337,475	337,475	337,475	337,475
Total	1,951,749	1,951,749	1,951,749	1,951,749	2,646,829	1,951,749	337,475	337,475	1,306,982	337,475
NPV	$9,287,770									

Exhibit 8   Lifetime Value Of A Customer—NPV[1]

1. Assume major upgrades, worth 1/3, (1/2) occur once every 3-4 years, and require substantial services also at 1/3 initial value
2. License contribution included in initial sale revenue

155

Armstrong recognized that many of the longer term figures he was estimating were approximate at best, but he also knew that if he included only the tangible, short-term values, he would be making a decision without complete information.

Armstrong also knew that he would also have to be creative about the structure of the proposal teams; resources were limited, and he wanted to minimize additional cost on similar work. He wondered whether or not the partners would be willing to negotiate about firewall requirements as from a software perspective, the solutions for the client were essentially the same. His rough calculations of the cost of the initial bid are outlined in Exhibit 9.

With the knowledge that any of the alternatives could be pursued, Armstrong felt it was time to make a decision. He opened his computer to draft his presentation to Aicklen, with the required costs/benefit analysis of the potential partnerships for the City of Winnipeg bid and discussion of the specific strategy and structure of the bid team(s).

NOTES

1. Source: Government Advantage: A Different Approach For Municipalities, DMS, Prosoft 2001.

2. In a typical municipal bid, there would be three or four vendors who would reach the discovery phase. Many of these prospective bidders would be alliances between software providers and consulting firms who would do the integration.

3. Wedbush Morgan Securities, Research Note—Prosoft, July 19, 2002.

4. City of Winnipeg Capital Projects Summary: 2002-2006 Five Year Capital Forecast, February 27, 2001.

5. Note: Only the portion of project budgets that are covered by the project bid are stated.

Resources	Est. Annual Salary	Time (months)	Time Allocation	Cost
Sales Representative	150,000	3.5	0.25	10,938
Product Consultant	100,000	3.5	0.08	2,333
Services (integration consultant)	150,000	3.5	0.08	3,500
RFP Coordinator	45,000	3.5	0.02	263
Management - @ 70% time	175,000	3.5	0.06	3,063
Travel and Administrative[2]	4,019			4,019
		Total Cost		24,115

Exhibit 9   Initial Bid Costs[1]

Source: Interview with Joseph Lo, Sept. 27, 2002

1. Figures do not include the opportunity cost of having resources involved in bid development instead of selling additional work or completing other projects
2. Travel and Administrative assumed to be 20% of total cost

CAMERON AUTO PARTS (A)—REVISED

Revised by Professor Paul Beamish
(originally prepared by Professor Harold Crookell)

Copyright © 2006, Ivey Management Services   Version: (A) 2006-01-10

Alex Cameron's first years in business were unusually harsh and turbulent. He graduated from a leading Michigan business school in 2001 when the American economy was just falling into a recession caused by the combination of the bursting of the telecom and dot.com bubble and the terrorist attacks of September 11. It was not that Alex had difficulty finding a job, however; it was that he took over the reins of the family business. His father timed his retirement to coincide with Alex's graduation and left him with the unenviable task of cutting back the workforce to match the severe sales declines the company was experiencing.

HISTORY

Cameron Auto Parts was founded in 1965 by Alex's father to seize opportunities created by the signing of the Auto Pact between Canada and the United States. The Auto Pact permitted the Big Three automotive manufacturers to ship cars, trucks and original equipment (OEM) parts between Canada and the United States tariff free, as long as they maintained auto assembly facilities on both sides of the border. The Pact had been very successful with the result that a lot of auto parts firms sprang up in Canada to supply the Big Three. Cameron Auto Parts prospered in this environment until, by 1999, sales had reached $60 million with profits of $1.75 million. The product focus was largely on small engine parts and auto accessories such as oil and air filters, fan belts and wiper blades, all sold as original equipment under the Auto Pact.

When Alex took over in 2001, the company's financial position was precarious. Sales in 2000 dropped to $48 million and for the first six months of 2001 to $18 million. Not only were car sales declining in North America, but the Japanese were taking an increasing share of the market. As a result, the major North American auto producers were frantically trying to advance their technology and to lower their prices at the same time. It was not a good year to be one of their suppliers. In 2000, Cameron Auto Parts lost $2.5 million, and had lost the same amount again in the first six months of 2001. Pressure for modernization and cost reduction had required close to $4 million in new investment in equipment and computer-assisted design and manufacturing systems. As a result, the company had taken up over $10 million of its $12 million line of bank credit at an interest rate which stood at 7.0 per cent in 2001.

Alex's first six months in the business were spent in what he later referred to as "operation survival." There was not much he could do about working capital management as both inventory and receivables were kept relatively low via contract arrangements with the Big Three. Marketing costs were negligible. Where costs had to be cut were in production and, specifically, in people, many of whom had been with the company for over 15 years and were personal friends of Alex's father. Nevertheless, by the end of 2001, the workforce had been cut from 720 to 470, the losses had been stemmed and the company saved from almost certain bankruptcy. Having to be the hatchet man, however, left an indelible impression on Alex. As things began to pick up during 2002 and 2003, he added as few permanent workers as possible, relying instead on overtime, part-timers or sub-contracting.

RECOVERY AND DIVERSIFICATION

For Cameron Auto Parts, the year 2001 ended with sales of $38 million and losses of $3.5 million (see Exhibit 1). Sales began to pick up in 2002, reaching $45 million by year-end with a small profit. By mid-2003, it was clear that the recovery was well underway. Alex, however, while welcoming the turnaround, was suspicious of the basis for it. Cameron's own sales hit $27 million in the first six months of 2003 and company profits were over $2 million. The Canadian dollar had dropped as low as 77 cents in terms of U.S. currency and Cameron was faced with more aggressive competition from Canadian parts manufacturers. The short-term future for Cameron, however, seemed distinctly positive, but the popularity of Japanese cars left Alex feeling vulnerable to continued total dependence on the volatile automotive industry. Diversification was on his mind as early as 2001. He had an ambition to take the company public by 2007 and diversification was an important part of that ambition.

Unfortunately, working as an OEM parts supplier to the automotive industry did little to prepare Cameron to become more innovative. The auto industry tended to standardize its parts requirements to the point that Cameron's products were made to precise industry specifications and consequently, did not find a ready market outside the industry. Without a major product innovation it appeared that Cameron's dependence on the Big Three was likely to continue. Furthermore, the company had developed no "in-house" design and engineering strength from which to launch an attempt at new product development. Because product specifications had always come down in detail from the Big Three, Cameron had never needed to design and develop its own products and had never hired any design engineers.

In the midst of "operation survival" in 2001, Alex boldly decided to do something about diversification. He personally brought in a team of four design engineers and instructed them to concentrate on developing products related to the existing

	2001	2002	2003
Net Sales	$38,150	$45,200	$67,875
Cost of goods sold:			
Direct materials	6,750	8,050	12,400
Direct labor	12,900	10,550	12,875
Overheads (including depreciation)	16,450	19,650	27,600
Total	36,100	38,250	52,875
Gross Profit	2,050	6,950	15,000
Expenses:			
Selling and administration (includes design team)	3,150	3,800	6,200
Other (includes interest)	2,400	2,900	3,000
Total	5,500	6,700	9,200
Net Profit before Tax	(3,450)	250	5,800
Income Tax	500	—	200
Net Profit after Tax	$(2,950)	$250	$5,600

Exhibit 1   Income Statements, For Years Ended December 31, 2001, 2002, 2003 ($000s)

Note: Alex expected total sales to reach $85 million in 2004 with profits before tax of $10 million. Flexible couplings were expected to contribute sales of $30 million and profits of $5 million on assets of $12 million.

line but with a wider "non-automotive" market appeal. Their first year together showed little positive progress, and the question of whether to fund the team for another year (estimated budget $425,000) came to the management group:

Alex: Maybe we just expected too much in the first year. They did come up with the flexible coupling idea, but you didn't seem to encourage them, Andy (production manager).

Andy McIntyre: That's right! They had no idea at all how to produce such a thing in our facilities. Just a lot of ideas about how it could be used. When I told them a Canadian outfit was already producing them, the team sort of lost interest.

John Ellis (Finance): We might as well face the fact that we made a mistake, and cut it off before we sink any more money into it. This is hardly the time for unnecessary risks.

Alex: Why don't we shorten the whole process by getting a production licence from the Canadian firm? We could start out that way and then build up our own technology over time.

Andy: The team looked into that, but it turned out the Canadians already have a subsidiary operating in United States—not too well from what I can gather—and they are not anxious to licence anyone to compete with it.

Alex: Is the product patented?

Andy: Yes, but apparently it doesn't have long to run.

At this point a set of ideas began to form in Alex's mind, and in a matter of months he had lured away a key engineer from the Canadian firm with an $110,000 salary offer and put him in charge of the product development team. By mid-2003, the company had developed its own line of flexible couplings with an advanced design and an efficient production process using the latest in production equipment. Looking back, in retrospect, Alex commented:

We were very fortunate in the speed with which we got things done. Even then the project as a whole had cost us close to $1 million in salaries and related costs.

MARKETING THE NEW PRODUCT

Alex continued:

We then faced a very difficult set of problems, because of uncertainties in the market place. We knew there was a good market for the flexible type of coupling because of its wide application across so many different industries. But, we didn't know how big the market was nor how much of it we could secure. This meant we weren't sure what volume to tool up for, what kind or size of equipment to purchase, or how to go about the marketing job. We were tempted to start small and grow as our share of market grew, but this could be costly too and could allow too much time for competitive response. Our Canadian engineer was very helpful here. He had a lot of confidence in our product and had seen it marketed in both Canada and the United States. At his suggestion we tooled up for a sales estimate of $30 million—which was pretty daring. In addition, we hired eight field sales representatives to back up the nation-wide distributor and soon afterwards hired several Canadian-based sales representatives to cover major markets. We found that our key Canadian competitor was pricing rather high and had not cultivated very friendly customer relations. We were surprised how quickly we were able to secure significant penetration into the Canadian market. It just wasn't being well-serviced.

During 2003, the company actually spent a total of $2.5 million on equipment for flexible coupling production. In addition, a fixed commitment of $1.5 million a year in marketing expenditures on flexible couplings arose from the hiring of sales representatives. A small amount of trade advertising was included in this sum. The total commitment represented a significant part of the company's resources and threatened serious damage to the company's financial position if the sales failed to materialize.

Sales by Market Sector ($ millions)				
	OEM Parts Sales	**Flexible Couplings Sales**	**Total Sales**	**After Tax Profits**
1999	60	Nil	60	1.75
2000	48	Nil	48	(2.50)
2001	38	Nil	38	(3.50)
2002	45	Nil	45	0.25
2003	58	10 (six months)	68	5.80

Figure 1   Sales by Market Sector ($000s)

"It was quite a gamble at the time," Alex added. "By the end of 2003, it was clear that the gamble was going to pay off." (See Figure 1.)

Cameron's approach to competition in flexible couplings was to stress product quality, service and speed of delivery, but not price. Certain sizes of couplings were priced slightly below the competition but others were not. In the words of one Cameron sales representative:

Our job is really a technical function. Certainly, we help predispose the customer to buy and we'll even take orders, but we put them through our distributors. Flexible couplings can be used in almost all areas of secondary industry, by both large and small firms. This is why we need a large distributor with wide reach in the market. What we do is give our product the kind of emphasis a distributor can't give. We develop relationships with key buyers in most major industries, and we work with them to keep abreast of new potential uses for our product, or of changes in size requirements or other performance characteristics. Then we feed this kind of information back to our design group. We meet with the design group quite often to find out what new types of couplings are being developed and what the intended uses are, etc. Sometimes they help us solve a customer's problem. Of course, these 'solutions' are usually built around the use of one of our products.

FINANCING PLANT CAPACITY

When Alex first set his diversification plans in motion in 2001, the company's plant in suburban Detroit was operating at 50 per cent capacity. However, by early 2004, sales of auto parts had recovered almost to 1999 levels and the flexible coupling line was squeezed for space. Andy McIntyre put the problem this way:

I don't see how we can get sales of more than $85 million out of this plant without going to a permanent two-shift system, which Alex doesn't want to do. With two full shifts we could probably reach sales of $125 million. The problem is that both our product lines are growing very quickly. Auto parts could easily hit $80 million on their own this year, and flexible couplings! Well, who would have thought we'd sell $10 million in the first six months? Our salespeople are looking for $35 million to $40 million during 2004. It's wild! We just have to have more capacity.

There are two problems pressing us to consider putting flexible couplings under a different roof. The first is internal: we are making more and more types and sizes, and sales are growing to such a point that we may be able to produce more efficiently in a separate facility. The second is external: The Big Three like to tour our plant regularly and tell us how to make auto parts cheaper. Having these flexible couplings all over the place seems to upset them, because they have trouble determining how much of our costs belong to Auto Parts. If it were left to me I'd just let them be upset, but Alex feels differently. He's afraid of losing orders. Sometimes I wonder if he's right. Maybe we should lose a few orders to the Big Three and fill up the plant with our own product instead of expanding.

Flexible couplings were produced on a batch basis and there were considerable savings involved as batches got larger. Thus as sales grew, and inventory requirements made large batches possible, unit production costs decreased, sometimes substantially. Mr. McIntyre estimated that unit production costs would decline by some 20 per cent as annual sales climbed from $20 million to $100 million, and by a further 10 per cent at $250 million. Scale economies beyond sales of $250 million were not expected to be significant.

John Ellis, the company's financial manager, expressed his own reservations about new plant expansion from a cash flow perspective:

> We really don't have the balance sheet (Exhibit 2) ready for major plant expansion yet. I think we should grow more slowly and safely for two more years and pay off our debts. If we could hold sales at $75 million for 2004 and $85 million for 2005, we would be able to put ourselves in a much stronger financial position. The problem is that people only look at the profits. They don't realize that every dollar of flexible coupling sales requires an investment in inventory and receivables of about 30 cents. It's not like selling to the Big Three. You have to manufacture to inventory and then wait for payment from a variety of sources.

As it is, Alex wants to invest $10 million in new plant and equipment right away to allow flexible coupling sales to grow as fast as the market will allow. We have the space on our existing site to add a separate plant for flexible couplings. It's the money I worry about.

FOREIGN MARKETS

As the company's market position in North America began to improve, Alex began to wonder about foreign markets. The company had always been a major exporter to Canada, but it had never had to market there. The Big Three placed their orders often a year or two in advance, and Cameron just supplied them. As Alex put it:

> It was different with the flexible coupling. We had to find our own way into the market. We did, however, start getting orders from Europe and South America, at first from the subsidiaries of our U.S. customers and then from a few other firms as word

	2001	2002	2003
Assets			
Cash	$615	$430	$400
Accounts Receivable	5,850	6,850	10,400
Inventories	4,995	4,920	7,500
Total Current Assets	11,460	12,200	18,300
Property, plant and equipment (net)	10,790	11,800	13,000
Total Assets	22,250	24,000	31,300
Liabilities			
Accounts Payble	4,850	5,900	9,500
Bank loan	11,500	12,000	10,000
Accrued Items (Including taxes)	450	400	500
Total Current Liabilities	16,800	18,300	20,000
Common Stock (Held by Cameron family)	500	500	500
Retained Earnings	4,950	5,200	10,800
Total Equity	5,450	5,700	11,300
Total Liabilities	$22,250	$24,000	$31,300

Exhibit 2   Balance Sheets for Years Ended December 31, 2001, 2002, 2003 ($000s)

got around. We got $40,000 in orders during 2003 and the same amount during the first four months of 2004. This was a time when we were frantically busy and hopelessly understaffed in the management area, so all we did was fill the orders on an FOB, Detroit basis. The customers had to pay import duties of approximately three per cent into most European countries, and a value added tax of about 20 per cent (20 to 50 per cent into South America), on top of the freight and insurance, and still orders came in.

Seeing the potential in Europe, Alex promptly took a European Patent from the European Patent Office in the United Kingdom. The cost of the whole process was under $10,000.

A LICENSING OPPORTUNITY

In the spring of 2004, Alex made a vacation trip to Scotland and decided while he was there to drop in on one of the company's new foreign customers, McTaggart Supplies Ltd. Cameron Auto Parts had received unsolicited orders from overseas amounting to $40,000 in the first four months of 2004, and over 10 per cent of these had come from McTaggart. Alex was pleasantly surprised at the reception given to him by Sandy McTaggart, the 60-year-old head of the company.

Sandy: Come in! Talk of the devil. We were just saying what a shame it is you don't make those flexible couplings in this part of the world. There's a very good market for them. Why my men can even sell them to the English!

Alex: Well, we're delighted to supply your needs. I think we've always shipped your orders promptly, and I don't see why we can't continue. . . .

Sandy: That's not the point! Those orders are already sold before we place them. The point is we can't really build the market here on the basis of shipments from America. There's a three per cent tariff coming in, freight and insurance cost us another 10 per cent on top of your price, then there's the matter of currency values.

I get my orders in pounds (£)[1] but I have to pay you in dollars. And on top of all that, I never know how long the goods will take to get here, especially with all the dock strikes we have to put up with. Listen, why don't you license us to produce flexible couplings here?

After a lengthy bargaining session, during which Alex secured the information shown in Exhibit 3, he came round to the view that a license agreement with McTaggart might be a good way of achieving swift penetration of the U.K. market via McTaggart's sales force. McTaggart's production skills were not as up-to-date as Cameron's, but his plant showed evidence of a lot of original ideas to keep manufacturing costs down. Furthermore, the firm seemed committed enough to invest in some new equipment and to put a major effort into developing the U.K. market. At this point the two executives began to discuss specific terms of the license arrangements:

Alex: Let's talk about price. I think a figure around three per cent of your sales of flexible couplings would be about right.

Sandy: That's a bit high for an industrial license of this kind. I think one and a half per cent is more normal.

Alex: That may be, but we're going to be providing more than just blueprints. We'll have to help you choose equipment and train your operators as well.

Sandy: Aye, so you will. But we'll pay you for that separately. It's going to cost us £500,000 in special equipment as it is, plus, let's say, a $100,000 fee to you to help set things up. Now you have to give us a chance to price competitively in the market, or neither of us will benefit. With a royalty of one and a half per cent I reckon we could reach sales of £500,000 in our first year and £1 million in our second.

Alex: The equipment will let you produce up to £4 million of annual output. Surely you can sell more than a million. We're getting unsolicited orders without even trying.

Sandy: With the right kind of incentive, we might do a lot better. Why don't we agree to a royalty of two and a half per cent on the first million in sales and one and a half per cent after that. Now mind you, we're to become exclusive agents for the U.K. market. We'll supply your present customers from our own plant.

Alex: But just in the United Kingdom! Now two per cent is as low as I'm prepared to go. You make those figures three per cent and two

per cent and you have a deal. But it has to include a free technology flow-back clause in the event you make any improvements or adaptations to our manufacturing process.

Sandy: You drive a hard bargain! But it's your product, and we do want it. I'll have our lawyers draw up a contract accordingly. What do you say to a five-year deal, renewable for another five if we are both happy?

Alex: Sounds good. Let's do it.

2003 Sales	£35 million (down from £44 million in 2001)	
Total Assets	£11 million: Equity £6.5 million	
Net profit after tax	± £1.5 million	
Control	McTaggart Family	
Market coverage	15 sales representatives in United Kingdom, two in Europe, one in Australia, one in New Zealand, one in India.	
Average factory wage rate	£8.00 per hour (which is below the U.K. mean of £12.00 due to the factory being located in a depressed area) (versus $18.00 in America).	
Factory	Old and larger than necessary. Some very imaginative manufacturing know-how in evidence.	
Reputation	Excellent credit record, business now 130 years old, good market contacts (high calibre sales force).	
Other	Company sales took a beating during 2001–2002 as one of the company's staple products was badly hurt by a U.S. product of superior technology. Company filled out its line by distributing products obtained from other manufacturers. Currently about one-half of company sales are purchased from others. Company has capacity to increase production substantially.	

Pricing	Index
Cameron's price to McTaggart	100
(same as net price to distributor in America)	
+ Import duty	3
+ Freight and insurance	10
Importer's Cost	113
+ Distributor's (McTaggart's) Margin (30%)	34
+ Value Added Tax (17.5% on cost plus margin)	26
= Price charged by McTaggart	173
vs. Price charged by American distributor in U.S.	120

Exhibit 3   Data on McTaggart Supplies LTD.

Note: Under the European Union agreement, all imports from non-EU countries were subject to common customs tariffs. In 2004, the common customs tariff for the flexible coupling had an import duty of 2.7 per cent. In addition to the import duty, all imported items were subjected to the value added tax (VAT) which was applied on all manufactured goods—both imported as well as locally made. The VAT was going through a harmonization process but was expected to take some years before a common VAT system was in place. As of 2004, the VAT for United Kingdom was 17.5 per cent, and France 19.6 per cent. Denmark, Hungary, and Sweden had the highest VAT at 25 per cent.

Alex signed the contract the same week and then headed back to America to break the news. He travelled with mixed feelings, however. On the one hand, he felt he had got the better of Sandy McTaggart in the bargaining, while on the other, he felt he had no objective yardstick against which to evaluate the royalty rate he had agreed on. This was pretty much the way he presented the situation to his executive group when he got home.

Alex: . . . so I think it's a good contract, and I have a cheque here for $100,000 to cover our costs in helping McTaggart get set up.

John: We can certainly use the cash right now. And there doesn't seem to be any risk (finance) involved. I like the idea, Alex.

Andy (production): Well, I don't. And Chuck (head of the Cameron design team) won't either when (production) he hears about it. I think you've sold out the whole U.K. market for a pittance. I thought you wanted to capture foreign markets directly.

Alex: But Andy, we just don't have the resources to capture foreign markets ourselves. We might as well get what we can through licensing, now that we've patented our process.

Andy: Well, maybe. But I don't like it. It's the thin edge of the wedge if you ask me. Our know-how on the production of this product is pretty special, and it's getting better all the time. I hate to hand it over to old McTaggart on a silver platter. I reckon we're going to sell over $20 million in flexible couplings in the United States alone during 2004.

NOTE

1. One pound was equivalent to US$1.83 in 2004.

3

Negotiating and Designing an Alliance

In Brief

The design and negotiation of an alliance is both a critical and pivotal point in the alliance process. Beyond establishing a win-win arrangement, this phase of building alliances sets the tone of the future relationship. Many signals are communicated during this stage as to whether or not an alliance is likely to become a collaborative, enduring partnership.

The negotiation process involves prenegotiation preparations such as putting together the negotiating team, conducting the negotiation itself, and finalizing the ultimate agreement. The agreement should address, among other things, the mission of the alliance, its structure and governance, ownership and control details, identification of performance objectives and milestones, conflict resolution procedures, and provision for termination of the partnership.

Finally, key to a successful alliance is a strong relationship between the partners supported by mutual trust and commitment. A good contract is no substitute for a good relationship.

The basis for effective long-term collaboration is established at the negotiation stage. But alliance negotiations can be challenging to executives steeped in the adversarial, position-maximizing style of negotiating that characterizes many types of business arrangements. Approaching alliance negotiations from an adversarial or winner-take-all perspective is an invitation to trouble. In both their tone and approach, alliance negotiations should reflect the desire of the parties to create a solid foundation for their relationship and a positive atmosphere for the partnership. Negotiations should be considered first and foremost as a means of building the linkages that will support effective collaboration between the partner companies.

Alliance negotiations should endeavor to accomplish three things:

1. Establish the potential partners' mutual interest and test their strategic fit
2. Provide an opportunity to create a foundation of trust and to develop a problem-solving attitude
3. Establish a business and operational plan for the proposed enterprise

At the end of the process, both parties should be perceiving the benefits to be high and the risks equally shared. A venture with unhappy partners at the outset is unlikely to endure for very long.

The negotiation process is an excellent vehicle for developing some unique insights into how the other party does business. It is a good place to test compatibility and personal chemistry between key personalities. The style and approach exhibited by the key players at the negotiating table can be a good indicator of the nature of the eventual relationship.

Alliance negotiations typically deal with conflicting aims. While they must focus on achieving the greatest possible competitive advantage for the joint venture itself, each party also looks at how to get the best deal for their company. No matter how cooperative the intent, the negotiation phase is inevitably loaded with power issues and a heightened sensitivity to misunderstanding. This dilemma is most effectively mitigated when both partners negotiate generously with their primary objective so that both partners achieve a good deal. This strategy often entails suboptimizing on the immediate deal but at the same time laying the groundwork for optimizing long-term success.[1]

In alliance negotiations, several areas require particular attention, including putting together the negotiating team, prenegotiation preparations, the negotiation process itself, and formalizing the ultimate agreement.

PUTTING THE TEAM TOGETHER

There is no recipe for determining who should be at the negotiating table. There is value, however, in using a two-track approach involving both senior executives and middle-level or operational managers in the negotiation process when the size of companies warrants it (see Figure 3.1). (This may be difficult in partnerships between small firms and large multinationals, but to the extent possible, attempts should be made to structure it this way.)

The executive-level team establishes the commitment and strategic parameters of the negotiation. Discussions between CEOs or senior managers are usually focused on issues related to *strategic and financial fit* of the companies involved and the forms of cooperation that might be feasible. CEO involvement and visible commitment at the early stage provide important cues for middle management and staff about commitment to the venture's strategic importance, and this backing can be an important factor in mobilizing lower-level support.

The second-level team typically comprises division heads and middle managers as well as legal, financial, market, and technical experts.[2] This team focuses on *operational fit* and the day-to-day issues related to the venture's implementation. This team works out the details of the contract, its structure, partner contributions, management, and so on. The participation of, and early buy-in of, key operational managers should also help pave the way for the venture to be implemented quickly. If the people who may be involved in the implementation of the proposed venture are uncomfortable with some aspect of it, the chances of success may be greatly diminished.

Figure 3.1 Roles of the Negotiation Team

The involvement of operational managers at this point can also help to temper inflated expectations that sometimes develop during negotiations. People who will be required to live up to the commitments made by the partners are less likely to allow them to escalate. This also provides the individual or individuals who will be ultimately responsible for the alliance an opportunity to see if they are compatible with their potential partners.

WHO SHOULD BE ON THE TEAM

Beyond identifying CEO-level and key operational managers discussed above, managers need to keep the following considerations in mind when rounding out the negotiating team with legal, financial, and other resources:

- **Experience is a definite asset.** Negotiations can be stressful and managers want to be confident that their team members will conduct themselves with poise and in a non-adversarial manner. With inexperienced members, additional role-playing in advance of the negotiations would likely be beneficial.

- **Having a "contrarian" on the team.** This is someone who can identify and counter "group think" and can cut through some of the ego involvement that takes place in negotiations. The role is to challenge assumptions and take a close look at potential problems and ensure negotiators are realistic and objective in assessing the proposal.

- It is best to **avoid involving legal counsel as a negotiator.**[3] Legal and tax professionals have a very important role to play in putting a partnership together; however, their role is largely behind the scenes. Negotiations aim first to establish the business framework for the alliance. Once agreed to in principle, legal counsel should be brought in to draw up a sound document to protect both parties and provide the partnership a solid foundation. Similarly, tax advisers can help structure the deal for maximum financial benefit, but presence at the negotiating table may encourage similar self-interest from the potential partners and lead to an adversarial climate. Moreover, in some foreign cultures (particularly in some Asian countries), having legal counsel at the negotiating table may be interpreted as a sign of mistrust.

NEGOTIATING IN A FOREIGN BUSINESS CULTURE

When dealing in a foreign business culture, managers may want to find specialized consultants to assist in the negotiations. Consultants knowledgeable in the culture and business practices of the foreign environment and who have credibility and contacts in the area of the proposed venture can sometimes be of enormous benefit in both better understanding the potential deal and in facilitating it. It is always best, however, to avoid relying on a consultant to put the deal together. If a company doesn't have the capability to make the strategic and business decisions leading up to the deal, it is unlikely to have the ability to implement it effectively.

If interpreters are required, it is important that they be briefed on the proposed deal and the company's expectations. A well-briefed interpreter can help avoid some of the miscommunications and misunderstandings that frequently occur in cross-cultural negotiations. Using a senior executive as an interpreter could, in some cultures, diminish the perception of the executive's status and role in the eyes of the foreign partner and undermine his or her ability to make a substantive contribution to the negotiations.

PRENEGOTIATION PREPARATION

Coming to the table well prepared can smooth negotiations and substantially reduce the time it takes to put the deal together. Good preparation results in clarity of the company's expectations for the venture and the commitments that it is willing to make as well as those that it is expecting from its partner. Advanced preparation should also help assess bargaining power, understand the concessions to be made, and forecast issues that might arise.

Figure 3.2 has been designed to help in preparing for a negotiation. Responding to the first set of questions related to one's negotiating position is easy once the strategic analysis is complete. The next step entails overlaying the perceptions and expectations of the partner.

THE NEGOTIATION PROCESS

Good negotiations are characterized by honesty and an open flow of information between the partners. The parties focus on what they have in common rather than on their differences, and they actively seek solutions that meet both sides' primary goals. Figure 3.3 outlines steps in the negotiation process.

The initial meetings between the parties should focus on identifying mutual interests and building consensus on the basic strategic objectives of the alliance. There should be no pressure to close a deal. Efforts to conclude a deal quickly can lead negotiators to focus their attention on legal and financial aspects of the partnership while ignoring the relational and operational issues involved in managing the venture. Spelling out mutual benefits can also help negotiators uncover unrealistic expectations.

Our Company	The Alliance	Our Partner
Conditions of Negotiation ❑ What are our objectives for the alliance? ❑ How does this alliance fit with our strategy? ❑ What are we expecting from this alliance? ❑ How do we measure success? ❑ What strengths do we bring to this alliance? ❑ What are the essential requirements for the alliance to meet our objectives? ❑ What potential obstacles may prevent the alliance from meeting our objectives?	❑ What should be the objectives of the alliance? ❑ What should be the alliance's strategy? ❑ What are appropriate measures for alliance success (over time)? ❑ What will be the unique strengths of the alliance as a result? ❑ What risk factors may hamper the likelihood of success?	❑ What do we think are the objectives of our partner? ❑ How does this alliance fit with its strategy? ❑ What do we think our partner is expecting from this alliance? ❑ How do we think our partner measures success? ❑ What strengths does our partner bring to this alliance? ❑ What are the essential requirements for the alliance to meet our partner's objectives? ❑ What potential obstacles may prevent the alliance from meeting our partner's objectives?
Negotiating Levers ❑ What needs to be safely guarded? (e.g., intellectual property) What are *sacred cows*? ❑ What concessions can we offer freely that we think they will want?	❑ What negotiations are in the best interest of the alliance?	❑ What concessions do we think our partner will request? How can we accommodate them? ❑ What concessions will we want from our partner? Which ones are deal breakers?

Figure 3.2   Preparing for a Negotiation

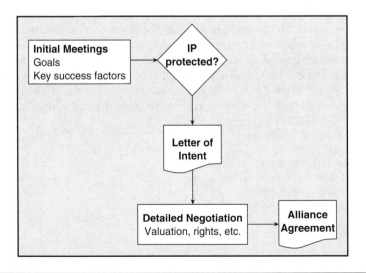

Figure 3.3   Topics for Negotiation

The early negotiations should allow the parties to get to know each other, clarify expected benefits, and identify shared goals and objectives. At this stage, it is best to try to avoid placing too much emphasis on legal issues and technicalities, decision-making processes, and ownership formulas. Rather, focus discussions on operations planning, clarity of goals, personnel selection, resource needs, reporting systems, cost controls, and desired results.[4]

The prenegotiation stage should have identified proprietary knowledge that needs to be protected, so before disclosing proprietary data, managers should ensure their competitive advantage is adequately protected and make certain the negotiators have been well briefed on what is appropriate to share and when. Technology to be disclosed should ideally be patented, and confidentiality agreements should be signed to cover sensitive information to preclude prospective partners from using disclosures in a competitive manner. A good approach is to balance the amount of capabilities and information unveiled with what the partner unveils. A partner's negotiating history, usually known and discussed within industry circles, can be a valuable guide to decide how to approach the handling of competitive or proprietary information. If, for example, a company has previously entered negotiations in bad faith simply to obtain competitive intelligence, the industry will likely have talked about it.

There should be no pressure to rush to do the deal. It is important to take a hard look at the partner and the deal at each stage of the negotiation process and to stay attuned to warning signals, such as demands for quick commitments or partners not willing to discuss their strategic agenda.

At the end of the day, managers hope to emerge from these negotiations with a clear focus on goals and a plan for achieving them. Clarity is vital. Ambiguous goals, fuzzy directions, or uncoordinated activities will lead to disappointment. The definition of the partnership should be precise enough to ensure commitment but not so rigid that there is no potential for learning and growth.

Figure 3.4 summarizes some key issues to address during the negotiation.

LETTER OF INTENT

Once the mutual benefits and general objectives have been set out, the concepts of the venture can begin to be transferred to a nonbinding letter of intent. This document is used to move the negotiations beyond the initial conceptual stages to an operational stage where the alliance starts to have a clear description. The key players of both parties should jointly draft this document. A good letter of intent will greatly facilitate the drafting of a binding legal agreement.

Elements of the letter of intent typically include the following elements:

- Purpose of the alliance
- Scope of activity
- Key objective and responsibilities
- Method for decision making
- Resource commitments
- Assumption of risk and division of rewards
- Rights and exclusions
- Proposed structure of the alliance or venture

In some jurisdictions, a nonbinding letter of intent may, in fact, be binding. Before signing a letter of intent, check the legal ramifications of signing any documents in the course of the negotiations.

Technological Issues	Market Issues	Alliance Structure
❏ Ownership of technologies developed by the alliance. ❏ Rights to use and market core technologies, future technologies to be developed, and those from outside sources. ❏ Royalty rights if partner markets developed technology in other markets. ❏ Ownership and rights of future technology enhancements. ❏ Applicable decision-making process where new technology concerned. ❏ Legal rights in case of third party infringement of joint technology.	❏ Decision-making process on new product definition. ❏ Identification of product management roles including product design, naming, quality assurance. ❏ Identification of roles and cost sharing of marketing campaigns. ❏ Decision-making process on product evolution (improvements, additions, etc.). ❏ Identification of legal liabilities including warranty obligation, customer injury, or technology infringement. ❏ Marketing rights of products and technologies if the partnership ends.	❏ Management representation and, in case of a joint venture, board representation of the alliance. ❏ Identification of resources to be used (e.g. new, dedicated staff or resources assigned from each partner). ❏ Mechanisms for possible future business expansion. ❏ Mechanisms for a partner to extract themselves from the alliance. ❏ Decision-making process in the event of partner dissolution as well as division of assets and technology.

Figure 3.4   What Needs to Be Negotiated?

Source: Adapted from Marlee Myers, "Strategic Partnerships," *Pittsburgh High Technology Journal,* May 1989, 5–6.

PARTNER CONTRIBUTION VALUATION

Valuing the partners' contributions tends to be one of the most difficult and contentious issues in alliance negotiations.[5] The assessment of a partner's value will depend on an estimate of its present and future contributions and will vary in its measurability on the choice of alliance form and the nature of the assets involved. Typical areas of contribution to be valued are as follows:

- Fixed assets
- Working capital
- Expertise
- Contact network (e.g., access to customers)
- Brand and associated goodwill
- Expected technology transfer

Partner contribution valuation is not an exact science. A partner company's attitude to alliances and how they should be controlled and managed, as well as its expectations about how a particular venture will evolve, heavily influences its approach to valuation. For example, if one or both partners bring to the valuation process a power or competitive attitude, an agreement will likely be harder to reach. The partners' relative power is generally not a key ingredient in the success of the alliance. It is more effective to start with the definition of what constitutes a contribution in light of the key success factors for the alliance and the potential payoffs that a partner expects to derive from the collaboration. In some cases, companies will not fight over the valuation of their contribution when they have determined that the tangible and intangible returns that they expect from the alliance will at least meet their initial expectations.

Resolving divergent positions on valuation, particularly non-market-based contributions such as expertise, can become a delicate matter. While some partners can agree on simple methodologies such as "splitting the difference," others may pursue much more sophisticated methodologies, including the following:

- *Discounted cash flows (DCF)* value the prospective future cash flows of the venture in terms of present-day value.
- A *capitalization approach* measures the asset value of contributions to the alliance based on the projected net income and expected rate of return.
- The *cost approach* takes into consideration the cost needed to substitute an alternative contribution that would meet the objectives of the alliance.
- An *industry benchmarking approach* places emphasis on the past valuation of similar ventures within the same industry. This approach factors in the competitive forces that would influence partner valuation.

Regardless of the approach, it is advisable to first agree on a process for resolution such as deferring to a mutually agreed-upon third party.

THE AGREEMENT

Informal alliances often do not require binding agreements. Rather, the partners maintain individual control over specific areas of responsibility but share the results jointly. Most arrangements, however, are cemented by a contractual agreement. The complexity of the agreement will be related to the proposed scope and structure of the venture.

Two companies that have never worked together before may want to consider a less formal alliance as a first step in collaboration. This could be a narrowly focused agreement that defines a small project, which allows the partners to see how the two companies interact and establish mutual trust on which to base a broader

---

When Negotiations Should Stop

Springboard Wireless Networks, a spin-off of Toronto-based Kasten Chase, had developed a world-leading communications system for managing the flow of subways and trains more efficiently. While most land-based traffic systems were based on a "fixed-block" queuing approach, Springboard was set to revolutionize flow management with a wireless communications system that would support much more efficient "moving block" systems. In 1999, the City of New York subway system—known for setting global industry standards in underground transportation— was impressed with the technology and incorporated it in its reference specification for a pilot project it was about to launch. Collaboration promptly began with Alstom, Alcatel, and Siemens, which were competing for the New York project. A strong relationship emerged with Alstom representatives, and the two companies embarked on alliance discussions. For Springboard, the alliance represented an exceptional opportunity to accelerate growth in the 25-person company, and management was not opposed to acquisition as an eventual outcome. The primary concern, however, was that Springboard retain sufficient control to enable it to continue to work with the remaining two competitors in the short term and retain the option of an initial public offering (IPO) should acquisition not occur. Negotiations began well, based on their relationship foundation. As executives from France headquarters became involved, however, Springboard sensed the emergence of conflicting agendas. French executives were interested in making a small investment but were insistent on assuming effective management control. After careful consideration, Springboard concluded that the control issue presented far too much risk that directly contravened its strategic goals. Negotiations promptly terminated.

partnership. Terminating a small alliance that is not working is infinitely easier than disengaging from a large one.

Legal agreements should be well written and set out the purpose, terms, duration, warranties, obligations, and other key understandings on which the relationship is based. They should be designed to reinforce the business objectives of the partnership and, at the same time, protect the partners. Some of the best agreements, while setting out clearly articulated ground rules, leave a lot of room for the relationship to grow and deal with changes. The following suggest areas applicable to an alliance legal agreement:

- The venture's objectives
- The level of commitments and contribution of both parties
- An organizational structure congruent with the venture's strategy with an appropriate incentive and reward structure
- Benchmarks, performance objectives, and review process
- A description of the roles and responsibilities of the parties
- An implementation plan
- Formulas for transfer pricing, earnings, and equity
- Detailed penalty, arbitration, and termination clauses
- Provisions for expansion of activity
- Procedures for adapting to change
- Conflict resolution procedures
- Mechanisms and procedures for governance of the venture
- Provisions for control (in the case of joint venture)
- Finance, tax, and legal considerations

The remainder of this section focuses on six aspects of the alliance agreement that merit particular attention: mission, structure and governance, ownership and control, establishing performance objectives, providing for termination, and establishing conflict resolution procedures.

1. Mission

Managers need to be painstakingly thorough in describing the mission or scope of the venture's activity. They should ensure that matters important to them such as business mission, access to technology, learning, financing, and dividend policy are covered to their satisfaction in the written agreement.

2. Structure and Governance

The alliance's structure provides the context for the interaction among partners. The strategic and operational objectives of the partners can only be achieved if facilitated by the alliance structure. For example, in an alliance where learning is a key objective, the venture's structure will be a determining factor in the nature of the partner interaction and the types and amounts of the information to be transferred.

As a minimum, alliance structure and governance should address the board configuration, roles, responsibilities and lines of authority, frequency of meetings, and other expected forms of communications. The key word to an alliance structure that is operationally feasible is *simplicity.* The ideal structure is one that is uncomplicated with clear lines of authority, communication, and decision making. Alliances that have very ambitious goals and involve significant interactions between partners or complex interdependencies run a higher risk of failure, especially if partners are new to each other or have little experience managing alliances.

There are numerous possible tools for structuring a venture. While each varies in complexity and commitment, there are advantages and disadvantages to be considered. Lynch outlines the following approaches to structuring an alliance.[6]

- A *handshake* is used more often than imagined in nonequity arrangements, even by some very large corporations. This approach tends to be used where a high level of trust already exists between the partners and where no legal or contractual documentation is necessary. It may also be an interim arrangement where there is a desire to get the venture up and running before contracts or legal documents are prepared. Handshake agreements are not recommended where corporate or staffing changes may jeopardize the memory and understanding of the arrangement.

- *Contracts and written agreements* maintain an arm's-length relationship between the parties. Each outlines how the revenue is to be divided and who is responsible for specific performance tasks and deliverables. This approach is typically used for short-term relationships (under 3–5 years), where daily or close coordination is not required, or where capital investments are separately made by both parties for their own activities.

- *Partnership* is a legal structure that allocates investment, profits, losses, and operational responsibilities while maintaining the autonomy of the participants. Small entrepreneurial companies commonly choose this arrangement or in cases where the alliance is project oriented, requiring high levels of commitment and interaction for limited periods of time (likely to endure less than 5 years). It is appropriate when a separate business entity is required but there is no need for separate management. It has a great range of flexibility in what is often an uncertain environment.

- *Joint venture* is the most formal of alliance structures. It involves the parties coming together and creating a separate or stand-alone entity in which they all have an equity interest. Joint ventures—described by some as permanent solutions to temporary problems—are best used when the project is large or complex enough to require its own internal management and when the goal of the venture is long term. The structure works best when it has a certain amount of autonomy while being strategically driven by the founding parents.

The issue of equity involvement should be a strategic consideration when establishing a venture's structure. Numerous alliances operate successfully without an equity link. Equity participation can permit some control over ventures that are central to a partner's long-term competitive success or involve a substantial contribution of technological resources and shared information. The decision needs to be made in the context of balancing control and preserving agility. A company needs to be careful about locking into an equity-based alliance in an environment where technology, market conditions, and strategy are constantly evolving.

3. Ownership and Control

In equity-based joint ventures, ownership and control should be treated as separate issues. Control is about the ability to influence behaviors and decisions in a partnership (see Figure 3.5 for examples of control mechanisms). For instance, a company in a minority equity position may still be able to control key decisions. Many executives believe that, irrespective of the ownership structure of a joint venture, it should be run as much as possible as if it was a 50/50 arrangement. The power associated with majority ownership should be used very selectively to preserve the spirit of the partnership, although, where compromise is not possible, the majority partner needs to exercise his or her voting authority to ensure the continuation of the joint venture's affairs.

But even with 50/50 ownership, one partner should be clearly responsible for ultimate management control. In some cases, partners agree to maintain control over specific functions of the venture that are critical to them. In fact, a 2002 study of international joint ventures in Korea found that split control yielded higher performance than shared control.[7] It is noteworthy that the McKinsey and Company study also found no instances of a successful joint venture where management control was shared evenly between the owners.

The resolution of the control issue, particularly in joint venture agreements, should result in a decision-making structure that is efficient, collaborative, and synergistic. Control should be a business decision first and a legal decision second. Control should not be approached in terms of who has more or less control but rather in terms of three key questions:

- Who should control what?
- How should control be exercised over key areas?
- When should control be exercised?

Addressing these questions forces both partners to determine who is in the best position to contribute to areas critical to the alliance's success and to allocate responsibilities accordingly.

4. Establishing Performance Objectives

Successful partnerships require regular and frequent care and attention. Periodic reviews based on prespecified benchmarks allow both parties to assess the progress and

Hard Mechanisms	Soft Mechanisms
Design/participate in planning process	Board of Directors
Design/approve capital appropriation	Approval requirements for
Formulation of policies & procedures	• Specific decisions
Staffing: Alliance general manager, Key functional executives	• Plans, budgets
Set objectives for alliance GM	• Resource allocation
Reporting structure	Appointment of alliance GM
Training programs	Screening of issues before discussion with partner
Staff services	
Set performance measurement	
Set compensation formula	

Figure 3.5   What Control Mechanisms Work Best?

identify problem areas. They also help manage expectations and enable partners to make any necessary adjustments early rather than wait until deviations become substantial and the alarm bells ring. Benchmarks can also be used to manage infusions of capital and technology transfer in ways that protect partner interests. Some companies use performance objectives to build trust and enthusiasm by moving from simple to more complex interdependencies throughout a series of easily achievable milestones.

5. Providing for Termination

A good relationship and a well-conceived agreement make provisions for changing circumstances and the possibility that the alliance will be terminated. Relationships can outlive their usefulness even when they have a mutually productive and beneficial history. The directions of companies change. New management may have a different vision for the corporation. The founder of a company may decide it's time to sell out and do something different. Hence, it is important to insist on a termination clause that details how separation occurs if one partner wants out. It is always a painful process to work through a separation without guidance from an agreement.[8]

Termination should include agreement on the allocation of rights and assets emerging from the alliance. One way to avoid unmet expectations is to spell out, in the contract, the terms and conditions for continuation of the relationship. Put in writing the outcomes that must be achieved for the partnership to continue and list things that can lead to the termination of the arrangement. A requirement that the principals meet at least every year, review progress, agree on future plans and goals for the collaboration, and revise terms and conditions for renewal and termination as needed is also a useful way to ensure the relationship continues to benefit both parties. If there are phases or stages in the contract, the collaboration agreement needs to say what they are.

6. Establishing Conflict Resolution Procedures

Strategic alliances often involve partners with different corporate and national cultures, capabilities, and, in some cases, ultimate objectives. A certain amount of conflict, therefore, is inevitable. However, to minimize their consequences, companies incorporate in contracts clauses that spell out the handling of disputes.

A moderate degree of conflict in an alliance can be quite healthy and a stimulus to creativity and improved performance. As a first step, partners should look at mitigating potential conflicts structurally or managerially. Where the potential exists for a high level of conflict, it may be best to start off with a highly focused venture with a simple structure and work on building the relationship. Work to find solutions to potential conflicts before attempting a more complex arrangement.

A mutually agreed-to, clearly articulated alliance strategy will divert many conflicts, and asking, "What is in the best interest of the alliance strategy?" will often eliminate the conflict. Similarly, consistent and mutually agreed-upon management principles for the venture will help as many of the conflicts that arise during alliances are the result of misunderstandings between the partners.

A 1999 study among 40 Russian-based international joint ventures revealed nine successful strategies for minimizing conflict, many of which are discussed here.[9] Of particular interest is the recommendation to have a process in place *before* real conflicts arise. A process could include dialogs, written statements, parent intervention, and ultimately arbitration. A formal method for resolving disputes should be outlined within the agreement and be consistent with the nature of the venture and the resources of the partners.

In closing, good contracts, whether formal or informal, are essential to alliances; however, no contract can specify all of the eventualities and anticipate all of the future opportunities. The key to a successful alliance is a strong relationship between the partners supported by mutual trust and commitment. These relationship factors will greatly facilitate getting access to the partner capabilities needed and overcoming some of the rough spots that the alliance will go through during its lifetime. A good contract is no substitute for a good relationship.

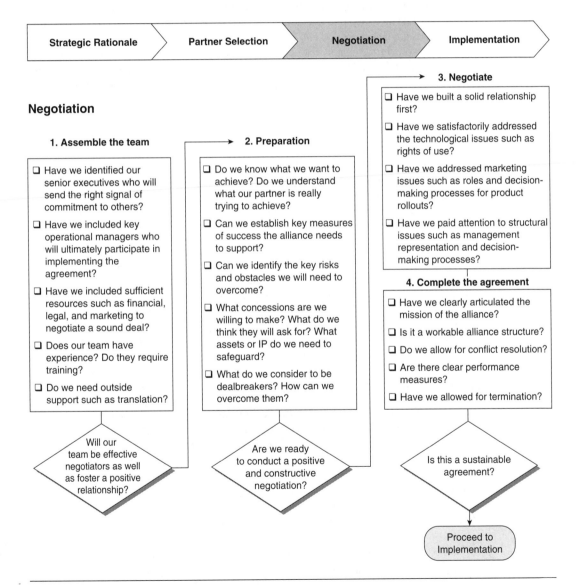

Figure 3.6   Negotiation Flowchart

CASES

Blue Ridge Spain

Blue Ridge Spain was a joint venture established between a well-known U.S. fast-food chain and an "old guard" family-run agricultural company that was seeking to diversify in the wake of Spain's entry into the European Union. The European regional director of the company has been dealt an unexpected professional blow. After several years of fostering a successful joint venture, the regional director is stunned to find out that the new owners of Blue Ridge want out of the arrangement. Despite the fact that this particular joint venture has been profitable since its inception and the company has experienced brisk growth during that time, the new owners are determined to end the partnership. The regional director is left examining how he is to respond to a request that he feels is not only detrimental to his company but also contrary to his principles. He questions the ethics of secretly undermining the joint venture in order to achieve the upper hand in buyout negotiations. As a Greek, the importance of personal relationships and social contracts only adds to his dilemma.

Assignment Questions

1. What led the joint venture partners to this impasse? What were the major difficulties between the joint venture partners over the years?

2. Be prepared to argue for an action plan from the perspectives below (you will be assigned to one of them). You also want to think about some of the following:
   - As Sodergran and Dryden, representing Delta, how much is Blue Ridge Spain worth to Delta? Would you push ahead with the dissolution strategy? Why or why not? What implementation issues should you consider, and how would you address them? Be prepared to negotiate the price and conditions for ending the joint venture.
   - As Terralumen management, if Delta pursues the dissolution strategy, what would you do? How much is the company worth, and how much do you want for your share of the company? What other issues should they consider? Be prepared to negotiate the price and conditions for ending the joint venture.

3. As Costas, would you go ahead and develop a dissolution strategy for the joint venture? Why or why not? Would you do something else? What issues should you consider in making your decision? What would you do as Costas?

TeqSwitch Inc.: Business in Buenos Aires

Engineers formed TeqSwitch Inc. to design and produce faster networking equipment. Five years after they began, the company has 120 employees in Canada, England, and Australia and sales in the tens of millions. The company decided to expand into Latin America and has worked out a $15 million joint venture with Unitas in Argentina to sell components. TeqSwitch establishes an office in Buenos Aires and works with Unitas to develop sales personnel and business processes. As the company is about to launch its next generation of products, the vice president international of TeqSwitch receives information from the joint venture partner about terminating the agreement. He must determine what has gone wrong.

Assignment Questions

1. Why did this joint venture fail?

2. What advice would you give to TeqSwitch for its next Argentinean joint venture?

Textron Ltd.

Textron Ltd. is a family-owned manufacturer of cotton- and sponge-fabricated items. The company wants to expand its business with an offshore manufacturing enterprise that will fit with the company's policy of caring for its employees and providing quality products. The company is looking at two options: a guaranteed outsourcing purchase agreement or a joint venture. After several meetings with offshore alliance candidates, the vice president of the company must analyze the cross-cultural differences to established corporate guidelines of global ethics and social responsibility that the company can use in its negotiations with a foreign manufacturing firm.

Assignment Questions

1. As an outside consultant brought into the situation to address all issues, advise Gary Case as to appropriate action he should contemplate taking.

2. As a member of the board of directors of Textron Ltd., what guidance would you offer to the executive involved?

3. Draft a corporate code of conduct as a model for global companies built around the *absolute* business practices (*core human values* practiced through the doctrine of *ethical imperialism*). These are the points that shall not be compromised regardless of which host country a multinational enterprise operates in. It should recognize *relative* business practices (respect for local traditions and context practiced via the doctrine of cultural relativism) that recognize the differences in economic and social environments that multinational firms locate their activities within.

Nora-Sakari: A Proposed JV in Malaysia (Revised)

This case presents the perspective of a Malaysian company, Nora Bhd, which was in the process of trying to establish a telecommunications joint venture with a Finnish firm, Sakari Oy. Negotiations have broken down between the firms, and students are asked to try and restructure a win-win deal. The case examines some of the most common issues involved in partner selection and design in international joint ventures.

Assignment Questions

1. How important is the joint venture to Nora and Sakari?

2. If the joint venture is important, why have the negotiations failed to this point?

3. Should Nora and Sakari renegotiate? If yes, how should they restructure the deal to reach a win-win situation?

Majestica Hotel in Shanghai?

Majestica Hotels Inc., a leading European operator of luxury hotels, was trying to reach an agreement with Commercial Properties of Shanghai (CPS) regarding the management contract for a new hotel in Shanghai. A series of issues requires resolution for the deal to proceed, including length of contract term, name, staffing, and many other control issues. Majestica was reluctant to make further concessions for fear that doing so might jeopardize its service culture, arguably the key success factor in this industry. At issue was whether Majestica should adopt a contingency approach and relax its operating philosophy or stick to its principles, even if it meant not entering a lucrative market.

Assignment Questions

1. How many issues require resolution between Majestica and CPS?

2. As Majestica, where, if anywhere, would you make concessions?

3. As CPS, if Majestica refuses to make concessions, will you walk away?

Eli Lilly in India: Rethinking the Joint Venture Strategy

Eli Lilly and Company is a leading U.S. pharmaceutical company. The new president of intercontinental operations is reevaluating all of the company's divisions, including the joint venture with Ranbaxy Laboratories Limited, one of India's largest pharmaceutical companies. This joint venture has run smoothly for a number of years despite their difference in focus, but recently, Ranbaxy was experiencing cash flow difficulties due to its network of international sales. In addition, the Indian government was changing regulations for businesses in India, and joining the World Trade Organization would have an effect on India's chemical and drug regulations. The president must determine if this international joint venture still fits Eli Lilly's strategic objectives.

Assignment Questions

1. Did Eli Lilly pursue the right strategy to enter the Indian market?

2. Carefully consider the evolution of the joint venture. Evaluate the three successive international joint venture (IJV) leaders. Identify the unique challenges faced by each.

3. How would you assess the overall performance of the joint venture (JV)? What did the partners learn from the IJV?

4. What action would you recommend regarding the Ranbaxy partnership? What are the implications of your recommendation? How would you implement this?

NOTES

1. J. Child and D. Faulkner, *Strategies of Cooperation* (Oxford, UK: Oxford University Press, 1998), 145.

2. R. Lynch, *Business Alliance Guide* (New York: John Wiley, 1993), 275.

3. For a discussion on the role of lawyers in alliance negotiations, see James W. Botkin and Jana B. Matthews, *Winning Combinations: The Coming Wave of Entrepreneurial Partnerships Between Large and Small Companies* (New York: John Wiley, 1992), 132–4.

4. R. Lynch, "Building Alliances to Penetrate the European Market," *Journal of Business Strategy,* March/April 1990, 25.

5. For a discussion of valuation issues, see Child and Faulkner, *Strategies of Cooperation,* 157–60; Y. Doz and G. Hamel, *Alliance Advantage: The Art of Creating Value Through Partnering* (Boston: Harvard Business School Press, 1998), 66–72; R. Spekmam, L. Isabella, and T. MacAvoy, *Alliance Competence* (New York: John Wiley, 2000), 147–8.

6. R. Lynch, *Business Alliance Guide* (New York: John Wiley, 1993), 251–6.

7. Chang-Brn Choi and Paul Beamish, "Split Management Control and International Joint Venture Performance," *Journal of International Business Studies* 35, no. 3 (2004): 201.

8. For a discussion of exit and termination clauses, see Spekman, Isabella, and MacAvoy, *Alliance Competence,* 163–80.

9. Carl F. Fey and Paul W. Beamish, "Strategies for Managing Russian International Joint Venture Conflict," *European Management Journal* 17, no. 1 (1999): 99–106.

BLUE RIDGE SPAIN

Prepared by Jeanne M. McNett under the supervision of
David Wesley and Professors Nicholas Athanassiou and Henry W. Lane

Yannis Costas, European managing director of Blue Ridge Restaurants, found it difficult to control the anger welling up inside him as he left the meeting with the company's regional vice-president (VP) earlier in the day. That evening, he began to reflect on the day's events in the relative peace of his London flat. "Ten years work gone down the drain," he thought to himself, shaking his head. "What a waste!"

Costas recalled the many years he had spent fostering a successful joint venture between his company, Blue Ridge Restaurants Corporation, and Terralumen S.A., a mid-sized family-owned company in Spain. Not only had the joint venture been profitable, but it had grown at a reasonably brisk pace in recent years. Without a doubt, partnering with Terralumen was a key reason for Blue Ridge's success in Spain. Therefore, Costas was somewhat dismayed to find out that Delta Foods Corporation, Blue Ridge's new owner, wanted out. Yes, there had been recent tension between Terralumen and Delta over future rates of growth (see Exhibits 2 and 3), but the most recent round of talks had ended in an amicable compromise—he thought. Besides, Delta's senior managers should have realized that their growth targets were unrealistic.

They had gone over the arguments several times, and Costas tried every angle to convince his superiors to stick with the joint venture, but to no avail. To make matters worse, Costas had just been assigned the unpleasant task of developing a dissolution strategy for the company he had worked so hard to build.

BLUE RIDGE RESTAURANTS CORPORATION

Blue Ridge was founded in Virginia in 1959, and quickly established a reputation for quality fast food. In 1974, after establishing more than 500 food outlets in the United States and Canada, Blue Ridge was sold to an investment group for US$4 million.

Over the next five years, the company experienced sales growth of 96 per cent annually. However, international sales were haphazard and there was no visible international strategy. Instead, whenever a foreign restauranteur wanted to begin a Blue Ridge franchise, the foreign company would simply approach Blue Ridge headquarters with the request. As long as the franchise delivered royalties, there was little concern for maintaining product consistency or quality control in foreign markets.

In 1981, Blue Ridge was acquired by an international beverages company for US$420 million. Under new ownership, the company made its first major foray into international markets, and international operations were merged with the parent company's existing international beverage products under a new international division.

The strategy at the time was to enter into joint ventures with local partners, thereby allowing Blue Ridge to enter restricted markets and draw on local expertise, capital and labor. Partnering also significantly reduced the capital costs of opening new stores. The strategy of local partnering combined with Blue Ridge's marketing know-how and operations expertise, quickly paid off in Australia, Southeast Asia and the United Kingdom, where booming sales led to rapid international expansion.

On the other hand, there were some glaring failures. By 1987, Blue Ridge decided to pull out of France, Italy, Brazil and Hong Kong where infrastructure problems and slow consumer acceptance resulted in poor performance. Some managers, who had been accustomed to high margins and short lead times in their alcoholic beverages division, did not have the patience for the long and difficult road to develop these markets and would tolerate only those ventures that showed quick results.

These early years of international expansion provided important learning opportunities as more managers gained a personal understanding of the key strategic factors behind successful foreign entry. The success of the company's international expansion efforts helped Blue Ridge become the company's fastest growing division. When Blue Ridge was sold to Delta Foods in 1996 for US$2 billion, it was one of the largest fast-food chains in the world and generated sales of US$6.8 billion.

Delta was a leading soft drink and snack food company in the United States, but at the time of the Blue Ridge acquisition, it had not achieved significant success internationally. It had managed to establish a dominant market share in a small number of countries with protected markets in which its main competitors were shut out. For example, one competitor was shut out of many Arabic countries after deciding to set up operations in Israel.

The company's senior managers disliked joint ventures, in part because they were time-consuming, but also because they were viewed as a poor way to develop new markets. Delta was an aggressive growth company with brands that many believed were strong enough to support entry into new overseas markets without the assistance of local partners. When needed, the company either hired local managers directly or transferred seasoned managers from the soft drink and snack food divisions.

Delta also achieved international growth by directly acquiring local companies. For example, in the late 1990s, Delta acquired the largest snack food companies in Spain and the United Kingdom. However, given that joint ventures had been the predominant strategy for Blue Ridge, and that some countries, such as China, required local partnering, Delta had no choice but to work with joint venture partners.

Yannis Costas

Yannis Costas was an American-educated Greek who held degrees in engineering and business (MBA) from leading U.S. colleges. Although college life in a foreign country had its challenges, it afforded him an opportunity to develop an appreciation and understanding of American culture and business practices. Therefore, upon completing his MBA, Costas turned-down several offers of employment from leading multinational corporations that wanted him to take management positions in his native country. Such positions, however appealing they may have been at the time, would have doomed him to a career as a local manager, he thought. He chose instead to accept a position in international auditing at Blue Ridge headquarters in Virginia, mainly because of the opportunity for extended foreign travel.

The transition from university to corporate life was a difficult one. Social life seemed to revolve around couples and families, both at Blue Ridge and in the larger community. Although Costas met some single women from the local Greek community, his heavy travel schedule prevented him from establishing any meaningful relationships. Instead, he immersed himself in his work as a way to reduce the general feeling of isolation.

Costas was fortunate to have an office next to Gene Bennett, the company's director of business development. Bennett had served as a lieutenant in the U.S. Navy before working in the pharmaceutical industry setting up joint ventures in Latin America and Europe. He was hired by Blue Ridge specifically to develop international joint ventures. As Costas' informal mentor, Bennett passed on many of the lessons Costas would come to draw on later in his career.

It was at the urging of Bennett that Costas applied for a transfer to the international division in 1985. Three years later, Costas was asked to relocate to London, England, in order to take on the role of European regional director for Blue Ridge. In this position, he became responsible for joint ventures and franchises in Germany, the Netherlands, Spain, Northern Ireland, Denmark, Sweden and Iceland.

In 1993, Costas was transferred to Singapore where, under the direction of the president of Blue Ridge Asia,[1] he advanced in his understanding of joint ventures, market entry and teamwork. Over the next five years, Costas built a highly productive management team and successfully developed several Asian markets. He was eager to apply these new skills when he returned to London in 1998 to once again take up the role of European director (see Exhibit 1 for a summary of Costas' career).

Year	Blue Ridge Restaurants	Yannis Costas
1959	Company founded in Virginia	
1974	Blue Ridge Sold for $4 million	
1975–1980	96 per cent annual growth	Leaves Greece to study in United States
1981	Blue Ridge sold for $420 million	
1982	International expansion	Completes his BS in United States
1983	Begin negotiations for JV in Spain	
1984		Completes MBA and is hired by Blue Ridge; moves to Virginia
1985	JV agreement with Terralumen S.A.	Applies for transfer to International Div.
1986	Rodrigo appointed managing director of Blue Ridge Spain	
1987	Company pulls out of France, Brazil, Hong Kong and Italy	
1988		Promoted to European regional director; moves to London
1988–1993	Spanish JV grows slower than expected	
1993	U.S. manager sent to oversee Spanish JV	Transfer to Singapore
1995	Rodrigo replaced by Carlos Martin	
1996	Blue Ridge sold to Delta for $2 billion	
1995–1998	Spanish JV grows more rapidly	
1998	5-year plan for 50 restaurants in Spain, Blue Ridge has 600 stores in Europe/ME	Costas asked to return to London
Jan. 1999		Rescues JV in Kuwait
May 1999	Södergran hired as Delta VP for Europe	
June 1999	Directors meeting for Spanish JV	
December 1999	Dryden withholds Delta payment to JV; Alvarez sells prime Barcelona property	
January 2000		Asked to develop dissolution strategy for Spain

Exhibit 1   Timeline

THE SPANISH DECISION

When the decision was first made to enter the Spanish market, Bennett was sent overseas to meet with real estate developers, construction companies, retail distributors, agribusiness companies, lawyers, accountants and consumer product manufacturers in order to gather the preliminary knowledge needed for such an undertaking. Bennett soon realized that Blue Ridge would need a credible Spanish partner to navigate that country's complex real estate and labor markets.

Few Spaniards among Bennett's peer generation spoke English. However, Bennett had a basic knowledge of Spanish, a language that he had studied in college, and this helped open some doors that were otherwise shut for many of his American colleagues. Still, Bennett knew that finding a suitable partner would be difficult, since Spaniards frequently appeared to distrust foreigners. The attitude of one investment banker from Madrid was typical:

> Many Spaniards do not want to eat strange-tasting, comparatively expensive American food out of paper bags in an impersonal environment. We have plenty of restaurants with good inexpensive food, a cozy atmosphere and personal service, and our restaurants give you time to enjoy your food in pleasant company. Besides, we don't even really know you. You come here for a few days, we have enjoyable dinners, I learn to like you, and then you leave. What kind of relationship is that?

Luckily, Bennett had a banker friend in Barcelona who recommended that he consider partnering with Terralumen.

TERRALUMEN S. A.

Terralumen was a family-owned agricultural company that had later expanded into consumer products. In doing so, Terralumen entered into several joint ventures with leading American companies. In recent years, Terralumen had also begun to experiment with the concept of establishing full-service restaurants.

Bennett was introduced to Francisco Alvarez, Terralumen's group vice-president in charge of restaurant operations and the most senior non-family member in the company. In time, Bennett had many opportunities to become well acquainted with Terralumen and its managers. On weekends he stayed at Alvarez's country home, attended family gatherings in Barcelona and had family members visit him in Virginia. Over the span of their negotiations, Bennett and Alvarez developed a solid friendship, and Bennett began to believe that Terralumen had the type of vision needed to be a successful joint venture partner.

After two years of negotiations, Blue Ridge entered into a joint venture with Terralumen to establish a Blue Ridge restaurant chain in Spain. Upon returning to Virginia, Bennett could not hold back his euphoria as he related to Costas the details of what he considered to be the most difficult joint venture he had ever negotiated.

BLUE RIDGE SPAIN

Alvarez hired Eduardo Rodrigo to head up the joint venture as its managing director. An accountant by trade, Rodrigo was a refined and personable man who valued his late afternoon tennis with his wife and was a professor at a university in Barcelona. He also spoke fluent English.

Before assuming his new role, Rodrigo and another manager went to Virginia to attend a five-week basic training course. Upon his return, Rodrigo's eye for detail became quickly apparent as he mastered Blue Ridge's administrative and operating policies and procedures. He knew every detail of the first few stores' operating processes and had an equally detailed grasp of each store's trading profile. As a result, Blue Ridge Spain began to show an early profit.

Profitability was one thing; growth was another. Although the Blue Ridge concept seemed to be well received by Spanish consumers, Rodrigo was cautious and avoided rapid expansion. Moreover, one of the most important markets in Spain was Madrid. Rodrigo, who was Catalan,[2] was not fond of that city and avoided travelling to Madrid whenever possible. As personal contact with real estate agents, suppliers and others was necessary to develop new stores, Blue Ridge's expansion efforts remained confined to the Barcelona area. Terralumen, becoming impatient with Blue Ridge's sluggish growth, decided to focus more resources on its consumer product divisions and less on the restaurant business.

For Costas, one of the challenges during his first assignment as European director was to convince Terralumen to focus more on the joint venture and support faster growth. Rodrigo positively opposed more rapid growth, even though Alvarez, his direct superior, voiced support for the idea. Although he had been very cordial in his interactions with his American counterparts, Rodrigo believed himself to be in a much better position to judge whether or not the Spanish market would support faster growth.

In 1993, shortly after Costas was transferred to Singapore, Blue Ridge decided to send one of its own managers to oversee the Spanish joint venture. Under pressure, Rodrigo began to ignore criticism about the company's lack of growth. On one occasion, Rodrigo decided to close the Blue Ridge offices for an entire month just as Blue Ridge's international director of finance arrived in Barcelona to develop a five-year strategic plan.[3]

Terralumen finally replaced Rodrigo with a more proactive manager who had just returned from a successful assignment in Venezuela. Under the new leadership of Carlos Martin, Blue Ridge Spain began to prosper. Soon everyone was occupied with the difficult task of acquiring new sites, as well as recruiting and training employees.

COSTAS RETURNS TO EUROPE

In late 1998, Costas was transferred from Singapore to London to resume the role of European managing director. The previous director had performed poorly and it was felt that Costas had the experience needed to repair damaged relations with some of Blue Ridge's Middle Eastern joint venture partners. By this time, Blue Ridge had more than 600 stores in Europe and the Middle East.

One of Blue Ridge's more lucrative joint ventures was in Kuwait. However, the partners were threatening to dissolve the enterprise after the previous managing director became upset that the Kuwaitis were not meeting growth targets. The partners were especially concerned when they discovered that he had begun to seek other potential partners.

Costas decided to schedule a visit to Kuwait in early January. The partners counselled against the visit since Costas would be arriving during Ramadan,[4] and therefore would not be able to get much work done. Nevertheless Costas went to Kuwait, but spent nearly all of his time having dinners with the partners. He recalled:

> Most American managers would have considered my trip to be a waste of time, since I didn't get much "work" done. But it was a great opportunity to get to know the partners and to re-establish lost trust, and the partners felt good about having an opportunity to vent their concerns.

Costas returned to London confident that he had reassured the Kuwaiti partners that Blue Ridge was still committed to the joint venture.

Costas was also happy to be working with his old friend Alvarez again, as the two began working on an ambitious plan to develop a total of 50 stores by 2002 (see Exhibit 2).[5] As Blue Ridge Spain continued to grow, stores were opened in prime locations such as the prestigious Gran Via in Madrid and Barcelona's famous Las Ramblas shopping district. Costas and Alvarez, both of whom had been involved from the beginning of the joint venture, were delighted to see how far the company had come.

EUROPEAN REORGANIZATION

Delta began to take a more direct and active role in the management of Blue Ridge. In Europe, for example, Delta created a new regional VP position with responsibility for Europe, the Middle East and South Africa. When Costas became aware of the new position, he asked

	1998	2000	2001	2002	2003	2004
No. of Stores	12	24	37	50	65	80
Avg. Annual Sales	700	770	847	932	1,025	1,127
Gross Sales	$8,400	18,480	31,339	46,600	66,625	90,160
Cost of Goods Food	1,680	3,322	5,474	8,141	11,639	15,770
Cost of Goods Direct Labor	1,680	3,323	5,641	8,374	11,646	15,766
Advertising/Promotion	504	1,109	1,880	2,796	3,998	5,410
Occupancy Costs	1,260	1,848	3,129	4,660	6,663	9,016
Fixed Labor	840	1,478	2,507	3,728	5,330	7,213
Miscellaneous	168	277	470	699	999	1,352
Royalties to Blue Ridge U.S.	420	924	1,560	2,330	3,331	4,508
Total Costs	6,552	12,281	20,662	30,728	43,606	59,035
Contribution to G&A	1,848	6,199	10,677	15,872	23,019	31,125
Salaries and Benefits	875	1,531	2,641	3,493	4,580	5,899
Travel Expenses	120	240	300	375	469	586
Other	240	312	406	527	685	891
Occupancy Costs	240	720	828	952	1,095	1,259
Total G&A	1,475	2,803	4,175	5,347	6,829	8,635
Earnings Before Interest/Tax	$ 373	3,396	6,502	10,525	16,190	22,490
% of Gross Sales	4.44	18.38	20.75	22.59	24.30	24.94
Office Employees (Spain)	10	20	30	35	40	45

Exhibit 2   Development Plan Agreed Between Blue Ridge Restaurants and Terralumen (as of December 1998) (in US$000s)

Source: Company files.

- This plan was agreed before Yannis Costas' appointment to Blue Ridge Europe in late 1998.
- End 2004 plan: 20 stores in Barcelona, 30 in Madrid, 30 in other cities
- Capital Investment per store $700,000 to $1 million
- Site identification, lease or purchase negotiation, permits, construction: 18 to 24 months. Key Money is a part of occupancy costs. It is a sum paid to property owner at signing; varies by site $100,000 plus. Up to 1999, many owners wanted Key Money paid off the books, often in another country.
- Store Staffing (at the average sales level):
  - One manager, two assistants full time (larger stores three to four assistants)
  - 10 to 12 employees per eight-hour shift (40 hours per week); 980 employee hours per week
- Store employees needed by end of 1999: 300; by the end of 2004: 2,250 (approx.)
- Store employee attrition: approximately 25 per cent per year
- Dividends from earnings were declared periodically and then were shared equally between partners.

whether or not he was being considered, given his extensive experience in managing international operations. The human resources department in the United States explained that they wanted to put a seasoned Delta manager in place in order to facilitate the integration of the two companies.

Although disappointed, Costas understood the logic behind the decision. He also considered that by working under a seasoned Delta manager, he could develop contacts in the new parent company that might prove favorable to his career at some future date.

In May 1999, Costas received a phone call from Bill Sawyer, Blue Ridge's director of human resources, whom Costas had known for many years.

Sawyer: We hired someone from Proctor and Gamble. He's 35 years old and has a lot of marketing experience, and he worked in Greece for three years. You'll like him.

Costas: That's great. Have your people found anyone for the VP job yet?

The line was silent, then Sawyer replied in an apologetic tone, "He *is* the new VP." Costas was dumbfounded.

Costas: I thought you said you were planning to transfer a Delta veteran to promote co-operation.

Sawyer: Nobody from Delta wanted the job, so we looked outside the company. Kinsley (president, international division) wanted a "branded" executive, so we stole this guy from P&G.

Sawyer went on to explain that Mikael Södergran, who was originally from Finland, had no background in restaurant management, but had achieved a reputation for results in his previous role as a P&G marketing manager for the Middle East and Africa. He had recently been transferred from Geneva, Switzerland to P&G European headquarters in Newcastle upon Tyne.[6] Södergran was not happy in Newcastle and saw the Delta position both as an opportunity to take on greater responsibility and to move back to the civilization of London.

"You couldn't find anyone better than *that?*" Costas exclaimed. He was furious, not only for having been deceived about the need to have a Delta manager as VP, but also that he, with 10 years experience managing international operations, had been passed over in favor of someone with no experience managing operations, joint ventures or a large managerial staff. Nevertheless, the decision had been made, and Södergran was scheduled to start in two weeks.

THE DIRECTORS' MEETING

It was Södergran's first day on the job when he met with Blue Ridge Spain's board of directors to discuss a recently drafted consultants' report and negotiate new five-year growth targets (see Exhibit 3). The study, which was conducted by a leading U.S.-based management consulting firm, projected significant expansion potential for

	1998	2000	2001	2002	2003	2004
Stores						
Spain	12	30	65	100	135	170
France	0	10	20	55	90	130
Germany	3	15	30	65	100	150
Total	**15**	**55**	**115**	**220**	**325**	**450**
Regional Managers (London)	1	15	20	22	24	26
Country Staff/Managers	12	40	90	180	220	250
Store Employees	215	1,650	3,450	6,600	9,750	13,500

Exhibit 3 Consultants' Recommendations, Blue Ridge European Expansion (Selected Markets)

Source: Company files.

Blue Ridge in Spain, as well as in France and Germany, where Blue Ridge had no visible presence.[7] Delta also wanted to increase the royalties and fees payable from the joint venture partner in order to cover the cost of implementing new technologies, systems and services (see Exhibit 4).

Other Blue Ridge managers at the meeting included Yannis Costas and Donald Kinsley, Blue Ridge's new international president. Although Kinsley had formerly been president of a well-known family restaurant chain in the United States, this was his first international experience. Terralumen was represented by company president Andres Balaguer, Francisco Alvarez and Carlos Martin, Blue Ridge Spain's managing director.

Even before the meeting began, Delta's management team assumed that Terralumen was content to keep growth rates at their current levels and would have to be pressed to accept more aggressive targets. As expected, Martin protested that his team of 10 managers could not handle the introduction of 30 new stores a year, as suggested by the study. The meeting's cordial tone quickly dissolved when Södergran unexpectedly began to press the issue. His aggressive stance was not well received by Terralumen, who in turn questioned

	Blue Ridge U.S. Desired Objective	Blue Ridge Spain - Variance
Joint Venture Outlets		
Royalty	At least 4 per cent	No royalty
Fees	$20,000	$5,000
Term	10 years	5 years
Exclusivity	Avoid exclusivity	Spain, Canary Islands, Spanish Sahara, Beleares Islands
Advertising	5 per cent, right of approval	No obligations
Outlet Renewal Requirements	Renewal fee at least $2,000; Upgrading or relocation	No fee or other specific requirements
Delta Products	Required	No requirement
Development Program	Schedule for required development of territory	No requirement
Non-Competition	Restrictions on similar business	No provision
Assignment	First refusal right; approval of assignee	No provision
Sub-Franchising		
Contract privity	Blue Ridge U.S. should be a party and successor to franchisor	Blue Ridge cited; Blue Ridge succeeds on JV dissolution
Royalty	At least 4 per cent	None
Fees	$20,000	None
Joint Venture Operation		
Equity Participation	More than 50 per cent	50 per cent
Profit Distribution	At least 50 per cent	Additional 20 per cent when profits are greater than 20 per cent
Actual Management	Blue Ridge U.S. should appoint General Manager	General Manager is from JV partner
Board Control	Blue Ridge U.S. should have majority	Equal number of board members

Exhibit 4   Blue Ridge Spain, Exceptional Term Highlights

Source: Company files.

the ability of the consulting firm's young freshly minted American MBAs to understand the intricacy of the Spanish fast-food market. Balaguer simply brushed off the study as "a piece of American business school cleverness."

Södergran became visibly annoyed at Balaguer's refusal to consider Delta's targets. "The contract says that you are required to grow the markets," Södergran demanded. Balaguer, a tall, elegant man, slowly stood up, lifted a sheaf of papers and replied, "If this is your contract, and if we rely on a contract to resolve a partnership problem, well, here is what I think of it and of you." He walked across the room and dropped the papers into a garbage can. Then upon returning to his seat, he remarked in Spanish, "If this meeting had been conducted in my language, you would have known what I *really* think of you," in reference to Södergran.

After a long pause, Costas tried to mend the situation by pointing out that Terralumen had already committed to considerable growth, and had therefore already come some way toward Delta's expansions goals. He suggested that the two companies break to consider alternatives.

A few weeks later, Costas sent an e-mail to Södergran outlining his recommendations (see Exhibit 5).

EMERGING CONFLICTS

Costas tried his best to keep an open mind with regard to Södergran and to support him as best he could. However, as time went on, Costas began to seriously question Södergran's ability. He never seemed to interact with anyone except to conduct business. On one occasion Costas suggested that they have dinner with the joint venture partners. Södergran replied, "Oh, another dinner! Why don't we get some work done instead?"

Costas became more concerned after Södergran rented a suite two floors below the company offices "in order to have some peace and quiet." Some of the regional headquarters staff began to wonder if Södergran had taken on too much responsibility and whether he was avoiding them because of the pressure he was

under. Costas also believed that Södergran was uncomfortable with him, knowing that he resented not being offered the VP position.

In October 1999, Delta sent a finance manager from the snack foods division to become the company's new VP of finance for Europe. Geoff Dryden had no overseas experience, but when he was in the United States, he had been involved in several large international acquisitions. Dryden, who was originally from North Carolina, was pleasant, well polished in his manners and dress, and very proud of his accomplishments at Delta. For him, the European assignment was an opportunity to move out of finance and, if all went well, to assume greater managerial responsibilities.

Costas, who had specialized in finance when doing his MBA, had always done his own financial projections and was not very fond of the idea of surrendering this responsibility to someone else. Still, he helped Dryden as much as needed to make accurate projections, taking into account the unique aspects of each market.

A NEW STRATEGY

Over the next six months, the joint venture board of directors met four times. In the end, Terralumen committed to half the growth rate originally proposed by Delta and agreed to make upward revisions if market conditions proved favorable. Delta's managers were clearly becoming frustrated by what they perceived to be their partner's entrenched position.

After the final meeting, Södergran and Costas met with their European staff to discuss the results. Dryden asked why they put up with it. "Why don't we just buy them out?" he asked, calling to mind Delta's successful acquisition of a Spanish snack food company. Costas reminded Dryden that not only were snack foods and restaurants two very different enterprises, but all the joint venture managers had come from Terralumen, and most would leave Blue Ridge if Delta proceeded to buy out the partners.

After the meeting, Dryden discussed the situation privately with Södergran. Noting that a

---

From: Yannis Costas [Costas@deltafoods.co.uk]
Sent: Wednesday, July 7, 1999 10:16 AM
To: 'Sodergran@deltafoods.co.uk'
Subject: Key Issues – Here is what I believe we should be going for in Spain.

Mikael:
Here are my recommendations for Spain.

A. PRESERVE PARTNERSHIP
- Need a "real" market success while developing markets elsewhere in Europe.
  - Fuel interest of potential partners elsewhere.
  - Keep Blue Ridge and Delta believing in European potential.
  - Market for real testing of concepts and ideas.
  - No complete reliance on UK for "successes."

B. REVERSAL NOT EASY TO OVERCOME
- May have to pay a high premium to buy out joint venture.
- Will lose all key managers *(no substitutes on hand)*
- If we inherit "green field"
  - Down time close to 2 years.
  - Why? From decision to opening will take approximately nine months to one year.
  - In a new market this will be longer as we have no human resource experience to draw on.
  - Potential new partners need to be convinced about why we broke up with a "good" partner.
  - Real estate market does not want to deal with foreigners or raises the price.
- If the divorce is messy, we may be bound by the current contract for another year.

C. WORK TOWARDS ACHIEVING ACCEPTABLE INTEGRATION WITH OUR DESIRABLE CONTRACT FRAMEWORK OVER CURRENT DELTA PLANNING HORIZON (5 YEARS)
- Strong development schedule for joint venture.
- Royalty integration over mutually acceptable period.
- Designated "agency" for franchisees immediately, but fee flow indirectly to Blue Ridge only the amount *over* current terms with existing franchisees. Phase-in higher flow on schedule similar to royalties.
- Accept the notion of phasing in royalties as *we* phase in systems and services (If we *don't* phase them in there won't be much of a business anyhow!)

D. KEY RATIONALE
- We may have the perfect contract, but no stores to apply it to for three years – hence no income to cover overheads. *SO . . .*
- Accept half the current growth targets with the full expectation that by year 3 or 5, there will be a decent system for the contract's objectives to be meaningful.

Exhibit 5   Costas' Recommendations

---

major loan payment would soon be due to one of their creditors (a major Spanish bank), Dryden suggested holding back Delta's contribution, thereby forcing the joint venture company to default on the loan. If all went according to plan, the joint venture would have to be dissolved and the assets divided between the partners. This, he noted, would be much less expensive than trying to buy out their partner.

As expected, Terralumen requested matching funds from Delta, but Dryden simply ignored the request. However, unbeknownst to Dryden or anyone else at Delta, Alvarez proceeded to sell one of the company's prime real estate properties and lease back the store as a means of paying the loan.

Costas happened to be in Barcelona working on Blue Ridge Spain's marketing plan with Carlos Martin. One evening, Costas was dining with his counterparts from Terralumen when Alvarez mentioned the sale of the company's Barcelona property. Costas, who at the time was unaware of Dryden's strategy, was dismayed. Real estate values in Barcelona were expected to appreciate significantly over the short term. Selling now seemed illogical. Furthermore, Costas was surprised to discover that Alvarez had been given power of attorney to make real estate transactions on behalf of the joint venture. Alvarez explained:

> Quite a few years ago, when you were in Singapore, Blue Ridge decided to give Terralumen this authority in order to reduce the amount of travel required by your managers in the United States. Besides, as you know, it is not often that good properties become available, and when they do, we must act quickly.

On his return to London, Costas discussed the real estate transaction with Dryden, who, upon hearing the news, furiously accused Costas of "siding with the enemy." Costas was quick to remind Dryden that he had not been privy to the dissolution strategy and, besides, the whole thing was unethical. Dryden retorted, "Ethics? Come on, this is strategy, not ethics!"

Dryden was clearly surprised by the news, especially given the fact that Delta would never have given such powers of attorney to a joint venture partner. The company's lawyers could have warned Dryden, but he had not been very fond of the "old hands" at Blue Ridge's legal affairs department, and therefore had chosen to not disclose his plan. Now that his strategy had failed, an alternative plan would have to be devised.

Costas felt torn between his responsibility to his employer and his distaste for the company's new approach. This whole thing was a mistake, he believed. Costas discussed his views with Södergran:

> We cannot hope to take over the stores in Spain while simultaneously developing new markets in Germany and France. Where are we going to find suitable managerial talent to support this expansion? People in Europe don't exactly see the fast-food industry as a desirable place to grow their careers. And besides, Delta hasn't given us sufficient financial resources for such an undertaking.

Why don't we focus on France and Germany instead, and continue to allow Terralumen to run the Spanish operation? Revenue from Spain will help appease Delta headquarters while France and Germany suffer their inevitable growing pains. In the meantime, we can continue to press Terralumen for additional growth.

Södergran dismissed these concerns and instead gave Costas two weeks to develop a new dissolution strategy. Costas was furious that all his suggestions were so easily brushed off by someone who, he believed, had a limited understanding of the business.

On his way home that evening Costas recalled all the effort his former mentor, Gene Bennett, had put into the joint venture 16 years earlier, and all the good people he had had the privilege to work with in the intervening years. Just as all that work was about to pay off, the whole business was about to fall apart. Why hadn't he seen this coming? Where did the joint venture go wrong? Costas wondered what to do. Surely he had missed something. There had to be another way out.

NOTES

1. At the time, Blue Ridge Asia was one of the company's most successful operations with nearly 800 restaurants in Singapore, Malaysia, Taiwan and Thailand.

2. Catalonia, a state in northeast Spain, had a distinct culture and language (Catalan).

3. In Spain, the month of August was traditionally set aside for vacations.

4. Ramadan is the holy month of fasting ordained by the Koran for all adult Muslims. The fast begins each day at dawn and ends immediately at sunset. During the fast, Muslims are forbidden to eat, drink or smoke.

5. The plan to develop 50 stores was agreed to in 1998, prior to Costas' arrival.

6. Newcastle upon Tyne, United Kingdom, was an important industrial and transportation center located in northeast England (approximately 3 hours from London). It had a population of 263,000 (1991 census).

7. Large restaurant chains served only four per cent of fast food meals in Spain, compared with 15 per cent for the rest of Western Europe, and 50 per cent for the United States.

APPENDIX 1: MANAGEMENT STYLES FOR SELECTED NATIONALITIES[1]

Spain

In Spain, a strong differentiation of social classes and professional occupations exists. Business communication is often based on subjective feelings about the topic being discussed. Personal relationships are very important as a means to establish trust, and are usually considered more important than one's expertise. Established business contacts are essential to success in Spain. Therefore, it is important to get to know someone prior to conducting business transactions. Only intimate friends are invited to the home of a Spaniard, but being invited to dinner is usual.

Spaniards are not strictly punctual for either business or social events, and once a business meeting is started, it is improper to begin with a discussion of business. National pride is pervasive, as is a sense of personal honor. To call someone "clever" is a veiled insult. Only about 30 per cent of local managers speak English, while French is often the second language of choice for many older Spaniards.

Greece

Greek society employs a social hierarchy with some bias against classes, ethnic groups and religions. For Greeks, interpersonal relationships are very important when conducting business, and decisions are often based on subjective feelings. Much importance is placed on the inherent trust that exists between friends and extended families. Authority lies with senior members of any group, and they are shown great respect. They are always addressed formally.

While punctuality is important, it is not stressed. Greeks have a strong work ethic and often strive for consensus.

United States

Americans are very individualistic, with more stress placed on self than on others. Friendships are few and usually based on a specific need. Personal contacts are considered less important than bottom line results. Americans have a very strong work ethic, but a person is often considered to be a replaceable part of an organization. Great importance is placed on specialized expertise. Punctuality is important.

Business is done at lightning speed. In large firms, contracts under $100,000 can often be approved by a middle manager after only one meeting. Often companies and individuals have a very short-term orientation and expect immediate rewards. Small talk is very brief before getting down to business, even during dinner meetings and social gatherings.

Finland

Finns have a strong self orientation. More importance is placed on individual skills and abilities than on a person's station in life. Decisions are based more on objective facts than personal feelings. Privacy and personal opinions are considered very important. Finns often begin business immediately without any small talk. They are very quiet and accustomed to long periods of silence, but eye contact is important when conversing. Authority usually rests with the managing director. Punctuality is stressed in both business and social events.

---

1. Based on *Kiss, Bow, or Shake Hands: How to do Business in Sixty Countries,* Adams Media, 1994. The descriptions do not account for individual differences within each nationality or culture.

TEQSWITCH INC.: BUSINESS IN BUENOS AIRES

Prepared by Ken Mark under the supervision of Professor Christina Cavanagh

INTRODUCTION

It was the middle of August 2001, and Kyle Keppie, vice-president international of TeqSwitch Inc. had just received confusing news from their joint venture partner, Unitas S.A. in Buenos Aires, Argentina: Unitas was preparing to walk away from their Cdn$15 million agreement to sell TeqSwitch's networking equipment in Latin America.

The relationship between Toronto-based TeqSwitch and Unitas had seemed fine, thought Keppie. Early on, TeqSwitch had established an office in Buenos Aires to help Unitas sales personnel in the business development process. What in the world was wrong?

BACKGROUND OF THE JOINT VENTURE DEAL

In August 2000, James Munroe, vice-president international for TeqSwitch had signed a Memorandum of Understanding (MOU) with the partners of Unitas, a spinoff company of a well-known Argentinian consulting firm.

The MOU stipulated that TeqSwitch would sell Cdn$15 million of its cutting-edge networking equipment at 15 per cent less than Canadian wholesale prices to Unitas, over a period of two years. In addition, TeqSwitch would acquire a 15 per cent stake in Unitas by issuing stock options to the four partners at Unitas.

A final agreement was signed in September and the news media were notified. TeqSwitch's stock soared 20 per cent to Cdn$12.20 that day.

Through his network of contacts, Keppie had hired Rick Lang, a consultant who had worked in Mexico for the last eight years, to be TeqSwitch's contact with Unitas. While in Mexico, Lang had worked for a large multinational telecommunications company, dealing extensively with Mexican government officials and large Mexican businesses. Essentially, Keppie wanted Lang to represent TeqSwitch in Argentina, to monitor the operations of Unitas and ultimately to guide Unitas representatives along in the sales process.

TEQSWITCH

Founded in 1993, TeqSwitch was the brainchild of two Bell Canada engineers, Kyle Keppie and David Jacobson, who believed they could design, produce and market faster networking equipment. Technology available at that time could only transmit at two megabits per second— Keppie and Jacobson knew that they could design equipment to transmit at more than 50 megabits per second. Frustrated by the bureaucratic new product approval process at Bell, they decided to start their own company, luring away six fellow engineers. After securing seed financing from a regional venture capital firm, they were able to produce and launch their new product, the TS-30 (transmitting at 30 megabits per second) within two years. Within four years, they went public.

Five years after they began, TeqSwitch counted 120 employees in three countries: Canada, England and Australia. Their sales grew into the tens of millions. Careful about managing their cash flow, Keppie and Jacobson were able to survive the stock market decline from mid-2000 to 2001 without having to return to the capital markets.

Interested in diversifying their customer base, Keppie instructed that TeqSwitch's business development efforts were to focus on Latin America. Here, he thought, was a market prime for TeqSwitch's advanced products. Most large multinational corporations were enamored with the Asian markets, including China, Japan, South Korea and Southeast Asia. Keppie had noticed that there were very few companies targeting Latin American countries. Coupled with the fact that he had contacts in Argentina (and no contacts in Asia), Keppie was confident that TeqSwitch could first expand into Latin America.

The telecommunications equipment market in Latin America was nascent—most companies were using equipment that dated from the early 1990s—Keppie thought that there lay a tremendous opportunity to establish a lead in the market.

EXPANSION PLANS

Keppie explained:

> We cannot do everything, enter every market, pitch every customer, we have a current list of North American companies we'd like to have relationships with—potential co-marketers, manufacturers and service providers. But the real growth will be partnering with firms in Latin America.

"Relationships are the foundation of international business and we know that. It's all about people who know people," mentioned Munroe. Through their Australian business contacts, Keppie and Munroe got to know four Argentinian immigrants who were working in the telecommunications industry. By 1999, these four were lured back to Buenos Aires by a major strategy consulting company.

Keppie decided to entice the four Argentinians into starting up a sales company selling TeqSwitch components. The four were very receptive and began a dialogue that lasted eight months.

WORKING OUT AN AGREEMENT

TeqSwitch believed that it would enjoy steady growth, with (long-term) growing demand for telecommunications equipment around the world outstripping supply. By signing a substantial deal in Latin America, TeqSwitch would take steps towards gaining credibility outside of the English-speaking world. Thus, Keppie decided to work on a deal with the four Argentinians, who now called their startup Unitas S.A. The four partners assured Keppie that they had a general director, a sales manager and one information technology (IT) support person. Even with this force, Unitas was by no means a large entity, however, the partners assured TeqSwitch that they could draw upon their own network of contacts, in the event that additional personnel were needed.

Negotiations between TeqSwitch and Unitas stalled in late 1999 and early 2000, as both parties disagreed on terms such as revenue progression and exclusivity. Keppie began to worry that these disagreements might be a precursor of things to come, but he needed to drive ahead to gain market presence in Argentina.

Because of the need to move quickly, TeqSwitch was willing to make concessions. In exchange for exclusivity, TeqSwitch wanted to extract volume commitments from Unitas. Since options for TeqSwitch stock were to be granted to Unitas, Keppie wanted guarantees in return. Unitas was also looking for favorable discounts, an increase of between 10 per cent to 30 per cent, relative to what TeqSwitch was selling to other carriers and customers. Effectively, Unitas wanted to be able to sell to their customers at the same prices that TeqSwitch was selling to its customers. From Unitas, TeqSwitch wanted strict quarterly performance targets for revenue progression, but Unitas balked, only wanting to commit to a total of Cdn$15 million over two years.

POST-AGREEMENT

In July 2000, Unitas returned to the negotiating table and a compromise was worked out to eliminate the "show stoppers." Moving on from the MOU, Munroe wanted to start understanding Unitas's business plan, sales strategy, target customers and the resources that it would allocate to its plan to become part of the TeqSwitch network. Munroe was assured that everything would go smoothly—a copy of the Unitas business plan would be forwarded to him as soon as possible. By September, Munroe received the extensively detailed business plan and was pleased. He shared the plan with his senior management in Toronto.

Keppie was cautiously optimistic, and decided to proceed with establishing a "beach head" office in Buenos Aires, in close proximity to Unitas. Lang, freshly hired, was fluent in Spanish, and was assigned the task of being TeqSwitch's representative in Buenos Aires. His task was to ensure that Unitas "learned the ropes" with as little trouble as possible.

"We need Unitas to be TeqSwitch Latin America," said Munroe. "We needed to issue options tied to revenue to drive motivation. To facilitate communication, I expect to fly to Buenos Aires at least once per month to handle the details."

TeqSwitch's Partner Management Strategy

Keppie and Munroe believed that the two biggest issues in their minds were trust and turnover. They needed to know that both parties (referring to Lang and the salespeople at Unitas) were working with TeqSwitch's interests in mind. They were careful to set incentives and sales targets in collaboration with Unitas, ensuring that a solid commitment was achieved.

TeqSwitch management also believed that recognition played a large role in motivating sales. They considered updates to each other's companies regarding the progress the salespeople would be making.

Slow Startup Process

Lang was in daily contact with Keppie and Munroe, keeping a log of his meetings with Unitas representatives. He assured them that the training was on track.

Keppie and Munroe expected that it would take a few months for Unitas to begin selling. By April 2001, TeqSwitch was beginning to get frustrated with the "lack of action." Munroe's frequent visits had led him to believe that things were going as planned. Whenever he inquired about the progress Unitas was making towards sales of the Cdn$15 million worth of equipment in the year and a half that remained, he was told:

> My friend, you have to put aside your North American business attitude. This is Latin America and we do things differently here. Business is based on trust, and trust is not gained in a day, or a week. It takes time. We are motivated to sell, yes, but we've got to do it our way.

Now What

In August 2001, Keppie was preparing to welcome the four Unitas partners for their second visit to Toronto (the first meeting in Toronto had taken place during the initial negotiations). TeqSwitch was ready to launch its next generation of products, the TS-50 (50 megabits per second) and the partners at Unitas had hinted that they were interested in attending the launch.

Two days before they were scheduled to arrive, Keppie received an e-mail message:

> Dear Kyle,
>   We regret to inform you that our efforts to sell your TeqSwitch products have not been successful. Believe me, we've tried our best. We don't believe that your product meets the requirements of telecommunications firms here in Latin America. Because of this, we have decided to request termination of our previously signed agreement. It is in both our best interests.

TEXTRON LTD.

Prepared by Lawrence A. Beer

        Version: (A) 2002-01-24

INTRODUCTION

Gary Case, executive vice-president of Textron Ltd., sat at his desk and slowly drew a circle around the words *ethics* and *social responsibility*. Above the circle he wrote in bold letters the phrase "public opinion," and sat back to ponder his symbolic illustration of a potential problem that only he seemed to envision.

Case was thinking ahead and letting his mind focus on an issue that seemed out of the realm of the tenants of basic managerial principles that his undergraduate and MBA studies had prepared him for during his scholastic years. While he well appreciated the strategic decision-making concepts of running a transnational business, he felt himself personally wondering how to approach the complex subject of applying global ethics and social responsibility to an international venture that was being pushed on his company.

BACKGROUND

Textron Ltd. was a 65-year-old, family-held business based in Youngstown, Ohio. As a producer of cotton and sponge fabricated items for the beauty trade, selling to intermediate users as components in their make-up compact cases as well as direct to the retail trade for onward sale to consumers, the company was under constant attack from Far Eastern manufacturers. The need to enter into some type of offshore manufacturing enterprise was now evident in order to maintain a cost competitive position for the firm to continue to prosper and grow.

As a maker of cotton puffs for the application of make-up cosmetics, the company had grown from a loft in Brooklyn, New York, back in the mid-1930s to a medium-sized enterprise with sales of $25 million and pre-tax earnings of $1 million plus. In the category of cosmetic applicators, Textron's fine reputation had been built on years of excellent service to the trade with attention to detail. Using at first the hand sewing abilities of seamstresses from the garment centres of lower Manhattan, the company had been a pioneer in developing customized machinery to produce quality cotton puffs to the precise custom requirements of modern cosmetic manufacturers. Today, 100 per cent virgin cotton rolls would enter Textron's factory at one end and exit as soft velour pads in numerous shapes, contoured sizes and colors at the other end of the process.

These puffs would be either sewn or glued with ribbon bands and satin coverings bearing the well-known brand names of the major franchised cosmetics companies of the world from Revlon, Estee Lauder, Maybelline and Max Factor as well as numerous others. They might also contain the names of retail store house brands or the internationally recognized trademarks of their own company. Currently, a new collection had been created through a licensing arrangement bearing the name of a highly respected fashion beauty magazine, whose instant recognition with the teenage trade was propelling the company to new sales levels. While historically Textron Ltd. primarily had produced components, supplying cosmetic companies with custom applicators tailored to their cosmetic ingredient requirements, the growth of its retail business in this sub-category was developing at a rapid pace. Major drug store chains, supermarkets and specialty shops featured Textron brands and their lines were becoming synonymous with the best in cosmetic applicators and assorted beauty accessories. With the launch of an additional range under the guise of a high fashion authority, featuring highly stylized "cool shapes" and "hot colors" designed to entice younger adolescent buyers, their reputation was achieving enhanced public notice. Such products using uniquely descriptive trendy phrases evoked an image of "hip to use applicators" and a whole new generation of teenage users was being developed.

The firm also was a key purveyor to the entertainment industry directly servicing the Hollywood movie and TV production companies, Broadway and the theatrical community, along with indirect sales to professional make-up artists and modeling studios thanks to the quickly developing beauty store trade. All in all, the future for Textron Ltd. was most promising.

Gary Case, a college friend of the company's president and principal owner, was brought into the business because of his experience at the retail sales and marketing level. The chief executive officer, who possessed an engineering background, was more than capable of overseeing the manufacturing side of the business; however, the strong movement of the organization into direct consumer goods, coupled with the overall expansion of the company, necessitated Case's hiring.

As the company began to prosper in the early 1970s, other stateside competitors emerged, but none could match the quality and inherent reputation of Textron Ltd. Their attention to detail and expertise of their original equipment manufacturer (OEM) sales staff servicing the franchise cosmetic companies gave Textron a competitive edge. They were called upon to work closely with their industrial customers to develop cotton puffs that matched the trends in new cosmetic ingredients and application methods at the research and development (R&D) stage of such developments. Such progressive fashion-oriented but facially skin-sensitive cosmetic formulas required applicators that matched the demanding specifications of these new advances in the cosmetic field. Cotton materials were needed to sustain the look on the skin and provide the user with the same result that the cosmetic cream, lotion or powder promised. While women, the prime purchasers of such products, wanted to obtain the dramatic results

the franchise cosmetic companies advertised, professional make-up artists had long known that the choice of applicators to transfer the pressed powder in the compact, the lotion in the bottle or the cream in the jar, was the key to the process. The right puff was therefore needed to compliment the make-up process.

In the late 1980s, Far Eastern manufactures of cosmetic applicators began to emerge, offering cheaper versions of such items. While the detailed processing of the raw cotton material used in such production was inferior to the quality and exacting details of those manufactured by Textron Ltd., the cost considerations necessitated a strong consideration of their offerings by the company's clients. As textile manufacturing began to develop in the Indochina region and more and more American firms brought their expertise to the area, the overall quality of goods as well as the base materials used began to improve. As an outgrowth of improvements in the generic textile business emerged, better methods of production, selection of raw materials and attention to quality filtered down into the cosmetic cotton applicator category.

Case, along with the president of the company, David Grange, and the head of product development group, Nancy Adams, had made periodic trips to the Hong Kong Beauty Exhibition to constantly gauge Far Eastern competitors. For many years, they observed a display of poor offerings and found themselves returning from such trips visits confident that the threat of offshore competition was not yet emerging as a viable alternative for their clients. Their regular customers, both beauty companies and retailing organizations, were rarely evident at such conventions and hence their positive feelings were continuously strengthened.

CURRENT ISSUES

Over the last few years, however, it became evident that startup companies, beginning as derivative plants of the large textile manufacturers throughout China, Taiwan, Korea and Thailand, could become a real danger to their ever-growing global business. While many of these enterprises still produced inferior merchandise, Textron noticed that a number of their American competitors were now forming alliances with such organizations. These associations brought with them the knowledge of how to deal with the beauty industry both in America and Europe, instilling in them a deep appreciation for quality and endurance of raw materials to work with the new cosmetic preparations. Once such considerations took a foothold and a reputation for delivering such competitively detailed quality merchandise with vastly lower costs was discovered by Textron's clients, the company could be in for some rough times ahead. During the last visit to the Hong Kong show, Grange had bumped into a number of his key franchise cosmetic component buyers as well as a few of his retail chain merchandise managers. They had all acknowledged the quality advances made by these emerging new players. It was felt however that the distance of such suppliers from their own factories and key decision-making staffs and the fact that the shapes and designs were still not up to the innovative expertise of the Textron company created a hesitation among clients wanting to deal with them. Grange knew full well however that with advanced global communication technology and the alliances with American-based representative organizations, the gap would be closed shortly. If such alterations were made and a fully competitive quality product could be offered with the inherent deep labor and overhead cost advantages that Far Eastern firms possessed, Textron was due for some major sales competition in the future.

After their last trip to the Asian convention in September of 1999, Grange and Case spent the hours on the return trip discussing strategic alternatives for the company in the years ahead. This wasn't the first time such matters were approached and, in fact, two years earlier, the company entered into an alliance with a United Kingdom manufacturer for the production on a joint basis of cosmetic sponges. Grange had always been reluctant to place his production

facilities out of his geographical everyday domain. He was a "hands on" entrepreneur who felt strongly that all facets of one's business should be at arm's reach. Grange was deeply committed to his people and his door was always open to everyone in his organization. He was involved in every area of the business and it was not until Case joined Textron that Grange began to relinquish control over selective daily operations. This desire to closely preside over and monitor his people was born out of a heritage of family involvement as exemplified by his father. His dad had instilled in Grange a great empathy for workers and staff, and even today the company's culture still carried such roots of benevolent carrying.

When the firm had moved from the greater New York area to Youngstown, key personnel were given liberal incentives to move to the new location, and great care was given to those who could not make the journey. Still today, the company showed great pride in its relationship with employees. Textron's human resources department was not merely a conduit for processing applications for employment and overseeing payroll but a large fully functional multitalented group that ran off-site improvement seminars and cross training exercises. Besides offering a full array of benefit packages, the company had a well-supervised child-care facility on the premises at no charge to employees. The human resources director attended all managerial meetings, thereby maintaining a strong presence in all company decision-making and the position was considered on par with senior management executives. The commitment to maintaining hands-on control of his organization and the strong, caring relationship with his people made for a close-knit family and a kind of patriarchal role for Grange. He prided himself on the fact that union attempts to organize his factory labor force never got off the ground, as his employees felt that they were best represented by Grange himself.

Years ago, a satellite retail packaging assembly plant and distribution facility in San Antonio, Texas, which had been part of the purchase of a small professional beauty applicator business, was dissolved in favor of consolidating all operations in Youngstown. All personnel at this redundant factory were given an opportunity to relocate in Youngstown or they received good termination benefits.

The United Kingdom alliance was finalized due to Grange's long and valued friendship with the principal of that company. The two also shared similar feelings about managing people and a common cultural background. Both parties had spent many years working together and enjoyed a special relationship, which had been fostered by the fact that the U.K. managing director's family resided in Ohio, thereby bringing the two executives together on a monthly basis as the Englishman came home often. Grange also visited the British facility every two months and the two executives spoke weekly on the phone. Both men viewed the alliance as more of a partnership than an arm's length sourcing arrangement.

Grange always felt that one of his prime differentiated product marketing characteristics was that up until the U.K. association for sponge material applicators, all his products were made in the United States. He believed that such designation symbolized quality of material and manufacturing excellence as well as innovative styling and technologically advanced, state-of-the-art compliance. Even with the English sponge production unit, all the cotton puff applicators were still made in the States. To drive home this important selling issue, all packages of retail cotton finished goods bore the American flag proudly stamped on them next to the words "Made in the U.S.A." Grange had recently seen consumer products bearing the slogan "Designed in America" as well as "Product Imported From China and Packaged in the U.S.A." but felt that the global customer still valued the U.S.A. slogan indicating the country of origin on his retail line. But in Grange's recent discussions with component buyers in the cosmetic and fragrance industry, such designation did not seem so important, given the fact that both the sponges and cotton puffs were slightly undistinguishable or hidden parts in the total presentation of the

makeup compact, the accent being on the brand name, ingredients and plastic case; imported items could be utilized if quality was maintained. The recent acceptance of the sponges made in England by Textron's clients gave credence to the fact that quality, price and service were the prime criteria for the industry, rather than the country of origin.

DECISION-MAKING TIME

Following the conference on the plane ride home from the Orient, Grange and Case had assembled their managerial staff and charged them with putting together a preliminary plan to form an association with a Far Eastern manufacturer of cotton puffs. At the initial briefing meeting, samples of cotton puff merchandise collected from a variety of Far Eastern producers were evaluated by the manufacturing quality control people as well as by representatives of the marketing and sales groups from the retail and OEM divisions. The immediate consensus was that with a little direction in fashion styling composition and adjustment in fixative dyes to sustain color in the cotton velour, a quality comparative range to supplement their domestic manufacturing output could be produced abroad. When Case presented the factory cost quotations for the samples being reviewed, the vice-president of finance exclaimed, "Such values were way below our own manufacturing standard costs before administrative overhead." He further added that "even with anticipated duty and freight via containerized shipments, the projected landed price at our door would eclipse our costs by a good 20 per cent or more reduction." When Case noted that, "These foreign price quotations were based on minimum quantities and could be subject to economies of scale discounting," all participants quickly realized that their projected stock keeping unit (SKU) sales for 2000 would easily allow for even greater margins.

When the meeting broke up, Chris Jenkins, the vice-president of finance, cornered Grange and Case in the hallway.

Guys, if these numbers can be confirmed, and if future production of these Chinese puffs can be modified to accommodate our quality stability color standards and slightly altered for design modification, we need to jump on this as soon as possible. Better still, if we can manufacture over there ourselves via our own factory or through a joint venture, our profit potential would be magnified at least three times.

ALTERNATIVE PROPOSALS

It was now six months since that initial meeting. In the interim, Case had been back and forth a number of times, holding substantial discussions with what was now a short list of two potential alliance candidates, both of which were co-operative ventures, with local Chinese governmental bodies holding a share in them. While these companies' abilities to alter their production to accommodate changes in the color additive process and make design modifications were verified, and the exchange of cost quotations were proceeding well, Case had not yet proposed the final type of alliance he wanted.

In the back of his mind, Case wanted to form his own subsidiary but felt that such initial market entry strategy was both costly and risky, given the large investment required. Besides Case and Grange, the company did not have any other executives familiar with managing abroad. Given such considerations, Case's discussions to date with his Chinese associates had produced only two feasible alternatives to begin the relationship:

1. An initial three-year guaranteed outsourcing purchase agreement wherein, following the detailed specifications of Textron Ltd., supplies of cotton powder puffs would be produced at base prices. Such quotations would be subject to preset quantity discounting but offset slightly by an inflationary yearly adjustment. The right to pre-approve the samples of each and every shipment before departure would also be included in the arrangement. In essence a simplistic arm's-length purchasing association was contemplated.

2. The creation of a joint venture wherein Textron Ltd. would own 48 per cent of the company and the alliance partner would own the rest. Textron would be primarily responsible for sales and marketing worldwide along with periodic on-site technical assistance as to product design, quality assurances and engineering considerations by their technical staff. The plant facility, the manufacturing process itself and everyday operations would be under the direct control of the Chinese partner. Textron Ltd. would contribute a yet-to-be-finalized small dollar investment to help upgrade machinery and in general modernize the physical facilities. The partners would share the revenue generated by the sales efforts of Textron for the items produced in the plant.

Although exacting details of either proposed strategy needed to be worked out, with the former option requiring more legal and regulatory considerations, Case was confident that both situations could be accomplished. With the additional help of some local Chinese alliance specialists whom Case had utilized during the days when he had actually lived and worked in Hong Kong for a former employer, all seemed to be progressing nicely. Case knew he had to give additional thought to many other operational and administrative issues, and he wanted to obtain some sound advice from his internal teams before deciding which alternative to pursue. Questions as to the capital investment and how such funds would be utilized would require more discussions with the potential partners if the joint-venture route was chosen, but such issues would be addressed during Case's next trip to the Far East.

CHINA AS THE PRIME CHOICE OF SUPPLY

The focus on China was due mainly to Case's familiarity with the people and business environment. He felt very comfortable, given his prior experiences in the region and his knowledgeable appreciation of the culture and the way relationships were constructed. Beyond Case's personal considerations, the Chinese manufacturers he had encountered already had the necessary machinery and were well versed in the production of cotton puffs. Many already supplied the worldwide beauty trade, but did not possess the sophisticated marketing and sales competencies practised by Textron, nor had they gained the reputation Textron historically enjoyed with the franchise cosmetic industry. An alliance with Textron would enhance the Chinese manufacturers' technical abilities and provide them with a wider entrée to the trade. The annual beauty show in Hong Kong attracted a global following, which would allow Textron to even create an offshore sales office and showroom close to the prime production facility to entertain prospective clients. Besides the Chinese connection, Case had opened initial discussion with makers of sponge applicators and other beauty accessories in Japan and Korea so that his trips to the China could be combined with other business opportunities he wanted to pursue in the Far East.

Case had entertained pursuing a Mexican manufacturer, as he had had prior dealings with companies producing a variety of cotton products in Mexico. Given the background of many of them in the cotton and aligned textile trade, this seemed a natural consideration, especially given the NAFTA accords and geographical proximity to Textron's major market, the United States. All potential companies Case visited, however, were located in the central part of the country, none near the border where the *Maquiladores* were available. Case's Mexican contacts were not familiar with the specific production of cotton puff applicators as their cotton experience was in the manufacturing of surgical dressings, bandages, feminine hygiene pads and simple cotton balls. They would need to buy machinery and train a staff in such manufacturing operations. If Textron would fund such investment and provide technical assistance, a number of them agreed to manage such a facility on the U.S.-Mexican border through a joint venture. Case was hesitant to provide the

funding, and he was worried that starting up a new plant would not let Textron achieve the inherent historical benefits that the more mature existing production in China would instantly allow.

Besides the economic considerations, Case found the Mexican manager's attitude a bit troublesome. Textron had once used a Mexican plant to supply, in final packaged form, cotton pads for the removal of facial cosmetic make-up. While his dealings with the principals of this family owned and operated business was most cordial and personally gratifying, Case had found that their attention to manufacturing details left much to be desired. The quality inspection of the raw cotton coming into their plants had given Case cause for concern. Many openly told him they mixed first quality fibres with "seconds" and remnants from the textile manufacturers in their local areas to achieve cost efficient production. As Textron always claimed its materials for cotton puff applicators were of "100 per cent virgin cotton," such an assertion using might be difficult to enforce and supervise, given the pronouncements by his prior supplier. When discussions as to the importance of schedules to insure timely supply arose, the Mexican sources seemed to give the impression that they would do their best to comply. This slight hesitation bothered Case, as his component buyers demanded on-time delivery and were always changing specifications at the last minute.

Case had deep reservations on the business competencies exhibited by such Mexican firms, as his communications with them in the past, wherein days would go by before he heard from them, had left a poor impression on him. Many times, when he had repetitively inquired by e-mail, fax and telephone as to shipping dates for packaged finished products, he was eventually told that third-party suppliers of the packaging materials for the cotton pads caused the assembly delay. Inquiring further, during a visit with his Mexican supplier, Case learned that when local Mexican firms contract with each other, time promises are flexible and it seemed that an attitude of "when they are available, we get them" took precedence over definite schedules. During the year the company utilized the Mexican supplier, not one shipment was dispatched within the required period, and Case had given up contacting them, even paraphrasing the Mexican explanation when queried by his own inventory/warehouse manager.

The decision to go with a Chinese partner in some format seemed to be the best solution.

CASE'S PERSONAL REFLECTIONS

As Case pondered what other matters needed to be resolved, his mind began to focus on his three-year posting, back in the early 1990s in Hong Kong, with an electronics manufacturer to oversee their Chinese network of suppliers. When Case and his family had first arrived in the then-British colony, the excitement of this new foreign land and its unique culture had made a lasting impression on him. He had marveled at the sights, sounds, smells and overall ambience of the city state that mixed East and West. Coming from a middle class American lifestyle, the treatment the family received was like being transformed into a rich conclave of the elite. His children went to a specialized English-type boarding school and rarely mixed with local natives of their own age. In fact, such young Chinese children were lucky to get a basic elementary school education before being forced out into the real world and into the working community. The outskirts of the city, and even sections within, contained deep pockets that were below some extreme poverty levels Case had seen in other depressed regions of the world. Within a severely overpopulated area that was strained every day with new immigrants from the mainland, the concept of work, any job, took on a new meaning. People would work for what seemed like slave wages to Case, and he wondered how they survived, just attaining a mere sustenance level. His wife could afford household maids and cooks that were more like indentured servants than domestic employees. They worked long hours at meagre wages and never complained.

During Case's visits to plants in mainland China, both during his expatriate posting years and subsequent trips back in the mid-1990s, the conditions at such facilities had initially deeply disturbed him. The environments he witnessed were nothing like he had ever seen in the United States. Factories were like prison compounds. The laborers seemed to toil at their job stations never looking up, never smiling and always looked like they were staring out with blank facial expressions. Rarely had Case seen them take a break, with many workers eating lunch at their desks and at their worktables or machinery. He seldom witnessed the laborers even taking bathroom breaks. The air in the facilities was always stale with no ventilation except for a few fans, and it was always very hot or very cold, depending on the outside temperature. He witnessed children, younger it seemed than his two adolescent kids, toiling in the plants alongside the elderly. He watched infants placed alongside their mothers on the floor of the factories being rocked by feet as the mothers' hands moved on the table above them. As these visits become more frequent, Case's disdain for such initially horrific working conditions began to lessen and he began to accept what he saw.

Many times, in social conversations with other executives and managers, Case had voiced his concerns about the treatment of the workers. He listened as they tried to get him to understand and appreciate that while the conditions were terrible, the alternative might be even worse. With the expanded population, growing at a massive rate, the supply of people outstripped employment opportunities. In order to survive, people would take any job and children as well as the elderly all had to work. Public governmental assistance was not only inadequate but almost impossible to administer, even if the resources could be found. The old communist philosophy of all society working for the good of the common proletariat, and hence the state, had been indoctrinated with the birth of the Mao regime; people saw it as their duty and obligation to endure hard times.

Case's Chinese friends had often remarked that if China were to catch up to the Western capitalistic nations and be a participant in the world's expanded trading economies, its people were its greatest competitive asset. In order to be a member in the world community and to provide enrichment for future generations, sacrifices had to be made. Capital for the improvement of factory environmental conditions was secondary to the need to update basic machinery and gain technology. The government had to build a sound internal infrastructure of roadways, rail and port facilities to ship its goods before the physical welfare of its people could be considered. With power still a scarce commodity, any electricity flowing into a factory needed to be first used to run the machinery and not for hot or cool air to be produced. The only way to achieve the goal of making mainland China competitive with the rest of the world was through the exportation route which was founded in the country's ability to produce cheaper goods than the rest of the globe. This simple fact necessitated low labor and overhead operating costs that contributed to poor working conditions in the factories.

Obviously, Case understood this economic argument was the main reason his company—and therefore he himself—had come to the region. In order for his own organization to remain competitive in the cotton puff business both at home and abroad, it would have no choice but to locate a portion of its operations in China or some other emerging nation.

Case had seen the TV footage of the protesters at the 2000 WTO conference in Seattle who had destroyed that meeting and in latter months had done the same in Washington, D.C., and Ottawa, Canada. He heard them voicing and physically demonstrating their deep concerns against governments and transnational companies as to worker rights and environmental conditions in emerging and developing nations. Case was well aware of the attention the press gave to large multinational companies like Levi Strauss, Reebok and others over their treatment of employees accusing them of almost slavelike practices in their foreign factories. Even personalities that lent their names to the labels of garments, like Kathy Lee Gifford, had come under strong pressure for allowing their third party licensees in the United States to operate sweat shops and mistreat workers. Companies that did not even have a direct relationship wherein they exercised straight control over employee conditions were still questioned about the suppliers they used

abroad as the social conscience of the world seem to be focused on these issues.

Although Case himself deplored the hiring of adolescent children, he understood the economic and social context that existed in China for their use. China wasn't America. Young kids grew up much faster and much more was expected of them as contributors to the family unit. Even with the government mandate, made within the framework of the message of a collective good of the nation for families to have only one child, did not alleviate the problem. In fact, in many families it just made the burden deeper. Most Chinese families were made up of extended relatives who grouped together to pool their resources for their common survival. In these family units, all members had to work. The simple luxury of going to a public school, playing games and watching TV, as American children enjoyed, was not part of their world. In numerous families, children, mostly young girls, were sent away from their rural villages to emerging urban industrial centres to look for work. After paying large portions of their meagre weekly salaries back to their employees for dormitory housing and food within the confines of the factory compound, any amount left over was sent to the family.

Even the elderly felt such pressure to work, as retirement after years of service and a reasonable pension was almost a non-existent consideration. No true governmental program like social security existed, and the family had to care for the elderly in their homes, putting a great burden on the whole extended unit. Political dissidents and even criminals were conscripted into the labor force to help offset the cost of the State having to provide for them. Plant conditions, treatment of workers and even caring about the environment were not primary issues for an emerging country trying to first find work for its population during the transformation process into a competitive world economic nation.

Case pondered if it was time for the company to prepare a written corporate moral compass. Should it publish a code of ethics, as many transnational firms had been doing? What should it consist of, what specific criteria defining norms of behavior should be stated? and should it be incorporated as an obligation in the arm's length purchasing agreement being considered with the Chinese supplier? If the announced provisions were violated, should this be viewed as an automatic right for Textron to terminate the agreement, or should there be a time frame in which to cure such conditions? Case also wondered how his firm could monitor such matters to ensure compliance. If the alternative joint venture were chosen, how should such values be incorporated into the partnership agreement and how should Case process such matters during the negotiation?

Case was comfortable with discussions on costs, quality and delivery specifications as they had a finite measurable logic to them. Social responsibility and ethics touched upon many emotional areas that were harder to define. He had seen firsthand how different cultures approached them from divergent viewpoints, and he had gained a respect for the saying "when in Rome do as the Romans do." He also, however, maintained the feeling that there were core human values that at times transcended such local traditions and social context.

Moral Dilemmas— Unanswered Questions

What worried Case was even if the business decision were the right one, could the company be entering a relationship that might some day backfire? If a factory that Textron brought merchandise from or, because of the joint venture, was more deeply involved in was alleged to be mistreating employees, would public opinion injure the company's reputation? Was the focus of the world now on China and its historic practices of human rights abuse? Would someone be watching companies more closely that associated themselves with Chinese partners in any form?

What if Textron's buyers of components, the franchised cosmetic houses, were themselves chastised for using slave-type labor in the supplies used in their own manufacturing of their brand named products? Would they in turn cease to buy from Textron Ltd.? What if consumers of the retail packaged lines decided to boycott the products for similar reasons? What if the licensor of the new collection felt that such foreign sourcing of items bearing their trademark was injurious to their image and reputation, and they objected?

Given his company's strong traditional organizational culture of placing employees first, Case also wondered what effect any such ethical and socially responsibility issues stemming from a Chinese association could have on his own domestic operational employees.

He wondered about such matters again as he thought to himself that going global was more than just an exercise in financial, legal and operational logistical decision making; it involved taking a moral position in Textron's commercial relationships with overseas entities.

Nora-Sakari: A Proposed JV in Malaysia (Revised)

Prepared by R. Azimah Ainuddin under the supervision of Professor Paul Beamish

     Version: (A) 2005-11-28

On Monday, July 15, 2003 Zainal Hashim, vice-chairman of Nora Holdings Sdn Bhd[1] (Nora), arrived at his office about an hour earlier than usual. As he looked out the window at the city spreading below, he thought about the Friday evening reception which he had hosted at his home in Kuala Lumpur (KL), Malaysia, for a team of negotiators from Sakari Oy[2]

(Sakari) of Finland. Nora was a leading supplier of telecommunications (telecom) equipment in Malaysia while Sakari, a Finnish conglomerate, was a leader in the manufacture of cellular phone sets and switching systems. The seven-member team from Sakari was in KL to negotiate with Nora the formation of a joint-venture (JV) between the two telecom companies.

This was the final negotiation which would determine whether a JV agreement would materialize. The negotiation had ended late Friday afternoon, having lasted for five consecutive days. The JV Company, if established, would be set up in Malaysia to manufacture and commission digital switching exchanges to meet the needs of the telecom industry in Malaysia and in neighbouring countries, particularly Indonesia and Thailand. While Nora would benefit from the JV in terms of technology transfer, the venture would pave the way for Sakari to acquire knowledge and gain access to the markets of South-east Asia.

The Nora management was impressed by the Finnish capability in using high technology to enable Finland, a small country of only five million people, to have a fast-growing economy. Most successful Finnish companies were in the high-tech industries. For example, Kone was one of the world's three largest manufacturers of lifts, Vaisala was the world's major supplier of meteorological equipment, and Sakari was one of the leading telecom companies in Europe. It would be an invaluable opportunity for Nora to learn from the Finnish experience and emulate their success for Malaysia.

The opportunity emerged two and half years earlier when Peter Mattsson, president of Sakari's Asian regional office in Singapore, approached Zainal[3] to explore the possibility of forming a cooperative venture between Nora and Sakari. Mattsson said:

> While growth in the mobile telecommunications network is expected to be about 40 per cent a year in Asia in the next five years, growth in fixed networks would not be as fast, but the projects are much larger. A typical mobile network project amounts to a maximum of € 50 million, but fixed network projects can be estimated in hundreds of

millions. In Malaysia and Thailand, such latter projects are currently approaching contract stage. Thus it is imperative that Sakari establish its presence in this region to capture a share in the fixed network market.

The large potential for telecom facilities was also evidenced in the low telephone penetration rates for most South-east Asian countries. For example, in 1999, telephone penetration rates (measured by the number of telephone lines per 100 people) for Indonesia, Thailand, Malaysia and the Philippines ranged from three to 20 lines per 100 people compared to the rates in developed countries such as Canada, Finland, Germany, United States and Sweden where the rates exceeded 55 telephone lines per 100 people.

THE TELECOM INDUSTRY IN MALAYSIA

Telekom Malaysia Bhd (TMB), the national telecom company, was given the authority by the Malaysian government to develop the country's telecom infrastructure. With a paid-up capital of RM2.4 billion,[4] it was also given the mandate to provide telecom services that were on par with those available in developed countries.

TMB announced that it would be investing in the digitalization of its networks to pave the way for offering services based on the ISDN (integrated services digitalized network) standard, and investing in international fibre optic cable networks to meet the needs of increased telecom traffic between Malaysia and the rest of the world. TMB would also facilitate the installation of more cellular telephone networks in view of the increased demand for the use of mobile phones among the business community in KL and in major towns.

As the nation's largest telecom company, TMB's operations were regulated through a 20-year licence issued by the Ministry of Energy, Telecommunications and Posts. In line with the government's Vision 2020 program which targeted Malaysia to become a developed nation by the year 2020, there was a strong need for the upgrading of the telecom infrastructure in the rural areas. TMB estimated that it would spend more than

RM1 billion each year on the installation of fixed networks, of which 25 per cent would be allocated for the expansion of rural telecom. The objective was to increase the level of telephone penetration rate to over 50 per cent by the year 2005.

Although TMB had become a large national telecom company, it lacked the expertise and technology to undertake massive infrastructure projects. In most cases, the local telecom companies would be invited to submit their bids for a particular contract. It was also common for these local companies to form partnerships with large multinational corporations (MNCs), mainly for technological support. For example, Pernas-NEC, a JV company between Pernas Holdings and NEC, was one of the companies that had been successful in securing large telecom contracts from the Malaysian authorities.

NORA'S SEARCH FOR A JV PARTNER

In October 2002, TMB called for tenders to bid on a five-year project worth RM2 billion for installing digital switching exchanges in various parts of the country. The project also involved replacing analog circuit switches with digital switches. Digital switches enhanced transmission capabilities of telephone lines, increasing capacity to approximately two million bits per second compared to the 9,600 bits per second on analog circuits.

Nora was interested in securing a share of the RM2 billion contract from TMB and more importantly, in acquiring the knowledge in switching technology from its partnership with a telecom MNC. During the initial stages, when Nora first began to consider potential partners in the bid for this contract, telecom MNCs such as Siemens, Alcatel, and Fujitsu seemed appropriate candidates. Nora had previously entered into a five-year technical assistance agreement with Siemens to manufacture telephone handsets.

Nora also had the experience of a long-term working relationship with Japanese partners which would prove valuable should a JV be formed with Fujitsu. Alcatel was another potential partner, but the main concern at Nora was that the technical standards used in the French technology were not compatible with the British standards already adopted in Malaysia. NEC and Ericsson were not considered, as they were already involved with other local competitors and were the current suppliers of digital switching exchanges to TMB. Their five-year contracts were due to expire soon.

Subsequent to Zainal's meeting with Mattsson, he decided to consider Sakari as a serious potential partner. He was briefed about Sakari's SK33, a digital switching system that was based on an open architecture, which enabled the use of standard components, standard software development tools, and standard software languages. Unlike the switching exchanges developed by NEC and Ericsson which required the purchase of components developed by the parent companies, the SK33 used components that were freely available in the open market. The system was also modular, and its software could be upgraded to provide new services and could interface easily with new equipment in the network. This was the most attractive feature of the SK33 as it would lead to the development of new switching systems.

Mattsson had also convinced Zainal and other Nora managers that although Sakari was a relatively small player in fixed networks, these networks were easily adaptable, and could cater to large exchanges in the urban areas as well as small ones for rural needs. Apparently Sakari's smaller size, compared to that of some of the other MNCs, was an added strength because Sakari was prepared to work out customized products according to Nora's needs. Large telecom companies were alleged to be less willing to provide custom-made products. Instead, they tended to offer standard products that, in some aspects, were not consistent with the needs of the customer.

Prior to the July meeting, at least 20 meetings had been held either in KL or in Helsinki to establish relationships between the two companies. It was estimated that each side had invested not less than RM3 million in promoting the relationship. Mattsson and Ilkka Junttila, Sakari's representative in KL, were the key people in bringing the two companies together. (See Exhibits 1 and 2 for brief background information on Malaysia and Finland respectively.)

Malaysia is centrally located in South-east Asia. It consists of Peninsular Malaysia, bordered by Thailand in the north and Singapore in the south, and the states of Sabah and Sarawak on the island of Borneo. Malaysia has a total land area of about 330,000 square kilometres, of which 80 per cent is covered with tropical rainforest. Malaysia has an equatorial climate with high humidity and high daily temperatures of about 26 degrees Celsius throughout the year.

In 2000, Malaysia's population was 22 million, of which approximately nine million made up the country's labour force. The population is relatively young, with 42 per cent between the ages of 15 and 39 and only seven per cent above the age of 55. A Malaysian family has an average of four children and extended families are common. Kuala Lumpur, the capital city of Malaysia, has approximately 1.5 million inhabitants.

The population is multiracial; the largest ethnic group is the Bumiputeras (the Malays and other indigenous groups such as the Ibans in Sarawak and Kadazans in Sabah), followed by the Chinese and Indians. Bahasa Malaysia is the national language but English is widely used in business circles. Other major languages spoken included various Chinese dialects and Tamil.

Islam is the official religion but other religions (mainly Christianity, Buddhism and Hinduism) are widely practised. Official holidays are allocated for the celebration of Eid, Christmas, Chinese New Year and Deepavali. All Malays are Muslims, followers of the Islamic faith.

During the period of British rule, secularism was introduced to the country, which led to the separation of the Islamic religion from daily life. In the late 1970s and 1980s, realizing the negative impact of secularism on the life of the Muslims, several groups of devout Muslims undertook efforts to reverse the process, emphasizing a dynamic and progressive approach to Islam. As a result, changes were introduced to meet the daily needs of Muslims. Islamic banking and insurance facilities were introduced and prayer rooms were provided in government offices, private companies, factories, and even in shopping complexes.

Malaysia is a parliamentary democracy under a constitutional monarchy. The Yang DiPertuan Agung (the king) is the supreme head, and appoints the head of the ruling political party to be the prime minister. In 2000 the Barisan Nasional, a coalition of several political parties representing various ethnic groups, was the ruling political party in Malaysia. Its predominance had contributed not only to the political stability and economic progress of the country in the last two decades, but also to the fast recovery from the 1997 Asian economic crisis.

The recession of the mid 1980s led to structural changes in the Malaysian economy which had been too dependent on primary commodities (rubber, tin, palm oil and timber) and had a very narrow export base. To promote the establishment of export-oriented industries, the government directed resources to the manufacturing sector, introduced generous incentives and relaxed foreign equity restrictions. In the meantime, heavy investments were made to modernize the country's infrastructure. These moves led to rapid economic growth in the late 1980s and early 1990s. The growth had been mostly driven by exports, particularly of electronics.

The Malaysian economy was hard hit by the 1997 Asian economic crisis. However, Malaysia was the fastest country to recover from the crisis after declining IMF assistance. It achieved this by pegging its currency to the USD, restricting outflow of money from the country, banning illegal overseas derivative trading of Malaysian securities and setting up asset management companies to facilitate the orderly recovery of bad loans. The real GDP growth rate in 1999 and 2000 were 5.4% and 8.6%, respectively (Table 1).

Malaysia was heavily affected by the global economic downturn and the slump in the IT sector in 2001 and 2002 due to its export-based economy. GDP in 2001 grew only 0.4% due to an 11% decrease in exports. A US $1.9 billion fiscal stimulus package helped the country ward off the worst of the recession and the GDP growth rate rebounded to 4.2% in 2002 (Table 1). A relatively small foreign debt and adequate foreign exchange reserves make a crisis similar to the 1997 one unlikely. Nevertheless, the economy remains vulnerable to a more protracted slowdown in the US and Japan, top export destinations and key sources of foreign investment.

In 2002, the manufacturing sector was the leading contributor to the economy, accounting for about 30 per cent of gross national product (GDP). Malaysia's major trading partners are United States, Singapore, Japan, China, Taiwan, Hong Kong and Korea.

Table 1   Malaysian Economic Performance 1999 to 2002

Economic Indicator	1999	2000	2001	2002
GDP per capita (US$)	3,596	3,680	3,678	3,814
Real GDP growth rate	5.4%	8.6%	0.4%	4.2%
Consumer price inflation	2.8%	1.6%	1.4%	1.8%
Unemployment rate	3.0%	3.0%	3.7%	3.5%

Source: IMD. Various years. "The World Competitiveness Report."

Exhibit 1   Malaysia Background Information

Sources: Ernst & Young International. 1993. "Doing Business in Malaysia." Other Online Sources.

NORA HOLDINGS SDN BHD

The Company

Nora was one of the leading companies in the telecom industry in Malaysia. It was established in 1975 with a paid-up capital of RM2 million. Last year, the company recorded a turnover of RM320 million. Nora Holdings consisted of 30 subsidiaries, including two public-listed companies: Multiphone Bhd, and Nora Telecommunications Bhd. Nora had 3,081 employees, of which 513 were categorized as managerial (including 244 engineers) and 2,568 as non-managerial (including 269 engineers and technicians).

The Cable Business

Since the inception of the company, Nora had secured two cable-laying projects. For the latter project worth RM500 million, Nora formed a JV with two Japanese companies, Sumitomo Electric Industries Ltd (held 10 per cent equity share) and Marubeni Corporation (held five per cent equity share). Japanese partners were chosen in view of the availability of a financial package that came together with the technological assistance needed by Nora. Nora also acquired a 63 per cent stake in a local cable-laying company, Selangor Cables Sdn Bhd.

The Telephone Business

Nora had become a household name in Malaysia as a telephone manufacturer. It started in 1980 when the company obtained a contract to supply telephone sets to the government-owned Telecom authority, TMB, which would distribute the sets to telephone subscribers on a rental basis. The contract, estimated at RM130 million, lasted for 15 years. In 1985 Nora secured licenses from Siemens and Nortel to manufacture telephone handsets and had subsequently developed Nora's own telephone sets—the N300S (single line), N300M (micro-computer controlled), and N300V (hands-free, voice-activated) models.

Upon expiry of the 15-year contract as a supplier of telephone sets to the TMB, Nora suffered a major setback when it lost a RM32 million contract to supply 600,000 N300S single line telephones. The contract was instead given to a Taiwanese manufacturer, Formula Electronics, which quoted a lower price of RM37 per handset compared to Nora's RM54. Subsequently, Nora was motivated to move towards the high end feature phone domestic market. The company sold about 3,000 sets of feature phones per month, capturing the high-end segment of the Malaysian market.

Nora had ventured into the export market with its feature phones, but industry observers predicted that Nora still had a long way to go as an exporter. The foreign markets were very competitive and many manufacturers already had well-established brands.

The Payphone Business

Nora's start-up in the payphone business had turned out to be one of the company's most profitable lines of business. Other than the cable-laying contract secured in 1980, Nora had a 15-year contract to install, operate and maintain payphones in the cities and major towns in Malaysia. In 1997, Nora started to manufacture card payphones under a license from GEC Plessey Telecommunications (GPT) of the United Kingdom. The agreement had also permitted Nora to sell the products to the neighbouring countries in South-east Asia as well as to eight other markets approved by GPT.

While the payphone revenues were estimated to be as high as RM60 million a year, a long-term and stable income stream for Nora, profit margins were only about 10 per cent because of the high investment and maintenance costs.

Other Businesses

Nora was also the sole Malaysian distributor for Nortel's private automatic branch exchange (PABX) and NEC's mobile telephone sets. It was also an Apple computer distributor in Malaysia

Finland is situated in the north-east of Europe, sharing borders with Sweden, Norway and the former Soviet Union. About 65 per cent of its area of 338,000 square kilometres is covered with forest, about 15 per cent lakes and about 10 per cent arable land. Finland has a temperate climate with four distinct seasons. In Helsinki, the capital city, July is the warmest month with average mid-day temperature of 21 degrees Celsius and January is the coldest month with average mid-day temperature of –3 degrees Celsius.

Finland is one of the most sparsely populated countries in Europe with a 2002 population of 5.2 million, 60 per cent of whom lived in the urban areas. Helsinki had a population of about 560,000 in 2002. Finland has a well-educated work force of about 2.3 million. About half of the work force are engaged in providing services, 30 per cent in manufacturing and construction, and eight per cent in agricultural production. The small size of the population has led to scarce and expensive labour. Thus Finland had to compete by exploiting its lead in high-tech industries.

Finland's official languages are Finnish and Swedish, although only six per cent of the population speaks Swedish. English is the most widely spoken foreign language. About 87 per cent of the Finns are Lutherans and about one per cent Finnish Orthodox.

Finland has been an independent republic since 1917, having previously been ruled by Sweden and Russia. A President is elected to a six-year term, and a 200-member, single-chamber parliament is elected every four years.

In 1991, the country experienced a bad recession triggered by a sudden drop in exports due to the collapse of the Soviet Union. During 1991-1993, the total output suffered a 10% contraction and unemployment rate reached almost 20%. Finnish Markka experienced a steep devaluation in 1991-1992, which gave Finland cost competitiveness in international market.

With this cost competitiveness and the recovery of Western export markets the Finnish economy underwent a rapid revival in 1993, followed by a new period of healthy growth. Since the mid 1990s the Finnish growth has mainly been bolstered by intense growth in telecommunications equipment manufacturing. The Finnish economy peaked in the year 2000 with a real GDP growth rate of 5.6% (Table 2).

Finland was one of the 11 countries that joined the Economic and Monetary Union (EMU) on January 1, 1999. Finland has been experiencing a rapidly increasing integration with Western Europe. Membership in the EMU provide the Finnish economy with an array of benefits, such as lower and stable interest rates, elimination of foreign currency risk within the Euro area, reduction of transaction costs of business and travel, and so forth. This provided Finland with a credibility that it lacked before accession and the Finnish economy has become more predictable. This will have a long-term positive effect on many facets of the economy.

Finland's economic structure is based on private ownership and free enterprise. However, the production of alcoholic beverages and spirits is retained as a government monopoly. Finland's major trading partners are Sweden, Germany, the former Soviet Union and United Kingdom.

Finland's standard of living is among the highest in the world. The Finns have small families with one or two children per family. They have comfortable homes in the cities and one in every three families has countryside cottages near a lake where they retreat on weekends. Taxes are high, the social security system is efficient and poverty is virtually non-existent.

Until recently, the stable trading relationship with the former Soviet Union and other Scandinavian countries led to few interactions between the Finns and people in other parts of the world. The Finns are described as rather reserved, obstinate, and serious people. A Finn commented, "We do not engage easily in small talk with strangers. Furthermore, we have a strong love for nature and we have the tendency to be silent as we observe our surroundings. Unfortunately, others tend to view such behaviour as cold and serious." Visitors to Finland are often impressed by the efficient public transport system, the clean and beautiful city of Helsinki with orderly road networks, scenic parks and lakefronts, museums, cathedrals, and churches.

Table 2   Finnish Economic Performance 1999 to 2002

Economic Indicator	1999	2000	2001	2002
GDP per capita (US$)	24,430	23,430	23,295	25,303
Real GDP growth rate	3.7%	5.6%	0.4%	1.6%
Consumer price inflation	1.2%	3.3%	2.6%	1.6%
Unemployment	10.3%	9.6%	9.1%	9.1%

Source: IMD. Various years. "The World Competitiveness Report."

Exhibit 2   Finland: Background Information

Sources: Ernst & Young International. 1993. "Doing Business in Finland." Other Online Sources.

and Singapore. In addition, Nora was involved in: distributing radio-related equipment; supplying equipment to the broadcasting, meteorological, civil aviation, postal and power authorities; and manufacturing automotive parts (such as the suspension coil, springs, and piston) for the local automobile companies.

The Management

When Nora was established, Osman Jaafar, founder and chairman of Nora Holdings, managed the company with his wife, Nora Asyikin Yusof, and seven employees. Osman was known as a conservative businessman who did not like to dabble in acquisitions and mergers to make quick capital gains. He was formerly an electrical engineer who was trained in the United Kingdom and had held several senior positions at the national Telecom Department in Malaysia.

Osman subsequently recruited Zainal Hashim to fill in the position of deputy managing director at Nora. Zainal held a master's degree in microwave communications from a British university and had several years of working experience as a production engineer at Pernas-NEC Sdn Bhd, a manufacturer of transmission equipment. Zainal was later promoted to the position of managing director and six years later, the vice-chairman.

Industry analysts observed that Nora's success was attributed to the complementary roles, trust, and mutual understanding between Osman and Zainal. While Osman "likes to fight for new business opportunities," Zainal preferred a low profile and concentrated on managing Nora's operations.

Industry observers also speculated that Osman, a former civil servant and an entrepreneur, was close to Malaysian politicians, notably the Prime Minister, while Zainal had been a close friend of the Finance Minister. Zainal disagreed with allegations that Nora had succeeded due to its close relationships with Malaysian politicians. However, he acknowledged that such perceptions in the industry had been beneficial to the company.

Osman and Zainal had an obsession for high-tech and made the development of research and development (R&D) skills and resources a priority in the company. About one per cent of Nora's earnings was ploughed back into R&D activities. Although this amount was considered small by international standards, Nora planned to increase it gradually to five to six per cent over the next two to three years. Zainal said:

> We believe in making improvements in small steps, similar to the Japanese kaizen principle. Over time, each small improvement could lead to a major creation. To be able to make improvements, we must learn from others. Thus we would borrow a technology from others, but eventually, we must be able to develop our own to sustain our competitiveness in the industry. As a matter of fact, Sakari's SK33 system was developed based on a technology it obtained from Alcatel.

To further enhance R&D activities at Nora, Nora Research Sdn Bhd (NRSB), a wholly-owned subsidiary, was formed, and its R&D department was absorbed into this new company. NRSB operated as an independent research company undertaking R&D activities for Nora as well as private clients in related fields. The company facilitated R&D activities with other companies as well as government organizations, research institutions, and universities. NRSB, with its staff of 40 technicians/engineers, would charge a fixed fee for basic research and a royalty for its products sold by clients.

Zainal was also active in instilling and promoting Islamic values among the Malay employees at Nora. He explained:

> Islam is a way of life and there is no such thing as Islamic management. The Islamic values, which must be reflected in the daily life of Muslims, would influence their behaviours as employers and employees. Our Malay managers, however, were often influenced by their western counterparts, who tend to stress knowledge and mental capability and often forget the effectiveness of the softer side of management which emphasizes relationships, sincerity and consistency. I believe that one must always be sincere to be able to develop good working relationships.

SAKARI OY

Sakari was established in 1865 as a pulp and paper mill located about 200 kilometres northwest of Helsinki, the capital city of Finland. In the 1960s, Sakari started to expand into the rubber and cable industries when it merged with the Finnish Rubber Works and Finnish Cable Works. In 1973 Sakari's performance was badly affected by the oil crisis, as its businesses were largely energy-intensive.

However, in 1975, the company recovered when Aatos Olkkola took over as Sakari's president. He led Sakari into competitive businesses such as computers, consumer electronics, and cellular phones via a series of acquisitions, mergers and alliances. Companies involved in the acquisitions included: the consumer electronics division of Standard Elektrik Lorenz AG; the data systems division of L.M. Ericsson; Vantala, a Finnish manufacturer of colour televisions; and Luxury, a Swedish state-owned electronics and computer concern.

In 1979, a JV between Sakari and Vantala, Sakari-Vantala, was set up to develop and manufacture mobile telephones. Sakari-Vantala had captured about 14 per cent of the world's market share for mobile phones and held a 20 per cent market share in Europe for its mobile phone handsets. Outside Europe, a 50-50 JV was formed with Tandy Corporation which, to date, had made significant sales in the United States, Malaysia and Thailand.

Sakari first edged into the telecom market by selling switching systems licensed from France's Alcatel and by developing the software and systems to suit the needs of small Finnish phone companies. Sakari had avoided head-on competition with Siemens and Ericsson by not trying to enter the market for large telephone networks. Instead, Sakari had concentrated on developing dedicated telecom networks for large private users such as utility and railway companies. In Finland, Sakari held 40 per cent of the market for digital exchanges. Other competitors included Ericsson (34 per cent), Siemens (25 per cent), and Alcatel (one per cent).

Sakari was also a niche player in the global switching market. Its SK33 switches had sold well in countries such as Sri Lanka, United Arab Emirates, China and the Soviet Union. A derivative of the SK33 main exchange switch called the SK33XT was subsequently developed to be used in base stations for cellular networks and personal paging systems.

Sakari attributed its emphasis on R&D as its key success factor in the telecom industry. Strong in-house R&D in core competence areas enabled the company to develop technology platforms such as its SK33 system that were reliable, flexible, widely compatible and economical. About 17 per cent of its annual sales revenue was invested into R&D and product development units in Finland, United Kingdom and France. Sakari's current strategy was to emphasize global operations in production and R&D. It planned to set up R&D centres in leading markets, including South-east Asia.

Sakari was still a small company by international standards (see Exhibit 3 for a list of the world's major telecom equipment suppliers). It lacked a strong marketing capability and had to rely on JVs such as the one with Tandy Corporation to enter the world market, particularly the United States. In its efforts to develop market position quickly, Sakari had to accept lower margins for its products, and often the Sakari name was not revealed on the product. In recent years, Sakari decided to emerge from its hiding place as a manufacturer's manufacturer and began marketing under the Sakari name.

In 1989 Mikko Koskinen took over as president of Sakari. Koskinen announced that telecommunications, computers, and consumer electronics would be maintained as Sakari's core business, and that he would continue Olkkola's efforts in expanding the company overseas. He believed that every European company needed global horizons to be able to meet global competition for future survival. To do so, he envisaged the setting up of alliances of varying duration, each designed for specific purposes. He said, "Sakari has become an interesting partner with

Rank	Company	Country	1998 telecom equipment sales (US$ billions)
1	Lucent	USA	26.8
2	Ericsson	Sweden	21.5
3	Alcatel	France	20.9
4	Motorola	USA	20.5
5	Nortel	Canada	17.3
6	Siemens	Germany	16.8
7	Nokia	Finland	14.7
8	NEC	Japan	12.6
9	Cisco	USA	8.4
10	Hughes	USA	5.7

Exhibit 3   Ten Major Telecommunication Equipment Vendors

Source: International Telecommunication Union. 1999. Top 20 Telecommunication Equipment Vendors 1998. http://www .itu.int/ITU-D/ict/statistics/at_glance/Top2098.html.

which to cooperate on an equal footing in the areas of R&D, manufacturing and marketing."

The recession in Finland which began in 1990 led Sakari's group sales to decline substantially from FIM22 billion[5] in 1990 to FIM15 billion in 1991. The losses were attributed to two main factors: weak demand for Sakari's consumer electronic products, and trade with the Soviet Union which had come to almost a complete standstill. Consequently Sakari began divesting its less profitable companies within the basic industries (metal, rubber, and paper), as well as leaving the troubled European computer market with the sale of its computer subsidiary, Sakari Macro. The company's new strategy was to focus on three main areas: telecom systems and mobile phones in a global framework, consumer electronic products in Europe, and deliveries of cables and related technology. The company's divestment strategy led to a reduction of Sakari's employees from about 41,000 in 1989 to 29,000 in 1991. This series of major strategic moves was accompanied by major leadership succession. In June 1992, Koskinen retired as Sakari's

President and was replaced by Visa Ketonen, formerly the President of Sakari Mobile Phones. Ketonen appointed Ossi Kuusisto as Sakari's vice-president.

After Ketonen took over control, the Finnish economy went through a rapid revival in 1993, followed by a new period of intense growth. Since the mid 1990s the Finnish growth had been bolstered by intense growth in telecommunications equipment manufacturing as a result of exploding global telecommunications market. Sakari capitalized on this opportunity and played a major role in the Finnish telecommunications equipment manufacturing sector.

In 2001, Sakari was Finland's largest publicly-traded industrial company and derived the majority of its total sales from exports and overseas operations. Traditionally, the company's export sales were confined to other Scandinavian countries, Western Europe and the former Soviet Union. However, in recent years, the company made efforts and succeeded in globalizing and diversifying its operations to make the most of its high-tech capabilities. As a result, Sakari emerged as a more influential player in the international market and had gained international brand recognition. One of Sakari's strategies was to form JVs to enter new foreign markets.

THE NORA-SAKARI NEGOTIATION

Nora and Sakari had discussed the potential of forming a JV company in Malaysia for more than two years. Nora engineers were sent to Helsinki to assess the SK33 technology in terms of its compatibility with the Malaysian requirements, while Sakari managers travelled to KL mainly to assess both Nora's capability in manufacturing switching exchanges and the feasibility of gaining access to the Malaysian market.

In January 2003, Nora submitted its bid for TMB's RM2 billion contract to supply digital switching exchanges supporting four million telephone lines. Assuming the Nora-Sakari JV would materialize, Nora based its bid on supplying Sakari's digital switching technology. Nora competed with seven other companies short listed by TMB, all offering their partners' technology—Alcatel, Lucent, Fujitsu, Siemens, Ericsson, NEC, and Samsung. In early May, TMB announced five successful companies in the bid. They were companies using technology from Alcatel, Fujitsu, Ericsson, NEC, and Sakari. Each company was awarded one-fifth share of the RM2 billion contract and would be responsible in delivering 800,000 telephone lines over a period of five years. Industry observers were critical of TMB's decision to select Sakari and Alcatel. Sakari was perceived to be the least capable in supplying the necessary lines to meet TMB's requirements, as it was alleged to be a small company with little international exposure. Alcatel was criticized for having the potential of supplying an obsolete technology.

The May 21 Meeting

Following the successful bid and ignoring the criticisms against Sakari, Nora and Sakari held a major meeting in Helsinki on May 21 to finalize the formation of the JV. Zainal led Nora's five-member negotiation team which comprised Nora's general manager for corporate planning division, an accountant, two engineers, and Marina Mohamed, a lawyer. One of the engineers was Salleh Lindstrom who was of Swedish origin, a Muslim and had worked for Nora for almost 10 years.

Sakari's eight-member team was led by Kuusisto, Sakari's vice-president. His team comprised Junttila, Hussein Ghazi, Aziz Majid, three engineers, and Julia Ruola (a lawyer). Ghazi was Sakari's senior manager who was of Egyptian origin and also a Muslim who had worked for Sakari for more than 20 years while Aziz, a Malay, had been Sakari's manager for more than 12 years.

The meeting went on for several days. The main issue raised at the meeting was Nora's capability in penetrating the South-east Asian market. Other issues included Sakari's concerns over the efficiency of Malaysian workers in the JV in manufacturing the product, maintaining product quality and ensuring prompt deliveries.

Commenting on the series of negotiations with Sakari, Zainal said that this was the most difficult negotiation he had ever experienced. Zainal was Nora's most experienced negotiator and had single-handedly represented Nora in several major negotiations for the past 10 years. In the negotiation with Sakari, Zainal admitted making the mistake of approaching the negotiation applying the approach he often used when negotiating with his counterparts from companies based in North America or the United Kingdom. He said:

> Negotiators from the United States tend to be very open and often state their positions early and definitively. They are highly verbal and usually prepare well-planned presentations. They also often engage in small talk and 'joke around' with us at the end of a negotiation. In contrast, the Sakari negotiators tend to be very serious, reserved and 'cold.' They are also relatively less verbal and do not convey much through their facial expressions. As a result, it was difficult for us to determine whether they are really interested in the deal or not.

Zainal said that the negotiation on May 21 turned out to be particularly difficult when Sakari became interested in bidding a recently-announced tender for a major telecom contract in the United Kingdom. Internal politics within Sakari led to the formation of two opposing "camps." One "camp" held a strong belief that there would be very high growth in the Asia-Pacific region and that the JV company in Malaysia was seen as a hub to enter these markets. Although the Malaysian government had liberalized its equity ownership restrictions and allowed the formation of wholly-owned subsidiaries, JVs were still an efficient way to enter the Malaysian market for a company that lacked local knowledge. This group was represented mostly by Sakari's managers positioned in Asia and engineers who had made several trips to Malaysia, which usually included visits to Nora's facilities. They also had the support of Sakari's vice-president, Kuusisto, who was involved in most of the meetings with Nora, particularly when Zainal was present. Kuusisto had also made efforts to be present at meetings held in KL. This group also argued that Nora had already obtained the contract in Malaysia whereas the chance of getting the U.K. contract was quite low in view of the intense competition prevailing in that market.

The "camp" not in favour of the Nora-Sakari JV believed that Sakari should focus its resources on entering the United Kingdom, which could be used as a hub to penetrate the European Union (EU) market. There was also the belief that Europe was closer to home, making management easier, and that problems arising from cultural differences would be minimized. This group was also particularly concerned that Nora had the potential of copying Sakari's technology and eventually becoming a strong regional competitor. Also, because the U.K. market was relatively "familiar" and Sakari has local knowledge, Sakari could set up a wholly-owned subsidiary instead of a JV company and consequently, avoid JV-related problems such as joint control, joint profits, and leakage of technology.

Zainal felt that the lack of full support from Sakari's management led to a difficult negotiation when new misgivings arose concerning Nora's capability to deliver its part of the deal. It was apparent that the group in favour of the Nora-Sakari JV was under pressure to further justify its proposal and provide counterarguments against the U.K. proposal. A Sakari manager explained, "We are tempted to pursue both proposals since each has its own strengths, but our current resources are very limited. Thus a choice has to made, and soon."

The July 8 Meeting

Another meeting to negotiate the JV agreement was scheduled for July 8. Sakari's eight-member team arrived in KL on Sunday afternoon of July 7, and was met at the airport by the key Nora managers involved in the negotiation. Kuusisto did not accompany the Sakari team at this meeting.

The negotiation started early Monday morning at Nora's headquarters and continued for the next five days, with each day's meeting ending late in the evening. Members of the Nora team were the same members who had attended the May 21 meeting in Finland, except Zainal, who did not participate. The Sakari team was also represented by the same members in attendance at the previous meeting plus a new member, Solail Pekkarinen, Sakari's senior accountant. Unfortunately, on the third day of the negotiation, the Nora team requested that Sakari ask Pekkarinen to leave the negotiation. He was perceived as extremely arrogant and insensitive to the local culture, which tended to value modesty and diplomacy. Pekkarinen left for Helsinki the following morning.

Although Zainal had decided not to participate actively in the negotiations, he followed the process closely and was briefed by his negotiators regularly. Some of the issues which they complained were difficult to resolve had often led to heated arguments between the two negotiating teams. These included:

1. Equity Ownership

In previous meetings both companies agreed to form the JV company with a paid-up capital of RM5 million. However, they disagreed on the equity share proposed by each side. Sakari proposed an equity split in the JV company of 49 per cent for Sakari and 51 per cent for Nora. Nora, on the other hand, proposed a 30 per cent Sakari and 70 per cent Nora split. Nora's proposal was based on the common practice in Malaysia as a result of historical foreign equity regulations set by the Malaysian government that allowed a maximum of 30 per cent foreign equity ownership unless the company would export a certain percentage of its products. Though these regulations were liberalized by the Malaysian government effective from July, 1998 and new regulations had replaced the old ones, the 30-70 foreign-Malaysian ownership divide was still commonly observed.

Equity ownership became a major issue as it was associated with control over the JV company. Sakari was concerned about its ability to control the accessibility of its technology to Nora and about decisions concerning the activities of the JV as a whole. The lack of control was perceived by Sakari as an obstacle to protecting its interests. Nora also had similar concerns about its ability to exert control over the JV because it was intended as a key part of Nora's long-term strategy to develop its own digital switching exchanges and related high-tech products.

2. Technology Transfer

Sakari proposed to provide the JV company with the basic structure of the digital switch. The JV company would assemble the switching exchanges at the JV plant and subsequently install the exchanges in designated locations identified by TMB. By offering Nora only the basic structure of the switch, the core of Sakari's switching technology would still be well-protected.

On the other hand, Nora proposed that the basic structure of the switch be developed at the JV company in order to access the root of the switching technology. Based on Sakari's proposal, Nora felt that only the technical aspects in assembling and installing the exchanges would be obtained. This was perceived as another "screw-driver" form of technology transfer while the core of the technology associated with making the switches would still be unknown.

3. Royalty Payment

Closely related to the issue of technology transfer was the payment of a royalty for the technology used in building the switches. Sakari proposed a royalty payment of five per cent of the JV gross sales while Nora proposed a payment of two per cent of net sales.

Nora considered the royalty rate of five per cent too high because it would affect Nora's financial situation as a whole. Financial simulations prepared by Nora's managers indicated that Nora's return on investment would be less than the desired 10 per cent if royalty rates exceeded three per cent of net sales. This was because Nora had already agreed to make large additional investments in support of the JV. Nora would invest in a building which would be rented to the JV company to accommodate an office and the switching plant. Nora would also invest in another plant which would supply the JV with surface mounted devices (SMD), one of the major components needed to build the switching exchanges.

An added argument raised by the Nora negotiators in support of a two per cent royalty was that Sakari would receive side benefits from the JV's access to Japanese technology used in the manufacture of the SMD components. Apparently the Japanese technology was more advanced than Sakari's present technology.

4. Expatriates' Salaries and Perks

To allay Sakari's concerns over Nora's level of efficiency, Nora suggested that Sakari provide the necessary training for the JV technical employees. Subsequently, Sakari had agreed to provide eight engineering experts for the JV company on two types of contracts, short-term and long-term. Experts employed on a short-term basis would be paid a daily rate of US$1260 plus travel/accommodation. The permanent experts would be paid a monthly salary of US$20,000. Three permanent experts would be attached to the JV company once it was established and the number would gradually be reduced to only one, after two years. Five experts would be available on a short-term basis to provide specific training needs for durations of not more than three months each year.

The Nora negotiation team was appalled at the exorbitant amount proposed by the Sakari negotiators. They were surprised that the Sakari team had not surveyed the industry rates, as the Japanese and other western negotiators would normally have done. Apparently Sakari had not taken into consideration the relatively low cost of living in Malaysia compared to Finland. In 2000, though the average monthly rent for a comfortable, unfurnished three-bedroom apartment was about the same (660 US$) in Helsinki and Kuala Lumpur, the cost of living was considerably lower in KL. The cost of living index (New York = 100) of basket of goods in major cities, excluding housing, for Malaysia was only 83.75, compared to 109.84 for Finland.[6]

In response to Sakari's proposal, Nora negotiators adopted an unusual "take-it or leave-it" stance. They deemed the following proposal reasonable in view of the comparisons made with other JVs which Nora had entered into with other foreign parties:

Permanent experts' monthly salary ranges to be paid by the JV company were as follows:

(1) Senior expert (seven to 10 years experience) RM24,300–RM27,900

(2) Expert (four to six years experience) RM22,500–RM25,200

(3) Junior expert (two to three years experience) RM20,700–RM23,400

(4) Any Malaysian income taxes payable would be added to the salaries.

(5) A car for personal use.

(6) Annual paid vacation of five weeks.

(7) Return flight tickets to home country once a year for the whole family of married persons and twice a year for singles according to Sakari's general scheme.

(8) Any expenses incurred during official travelling.

Temporary experts are persons invited by the JV company for various technical assistance tasks and would not be granted residence status. They would be paid the following fees:

(1) Senior expert   RM1,350 per working day

(2) Expert   RM1,170 per working day

(3) The JV company would not reimburse the following:
   • Flight tickets between Finland (or any other country) and Malaysia.
   • Hotel or any other form of accommodation.
   • Local transportation.

In defense of their proposed rates, Sakari's negotiators argued that the rates presented by Nora were too low. Sakari suggested that Nora's negotiators take into consideration the fact that Sakari would have to subsidize the difference between the experts' present salaries and the amount paid by the JV company. A large difference would require that large amounts of subsidy payments be made to the affected employees.

5. Arbitration

Another major issue discussed in the negotiation was related to arbitration. While both parties agreed to an arbitration process in the event of future disputes, they disagreed on the location for dispute resolution. Because Nora would be the majority stakeholder in the JV company, Nora insisted that any arbitration should take place in KL. Sakari, however, insisted on Helsinki, following the norm commonly practised by the company.

At the end of the five-day negotiation, many issues could not be resolved. While Nora could agree on certain matters after consulting Zainal, the Sakari team, representing a large private company, had to refer contentious items to the company board before it could make any decision that went beyond the limits authorized by the board.

THE DECISION

Zainal sat down at his desk, read through the minutes of the negotiation thoroughly, and was disappointed that an agreement had not yet been reached. He was concerned about the commitment Nora had made to TMB when Nora was awarded the switching contract. Nora would be expected to fulfil the contract soon but had yet to find a partner to provide the switching technology. It was foreseeable that companies such as Siemens, Samsung and Lucent, which had failed in the bid, could still be potential partners. However, Zainal had also not rejected the possibility of a reconciliation with Sakari. He could start by contacting Kuusisto in Helsinki. But should he?

NOTES

1. Sdn Bhd is an abbreviation for Sendirian Berhad, which means private limited company in Malaysia.
2. Oy is an abbreviation for Osakeyhtiot, which means private limited company in Finland.
3. The first name is used because the Malay name does not carry a family name. The first and/or middle names belong to the individual and the last name is his/her father's name.
4. RM is Ringgit Malaysia, the Malaysian currency. As at December 31, 2002, US$1 = RM3.80.
5. FIM is Finnish Markka, the Finnish currency until January 1, 1999. Markka coins and notes were not withdrawn from circulation until January 1, 2002, when Finland fully converted to the Euro. As at December 31, 2000, US$1 = FIM6.31, and € 1 = FIM5.95.
6. IMD & World Economic Forum. 2001. The World Competitiveness Report.

MAJESTICA HOTEL IN SHANGHAI?

Prepared by Jane Lu under the supervision of Professor Paul W. Beamish

Copyright © 2005, Ivey Management Services   Version: (A) 2005-12-02

On March 20, 2005, Richard Roy, executive vice-president of Majestica Hotels Inc., was in China, for negotiations with Commercial Properties of Shanghai Limited (CPS). They were discussing a possible management contract under which Majestica would be the operator of a new luxury hotel there owned by Shanghai Industrial Holdings.

Majestica Hotels Inc. was one of the world's leading operators of luxury hotels. The expansion into mainland China had been on management's agenda since 1999. The opportunity emerged in late 2003 when a close friend of Majestica's chief executive officer (CEO) revealed that CPS was looking for an operator for its new luxury hotel under construction in Shanghai. Majestica immediately sent representatives to Shanghai to explore the possibility of becoming the operator. Majestica's proposal was welcomed by CPS, and a letter of intent was signed on August 20, 2004.

However, in discussions regarding the management contract, the two parties had reached a deadlock. The key issues to be resolved were the contract term, and the responsibilities and rights of Majestica as the operator, and CPS as the owner, of the hotel.

This Shanghai deal was important for Majestica's global expansion. It would not only provide Majestica with the opportunity to enter the China market but could also set a precedent for Majestica's future expansion in other emerging markets.

MAJESTICA HOTELS INC.

Majestica was founded in 1970 in western Europe. It focused exclusively on its niche of developing and operating luxury hotels with 200 to 450 rooms. In 1977, Majestica expanded to the United Kingdom. In 1984, Majestica entered the U.S. market via acquisition. Majestica's expansion in the U.S. market continued with properties in seven other major cities. By the end of the 1990s, Majestica had secured a strong position in the luxury hotel industry in North America, competing with such established chains as Four Seasons, Ritz-Carlton, Hilton, Hyatt, Marriott and Westin.

While Majestica expanded quickly in North America, it adopted a gradual expansion strategy in Asia. This gradual expansion strategy shifted when the opportunity arose to acquire a major competitor in Asia in 1998. This acquisition made Majestica one of the world's largest operators of luxury hotels and resort properties. More importantly, it provided Majestica with a much expanded position in Pacific Asia and an immediate presence in the greater China area. Majestica continued its international expansion by amassing a select portfolio of medium-sized luxury hotels in the world's commercial and financial centres. By the end of 2004, Majestica managed 40 properties in 15 countries with approximately 20,000 employees. The contribution of Majestica's properties in North America, Asia and Europe to its consolidated revenue was 54 per cent, 14 per cent and 32 per cent, respectively. Exhibit 1 provides a five-year review of the occupancy rate, average daily room rate (ADR) and average room revenue per available room (REVPAR) of Majestica hotels in these three regions and worldwide.

In 2004, Majestica had a market capitalization of $1.7 billion[1] and generated revenue of more than $2.3 billion (see Exhibit 2). Majestica earned revenue both from hotel management and hotel ownership operations. In the past five years, Majestica shifted away from owning hotels and focused on managing hotels. In 2004, 80 per cent of Majestica's earnings before other operating items were generated by its hotel management business.

Majestica followed a business strategy that offered business and leisure travellers excellent hotel and resort accommodation in each destination it served. Following this strategy, Majestica developed into a luxury hotel chain with service standards among the best in the industry. Majestica hotels and resorts were widely recognized for the exceptional quality of their guest facilities, service and atmosphere. The Majestica brand was generally considered one of the top luxury hotel chain brands in the world, and its hotels and resorts were named frequently among the world's best hotels and travel experiences by Institutional Investor, Condé Nast Traveler, AAA Five Diamond and others. Majestica's success was also reflected in consistently achieving above-market operating results for the properties under its management. During 2003, REVPAR (revenue per available room) for Majestica core hotels worldwide and in North America was 60 per cent higher than that of its competitors in the luxury segments worldwide and in North America. The room rate for a Majestica hotel in Chicago, for example, averaged $50 higher than those of Hyatt Regency, Hilton, Sheraton and Marriott (see Exhibit 3).

Majestica's superior hotel management results attracted the owners and developers of luxury hotels worldwide. By the end of 2004, in addition to the 40 hotels under its management, Majestica had 16 new hotels and resorts under construction or development, and it was evaluating dozens of additional management opportunities around the world. In summarizing the key success factors, the Majestica management pointed to a service culture that they had fostered for decades.

It emphasized anticipating travellers' needs and meeting those needs with superior hotel structures and a deeply instilled ethic of personal service. This service culture was built into every property, going beyond elegant hotel designs and finishes to the small, thoughtful touches that would add value for the guests. Every detail was deliberate, from mechanical systems that were as quiet as they were efficient to providing a disposable bathing suit in case hotel guests forgot to bring one. In addition, the design of the hotel rooms highlighted a use of space that enhanced the sense of luxury. On average, standard guest

	2004	2003	2002	2001	2000
Worldwide					
Occupancy	75.44%	74.50%	70.30%	69.50%	68.00%
ADR[1]	$380.18	$354.22	$312.24	$286.53	$239.85
REVPAR[2]	$280.38	$265.16	$223.93	$203.20	$162.15
Gross operating margin[3]	32.50%	33.10%	29.10%	26.70%	22.00%
North America					
Occupancy	76.40%	77.50%	78.00%	71.20%	68.90%
ADR	$413.69	$368.73	$328.87	$303.62	$251.84
REVPAR	$311.02	$277.72	$233.04	$211.71	$172.48
Gross operating margin	32.10%	33.10%	31.20%	25.40%	23.80%
Asia-Pacific					
Occupancy	69.90%	74.50%	73.80%	74.10%	67.80%
ADR	$288.44	$299.56	$267.36	$240.39	$195.80
REVPAR	$204.20	$220.02	$193.93	$175.69	$129.27
Gross operating margin	32.30%	34.50%	31.20%	29.60%	25.80%
Europe					
Occupancy	80.10%	82.30%	77.90%	70.10%	64.50%
ADR	$669.40	$637.95	$576.92	$428.95	$515.70
REVPAR	$530.01	$519.36	$455.44	$296.84	$331.49
Gross operating margin	42.10%	41.30%	39.80%	31.70%	34.10%

Exhibit 1   Hotel Occupancy, ADR and REVPAR (in US$ millions)

1. ADR is defined as average daily room rate per room occupied.
2. REVPAR is average room revenue per available room. It is a commonly used indicator of market performance for hotels and represents the combination of the average occupancy rate achieved during the period.
3. Gross operating margin represents gross operating profit as a percentage of gross revenues.

rooms in Majestica hotels were 25 per cent larger than those in Hyatt Regency, Hilton, Sheraton and Marriott.

More importantly, the service culture emphasized the depth of personal service. Majestica deemed ultimate luxury as not derived from furnishings but from personal service. The services at Majestica hotels were comprehensive and highly personalized. Guided by the service culture, Majestica's employees treated every interaction with guests as an opportunity to anticipate and satisfy a need. They provided services ranging from room service that felt like a fine dining experience to replacing worn shoelaces. The strong service culture ensured highly reliable services. For example, room service always arrived on time and conference arrangements were in place as promised.

	2004	2003	2002	2001	2000
Statements of Operations Data					
Consolidated revenues	268.80	135.18	151.87	143.92	113.23
Hotel Management Operations					
Fee revenues	118.72	106.06	99.12	89.49	67.54
Hotel management earnings before other operating items	71.34	62.38	58.02	51.41	31.25
Hotel Ownership Operations					
Revenues	151.54	19.71	47.60	48.27	42.56
Distribution from hotel investments	6.72	10.30	6.72	7.62	4.37
Hotel ownership earnings before other operating items	16.91	9.74	16.69	15.90	8.06
Earnings before other operating items	88.14	72.02	74.70	67.20	39.31
Net earnings (loss)	45.70	33.49	(83.55)	7.62	(135.30)
Earnings (loss) per share					
Basic and fully diluted	1.86	1.56	(3.92)	0.36	(6.49)
Weighted average number of shares (millions)	24.6	21.5	21.3	20.9	20.9
Balance Sheet Data					
Total assets	507.58	431.54	427.39	550.48	580.27
Total debt	157.02	268.80	299.71	345.63	400.40
Shareholders' equity	285.04	98.67	64.06	153.66	139.66
Other Data					
Total revenues of all managed hotels	2,373.73	2,129.68	2,058.45	1,901.98	1,514.13
Fee revenues as a % of consolidated revenues	44.20%	78.50%	65.30%	62.20%	59.60%
Percentage of Fee revenues derived outside North America	31.20%	38.30%	40.90%	38.80%	35.90%
Hotel management operating margin	60.10%	58.80%	58.50%	57.40%	46.30%
Hotel management earnings before other operating items as a % of earnings before other operating items	80.90%	86.60%	77.70%	76.50%	79.50%
EBITDA	88.14	72.02	74.70	67.20	39.31
Debt, net of cash	128.69	251.55	258.61	335.10	387.07
Market price per share at year-end	50.40	31.08	21.28	18.20	14.56
Shares outstanding (millions)	25.28	21.53	21.38	21.30	20.85
Market capitalization at year-end	1,699.49	892.86	606.26	517.33	404.43
Employees	24,640	23,520	24,080	24,080	22,456

Exhibit 2   Five-Year Financial Review (in US$ millions except per share amounts)

Name of Hotel	Affiliation	"Number of Guest rooms"	Room rate*
Four Seasons Hotel Chicago	Four Seasons Hotels & Resorts	343	435-535
The Ritz-Carlton Hotel Chicago	Four Seasons Hotels & Resorts	435	395-535
Park Hyatt Chicago	Hyatt International	203	375-425
Renaissance Chicago Hotel	Marriott International	513	204
The Drake	Hilton International	535	255-295
The Peninsula Chicago	Peninsula Hotel Group	339	445-455
Le Meridien	Le Meridien Group	311	249
Majestica Miracle Mile	Majestica Hotels	435	455

Exhibit 3   Major Luxury Hotels in Chicago (2005) (in US$)

Source: Company files.

*Ratings and pricing were obtained from Frommer's Hotel Guide online as of March 2005.

The service culture encouraged surpassing each guest's highest levels of expectation. Majestica employees would do everything possible to accomplish the guests' purpose of the trip. The stories of Majestica employees' responses to unusual requests were legendary.

It took Majestica decades to foster this unique service culture and to achieve the widely recognized outstanding service standards. The challenge Majestica faced in its global expansion was how to replicate the exceptional Majestica guest experience from hotel to hotel, no matter where it operated in the world. Maintaining consistency in the quality of guest experience across its portfolio was regarded as essential to Majestica's continuing success. Decades of experience in the luxury hotel market had taught Majestica that constancy built trust and loyalty. The challenge in Majestica's global expansion was how to export its service culture to new locations. Majestica successfully handled this challenge with the following two policies.

First, Majestica was careful about the pace of adding new hotels and resorts in the portfolio. Whether there was a compatible service culture in the new location was an important criterion in deciding the direction and pace of Majestica's international expansion. In fact, the perceived lack of service culture in Asia was one of the major reasons that Majestica adopted a gradual expansion strategy in Asia in the mid-1990s. This second mover strategy allowed Majestica to profit from the development of a service culture in Asia brought about by the earlier entrants, the major American hotels.

Second, it was Majestica's operating philosophy to have full control of the hotels under its management in order to cultivate its service culture and to maintain service consistency in new markets. Majestica's operating philosophy requested the owners of the Majestica hotels to adopt a hands-off approach, from the planning and designing of the hotels to the daily operating of the hotel such as purchasing hotel equipment, marketing and staffing. The non-interference from the hotel owners was important to the smooth fostering of Majestica's service culture in new markets. For example, the full authority in staffing enabled Majestica to carefully select the right people and imbue them with Majestica's service culture through various training programs and through leadership by example. Following this operating philosophy, Majestica's service culture was passed from one Majestica hotel to another so as to succeed in maintaining consistant service throughout its global expansion.

MAJESTICA IN THE ASIA-PACIFIC REGION

Asia was one of the fastest growing tourism destinations in the world. However, Asia's importance as a travel destination was not recognized by the major hotel companies in the world until the rising of Asia's tigers in the 1980s. Attracted by the unprecedented economic and construction boom in the region, a growing middle class, increases in passenger miles and an expanding economy, major hotel companies rapidly opened new properties in the Asia-Pacific region in an attempt to ensure a strong presence.

Among the major international luxury hotel chains, Hilton was the earliest entrant to the region. After its initial entry in 1948 with the 450-room Nagoya Hilton, Hilton International had 45 properties spreading across the region by 2000.

Through its 1995 acquisition of Westin Hotels & Resorts and ITT Sheraton Corp, Starwood Hotels & Resorts Worldwide gained a strong presence in the Asia-Pacific region. Prior to being acquired, both Westin and ITT Sheraton had been active in the Asia-Pacific region and were managing numerous properties.

Marriott and Hyatt were two of the later entrants to the Asia-Pacific region. Hyatt International managed 56 hotels and 18 resorts in 34 countries. In the Asia-Pacific region, it had 18 hotels in operation and 19 properties under development. Marriott entered the Asia-Pacific region in 1990 with its opening of the JW Marriott Hotel Hong Kong. Four more entries over the next seven years brought Marriott's total to five hotels, with a total of 1,941 rooms. Marriott had also secured management contracts for four additional hotels. The company was looking to add more hotels in the four- and five-star categories.

Another competitor, The Four Seasons, had 15 Asian-Pacific properties, with a total of 4,950 rooms. This total represented one-third of its rooms worldwide. In addition to these hotels, two more were scheduled to open in 2005. The company's Asian-Pacific portfolio was heavily concentrated in India, Indonesia, Singapore and Thailand.

The Ritz-Carlton Hotel Company was another upscale hotel firm that had targeted the region. In 1997, the company opened hotels in Osaka and Kuala Lumpur to complement its existing properties in Singapore, Hong Kong, Seoul and Sydney. The company also opened a resort in Bali, Indonesia, situated near one of Four Seasons' premier properties.

In addition to these competitors, Asian hotel companies such as Mandarin Oriental, Dusit Thani, CDL, Regal Hotels, Marco Polo, New World Hotels International and the Peninsula Group had been exploring opportunities for expansion in and around their bases in Asia. Hong Kong-based Shangri-La Hotels and Resorts was the most active Asian hotel company. It operated 32 hotels and resorts in China and Southeast Asia with plans for more.

Compared with the rapid expansion of these companies, Majestica had kept a low profile in the region. It had not entered Asia in the late 1980s because Majestica was not convinced that the political situation was stable and that a service culture existed there.

However, the 1990s brought a change in Majestica's strategy. In 1994, after two years of negotiation, Majestica acquired two Tokyo hotels, for its first properties in the region. In August 1996, with a solid capital base that had been built on the company's outstanding financial performance, Majestica acquired 100 per cent ownership of Le Roi Resorts, including its management contracts, trade names and trademarks. This transaction provided Majestica with a much expanded position in the Asia-Pacific region.

As 2005 approached, China was becoming the centre of Asia's fiercest competition in the hotel industry. With an annual Gross Domestic Product (GDP) growth rate of nine per cent for the past 20 years, China was the seventh largest economy and the 10th largest trading nation in the world. China's booming economy, coupled with its huge potential market comprising more than 1.2 billion people, had attracted many foreign investors. By the end of 2001, China ranked second to the United States as the largest foreign direct investment recipient in the world.

China's economic development and open door policy also attracted many foreign visitors. With over seven million foreign visitors (including people from Hong Kong, Macao and Taiwan) in 2000, China was the sixth most popular destination for business and leisure travel in the world. The World Tourism Organization predicted that China would become the No. 1 travel destination by 2020.

The hotel industry in China prospered with the boom in tourism. At the end of 2002, China had approximately 5,201 hotels, a growth rate of nearly 20 per cent since 1996. This represented a total of 701,700 available rooms in China. In 2000, the hotels sector recorded growth of over 10 per cent. Over half the hotels in China were categorized as tourist hotels.[2] Of the 1,669 hotels rated by the government, the majority were at the two- and three-star level, while just three per cent had been awarded five-star ratings. Most five-star hotels were operated by international luxury hotel chains such as Shangri-la Hotels & Resorts, ITT Sheraton Asia Pacific Group, Hilton International and Ritz-Carlton Hotels & Resorts.

COMMERCIAL PROPERTIES OF SHANGHAI LIMITED

Commercial Properties of Shanghai Limited (CPS), was a subsidiary of Commercial Properties Shanghai Investment (Holdings) Co., Ltd. (CPSIH), one of several overseas investment arms of the Shanghai municipal government. Incorporated in Hong Kong in October 1985, CPSIH expanded its businesses quickly and became a diversified conglomerate active in a wide range of businesses including international investment, manufacturing, real estate development and investment, banking and finance, trading and cultural activities. By the end of 2001, it was the largest overseas conglomerate wholly

owned by the Shanghai municipal government with interests in more than 200 companies in Shanghai, Hong Kong, other parts of China and in cities spanning the Americas, Europe, Australia, Africa and Asia.

Hotel development and management was one of the businesses in which CPSIH was engaged. It owned and managed three hotels: the Oceania Hotel situated on Hong Kong Island, Mandarin United Hotel situated in Pudong, Shanghai, and Peace Garden Hotel located near the Yuyuan Gardens in Shanghai. In addition, it also organized mainland China and Hong Kong tours from its properties. Although hotel development and management was a comparatively small business in the company's 2001 business portfolio, it was one of the focuses of the company's future business development. Development of the hotel industry fit well in the company's mission to promote Shanghai and served the need of the Shanghai municipal government for foreign currency. To strengthen its position in the hotel industry and enter the luxury hotel segment, CPSIH had invested $220 million in building the Oceania Hotel in Hong Kong.

CPS was listed on the Stock Exchange of Hong Kong in May 2000, and subsequently selected as a Hang Seng Index constituent stock in January 2002. At the time of the listing, the market capitalization of CPS was approximately $700 million. A majority of its shares were held by its parent, CPSIH.

Within the first year after the listing, CPS conducted several successful acquisitions. As well, the parent company also injected assets into CPS. These acquisitions and asset injections together were worth approximately $1.3 billion, making CPS one of the largest "red-chip" stocks listed on the Hong Kong stock market.

For the year ended 31st December, 2001, the company's turnover reached approximately HK$4,978 million (about $795 million), an increase of approximately 60 per cent over that in 2001. Profit for the year amounted to approximately HK$1,421 million (about $227 million), and earnings per share HK$1.79 (about $0.29), representing substantial increases over the results of 2000.

THE HOTEL INDUSTRY IN SHANGHAI

Situated in the middle of China's east coastline, Shanghai was China's economic and trade centre. In 2000, Shanghai had a population of 16.74 million and the highest per capita income in China. Shanghai and the surrounding provinces of Jiangsu and Zhejiang (Shanghai's manufacturing hinterland) formed the Yangtze River delta region. This region had a comprehensive industrial base and accounted for nearly one-third of China's industrial output. Moreover, it was home to one-quarter of all foreign investment in China. For these reasons, Shanghai was regarded not only as one of the main engines of China's economic growth but also as one of the leading markets in China. Given its strategic importance in China's economic development, its huge market potential and its popularity among tourists, Shanghai had long been recognized as a key site for companies that operated in the luxury hotel business.

According to the Shanghai Tourism Administrative Commission, Shanghai had 423 hotels at the end of 2004, with 68,000 rooms. By the end of 2005, the number of hotels was expected to rise to around 470 with the number of guest rooms rising to 75,000. The commission expected more than four million overseas tourists to stay at least one night in the city in 2005, an increase of 11 per cent from 2004. The commission also expected the number of domestic tourists visiting Shanghai to rise by five per cent, hitting 90 million. However, only a handful had a top rating of five-stars (see Exhibit 4). Portman Ritz-Carlton had been originally managed by Shangri-la Hotels & Resorts. However, at the end of 1997, the management contract expired and Ritz-Carlton took over the management of Portman. It was then renamed Portman Ritz-Carlton, and was Ritz-Carlton's first hotel in China.

In 1992, the Chinese government announced its initiative to develop Shanghai's Pudong District into Asia's finance centre. Local government offices, the Shanghai Stock Exchange, the Shanghai Cereal & Oil Exchange, and the Shanghai Real Estate Trading Market were all to move their offices across the Huangpu River to the Pudong District. Hotel developers quickly seized

Name of Hotel	Affiliation	"Number of Guest rooms"	Room rate*
St. Regis Shanghai	St. Regis Hotels International	318	320-340
Portman Ritz-Carlton Shanghai	Ritz-Carlton Hotels & Resorts	564	250
Westin Shanghai	Westin Hotels	301	320
Sheraton (fka Westin) Tai Ping Yang, Shanghai	Sheraton Hotels & Resorts	578	230-280
Grand Hyatt Shanghai	Hyatt International	555	320-335
Pudong Shangri-la	Shangri-la Hotels & Resorts	606	330-350
Hilton Shanghai	Hilton Hotels International	720	264
Four Seasons Shanghai	Four Seasons Hotels	439	312-362

Exhibit 4   Major Luxury Hotels in Shanghai (2005) (in US$)

Source: Company files.

*Ratings and pricing were obtained from Frommer's Hotel Guide online as of March 2005.

the opportunity created by this initiative and invested in the Pudong area. International luxury hotel chains soon followed and by mid-1998 Shangri-la opened the first five-star hotel in Pudong. Several months later, in the fall of 1998, Hyatt International opened its first Chinese Grand Hyatt in Pudong. This luxury hotel occupied the top 36 floors of Pudong's 88-story Jin Mao Tower, making it the tallest hotel in the world. Quickly, other luxury hotels followed these entries, and there was some thought among industry observers that the Shanghai luxury hotel market was saturated, even before Majestica's proposed entry.

MAJESTICA—CPS NEGOTIATION

Shanghai was an ideal location for Majestica's expansion into mainland China. First, the Shanghai location met Majestica's preference for locating in major commercial and financial centres. In fact, Shanghai ranked second to Paris on the company's list of attractive international location choices. Shanghai was also attractive for its investment infrastructure, especially in terms of the service mentality of the Shanghai people. The quality of people was important for the development of a service culture.

In addition to being an ideal location, Majestica was interested in the partner. The partner was seen as having both the appetite and resources and could provide the potential to enter into multiple cities in China in the future. Such an owner not only reduced Majestica's concern about the political risk in China but also ensured a long-term commitment to the city and the support of the Shanghai municipal government to the project. The fact that CPS was publicly listed in Hong Kong gave Majestica more confidence about business transparency and independence from government influence. Further, the fact that the hotel was under construction made the opportunity more attractive to Majestica.

Majestica's proposal to operate the luxury hotel satisfied CPS's ambition to build a pre-eminent hotel in Shanghai. Majestica's outstanding financial performance and reputation in

the luxury hotel industry convinced CPS that Majestica had the capability to provide the expected rate of return to its investment in the Hotel. CPS's confidence in Majestica was reflected in changing the original hotel design from 600 to 700 rooms (the Sheraton standard) to 375 to 450 rooms to meet the high standard of Majestica.

Majestica and CPS signed a letter of intent on August 20, 2004. After the signing of the letter of intent, the two parties started negotiation on the management contract. With respect to the fee structure, CPS was impressed by Majestica's above-market results for existing properties and was confident that the same could be achieved for the hotel. CPS agreed that Majestica would receive a base fee of three per cent of gross revenues of the hotel, as per its standard arrangement. In addition, Majestica would receive incentive fees based on the hotel's operating performance. Such incentives were in place for 90 per cent of the properties that Majestica managed.

The key issues in the negotiation that required resolution in March 2005 were the length of contract term and the control that Majestica could have over the management of the hotel.

Length of Contract Term

Most of the negotiation time was spent on the issue of the length of contract term. The length of the term of management contract was very important to Majestica. Majestica did not sign short-term management contracts. Based on its typical management contract term of 50 to 60 years elsewhere in the world, Majestica asked for a contract term of 55 years in its negotiation with CPS. CPS was shocked by this request; it had been prepared to offer only 12 years. In China, there were two levels of licensing in hotel development and management. The first level of licensing was from the government to the owner for the use of the land on which the hotel was built. The maximum length of land lease was 50 years. The second level of licensing was from the owner of the hotel to the operator who would manage the hotel on behalf of the owner. The normal hotel management term in China was only 10 years, since one of the objectives of the licensors was to learn hotel management and eventually manage the hotel themselves.

The big gap between the two parties on the contract length was a very difficult issue in the negotiation. After consultation with its parent company and presumably the Shanghai municipal government, CPS countered with an offer of 30 years. Majestica insisted that the hotel management contract term should be at least 50 years, the same as the land use right certificate term that CPS had received from the government. CPS argued that the hotel industry belonged to a sector which limited foreign investment, and government regulations would not allow the duration of hotel operation by foreign investors to be over 30 years. It further suggested that Majestica could enjoy a 30-year operation period, and the operation period could be extended when it expired, if both parties agreed to extend.

Pre-opening Assistance

Majestica assumed a substantial pre-opening role by sending senior people, such as its senior vice-president of design and construction, to help CPS in the design and constructing of the hotel. CPS welcomed Majestica's help but couldn't accept Majestica's request for retaining the approval right over all design aspects relating to the hotel, including the furniture, fixtures and equipment. Majestica argued that it requested this right to keep chain consistency, to make sure that the hotel would be developed and constructed as a world-class luxury hotel and to allow effective functioning of the hotel in operation.

Name of the Hotel

CPS suggested that the hotel be named "Shanghai Oceania—Majestica Hotel." Majestica insisted that the Hotel should be under the name "Majestica Hotel, Shanghai." This was essential to and consistent with Majestica's international strategic expansion program. Majestica believed that the Majestica brand was critical to the successful operation of the hotel as an international luxury hotel. Majestica would not agree to operate the hotel under any other name.

General Manager

Another major issue under debate was staffing the different levels of the hotel management (Exhibit 5). The hotel's general manager was responsible for the overall operation. In general, the two parties agreed that the general manager, upon the opening of the hotel, would be an expatriate. CPS, however, expressed the wish that in the near future, a Chinese general manager would be used. Majestica told CPS that in the selection of a general manager for the hotel, the competence of the general manager was a more important issue than their ethnic background and that while they could make every effort to locate a suitable person with Chinese background, they could not guarantee such an appointment. There was simply no history of Chinese nationals managing world class hotels at or near this level.

Expatriates

In discussions about the number of expatriates to be employed, the localization issue was raised again and was expressed more strongly. CPS could accept the use of any number of expatriates that Majestica considered necessary to get the hotel up and running. But they insisted that the number of the expatriate managers should be gradually reduced and local managers trained to replace them. The reasons were two-fold. First, such a move would cut down the overall operating costs, as it was very expensive to use expatriates. Second, learning how to operate a world class luxury hotel was one of CPS's objectives, and CPS expected Majestica to train the local employees and eventually use them to replace the expatriates.

Specifically, CPS requested that Majestica use a deputy general manager and a deputy financial controller sent by CPS. Majestica told CPS that Majestica would like to fill the positions of senior hotel personnel with local people, both from a cost

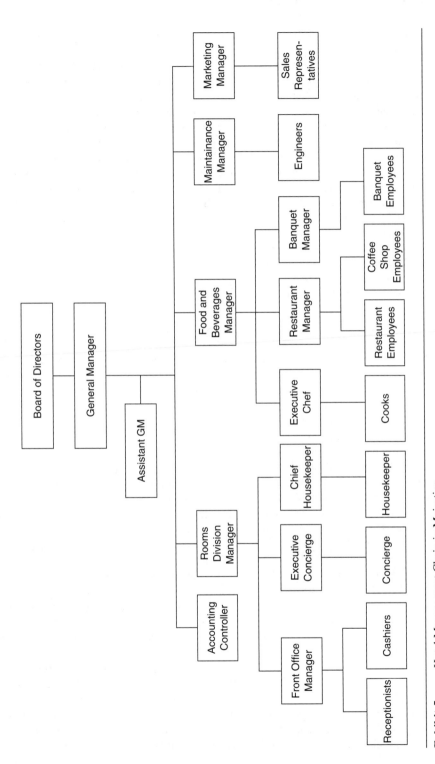

Exhibit 5   Hotel Management Chain in Majestica

Source: Company files.

and a cultural perspective. However, at this time, Majestica did not believe that local people would have the prerequisite experience (i.e. having held an equivalent position successfully in a world class luxury hotel) to perform their duties at the hotel on a basis consistent with its operation as an international world class luxury hotel. In addition, hotel management was a service business, and it took a long time to build a service culture. On average, it took 12 to 15 years for the culture to be absorbed by hotel professionals. Therefore, it was difficult to reduce the number of expatriates in the foreseeable future. In fact, staffing key positions in the new hotels with experienced hotel operations personnel was one of the secrets to Majestica's success. Richard Roy noted: "Exporting the Majestica work ethic does not depend on manuals, but on seeding new markets with those skilled at finding similar people in new places."

General Staffing

Closely related to the issues of the general manager and expatriates was the responsibility and authority of general staffing. Majestica insisted that it must have the exclusive responsibility and authority on the hiring, paying, supervising, relocating and discharging of all personnel of the hotel, and that CPS should unconditionally employ all the personnel selected and pay all the employment expenses. Majestica emphasized that selecting the appropriate employees and developing their attitudes and job performance in the context of Majestica's operating philosophy was critical to maintaining consistently high-quality performance. Therefore, Majestica should have exclusive authority in staffing to achieve a consistency of staff attitude and service standards. CPS argued that it was entitled to share the responsibility and authority in staffing as the ultimate employer of the hotel staff.

Purchasing

Majestica insisted that, commencing on the opening date, the hotel should participate in Majestica's centralized purchasing system for furniture, fixtures, operating equipment and supplies, and CPS should pay Majestica a modest fee relating to such centralized purchasing. Majestica argued that central purchasing could ensure standardized products, economies of scale and control over quality and design. CPS was concerned about the purchase prices and insisted that domestic purchasing should be a first priority.

With regard to personal property, other than the operating equipment and supplies, Majestica agreed that CPS could be responsible for the purchasing, subject to Majestica's approval right over the design of the personal property, as well as the firm used to purchase and install the personal property.

Owners' Access to Hotel Rooms

As the owner of the hotel, CPS requested access to hotel rooms or the use of some hotel rooms as offices. Majestica, however, insisted that the owner should not have any privileges over the use of hotel rooms as such an arrangement would cause confusion for the hotel management.

Arbitration

Another major issue discussed in the negotiation was related to arbitration. While both parties agreed to an arbitration process in the event of future disputes, they disagreed on the location for dispute resolution. Majestica insisted on a third country, following the norm commonly practised by the company. CPS, however, insisted that any arbitration should take place in China.

On top of the various issues in the negotiation of the management contract, CPS asked Majestica to take a minority equity position in the hotel. Generally, Majestica made only minority investments in properties where it was necessary and justified. It sought to limit its total capital exposure to no more than 20 per cent of the total equity required for the new property. The Foreign Investment Law in China, however, had stipulated until recently that the equity holdings by foreign investor(s) in an equity joint venture should be no less than 25 per cent. Thus, the request by CPS exceeded Majestica's upper limit on minority investment policy.

After many rounds of negotiation in the past three months, several issues remained unresolved. While CPS showed its flexibility and made concessions with a counter offer of 30-year contract term, it was clear that Majestica was expected to reciprocate CPS's flexibility and make some concessions in the next round of negotiations. However, Majestica found it difficult to make any concessions. Any requests made in the management contract were based on its operating philosophy for building a service culture, the key success factor in the luxury hotel industry.

THE DECISION

Thinking of the prolonged negotiation, Richard Roy felt disappointed because a lot of management time had been invested in this Shanghai project, but no decision had been reached. Reading through the minutes of the negotiation

again, it was clear to Roy that many of the issues under dispute reflected the conflict between Majestica's operating philosophy and CPS's hands-on approach as the owner of the hotel. The Shanghai deal was a great opportunity, particularly if the management contract could be settled quickly. Roy was unsure what position Majestica should take. Given the importance of the China market, should Majestica adopt a contingency approach and relax its operating philosophy at this time, or should it stick with its original philosophy, even if this meant not entering the Shanghai market?

NOTES

1. All amounts in US$ unless otherwise specified.
2. In China, there are two basic categories of hotels. Tourist hotels are licensed to receive foreigners. The rest are open only to domestic visitors. Tourist hotels are usually better built and better equipped than domestic hotels.

ELI LILLY IN INDIA: RETHINKING THE JOINT VENTURE STRATEGY

Prepared by Nikhil Celly under the supervision of Professors Charles Dhanaraj and Paul W. Beamish

Version: (A) 2005-12-02

In August 2001, Dr. Lorenzo Tallarigo, president of Intercontinental Operations, Eli Lilly and Company (Lilly), a leading pharmaceutical firm based in the United States, was getting ready for a meeting in New York, with D. S. Brar, chairman and chief executive officer (CEO) of Ranbaxy Laboratories Limited (Ranbaxy), India. Lilly and Ranbaxy had started a joint venture (JV) in India, Eli Lilly-Ranbaxy Private Limited (ELR), that was incorporated in March 1993. The JV had steadily grown to a full-fledged organization employing more than 500 people in 2001.

However, in recent months Lilly was re-evaluating the directions for the JV, with Ranbaxy signaling an intention to sell its stake. Tallarigo was scheduled to meet with Brar to decide on the next steps.

THE GLOBAL PHARMACEUTICAL INDUSTRY IN THE 1990S

The pharmaceutical industry had come about through both forward integration from the manufacture of organic chemicals and a backward integration from druggist-supply houses. The industry's rapid growth was aided by increasing worldwide incomes and a universal demand for better health care; however, most of the world market for pharmaceuticals was concentrated in North America, Europe and Japan. Typically, the largest four firms claimed 20 per cent of sales, the top 20 firms 50 per cent to 60 per cent and the 50 largest companies accounted for 65 per cent to 75 per cent of sales (see Exhibit 1). Drug discovery was an expensive process, with leading firms spending more than 20 per cent of their sales on research and development (R&D). Developing a drug, from discovery to launch in a major market, took 10 to 12 years and typically cost US$500 million to US$800 million (in 1992). Bulk production of active ingredients was the norm, along with the ability to decentralize manufacturing and packaging to adapt to particular market needs. Marketing was usually equally targeted to physicians and the paying customers. Increasingly, government agencies, such as Medicare, and health management organizations (HMOs) in the United States were gaining influence in the buying processes. In most countries, all activities related to drug research and manufacturing were strictly controlled by government agencies, such as the Food and Drug Administration (FDA) in the United States, the Committee on Proprietary Medicinal Products (CPMP) in Europe, and the Ministry of Health and Welfare (MHW) in Japan.

Patents were the essential means by which a firm protected its proprietary knowledge. The safety provided by the patents allowed firms to price their products appropriately in order to accumulate funds for future research. The basic reason to patent a new drug was to guarantee the exclusive legal right to profit from its innovation for a certain number of years, typically 20 years for a product patent. There was usually a time lag of about eight to 10 years from the time the patent was obtained and the time of regulatory approval to first launch in the United States or Europe. Time lags for emerging markets and in Japan were longer. The "product patent" covered the chemical substance itself, while a "process patent" covered the method of processing or manufacture. Both patents guaranteed the inventor a 20-year monopoly on the innovation, but the process patent offered much less protection, since it was fairly easy to modify a chemical process. It was also very difficult to legally prove that a process patent had been created to manufacture a product identical to that of a competitor. Most countries relied solely on process patents until the mid-1950s, although many countries had since recognized the product patent in law. While companies used the global market to amortize the huge investments required to produce a new drug, they were hesitant to invest in countries where the intellectual property regime was weak.

As health-care costs soared in the 1990s, the pharmaceutical industry in developed countries began coming under increased scrutiny. Although patent protection was strong in developed countries, there were various types of price controls. Prices for the same drugs varied between the United States and Canada by a factor of 1.2 to 2.5.[1] Parallel trade or trade by independent firms taking advantage of such differentials represented a serious threat to pharmaceutical suppliers, especially in Europe. Also, the rise of generics, unbranded drugs of comparable efficacy in treating the disease but available at a fraction of the cost of the branded drugs, were challenging the pricing power of the pharmaceutical companies. Manufacturers of generic drugs had no expense for drug research and development of new compounds and only had limited budgets for popularizing the compound with the medical community. The generic companies made their money by copying what other pharmaceutical companies discovered, developed and created a market for. Health management organizations (HMOs) were growing and consolidating their drug purchases. In the United States, the administration under President Clinton, which took office in 1992, investigated the possibility of a comprehensive health plan, which, among other things, would have allowed an increased use of generics and laid down some form of regulatory pressure on pharmaceutical profits.

Company	Origin	1992 Sales*	Company	Origin	2001 Sales**
Glaxo	US	8,704	Pfizer	USA	25,500
Merck	UK	8,214	GlaxoSmithKline	UK	24,800
Bristol-Myers Squibb	US	6,313	Merck & Co	USA	21,350
Hoechst	GER	6,042	AstraZeneca	UK	16,480
Ciba-Geigy	SWI	5,192	Bristol-Myers Squibb	USA	15,600
SmithKline Beecham	US	5,100	Aventis	FRA	15,350
Roche	SWI	4,897	Johnson & Johnson	USA	14,900
Sandoz	SWI	4,886	Novartis	SWI	14,500
Bayer	GER	4,670	Pharmacia Corp	USA	11,970
American Home	US	4,589	Eli Lilly	USA	11,540
Pfizer	US	4,558	Wyeth	USA	11,710
Eli Lilly	US	4,537	Roche	SWI	8,530
Johnson & Johnson	US	4,340	Schering-Plough	USA	8,360
Rhone Poulenc Rorer	US	4,096	Abbot Laboratories	USA	8,170
Abbot	US	4,025	Takeda	JAP	7,770
			Sanofi-Synthélabo	FRA	5,700
			Boehringer Ingelheim	GER	5,600
			Bayer	GER	5,040
			Schering AG	GER	3,900
			Akzo Nobel	NTH	3,550

Exhibit 1   World Pharmaceutical Suppliers 1992 and 2001 (US$ millions)

*Market Share Reporter, 1993.
**Pharmaceutical Executive, May 2002.

THE INDIAN PHARMACEUTICAL INDUSTRY IN THE 1990s

Developing countries, such as India, although large by population, were characterized by low per capita gross domestic product (GDP). Typically, healthcare expenditures accounted for a very small share of GDP, and health insurance was not commonly available. The 1990 figures for per capita annual expenditure on drugs in India were estimated at US$3, compared to US$412 in Japan, US$222 in Germany and US$191 in the United Kingdom.[2] Governments and large corporations extended health coverage, including prescription drug coverage, to their workers.

In the years before and following India's independence in 1947, the country had no indigenous capability to produce pharmaceuticals, and was dependent on imports. The Patent and Designs Act of 1911, an extension of the British colonial rule, enforced adherence to the international patent law, and gave rise to a number of multinational firms' subsidiaries in India, that wanted to import drugs from their respective countries of origin. Post-independence, the first public sector drug company, Hindustan Antibiotics Limited (HAL), was established in 1954, with the help of the World Health Organization, and Indian Drugs and Pharmaceutical Limited (IDPL) was established in 1961 with the help of the then Soviet Union.

The 1970s saw several changes that would dramatically change the intellectual property regime and give rise to the emergence of local manufacturing companies. Two such key changes were the passage of the Patents Act 1970 (effective April 1972) and the Drug Price Control Order (DPCO). The Patents Act in essence abolished the product patents for all pharmaceutical and agricultural products, and permitted process patents for five to seven years. The DPCO instituted price controls, by which a government body stipulated prices for all drugs. Subsequently, this list was revised in 1987 to 142 drugs (which accounted for 72 per cent of the turnover of the industry). Indian drug prices were estimated to be five per cent to 20 per cent of the U.S. prices and among the lowest in the world.[3] The DPCO also limited profits pharmaceutical companies could earn to approximately six per cent of sales turnover. Also, the post-manufacturing expenses were limited to 100 per cent of the production costs. At the World Health Assembly in 1982 Indira Gandhi, then Prime Minister of India, aptly captured the national sentiment on the issue in an often-quoted statement:

> The idea of a better-ordered world is one in which medical discoveries will be free of patents and there will be no profiteering from life and death.

With the institution of both the DPCO and the 1970 Patent Act, drugs became available more cheaply, and local firms were encouraged to make copies of drugs by developing their own processes, leading to bulk drug production. The profitability was sharply reduced for multinational companies, many of which began opting out of the Indian market due to the disadvantages they faced from the local competition. Market share of multinational companies dropped from 80 per cent in 1970 to 35 per cent in the mid-1990s as those companies exited the market due to the lack of patent protection in India.

In November 1984, there were changes in the government leadership following Gandhi's assassination. The dawn of the 1990s saw India initiating economic reform and embracing globalization. Under the leadership of Dr. Manmohan Singh, then finance minister, the government began the process of liberalization and moving the economy away from import substitution to an export-driven economy. Foreign direct investment was encouraged by increasing the maximum limit of foreign ownership to 51 per cent (from 40 per cent) in the drugs and pharmaceutical industry (see Exhibit 2). It was in this environment that Eli Lilly was considering getting involved.

ELI LILLY AND COMPANY

Colonel Eli Lilly founded Eli Lilly and Company in 1876. The company would become one of the largest pharmaceutical companies in the United States from the early 1940s until 1985 but it began with just $1,400 and four employees, including Lilly's 14-year-old son. This was accomplished with a company philosophy grounded in a commitment to scientific and managerial excellence. Over the years, Eli Lilly discovered, developed, manufactured and sold a broad line of human health and agricultural products. Research and development was crucial to Lilly's long-term success.

Before 1950, most OUS (a company term for "Outside the United States") activities were export focused. Beginning in the 1950s, Lilly undertook systematic expansion of its OUS activities, setting up several affiliates overseas. In the mid-1980s, under the leadership of then chairman, Dick Wood, Lilly began a significant

	1992	1994	1996	1998	2000
Gross domestic product (GDP) at current market prices in US$	244	323	386	414	481
Consumer price index (June 1982 = 100) in local currency, period average	77.4	90.7	108.9	132.2	149.3
Recorded official unemployment as a percentage of total labor force	9.7	9.3	9.1	9.2	9.2
Stock of foreign reserves plus gold (national valuation), end-period	8,665	23,054	23,784	29,833	48,200
"Foreign direct investment inflow (in US$ millions)[1]"	252	974	2,525	2,633	2,319
Total exports	19,563	25,075	33,055	33,052	43,085
Total imports	23,580	26,846	37,376	42,318	49,907

Year[2]	Population*
1991	846
2001	1,027

Exhibit 2   India Economy at a Glance

Source: The Economist Intelligence Unit.

1. United Nations Commission on Trade and Development
2. 1991, 2001 Census of India
*In millions.

move toward global markets. A separate division within the company, Eli Lilly International Corporation, with responsibility for worldwide marketing of all its products, took an active role in expanding the OUS operations. By 1992, Lilly's products were manufactured and distributed through 25 countries and sold in more than 130 countries. The company had emerged as a world leader in oral and injectable antibiotics and in supplying insulin and related diabetic care products. In 1992, Lilly International was headed by Sidney Taurel, an MBA from Columbia University, with work experience in South America and Europe, and Gerhard Mayr, an MBA from Stanford, with extensive experience in Europe. Mayr wanted to expand Lilly's operations in Asia, where several countries including India were opening up their markets for foreign investment. Lilly also saw opportunities to use

the world for clinical testing, which would enable it to move forward faster, as well as shape opinion with leaders in the medical field around the world; something that would help in Lilly's marketing stage.

RANBAXY LABORATORIES

Ranbaxy began in the 1960s as a family business, but with a visionary management grew rapidly to emerge as the leading domestic pharmaceutical firm in India. Under the leadership of Dr. Parvinder Singh, who held a doctoral degree from the University of Michigan, the firm evolved into a serious research-oriented firm. Singh, who joined Ranbaxy to assist his father in 1967, rose to become the joint managing director in 1977, managing director in 1982, and vice-chairman and managing director in 1987. Singh's visionary management, along with the operational leadership provided by Brar, who joined the firm in 1977, was instrumental in turning the family business into a global corporation. In the early 1990s, when almost the entire domestic pharmaceutical industry was opposing a tough patent regime, Ranbaxy was accepting it as given. Singh's argument was unique within the industry in India:

> The global marketplace calls for a single set of rules; you cannot have one for the Indian market and the other for the export market. Tomorrow's global battles will be won by product leaders, not operationally excellent companies. Tomorrow's leaders must be visionaries, whether they belong to the family or not. Our mission at Ranbaxy is to become a research based international pharmaceutical company.[4]

By the early 1990s, Ranbaxy grew to become India's largest manufacturer of bulk drugs[5] and generic drugs, with a domestic market share of 15 per cent (see Exhibit 3).

One of Ranbaxy's core competencies was its chemical synthesis capability, but the company had begun to outsource some bulk drugs in limited quantities. The company produced pharmaceuticals in four locations in India. The company's capital costs were typically 50 per cent to 75 per cent lower than those of comparable U.S. plants and were meant to serve foreign markets in addition to the Indian market. Foreign markets, especially those in more developed countries, often had stricter quality control requirements, and such a difference meant that the manufacturing practices required to compete in those markets appeared to be costlier from the perspective of less developed markets. Higher prices in other countries provided the impetus for Ranbaxy to pursue international

Company	1996*	Company	2000
Glaxo-Wellcome	4.97	Ranbaxy	20.00
Cipla	2.98	Cipla	12.00
Ranbaxy	2.67	Dr. Reddy's Labs	11.30
Hoechts-Roussel	2.60	Glaxo (India)	7.90
Knoll Pharmaceutical	1.76	Lupin Labs	7.80
Pfizer	1.73	Aurobindo Pharma	7.60
Alembic	1.68	Novartis	7.20
Torrent Pharma	1.60	Wockhardt Ltd.	6.80
Lupin Labs	1.56	Sun Pharma	6.70
Zydus-Cadila	1.51	Cadilla Healthcare	5.80
Ambalal Sarabhai	1.38	Nicholas Piramal	5.70
Smithkline Beecham	1.20	Aventis Pharma	5.30
Aristo Pharma	1.17	Alembic Ltd.	4.80
Parke Davis	1.15	Morepen Labs	4.70
Cadila Pharma	1.12	Torrent Pharma	4.40
E. Merck	1.11	IPCA Labs	4.20
Wockhardt	1.08	Knoll Pharma	3.70
John Wyeth	1.04	Orchid Chemicals	3.60
Alkem Laboratories	1.04	E Merck	3.50
Hindustan Ciba Geigy	1.03	Pfizer	3.40

Exhibit 3   Top 20 Pharmaceutical Companies in India by Sales, 1996 to 2000 (Rs billions)

Source: "Report on Pharmaceutical Sector in India," *Scope Magazine,* September 2001, p.14.

*1996 figures are from ORG, Bombay as reported in Lanjouw, J.O., www.oiprc.ox.ac.uk/EJWP0799.html, NBER working paper No. 6366.

markets; the company had a presence in 47 markets outside India, mainly through exports handled through an international division. Ranbaxy's R&D efforts began at the end of the 1970s; in 1979, the company still had only 12 scientists. As Ranbaxy entered the international market in the 1980s, R&D was responsible for registering its products in foreign markets, most of which was directed to process R&D; R&D expenditures ranged from two per cent to five per cent of the annual sales with future targets of seven per cent to eight per cent.

THE LILLY RANBAXY JV

Ranbaxy approached Lilly in 1992 to investigate the possibility of supplying certain active ingredients or sourcing of intermediate products to Lilly in order to provide low-cost sources of intermediate pharmaceutical ingredients. Lilly had had earlier relationships with manufacturers in India to produce human or animal insulin and then export the products to the Soviet Union using the Russia/India trade route, but those had never developed into on-the-ground relationships within the Indian market. Ranbaxy was the second largest exporter of all products in India and the second largest pharmaceutical company in India after Glaxo (a subsidiary of the U.K.-based firm).

Rajiv Gulati, at that time a general manager of business development and marketing controller at Ranbaxy, who was instrumental in developing the strategy for Ranbaxy, recalled:

> In the 1980s, many multinational pharmaceutical companies had a presence in India. Lilly did not. As a result of both the sourcing of intermediate products as well as the fact that Lilly was one of the only players not yet in India, we felt that we could use Ranbaxy's knowledge of the market to get our feet on the ground in India. Ranbaxy would supply certain products to the joint venture from its own portfolio that were currently being manufactured in India and then formulate and finish some of Lilly's products locally. The joint venture would buy the active ingredients and Lilly would have Ranbaxy finish the package and allow the joint venture to sell and distribute those products.

The first meeting was held at Lilly's corporate center in Indianapolis in late 1990. Present were Ranbaxy's senior executives, Dr. Singh, vice-chairman, and D.S. Brar, chief operating officer (COO), and Lilly's senior executives including Gene Step and Richard Wood, the CEO of Lilly. Rickey Pate, a corporate attorney at Eli Lilly who was present at the meeting, recalled:

> It was a very smooth meeting. We had a lot in common. We both believed in high ethical standards, in technology and innovation, as well as in the future of patented products in India. Ranbaxy executives emphasized their desire to be a responsible corporate citizen and expressed their concerns for their employees. It was quite obvious Ranbaxy would be a compatible partner in India.

Lilly decided to form the joint venture in India to focus on marketing of Lilly's drugs there, and a formal JV agreement was signed in November 1992. The newly created JV was to have an authorized capital of Rs200 million (equivalent of US$7.1 million), and an initial subscribed equity capital of Rs84 million (US$3 million), with equal contribution from Lilly and Ranbaxy, leading to an equity ownership of 50 per cent each. The board of directors for the JV would comprise six directors, three from each company. A management committee was also created comprising two directors, one from each company, and Lilly retained the right to appoint the CEO who would be responsible for the day-to-day operations. The agreement also provided for transfer of shares, in the event any one of the partners desired to dispose some or its entire share in the company.

In the mid-1990s, Lilly was investigating the possibility of extending its operations to include generics. Following the launch of the Indian JV, Lilly and Ranbaxy, entered into two other agreements related to generics, one in India to focus on manufacturing generics, and the other in the United States to focus on the marketing of generics. However, within less than a year, Lilly made a strategic decision not to enter the generics market and the two parties agreed to terminate the JV agreements related to the generics. Mayr recalled:

At that time we were looking at the Indian market although we did not have any particular time frame for entry. We particularly liked Ranbaxy, as we saw an alignment of the broad values. Dr. Singh had a clear vision of leading Ranbaxy to become an innovation driven company. And we liked what we saw in them. Of course, for a time we were looking at the generic business and wondering if this was something we should be engaged in. Other companies had separate division for generics and we were evaluating such an idea. However, we had a pilot program in Holland and that taught us what it took to be competitive in generics and decided that business wasn't for us, and so we decided to get out of generics.

The Start-up

By March 1993, Andrew Mascarenhas, an American citizen of Indian origin, who at the time was the general manager for Lilly's Caribbean basin, based in San Juan, Puerto Rico, was selected to become the managing director of the joint venture. Rajiv Gulati, who at the time spearheaded the business development and marketing efforts at Ranbaxy, was chosen as the director of marketing and sales at the JV. Mascarenhas recalled:

Lilly saw the joint venture as an investment the company needed to make. At the time India was a country of 800 million people: 200 million to 300 million of them were considered to be within the country's middle class that represented the future of India. The concept of globalization was just taking hold at Lilly. India, along with China and Russia were seen as markets where Lilly needed to build a greater presence. Some resistance was met due to the recognition that a lot of Lilly's products were already being sold by Indian manufacturers due to the lack of patent protection and intellectual property rights so the question was what products should we put in there that could be competitive. The products that were already being manufactured had sufficient capacity; so it was an issue of trying to leverage the markets in which those products were sold into.

Lilly was a name that most physicians in India did not recognize despite its leadership position in the United States, it did not have any recognition in India. Ranbaxy was the leader within India. When I was informed that the name of the joint venture was to be Lilly Ranbaxy, first thing I did was to make sure that the name of the joint venture was Eli Lilly Ranbaxy and not just Lilly Ranbaxy. The reason for this was based on my earlier experience in India, where "good quality" rightly or wrongly, was associated with foreign imported goods. Eli Lilly Ranbaxy sounded foreign enough!

Early on, Mascarenhas and Gulati worked getting the venture up and running with office space and an employee base. Mascarenhas recalled:

I got a small space within Ranbaxy's set-up. We had two tables, one for Rajiv and the other for me. We had to start from that infrastructure and move towards building up the organization from scratch. Rajiv was great to work with and we both were able to see eye-to-eye on most issues. Dr. Singh was a strong supporter and the whole of Ranbaxy senior management tried to assist us whenever we asked for help.

The duo immediately hired a financial analyst, and the team grew from there. Early on, they hired a medical director, a sales manager and a human resources manager. The initial team was a good one, but there was enormous pressure and the group worked seven days a week. Ranbaxy's help was used for getting government approvals, licenses, distribution and supplies. Recalled Gulati:

We used Ranbaxy's name for everything. We were new and it was very difficult for us. We used their distribution network as we did not have one and Lilly did not want to invest heavily in setting up a distribution network. We paid Ranbaxy for the service. Ranbaxy was very helpful.

By the end of 1993, the venture moved to an independent place, began launching products and employed more than 200 people. Within another year, Mascarenhas had hired a significant sales force and had recruited medical doctors and financial people for the regulatory group with assistance from Lilly's Geneva office. Mascarenhas recalled:

Our recruiting theme was 'Opportunity of a Lifetime' i.e., joining a new company, and to be part of its very foundation. Many who joined us, especially at senior level, were experienced executives. By entering this new and untested company, they were really taking a huge risk with their careers and the lives of their families.

However, the employee turnover in the Indian pharmaceutical industry was very high. Sandeep Gupta, director of marketing recalled:

Our biggest problem was our high turnover rate. A sales job in the pharmaceutical industry was not the most sought-after position. Any university graduate could be employed. The pharmaceutical industry in India is very unionized. Ranbaxy's HR practices were designed to work with unionized employees. From the very beginning, we did not want our recruits to join unions. Instead, we chose to show recruits that they had a career in ELR. When they joined us as sales graduates they did not just remain at that level. We took a conscious decision to promote from within the company. The venture began investing in training and used Lilly's training programs. The programs were customized for Indian conditions, but retained Lilly's values (see Exhibit 4).

Within a year, the venture team began gaining the trust and respect of doctors, due to the strong values adhered to by Lilly. Mascarenhas described how the venture fought the Indian stigma:

Lilly has a code of ethical conduct called the Red Book, and the company did not want to go down the path where it might be associated with unethical behavior. But Lilly felt Ranbaxy knew how to do things the right way and that they respected their employees, which was a very important attribute. So following Lilly's Red Book values, the group told doctors the truth; both the positive and negative aspects of their drugs. If a salesperson didn't know the answer to something, they didn't lie or make up something; they told the doctor they didn't know. No bribes were given or taken, and it was found that honesty and integrity could actually be a competitive advantage. Sales people were trained to offer product information to doctors. The group gradually became distinguished by this "strange" behavior.

Recalled Sudhanshu Kamat, controller of finance at ELR:

Lilly from the start treated us as its employees, like all its other affiliates worldwide. We followed the same systems and processes that any Lilly affiliate would worldwide.

Much of the success of the joint venture is attributed to the strong and cohesive working relationship of Mascarenhas and Gulati. Mascarenhas recalled:

We both wanted the venture to be successful. We both had our identities to the JV, and there was no Ranbaxy versus Lilly politics. From the very start when we had our office at Ranbaxy premises, I was invited to dine with their senior management. Even after moving to our own office, I continued the practice of having lunch at Ranbaxy HQ on a weekly basis. I think it helped a lot to be accessible at all times and to build on the personal relationship.

The two companies had very different business focuses. Ranbaxy was a company driven by the generics business. Lilly, on the other hand, was driven by innovation and discovery.

Mascarenhas focused his effort on communicating Eli Lilly's values to the new joint venture:

I spent a lot of time communicating Lilly's values to newly hired employees. In the early days, I interviewed our senior applicants personally. I was present in the two-day training sessions that we offered for the new employees, where I shared the values of the company. That was a critical task for me to make sure that the right foundations were laid down for growth.

The first products that came out of the joint venture were human insulin from Lilly and several Ranbaxy products; but the team faced constant challenges in dealing with government regulations on the one hand and financing the affiliate on the other. There were also cash flow constraints.

The ministry of health provided limitations on Lilly's pricing, and even with the margin the Indian government allowed, most of it went to the wholesalers and the pharmacies, pursuant to formulas in the Indian ministry of health. Once those were factored out of the gross margin, achieving profitability was a real challenge, as some of the biggest obstacles faced were duties imposed by the Indian government on imports

---

PEOPLE

"The people who make up this company are its most valuable assets"

- Respect for the individual
  - o Courtesy and politeness at all times
  - o Sensitivity to other people's views
  - o Respect for ALL people regardless of case, religion, sex or age
- Careers NOT jobs
  - o Emphasis on individual's growth, personal and professional
  - o Broaden experience via cross-functional moves

"The first responsibility of our supervisors is **to build men, then medicines**"

ATTITUDE

"There is very little difference between people. But that difference makes a BIG difference. The little difference is . . . Whether it is POSITIVE or NEGATIVE"

"Are we part of the PROBLEM or part of the SOLUTION?"

TEAM

"*None of us* is as smart *as all of us*"

INTEGRITY

- Integrity outside the company
  - a. "We should not do anything or be expected to take any action that we would be ashamed to explain to our family or close friends"
  - b. "The red-faced test"
  - c. "Integrity can be our biggest competitive advantage"
- Integrity inside the company
  - o With one another: openness, honesty

EXCELLENCE

- Serving our customers

  "In whatever we do, we must ask ourselves: how does this serve my customer better?"

- Continuous improvement

"Nothing is being done today that cannot be done better tomorrow"
- Become the Industry Standard

  "In whatever we do, we will do it so well that we become the Industry Standard"

Exhibit 4   Values at Eli Lilly Ranbaxy Limited

---

and other regulatory issues. Considering the weak intellectual property rights regime, Lilly did not want to launch some of its products, such as its top-seller, Prozac.[6] Gulati recalled:

We focused only on those therapeutic areas where Lilly had a niche. We did not adopt a localization strategy such as the ones adopted by Pfizer and Glaxo[7] that manufactured locally and sold at local prices. India is a high-volume, low price, low profit market, but it was a conscious decision by us to operate the way we did. We wanted to be in the global price band. So, we did not launch several patented products because generics were selling at 1/60th the price.

Product and marketing strategies had to be adopted to suit the market conditions. ELR's strategy evolved over the years to focus on two groups of products: one was off-patent drugs, where Lilly could add substantial value (e.g. Ceclor), and two, patented drugs, where there existed a significant barrier to entry (e.g. Reopro and Gemzar). ELR marketed Ceclor, a Ranbaxy manufactured product, but attempted to add significant value by providing medical information to the physicians and other unique marketing activities. By the end of 1996, the venture had reached the break-even and was becoming profitable.

The Mid-Term Organizational Changes

Mascarenhas was promoted in 1996 to managing director of Eli Lilly Italy, and Chris Shaw, a British national, who was then managing the operations in Taiwan, was assigned to the JV as the new managing director. Also, Gulati, who was formally a Ranbaxy employee, decided to join Eli Lilly as its employee, and was assigned to Lilly's corporate office in Indianapolis in the Business Development—Infectious Diseases therapeutic division. Chris Shaw recalled:

When I went to India as a British national, I was not sure what sort of reception I would get, knowing its history. But my family and I were received very warmly. I found a dynamic team with a strong sense of values.

Shaw focused on building systems and processes to bring stability to the fast-growing organization; his own expertise in operations made a significant contribution during this phase. He hired a senior level manager and created a team to develop standard operating procedures (SOPs) for ensuring smooth operations. The product line also expanded. The JV continued to maintain a 50-50 distribution of products from Lilly and Ranbaxy, although there was no stipulation to maintain such a ratio. The clinical organization in India was received top-ratings in internal audits by Lilly, making it suitable for a wider range of clinical trials. Shaw also streamlined the sales and marketing activities around therapeutic areas to emphasize and enrich the

knowledge capabilities of the company's sales force. Seeing the rapid change in the environment in India, ELR, with the support of Mayr, hired the management-consulting firm, McKinsey, to recommend growth options in India. ELR continued its steady performance with an annualized growth rate of about eight per cent during the late 1990s.

In 1999, Chris Shaw was assigned to Eli Lilly's Polish subsidiary, and Gulati returned to the ELR as its managing director, following his three-year tenure at Lilly's U.S. operations. Recalled Gulati:

When I joined as MD in 1999, we were growing at eight per cent and had not added any new employees. I hired 150 people over the next two years and went about putting systems and processes in place. When we started in 1993 and during Andrew's time, we were like a grocery shop. Now we needed to be a company. We had to be a large durable organization and prepare ourselves to go from sales of US$10 million to sales of US$100 million.

ELR created a medical and regulatory unit, which handled the product approval processes with government. Das, the chief financial officer (CFO), commented:

We worked together with the government on the regulatory part. Actually, we did not take shelter under the Ranbaxy name but built a strong regulatory (medical and corporate affairs) foundation.

By early 2001, the venture was recording an excellent growth rate (see Exhibit 5), surpassing the average growth rate in the Indian pharmaceutical industry. ELR had already become the 46th largest pharmaceutical company in India out of 10,000 companies. Several of the multinational subsidiaries, which were started at the same time as ELR, had either closed down or were in serious trouble. Das summarized the achievements:

The JV did add some prestige to Ranbaxy's efforts as a global player as the Lilly name had enormous credibility while Lilly gained the toehold in India. In 10 years we did not have any cannibalization of each other's employees, quite a rare event if you compare with the other JVs. This helped us build a unique culture in India.

	1998-1999	1999-2000	2000-2001
Sales	559,766	632,188	876,266
Marketing Expenses	37,302	61,366	96,854
Other Expenses	157,907	180,364	254,822
Profit after Tax	5,898	12,301	11,999
Current Assets	272,635	353,077	466,738
Current Liabilities	239,664	297,140	471,635
Total Assets	303,254	386,832	516,241
No. of Employees	358	419	460
Exchange Rate (Rupees/US$)	42.6	43.5	46.8

Exhibit 5   Eli Lilly-Ranbaxy India Financials 1998 to 2001 (Rs'000s)

Source: Company Reports.

Note: Financial year runs from April 1 to March 31.

THE NEW WORLD, 2001

The pharmaceutical industry continued to grow through the 1990s. In 2001, worldwide retail sales were expected to increase 10 per cent to about US$350 billion. The United States was expected to remain the largest and fastest growing country among the world's major drug markets over the next three years. There was a consolidation trend in the industry with ongoing mergers and acquisitions reshaping the industry. In 1990, the world's top 10 players accounted for just 28 per cent of the market, while in 2000, the number had risen to 45 per cent and continued to grow. There was also a trend among leading global pharmaceutical companies to get back to basics and concentrate on core high-margined prescription preparations and divest non-core businesses. In addition, the partnerships between pharmaceutical and biotechnology companies were growing rapidly. There were a number of challenges, such as escalating R&D costs, lengthening development and approval times for new products, growing competition from generics and follow-on products, and rising cost-containment pressures, particularly with the growing clout of managed care organizations.

By 1995, Lilly had moved up to become the 12th leading pharmaceutical supplier in the world, sixth in the U.S. market, 17th in Europe and 77th in Japan. Much of Lilly's sales success through the mid-1990s came from its antidepressant drug, Prozac. But with the wonder drug due to go off patent in 2001, Lilly was aggressively working on a number of high-potential products. By the beginning of 2001, Lilly was doing business in 151 countries, with its international sales playing a significant role in the company's success (see Exhibits 6 and 7). Dr. Lorenzo Tallarigo recalled:

When I started as the president of the intercontinental operations, I realized that the world was very different in the 2000s from the world of 1990s. Particularly there were phenomenal changes in the markets in India and China. While I firmly believed that the partnership we had with Ranbaxy was really an excellent one, the fact that we were facing such a different market in the 21st century was reason enough to carefully evaluate our strategies in these markets.

Ranbaxy, too, had witnessed changes through the 1990s. Dr. Singh became the new CEO in 1993 and formulated a new mission for

	1992	1994	1996	1998	2000
Net sales	4,963	5,711	6,998	9,236	10,862
Foreign sales	2,207	2,710	3,587	3,401	3,858
Research and development expenses	731	839	1,190	1,739	2,019
Income from continuing operations before taxes and extraordinary items	1,194	1,699	2,131	2,665	3,859
Net income	709	1,286	1,524	2,097	3,058
Dividends per share*	1.128	1.260	0.694	0.830	1.060
Current assets	3,006	3,962	3,891	5,407	7,943
Current liabilities	2,399	5,670	4,222	4,607	4,961
Property and equipment	4,072	4,412	4,307	4,096	4,177
Total assets	8,673	14,507	14,307	12,596	14,691
Long-term debt	582	2,126	2,517	2,186	2,634
Shareholder equity	4,892	5,356	6,100	4,430	6,047
Number of employees*	24,500	24,900	27,400	29,800	35,700

Exhibit 6   Lilly Financials, 1992 to 2000 (US$ millions)

Source: Company files.

*Actual value

the company: to become a research-based international pharmaceutical company with $1 billion in sales by 2003. This vision saw Ranbaxy developing new drugs through basic research, earmarking 20 per cent of the R&D budget for such work. In addition to its joint venture with Lilly, Ranbaxy made three other manufacturing/marketing investments in developed markets: a joint venture with Genpharm in Canada ($1.1 million), and the acquisitions of Ohm Labs in the United States ($13.5 million) and Rima Pharmaceuticals ($8 million) in Ireland. With these deals, Ranbaxy had manufacturing facilities around the globe. While China and Russia were expected to remain key foreign markets, Ranbaxy was looking at the United States and the United Kingdom as its core international markets for the future. In 1999, Dr. Singh handed over the reins of the company to Brar, and later the same year, Ranbaxy lost this visionary leader due to an untimely death. Brar continued Singh's vision to keep Ranbaxy in a leadership position.

However, the vast network of international sales that Ranbaxy had developed created a large financial burden, depressing the company's 2000 results, and was expected to significantly affect its cash flow in 2001 (see Exhibit 8). Vinay Kaul, vice-chairman of Ranbaxy in 2001 and chairman of the board of ELR since 2000, noted:

We have come a long way from where we started. Our role in the present JV is very limited. We had a smooth relationship and we have been of significant help to Lilly to establish a foothold in the market here in India. Also, we have opened up a number of opportunities for them to expand their network. However, we have also grown, and we are a global company with presence in a number of international markets including the United States. We had to really think if this JV is central to our operations, given that we have closed down the other two JV agreements that we had with Lilly on the generics manufacturing. It is common knowledge that whether we continue as a JV or not, we have created a substantial value for Lilly.

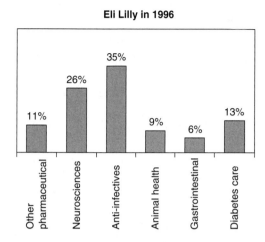

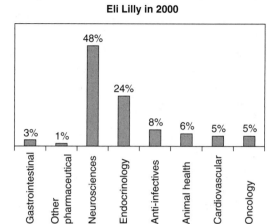

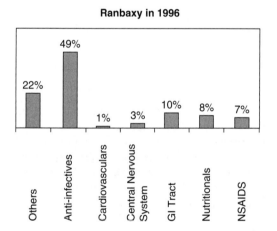

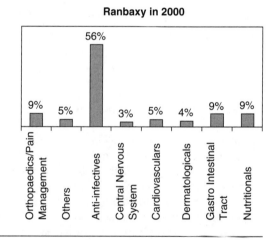

Exhibit 7 Product Segment Information, Lilly and Ranbaxy, 1996 and 2000

There were also significant changes in the Indian business environment. India signed the General Agreement on Tariffs and Trade (GATT) in April 1994 and became a World Trade Organization (WTO) member in 1995. As per the WTO, from the year 2005, India would grant product patent recognition to all new chemical entities (NCEs), i.e., bulk drugs developed then onward. Also, the Indian government had made

the decision to allow 100 per cent foreign direct investment into the drugs and pharmaceutical industry in 2001.[8] The Indian pharmaceutical market had grown at an average of 15 per cent through the 1990s, but the trends indicated a slowdown in growth, partly due to intense price competition, a shift toward chronic therapies and the entry of large players into the generic market. India was seeing its own internal consolidation

	1992-93	1994-95	1996-97	1998*	2000
Sales	4,607	7,122	11,482	10,641	17,459
Foreign sales	1,408	3,019	5,224	4,414	8,112
Profit before tax	358	1,304	1,869	1,240	1,945
Profit after tax	353	1,104	1,604	1,170	1,824
Equity dividend	66.50	199.80	379.10	560.10	869.20
Earnings per share (Rs)	16.21	25.59	32.47	13.46	15.74
Net current assets	1,737	5,790	9,335	8,321	8,258
Share capital	217.90	430.50	494.00	1,159.00	1,159.00
Reserves and surplus	1,028	6,000	11,056	12,849	16,448
Book value per share (Rs)	57.16	149.08	233.70	120.90	136.60
No. of employees	4,575	4,703	6,131	5,469	5,784
Exchange rate (US$1 = Rs)	29.00	31.40	35.90	42.60	46.80

Exhibit 8   Ranbaxy Financials 1992 to 2000 (Rs Millions)

Source: Company files.

*The financial year for Ranbaxy changed from April 1 to March 31 to calendar year in 1998. Also, the company issued a 1:2 bonus issue (see the changes in share capital and book value per share). The 1998 figures are based on nine months April to December 1998.

of major companies that were trying to bring in synergies through economies of scale. The industry would see more mergers and alliances. And with India's entry into the WTO and its agreement to begin patent protection in 2004-2005, competition on existing and new products was expected to intensify. Government guidelines were expected to include rationalization of price controls and the encouragement of more research and development. Recalled Gulati:

The change of institutional environment brought a great promise for Lilly. India was emerging into a market that had patent protection and with tremendous potential for adding value in the clinical trials, an important component in the pharmaceutical industry. In Ranbaxy, we had a partner with whom we could work very well, and one which greatly respected Lilly. However, there were considerable signals from both sides, which were forcing us to evaluate the strategy.

Dr. Vinod Mattoo, medical director of ELR commented:

We have been able to achieve penetration in key therapeutic areas of diabetes and oncology. We have created a high caliber, and non-unionized sales force with world-class sales processes. We have medical infrastructure and expertise to run clinical trials to international standards. We have been able to provide clinical trial data to support global registrations, and an organization in place to maximize returns post-2005.

EVALUATING STRATEGIC OPTIONS

Considering these several developments, Tallarigo suggested a joint task force comprising senior executives from both companies:

Soon after assuming this role, I visited India in early 2000, and had the pleasure of meeting Dr. Brar and the senior executives. It was clear to me that both Brar and I were in agreement that we needed to think carefully how we approached the future. It was there that I suggested that we create a joint task force to come up with some options that would help us make a final decision.

A task force was set up with two senior executives from Lilly's Asia-Pacific regional office (based in Singapore) and two senior executives from Ranbaxy. The task force did not include senior executives of the ELR so as to not distract the running of the day-to-day operations. Suman Das, the chief financial officer of ELR, was assigned to support the task force with the needed financial data. The task force developed several scenarios and presented different options for the board to consider.

There were rumors within the industry that Ranbaxy expected to divest the JV, and invest the cash in its growing portfolio of generics manufacturing business in international markets. There were also several other Indian companies that offered to buy Ranbaxy's stake in the JV. With India recognizing patent protection in 2005, several Indian pharmaceutical companies were keen to align with multinationals to ensure a pipeline of drugs. Although there were no formal offers from Ranbaxy, the company was expected to price its stakes as high as US$70 million. One of the industry observers in India commented:

I think it is fair for Ranbaxy to expect a reasonable return for its investment in the JV, not only the initial capital, but also so much of its intangibles in the JV. Ranbaxy's stock has grown significantly. Given the critical losses that Ranbaxy has had in some of its investments abroad, the revenue from this sale may be a significant boost for Ranbaxy's cash flow this year.

Gerhard Mayr, who in 2001 was the executive vice-president and was responsible for Lilly's demand realization around the world, continued to emphasize the emerging markets in India, China and Eastern Europe. Mayr commented on Ranbaxy:

India is an important market for us and especially after patent protection in 2005. Ranbaxy was a wonderful partner and our relationship with them was outstanding. The other two joint ventures we initiated with them in the generics did not make sense to us once we decided to get out of the generics business. We see India as a good market for Lilly. If a partner is what it takes to succeed, we should go with a partner. If it does not, we should have the flexibility to reconsider.

Tallarigo hoped that Brar would be able to provide a clear direction as to the venture's future. As he prepared for the meeting, he knew the decision was not an easy one, although he felt confident that the JV was in a good shape. While the new regulations allowed Lilly to operate as a wholly owned subsidiary in India, the partnership has been a very positive element in its strategy. Ranbaxy provided manufacturing and logistics support to the JV, and breaking up the partnership would require a significant amount of renegotiations. Also, it was not clear what the financial implications of such a move would be. Although Ranbaxy seemed to favor a sell-out, Tallarigo thought the price expectations might be beyond what Lilly was ready to accept. This meeting with Brar should provide clarity on all these issues.

NOTES

1. Estimates of industry average wholesale price levels in Europe (with Spanish levels indexed at 100 in 1989) were: Spain 100; Portugal 107; France 113; Italy 118; Belgium 131: United Kingdom 201; The Netherlands 229; West Germany 251. Source: T. Malnight, *Globalization of an Ethnocentric Firm: An Evolutionary Perspective*, Strategic Management Journal, 1995, Vol. 16 p.128.

2. Organization of Pharmaceutical Producers of India Report.

3. According to a study from Yale University, Ranitidine (300 tabs/10 pack) was priced at Rs18.53, whereas the U.S. price was 57 times more, and Ciprofloxacin (500 mg/4 pack) was at Rs28.40 in India, whereas the U.S. price was about 15 times more.

4. Quoted in *Times of India*, June 9, 1999.

5. A bulk drug is an intermediate product that goes into manufacturing of pharmaceutical products.

6. Used as an antidepressant medication.

7. An industry study by McKinsey found that Glaxo sold 50 per cent of its volume, received three per cent of revenues and one per cent of profit in India.

8. In order to regulate the parallel activities of a foreign company, which had an ongoing joint venture in India, the regulations stipulated that the foreign partner must get a "No objection letter" from its Indian partner, before setting up a wholly owned subsidiary.

4

IMPLEMENTING
WINNING CONDITIONS

In Brief

All the strategic analysis, negotiation, and implementation planning of a strategic alliance aims for the day the alliance can be formally launched. While much of the details depend on the specific nature of the agreement, there exist common practices that will take managers far down the path of successful alliance management. These include laying a positive foundation with the right team and establishing productive linkages across both organizations. It also includes dedicated focus on building trusted relationships in the early days and structuring alliance activities for some early successes. Alliances usually define success in terms of financial returns, but when the honeymoon is over, enduring and sustainable benefits will be more easily achieved through additional emphasis on effective communications, constructive conflict resolution, and continuous organizational learning—elements that support a productive relationship over time.

Finally, a sustainable alliance must accommodate the cyclical nature of relationships. Effective performance measurement combined with open discussion will signal the partners when their alliance is in need of renewal. Prompt attention to the signals will ensure continued benefits for as long as the alliance remains strategic.

Making the right decisions about strategy, partner, and structure is only the beginning. The real work starts when companies implement their alliance. While the chosen structure and scope of an alliance will significantly influence the kind of implementation required, the material covered in this section presents principles for creating winning conditions that are applicable to all.

LAY THE GROUNDWORK

Ideally, the negotiation and resulting alliance agreement will have formulated the higher-level aspects of the implementation plan, and it is now time to flesh out the details. Sufficient upfront planning will mitigate a large portion of the challenges faced in the early stages of alliance implementation. Accenture found that most companies unfortunately launch into alliances with high hopes but with no real plan to realize those hopes.[1] In most cases, emphasis is placed on the contractual elements of the deal while the day-to-day management and relationship aspects—that seed cooperation and collaboration—are ignored or are seriously underestimated.

SELECTING AN ALLIANCE MANAGER

Finding the best alliance manager to lead the venture is one of the most important decisions to be made as it will go a long way to positive results. An alliance manager should possess as many of the following qualities and characteristics as possible:

- Respect and credibility across all levels of all partners' organizations and an extensive personal network
- Ability to form good relationships with people in other organizations and possibly from different cultures
- A strong sense of diplomacy
- Creative problem-solving skills and strong negotiating skills
- Technical competence
- Comfort with navigating ambiguous circumstances; adaptability, flexibility, openness to learn from new situations
- Ability to work in and manage a team with diverse membership
- Clear understanding of the parent firms' strategies and the goals of the alliance

The alliance manager has several critical roles to play in the venture. The first involves establishing a positive tone for the relationship and creating the environment for effective collaboration. He or she is also responsible for monitoring the contributions that partners are making to the alliance and initiating appropriate corrective action if one side or the other is not living up to its commitments.[2]

The manager must be able to engage different groups within the partner firm for specific needs and should have strong interpersonal skills to do so. Organizational status, while important, is often insufficient. In many cases, the manager may have to work with large numbers of people over whom he or she have no clear authority but whom he or she may have to influence. This means the manager must have strong political and negotiating skills. How effectively the manager deals with his or her own organization is usually a good indication of how effectively he or she will interact with a partner's organization.

Continuity is an important consideration when selecting the alliance manager. Frequent management turnover can lead to instability in the alliance and be a major barrier to the establishment of the interpersonal relationships and trust required to make these arrangements work.

Appointment of an Alliance General Manager

While smaller-scale alliances may appoint an alliance manager from each organization to manage the relationship, larger ones, such as joint ventures (JV), will likely appoint one joint venture general manager (JVGM).

The JVGM finds himself or herself in a unique position of having to simultaneously meet the expectations and economic viability of the joint venture as well as the expectations of both parent companies. Frequently, parent company expectations are different, as is their corresponding metrics with which to assess JV performance. Reconciling these expectations can be further exacerbated by lack of autonomy when a parent's control practices constrain the JVGM.

JVGMs may ultimately find themselves playing the role of salesperson and mediator between the parent companies. The JVGM may need to sway reluctant parent companies to free up the promised resources that are critical to the joint venture's success. In addition, the JVGM may also need to help resolve differences between the parents, promote cross-company communications, and nurture parent relationships.

Successful JVGMs have found that the following practices help minimize these challenges:[3]

- Regardless of which organization the JVGM comes from, both partners should mutually approve the selected candidate, and the other partner should have the right to request removal of the JVGM should he or she ever be perceived as being biased or incompetent.

- Successful JVGMs see their allegiance to the joint venture first and to the parents second. This perspective promotes a win-win atmosphere.

- Ensure that reporting relationships to parent companies are in place to facilitate escalation of issues should it become necessary.

- Ensure that the JVGMs' performance and compensation package reflect the interests of the alliance and not the individual companies. Successful JVGMs report that they assess the success of the joint venture first on the relative strength of the relationship between parent companies and second on the basis of economic performance.

- While JVGMs need to be concerned about the long-term health of the partnership, short-term trade-off considerations that can bear immediate results should carry weight in decision making in order to fuel support from parent companies.

Establish Strategic and Operational Linkages

Partners need to consider where they will connect across the two organizations and how the interactions between them will be managed. Successful alliances involve numerous and reinforcing linkages at both the strategic and operational levels of the two organizations. This becomes particularly beneficial to smaller companies partnered with larger companies where turnover may be high. The more active links are at any given time, the greater the continuity and stability during times when new links and relationships need to be forged.[4]

The Strategic Interface

Designing the strategic interface between partners should take into consideration differences in organizational contexts. While it may be unrealistic to think that the executives of a small company can establish strong personal relationships with the CEO of a large multinational, creating linkages to key senior executives in the partner company is important. Senior management commitment is consistently ranked in studies as a key factor in the successful implementation of alliances.[5]

As with the negotiation phase, visible top-level commitment affects the achievement of alliance goals and signals its importance to operational managers and staff. The commitment by senior managers also enables operational managers, when required, to effectively escalate any issues that may arise.

Having a champion within the partner organization will be an enormous benefit, particularly for a small organization. Champions can help steer the venture through the bureaucracy, be credible defending the alliance against competing interests and priorities, and provide important insights in the broader perspectives of the partner company.

The Operational Interface

Numerous studies have highlighted the importance of strong linkages between middle management and operational levels in the partner companies.[6] It is hoped that building support and buy-in will have been started by key operational managers' involvement during the negotiation process.

A second step in building support entails instituting a communications and education program to establish an understanding of the reasons for the alliance and the benefits that will accrue. (Refer to "The First 6 Months" section for more details.)

When identifying the operational linkages between the two organizations, some best practices include the following:

- Look first for the *natural linkages* that will be required. For instance, a partner's sales force may need access to technical sales support personnel to assist with technical information.

- *Establish a process* for those links that will ensure smooth and predictable results. In the above example, you may want to consider whether a single sales support individual should be a primary contact to ensure consistent, quality information, or you may determine that a peer-to-peer relationship based on geographic location will better suit your needs.

- Within the linkages established, identify means of capturing and *tracking the quality of the linkages*. It could be logging communications or conducting random checks with partner personnel.

- Establish and communicate an *escalation procedure* such that if any personnel do not receive adequate support from the other partner, there is a "go to" process to follow.

- Beyond the natural linkages, *proactively introduce peripheral links* for the purpose of learning, awareness, and potential collaboration. A warehouse manager, for example, may have no direct role in the alliance, but introduction to your organization's product manager may stimulate valuable input into improving package design.

Although the companies may derive clear benefits from an alliance, certain individuals may feel they are losing out. As a result, the response to the alliance from some individuals may range from indifference to "not a priority" to outright bureaucratic sabotage. This needs to be managed proactively, helping along the individuals who simply require more education or assurance while extricating others who will never buy in.

Creating Special Teams and Task Forces

At times, partnerships between companies of substantially different sizes require creating a special operating environment. Even if the venture is between a small company and a particular business unit of a large company (as opposed to the larger company as a whole), the differences in bureaucratic cultures and operational practices may still prove stifling.

One way around this is to create task forces or horizontal teams with some decision-making capability. These teams are referred to as tiger teams, action teams, project teams, and so on, and they are created when managers realize that an alliance cannot be managed using their traditional corporate structures. In doing so, the team can actively develop the alliance, establishing strong linkages across key functions or activities that are relevant to the success of the alliance and jointly overcome some of the bureaucratic barriers they may encounter.

ROLES AND RESPONSIBILITIES

Being clear on how the alliance will be implemented within both organizations and who is going to be responsible for what is the basis of a manageable alliance. The framework for this should have been established in the alliance agreement, and, at the implementation phase, this will likely require documentation of more granular definitions of roles and work processes.

As several studies have suggested, doing so at the front end before the alliance is launched will ensure clarity in the implementation plan and prevent ambiguity. Robert Porter Lynch suggests developing a responsibility chart[7] that defines what tasks need to be performed, what decisions need to be made, and which group or individual does what. When assigning roles, the general rule of thumb is that tasks and responsibilities in an alliance should be allocated in a way that enables each party to do what it does best.

LINKAGE TO REMUNERATION POLICIES

Remuneration policies should reward alliance-supporting behavior. Individual performance objectives and associated compensation need to be consistent with the key performance measures identified in the negotiation process.

THE FIRST 6 MONTHS

All the strategic analysis, partner selection, negotiation, and implementation planning aims for the day the alliance can be formally launched into operation. Research on joint ventures finds an extremely high spike of failures in the early stages. A Bain & Company study found that out of 10 alliance agreements signed, 5 failed to meet the partners' expectations, and of the 5 that were deemed satisfactory, only 2 survived more than 5 years.[8] The first few months are therefore a critical formative period that requires earnest commitment and attention to get the relationship successfully off the ground.

CREATE THE CONDITIONS FOR COLLABORATION

The most pressing challenge facing managers in the initial stage is creating the conditions for collaboration, which involves creating a cooperative mind-set and fostering a positive working relationship between partners and those involved in the venture's operations.

No matter how ambitious a company's ultimate goals are, its initial focus should be on developing an early confidence in the alliance, building trust, improving mutual understanding, and defining tasks among the partners.

• *Senior managers should remain involved* in the early stages of implementation to ensure that the alliance has the resources, attention, and continued management support required.

• *Building trust should be the first priority.*[9] Alliance trust is defined as having sufficient confidence in a partner to commit valuable know-how and other resources to the venture. Numerous studies suggest that the early establishment of a trust-based relationship is critical in setting up the conditions for alliance success. Trust building takes time and is developed through positive experiences in the early stages and, more important, through joint problem solving over time. Managers should look for every opportunity to create a positive climate such as holding off-site team-building sessions or structuring smaller tasks for some "quick hits," as described next, and establishing a reliable flow of communications.

• *Create initial cooperative tasks that are achievable* and can provide quick or immediate feedback.[10] These can be extremely useful in this early stage because they provide actual collaborative experience and help identify potential obstacles that can be dealt with in a smaller situation where there is less at stake. For example, a joint effort to examine the competitive market environment may help partners develop mutual trust and shared understanding and also reduce the risk of inflated or misplaced expectations.

• Once the task has been completed, *step back and review* the quality of the collaboration, making sure to celebrate successes as well as identify areas for improvement.

Partners in successful alliances tend to increase their commitment in steps over time, once they perceive a balance between their commitments and related benefits.

ESTABLISH EFFECTIVE COMMUNICATIONS

The management of an alliance takes place through its communications processes, which are instrumental in managing joint activities, building a shared understanding of a venture's goals, and establishing mutual confidence and trust. Moreover, communications can overcome many of the barriers to success caused by the partner's differences in size, organizational complexity, unequal venturing experience, and different perspectives on the operational activities.[11]

Beyond internal and cross-organizational communications, timing of external communications should also be factored into the launch plans with the general rule being there should be no surprises for employees when details are disclosed in the media.

When an alliance is first launched, the following chronology of internal and external communications needs to be considered:

- If required, *briefings with operational managers* who have not been involved during the planning and negotiation phases should be made so they are familiar with the strategic and practical basis for the alliance.

- *Simultaneous executive-level announcements* should then be made within both organizations. This should ideally be done in person and supported by information tools such as newsletters, e-mail, and so on. People should be made aware of the rationale for the alliance; be shown clear, visible support from senior management; be given background on the partner; and, most important, understand the impact it will have on them as individuals.

- *Operational managers,* who have all been briefed, should then further discuss the impact of the alliance among their staff, reinforcing the benefits and the anticipated successes of the alliance. Reinforcement needs to be an ongoing effort if support is to be maintained.

- If planned, *external media announcements* detailing the strategic benefits of the alliance with contacts provided for both organizations should occur after the necessary internal information dissemination.

- *Continued and regular communications* coordinated through the alliance manager should occur to continually reinforce the benefits, successes, and commitment to the alliance.

The alliance manager should further ensure that communications channels are in place across the previously discussed linkages. Although a regular schedule for telephone calls or teleconferences for status reporting is a given, wherever feasible, face-to-face communications should be planned.

In particularly large or complex alliances, companies assign a dedicated individual on the alliance team to focus on internal and external communications. This can both radically improve the quality of communications as well as significantly offload the alliance manager.

DEVELOPING A SUSTAINABLE ALLIANCE

Both during and beyond the first 6 months, managers will likely be faced with new dimensions and circumstances that are unique to an alliance. How they respond to them could well determine whether the alliance thrives—or implodes. In particular, they should strive to maintain sensitivity to cultural differences, adopt constructive conflict resolution practices, manage the flow of sensitive information, and instill continuous learning throughout the organization.

OVERCOMING CULTURAL DIFFERENCES

Implementing and managing an alliance can often entail overcoming significant cultural differences between the partners, which is a common reason for alliance problems. A KPMG study found that cultural factors were responsible for 21% of prematurely disbanded alliances.[12] Other studies have found that cultural differences are more frequently the source of conflict in working relationships than operational or technical issues. Unfortunately, they have also noted that senior managers typically do not regard these differences as important.[13]

Differences can involve national cultures involving language, symbolism and meaning, large versus small company cultures, or manufacturing versus service company cultures. They may also involve functional cultures—for example, engineering versus marketing. Cultural differences can cause and/or exacerbate communications problems between partners and may stand in the way of developing the needed trust. Differences are likely to be particularly pronounced in the early stages of cooperation, especially when those involved have had little prior experience with each other.

Reconciling cultural differences can be approached in a number of different ways, depending on the extent of interaction between the partners and the extent of the differences involved.[14] The most extreme approaches involve one party adopting the other partner's culture as dominant or separating operations so as to minimize the interaction required. Limiting the "exchange surface" may circumvent the problem; however, these radical approaches limit the potential of the partners learning and benefiting from each other's culture.

> ### Culture Clash
>
> There are also numerous examples of the clash of national cultures occurring within strategic alliances. For example, the 25-month Corning (United States)–Vitro (Mexico) joint venture, described by some as a "marriage made in hell," was plagued with clashes, including differences in decision-making etiquette and styles and in perceptions of action timeframes. Conflict also occurred because of the perceived aggressiveness and directness of the U.S. executives by the Mexican managers, as well as the perceptions of U.S. managers that their Mexican counterparts were overly polite and unwilling to criticize. Cultural problems also plagued the start-up of the IBM, Toshiba, and Siemens AG chip venture. Here, language problems and differences in attitudes toward work practices made the building of joint engineering teams extremely difficult.

The more integrative approaches involve such things as partners participating in each other's executive development programs, cross-cultural and language training for staff involved in the venture, exchange visits, and cross-cultural workshops for people from the partner companies.

Cultural liaisons or cultural translators can also be helpful. For a small company, it may be useful to have cultural liaisons assigned to it from a larger partner. These individuals can then interpret or translate cultural norms and issues as required.

CONFLICT RESOLUTION

Some level of conflict is part of the everyday alliance experience, just as it is part of the everyday business experience. Conflicts may arise over hard financial or technical issues or soft cultural interpersonal issues. In some cases, these conflicts can be very positive, enhancing the creative tension of the alliances and resulting in new approaches, perspectives, or techniques. In other instances, they can be highly disruptive and undermine collaboration. For this reason, the conflict resolution process established in the initial alliance agreement will be invaluable.

In addition to the agreed-upon process, the following considerations will provide additional help in resolving conflicts:

• Conflict can be productive and a good learning experience. It should be *dealt with up-front* and not suppressed.

- If possible, conflicts should be *resolved where and when they surface* in order to maintain a healthy performing alliance. Only involve senior management when there are difficult issues or it affects the broader relationship.

- Conflicts can be more easily resolved by *understanding the position* and rationale of each party with the alliance's mutual objectives guiding decision making.

- *Don't allow operational disputes to become personal.* This will make them more difficult to resolve and could be very damaging to day-to-day operations.

- In extreme cases of impasse, consider *using a facilitator* who is trained in conflict resolution to help break down the barriers.

MANAGING INTELLECTUAL PROPERTY AND SENSITIVE INFORMATION

While some precautions against violations of intellectual property rights can be written into the alliance agreement, the potential for unintended skill transfer remains, and companies should be highly tuned to what their strategic information assets are.

Companies usually will have begun to address this issue when drafting their alliance contracts, but most agree that relying on patents or on the protection of the agreement is risky. Even if the law is on their side, they may get a hollow victory if excessive time and resources have been exhausted in litigation. Moreover, alliances with foreign partners can involve substantially different patent and legal systems or even cultural values regarding intellectual property (IP) rights. Prevention is therefore the best strategy.

There are several ways that companies can deal with the issue of the unplanned competency transfers.[15]

- *Increase awareness* among affected personnel. Ensure that managers and engineering staff are clear on the information and knowledge that can be shared with the partner and what knowledge is off limits. They should also be trained to monitor information flows. It may be useful to maintain a detailed record of information requests by the partner or operational staff. This practice will also safeguard against the "perils of familiarity," a side effect of good relationships.

- Sometimes, the outflow of proprietary information can be partially controlled by *partitioning tasks.* If partners possess distinct competencies in certain areas, these can be walled off into modular tasks, with each partner taking complete responsibility for its area of competency. This approach doesn't usually work where partner contributions are integrally related.

- Another approach is to *place joint activities in a third location.* This way, partners can decide which technologies to include and which to exclude. This may be preferred to carrying out joint venture activities within a parent firm as this method obviously limits its partner's access to ongoing processes and to nonrelated personnel.

- Finally, some companies *assign gatekeepers* or project managers to manage the information flow between partners. Gatekeepers consider all requests for information by the partner. By monitoring exchanges, the gatekeeper ensures skills are not unintentionally transferred to the partner. This will only work well in alliances involving limited interaction and information flow.

ESTABLISHING A LEARNING PROCESS

Learning is a principal way of extracting value from an alliance. While managers need to carefully manage the outflow of information, they also need to be vigilant about exploiting opportunities for learning from partners, particularly where different skills and capabilities exist.[16]

But learning will not happen without a proactive effort. It must be designed into the interaction between partners, thus providing a window on the skills and knowledge sought. Special procedures and attitudes need to be created to ensure that what needs to be learned is absorbed within the company's core operations (see Figure 4.1).

Some companies begin by establishing a learning agenda and translate their learning intentions into clear and actionable learning goals. They communicate this agenda to everyone who will interact with their partner. The next step is to create the systems that support the learning agenda so it can be integrated into the day-to-day interaction between partners. For example, the support system may involve creating an incentive and performance appraisal method to reward and reinforce acquisition, dissemination, and use of new knowledge. Finally, a review process would help determine what exactly has been learned.

Given the importance of alliances in general, firms should also use each alliance to develop an alliance knowledge base. They should ensure that experiences and expertise captured during one alliance is transferred to the next.

To do this, they must develop processes, determine best practices, develop repeatable tools such as contract templates, conduct postmortems, analyze case studies, and establish guidelines and training programs for staff.

Plan/Design	Implement	Review
❑ Confirm the learning goals you wish to achieve. ❑ How is information communicated in your firm? Are new processes required to support information transfer? ❑ Adjust individual performance evaluation criteria to reflect the learning objectives. ❑ Establish a knowledge base and supporting processes to capture alliance skills and expertise.	❑ Regularly communicate the learning intent to everyone who interacts with the partner. Everyone should be familiar with the broader strategies and specific learning goals. ❑ Assign specific people in your organization to be "learning officers" responsible for learning from your partner. ❑ Consider personnel rotation programs or cross-disciplinary seminars to disseminate knowledge. ❑ For international ventures develop/enhance key receptor skills such as language abilities, knowledge of host culture, etc.	❑ Schedule regular briefing and debriefing sessions with people visiting the partner to assess what has been learned. ❑ Look for external standards against which to benchmark your learning progress. ❑ As the alliance evolves, look for new learning opportunities. ❑ Transfer alliance skills and knowledge to the next alliance.

Figure 4.1   Learning From Alliances

Measuring Alliance Performance

Performance measurement is a key element of managing an alliance, yet many have trouble developing measures to monitor progress and performance. A consulting firm found that only 51% of alliances they studied used formal performance measures, and of those that did, just 20% believed the measures to be sufficient. They concluded that barely 10% had meaningful measures of performance.[17]

Although each partner may have its own metrics reflecting specific objectives and expectations, it is essential that the partners agree upon a common set of metrics to assess performance. This will go a long way to resolve differences in opinion about operational and strategic decisions.

The Balanced Scorecard Approach

Every venture has unique objectives, challenges, and parent company dynamics. Moreover, intangibles such as trust, culture, and communication—which can play an important role in alliance outcomes—suggest it is important to monitor performance from a variety of perspectives. A balanced scorecard approach to performance measurement is highly suitable as this approach is successful in evaluating cross-functional teams and other complex activities where multiple dimensions need monitoring.[18]

A balanced scorecard is based on the principle that performance measures should encompass a breadth of indicators as opposed to only a narrow few (which are commonly financial measures). The scorecard includes four measurement quadrants: financial, customer, internal systems, and employees.

Balanced Scorecard	
Financial	Customer
Internal	Employees

Figure 4.2   Balanced Scorecard

What Should Be Measured?

Selecting the most appropriate standard measures or crafting special measures to suit the characteristics of a venture should be done at the outset. The following steps may serve as a guide:

• *Measures should be developed for each quadrant* of the scorecard that supports each strategic objective of the alliance. The alliance agreement should be able to provide clear articulation of the overriding strategic objectives as well as some of the most tangible measures that represent their achievement.

• Establish *no more than 10 to 15* performance measures in all—3 or 4 per quadrant. The actual number should be large enough to incorporate the diverse aspects of the alliance but limited enough to easily monitor. The measures should try to provide a balanced combination of perspectives: financial and strategic measures, short-term and long-term measures, and measures that monitor progress and end results.

- Once these measures are developed, establish a baseline measure (what the current performance level is) and then attach *performance targets* and associated timeframes to each.

- *Measures should be explicit* and measurable. For instance, if management wants to include "customer satisfaction" as a measure, the baseline and targets should be expressed in terms of "xx% customer satisfaction," with satisfaction surveys used as the measurement instruments.

- Given the above, *be realistic about what can be measured.* There is no point establishing a measure, such as "increased knowledge," for which there are no means of measuring. Instead, consider a related indicator that can be easily quantified, such as "# of engineers using technology X," where technology X has been identified as a learning target.

- Finally, it is useful to elevate two or three of these performance measures as *red flags* that will quickly indicate when there are critical problems.

- Management should establish *regular performance review* sessions where the results are thoroughly assessed.

Alliance objectives:
1. Increase revenue through expanded service delivery offering (offer full life cycle)
2. Increase market reach through penetration into new industry verticals
3. Increase brand equity through broadened offering (one-stop shopping)

	Base	Target		Base	Target
Financial			**Customer**		
1. Services revenue generated from alliance	$10M	$45M	1. Increase customer satisfaction rate	85%	95%
2. Maintain healthy profit margin	30%	30%	2. Increase customer base from alliance	50 Tier1	60 Tier1
			3. Increase industry diversification (verticals)	3	5
Internal			**Employees**		
1. Standardized service delivery	Separate PM methodologies	Integrated PM by Q2	1. Product/service information training to 100% service fleet	20%	100%
2. Integrated customer support processes	Separate	Common screening and escalation	2. Alliance orientation program delivered to 100% service fleet	0%	100%
3. Integrated customer information database	Separate	Common data set by Q2	3. No change in morale due to alliance (from employee satisfaction survey)	80% emp. satisfaction	80% emp. satisfaction

Figure 4.3   Alliance Performance Scorecard

Figure 4.3 illustrates what a performance scorecard may look like for an alliance that involves two IT service companies looking to expand their reach and offering through an alliance partnership.

Measures should take the alliance's life cycle into consideration. In the early stage, managers may want to place more focus on soft measures—such as harmony among partners, morale, productivity, quality of the venture's staff, innovativeness, and so on. These are typically very qualitative, focusing on the process of cooperation and the quality and nature of partner interaction. (Note, however, that ideally, qualitative measures should still be expressed in quantitative ways.)

As the venture matures, the performance indicators can shift more toward outputs and more naturally quantitative measures such as cash flow or other financial markers. It is clear that many companies evaluate immature ventures too formally, placing too much emphasis on financial criteria at the early stage. The result of such action may be premature termination or a reduced level of commitment before the alliance has time to realize its potential.

ALIGN PERFORMANCE MEASURES WITH HR POLICIES

Performance measures don't get the attention they deserve without a reward system that reinforces them. Research has found that alliance-experienced companies create performance measures and link them to employment performance and compensation packages.[19]

Flexibility should be built into the measures to reflect the relative instability of the project. Once the measures are selected, devising appropriate rewards for alliance performance should be fairly straightforward.

The balanced scorecard can then be integrated into the performance evaluation process and employees sensitized to its dimensions. By doing so, every alliance participant will be actively involved in performance measuring and quite possibly flag needed improvements well in advance of formal reviews.

THE PROCESS NEVER ENDS

There will come a time when performance indicators suggest the alliance is delivering suboptimal results. The alliance audit in Figure 4.4 provides specific areas that managers may want to track. Responding to those indicators constructively and in a timely fashion can open doors to new innovation and continued alliance vitality. Managers can approach the performance indicators from a diagnostic perspective and celebrate the fact they are providing the necessary feedback. They should try to determine the root cause that may be at play, keeping the following thoughts in mind:

- *Revisit the original alliance objectives.* Have they possibly changed over time while the original agreement has not evolved with them? If yes, go back to the company's strategic rationale and evaluate current needs.

- *Look for changes that may have occurred with the partner.* Their strategy is likely not perfectly aligned, and it may be possible their circumstances have changed. Perhaps the alliance is of lesser strategic importance to

Measuring Performance

In NUMMI, the former alliance between General Motors (GM) and Toyota, GM's primary objective was to learn Toyota's production and manufacturing processes. The performance measures for GM were related to how effectively it appropriated and transferred the lessons learned throughout its entire manufacturing network and the degree to which this knowledge produced productivity gains and quality improvements throughout GM.

them today than it was before. If management suspects this to be the case, have candid discussions with the partner to get a realistic picture. If the strategic fit is no longer strong, it may be time to amend the alliance—or to exit the partnership gracefully.

• *Look for chronic issues* that may have continually surfaced over the life of the alliance. They may be pointing out an issue with the terms of the agreement or the operational linkages established that may have become embedded performance barriers.

• *Compare alliance performance measures against others* within the organization. If customer satisfaction is falling both within the alliance and with direct customers, management may have a bigger problem to address.

• *Continue to review and analyze the potential root cause of the performance decline* in the above manner. The following alliance audit provides specific areas of the alliance partnership to be examined.

Most important, managers need to be prepared to make changes as indicated, whether they are personnel changes, process changes, or amendments to the alliance agreement itself. The bottom line is that alliances will evolve as do companies. Good alliance management anticipates and supports those changes.

Performance	Strategic	Commitment
❑ Satisfaction with results in relation to objectives and expectations ❑ Growth ❑ Profitability ❑ Costs	❑ Understanding of alliance's objectives and strategic direction. ❑ Agreement with alliance's strategy. ❑ Fit of alliance's strategy with partners' corporate strategies.	❑ Support and involvement from all levels of partner organizations. ❑ Partners contribute resources and skills as expected. ❑ Partners perform respective roles as expected.

Compatibility	Equity	Relationship
❑ Time orientation ❑ Cultural compatibility ❑ Understanding and acceptance of differences.	❑ Equity in the allocation of benefits. ❑ Resources and skills committed by partners in line with benefits accrued.	❑ Satisfaction with relationship with partner at all levels. ❑ Satisfaction with relationship with alliance staff. ❑ Partners clear with allocation of roles and responsibilities.
Decision making		❑ Free flow of information between partners.
❑ Partners make decisions in the alliance's best interest. ❑ Partners involve each other in decisions when necessary. ❑ Mechanisms and processes exist for timely quality decisions. ❑ Conficts and disagreements are promptly and satisfactorily resolved.	**Alliance Audit**	❑ Free flow of information between alliance and partners. ❑ Appropriate amount of interaction between partners and with alliance.

Figure 4.4   Alliance Audit

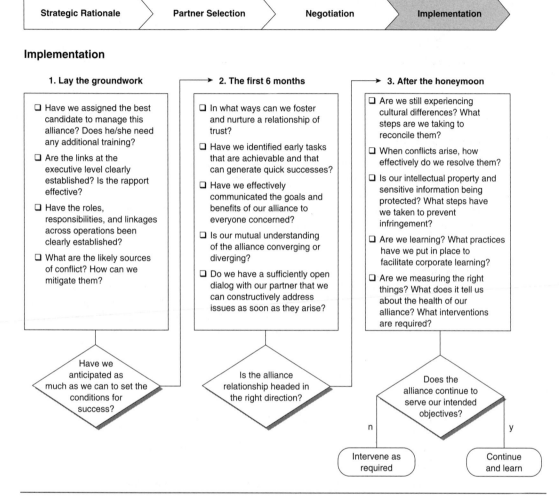

Implementation

Figure 4.5   Implementation Flowchart

CASES

Audible.com

Audible Inc. is one of the largest providers of audio content, such as books, magazines, and newspapers. The company has a large "library" of hours of content; strong alliances with partners, including Microsoft, Amazon, and Random House; and a growing customer base, but the company has lost money since it began. The chief executive officer and chief financial officer must decide how to raise funds to keep the company going while maintaining its partner and customer relationships.

Assignment Questions

1. What are the issues Audible faces? What options are open to the company?
2. Is this business worth saving?
3. Who is likely to want to purchase Audible outright? Why?
4. Who is likely to want to invest in this company? Why?
5. How can Audible become a profitable company?

Canadian Closures (A)

Canadian Closures was a JV between the Australian firm, Melbourne Closures (Melbourne), and Macklin Breweries (Macklin), which was based in Canada. The JV manufactured beer bottle caps based on Melbourne's technology; its only customer was Macklin's 10 breweries. Continuing product quality and performance problems resulted in the general manager being replaced. The new general manager was faced with the challenge of resolving these issues and balancing what was best for the parent companies in the short term and what was best for the JV in the long term. Macklin wanted reimbursement for faulty caps, which would have a significant impact on the profit objectives that both parent companies expected the JV to meet. The general manager had to find a solution that would satisfy both parent companies while minimizing negative impacts on the JV's results. The supplemental case, Canadian Closures (B), product 9B00M020, presents what happened and addresses another challenge later in the JV's life cycle.

Assignment Questions

1. What is your assessment of the situation confronting Canadian Closures and Bernard Kayvon, its general manager?
2. What do you see as the factors underlying this situation? What factors make it more difficult? Less difficult?
3. Why was this international joint venture (IJV) formed? What were the partners looking for? What did they contribute?
4. As Bernard Kayvon, what are your options? What do they entail? What would you do?

Cameco in Kyrgyzstan: Corporate Social Responsibility Abroad

Based in Saskatoon, Canada, Cameco was the world's largest uranium mining company. It had developed its policy for corporate social responsibility in northern Saskatchewan, where it had its major mining operations and where there were a large indigenous population of Cree and Dene Indians. The issue centers on whether the same corporate social responsibility policy can be applied to the company's joint venture with the Kyrgyzstan government to operate a gold mine in eastern Kyrgyzstan. Complicating the decision was a chemical spill that had occurred several months before, and relations with citizens in nearby communities were at an all-time low. The joint venture's vice president of human resources and corporate relations must decide which of the programs might be successfully implemented in Kyrgyzstan, what new programs might need to be developed, and how best to communicate company policy to the local community.

Assignment Questions

1. Who are the stakeholders, and what are their interests?

2. Given the recent evidence that the toxicity of the cyanide spill was relatively insignificant, what can and should Duret do to diffuse the negative reactions of the Kyrgyzstani people?

3. What actions should Duret take immediately to address the crisis?

4. What could Cameco do to rebuild its relationship with the nearby communities and the country?

5. Will the activities that Cameco initiated in Saskatchewan be as effective in Kyrgyzstan? Why or why not?

6. Is Cameco's corporate social responsibility policy adequate for northern Saskatchewan, Kyrgyzstan, or any other future operations?

7. Does Cameco get good value for its investment in corporate social responsibility? Are the shareholders' interests being looked after?

Wil-Mor Technologies: Is There a Crisis?

The CEO of Wilson Industries, a U.S. firm, is concerned about the performance of a joint venture between Wilson Industries and a Japanese firm, Morota Manufacturing. He wants the joint venture president to make some changes to improve financial performance. However, the president is unsure of what action to take because the Japanese partner, Morota, is satisfied with the performance and is considering expansion plans.

Assignment Questions

1. Why was this joint venture formed? Was there a good business case for the formation?

2. Describe the nature of the partner contributions. Who holds the bargaining power?

3. What are the major problems in the relationship between Wilson and Morota?

4. As Ron Berks, what are your options? What action would you take?

5. How do you think Morota, the Japanese partner, will respond to your decision?

The Wuhan Erie Polymers Joint Venture

The Erie Performance Polymers division manager in China and general manager of Wuhan Erie Polymers (WEP) joint venture has just received approval for his requested transfer to divisional headquarters in the United States. In preparing the division and joint venture for the change, a key decision concerns his successor. He has received information on six candidates under consideration and knows that his recommendation will carry heavy weight in the final decision. The general manager has attempted to inculcate in his mainly Chinese workforce an appreciation for Western business practices and ability to enact them. At the same time, acknowledging their substantial differences, he has tried to mix elements of both Chinese and Western values in creating a culture for the joint venture. He believes strongly that his successor must be responsive to the tensions between the relevant cultures. As he compares them, he wonders which candidate has the best set of qualities to succeed him as general manager.

Assignment Questions

1. How successful have Wong's efforts been to develop an effective JV at WEP? Why?

2. What responsibilities do Wong's positions carry? Rank them in order of importance. Which are the critical ones?

3. What challenges still face Wong and the company as he prepares for his transfer?

4. Who should be chosen to succeed Wong? Why?

NOTES

1. R. Freichs, "Partnerships and Prosperity: Survey of High-Tech Firms Finds Alliances Are Key to Survival in an Ever Changing Industry," *San Jose Mercury News,* January 31, 1999, 19.

2. M. Yoshino and U. Rangan, *Strategic Alliances: An Entrepreneurial Approach to Globalization* (Cambridge, MA: Harvard Business School Press, 1995), 23–146.

3. J.-L. Schaan and P. W. Beamish, "Joint Venture General Managers in LDCs," in *Cooperative Strategies in International Business,* edited by F. Contractor and P. Lorange (Lexington, MA: Lexington Books, D.C. Health & Co., 1998), 279–99.

4. For a discussion of design, see Y. Doz and G. Hamel, *Alliance Advantage: The Art of Creating Value Through Partnering* (Boston: Harvard Business School Press, 1998), 127–40.

5. J. Anderson and J. Narus, "A Model of Distribution Firms and Manufacturing Firms Working Partnerships," *Journal of Marketing* 54 (1990): 42–58. M. Kelly and J.-L. Schaan, *The Implementation and the Management of Strategic Alliances: The Experiences of Canadian Technology Executives* (Menlo Park, CA: SRI, 1996).

6. See J. Botkin and J. Matthews, *Winning Combinations* (New York: John Wiley, 1992), 136–7; M. L. Marks and H. Mirvis, *Joining Forces* (San Francisco: Jossey-Bass, 1998), 104–8; R. Spekman, L. Isabella, and T. MacAvoy, *Alliance Competence* (New York: John Wiley, 2000), 144–5.

7. R. P. Lynch, *Business Alliance Guide* (New York: John Wiley, 1993), 180–2.

8. See D. K. Rigby and R. W. T. Buchanan, "Putting More Strategy in Strategic Alliances," *Boards and Directors,* Winter 1994, 14–9.

9. For a discussion of building trust in alliances, see Spekman, Isabella, and MacAvoy, *Alliance Competence,* 46–7; Jordan Lewis, *Trusted Partners: How Companies Build Mutual Trust and Win Together* (New York: The Free Press, 1999); J. Child and D. Faulkner, *Strategies of Cooperation* (Oxford, UK: Oxford University Press, 1998), 45–64; A. Parkhe, "Understanding Trust in International Alliances," *Journal of World Business* 33, no. 3 (1998): 219–40; and A. Parkhe, "Building Trust in International Alliances," *Journal of World Business* 33, no. 4 (1998): 417–37.

10. Doz and Hamel, *Alliance Advantage,* 161–2.

11. K. R. Harrigan, "Keeping the Attraction Alive," *Directors and Boards* 18, no.2 (1994): 28–30.

12. G. Kok. and L. Wildeman, "Crafting Strategic Alliances: Building Effective Relationships." KPMG Report, 1998.

13. J. Harper and S. Cormeraie, "Mergers, Marriages and After: How Can Training Help," *Journal of European Industrial Training* 19 (1995): 24–9.

14. For a discussion of managing cultural differences, see M. L. Marks and H. Mirvis, *Joining Forces,* 187–210; and W. Hall, *Managing Cultures: Making Strategic Relationships Work* (New York: John Wiley, 1995).

15. See C. C. Baughn, J. G. Denekamp, J. H. Stevens, and R. N. Osborn, "Protecting Intellectual Capital in International Alliances," *Journal of World Business* 32, no. 2 (1997): 103–17.

16. See M. Crossan and A. Inkpen, "The Subtle Art of Learning Through Alliances," *Business Quarterly* 60, no. 2 (1995): 67–78; D. Lei, J. Slocum, and R. Pitts, "Building Cooperative Advantage: Managing Strategic Alliances to Promote Organizational Learning," *Journal of World Business* 32, no. 3 (1997): 203–23; and Child and Faulkner, *Strategies of Cooperation,* 283–313.

17. Andersen Consulting, "Dispelling the Myths of Alliances," 1999, www.ac.com/showcase/alliances.

18. See R. Kaplan and D. Norton, "Using the Balanced Scorecard as a Strategic Management System," *Harvard Business Review,* January–February 1996, 75–85; P. Migliorate, N. Nathan, and D. Norton, "A Scoring System for Creating Joint Ventures That Survive," *Mergers and Acquisitions,* January–February 1996, 45–50; and Spekman, Isabella, and MacAvoy, *Alliance Competence,* 234–40.

19. J. R. Harbison and P. Pekar, *Smart Alliances: A Practical Guide to Repeatable Success* (San Francisco: Jossey-Bass, 1998), 50.

AUDIBLE.COM[1]

Prepared by Ken Mark and Jordan Mitchell

Version: (A) 2004-06-22

INTRODUCTION

In late May 2003, Audible Inc.'s (Audible) chairman and chief executive officer (CEO), Donald Katz, faced a dilemma. There was only enough cash to survive for the third quarter of 2003.

Based in New Jersey, Audible considered itself the Internet's largest, most diverse provider of audio content (books, magazines, newspapers, etc.). Audible's customers could download content and either burn it on compact discs (CDs), or play it back on their personal computers or mobile devices.[2] Boasting more than 34,000 hours of content and 135 content partners, strategic alliances with Microsoft, Amazon and Random House, as well as a strong portfolio of products and a growing customer base, Audible seemed well-positioned for success. However, the company had experienced losses since it began in 1995 and had an accumulated deficit of US$113.9 million.[3] Sales of audio content were the fundamental driver of positive cash flow for Audible, according to chief financial officer Andrew Kaplan.[4] While Audible's revenue growth had been in the double digits historically, it had only been eight per cent in the last quarter.

Katz, together with Robert Kramer, president, and Andrew Kaplan, chief financial officer and vice-president, wondered what actions they could pursue.

AUDIO CONTENT TRENDS[5]

In 2003, the public demand for new media continued to grow. A study by Veronis, Suhler & Associates estimated that U.S. consumer spending on media and information would rise at a compound rate of 5.6 per cent per year reaching $180 billion in 2005, while spending on books was expected to grow at 2.8 per cent per year reaching $20.5 billion in 2006 from $17.8 billion in 2001.[6]

Some of the heaviest users of audio content were commuters and fitness enthusiasts. Both groups had begun to adopt audiobooks as an alternative to radio or music. There were 97 million people who drove alone to work, logging more than 550 million hours of drive-time each week. The average commute time was approximately 50 minutes, which represented a seven per cent increase since 1990. There were more than 50 million individuals in the United States who exercised regularly.[7]

In 2001, the Audio Publishers Association estimated that 23 million U.S. households listened to audiobooks, an increase of 7.5 per cent from 1999. An eBrain survey from 2002 found 20 per cent of their sample listened to audiobooks with an expectation of a 24 per cent increase in consumption in coming months. Children's audiobooks were estimated to represent 14 per cent of the entire $2 billion audiobook industry, which had grown more than 10 per cent since 1995.[8]

The one limitation of the audiobook was that it did not address the immediate time required content, such as newspapers, newsletters, magazines and journals. Audible addressed this problem by providing daily content to its subscribers from publications such as the *Wall Street Journal* and the *New York Times*.

THE IMPORTANCE OF HAVING HARRY POTTER

Having high quality audio content, particularly blockbuster content, was a necessary part of keeping audio customers engaged, yet content was usually exclusively controlled by one owner. An important example of this was *The Harry Potter* series of books, written by J.K. Rowling. The books were available on tape and CD, with the rights controlled by Listening Library until it was purchased by Random House Audio in 1999.

"Harry Potter catapulted our entire industry into a whole new realm," commented Heather Frederick, publisher of Audiobookshelf. The success of Harry Potter had a significant impact on growth in the children's audio category[9] and on bookseller's willingness to promote audiobooks.[10] By 2003, the digital rights to Harry Potter were not available for sale.

TECHNOLOGY TRENDS

By early 2003, the Internet had become a key source of education and entertainment with an estimated worldwide usage of more than 400 million people.[11] Wireless and digital transmission technologies were also growing, allowing users to download information and audio materials without going through a desktop. Worldwide sales of smart hand-held devices were estimated to reach $26 billion by 2004, as the number of cell phone subscribers grew by 255 million in 2001.[12]

More users were able to download content and burn it on CDs. The CD burner market was estimated to increase from 120 million in 2001 to 546 million in 2005 and sales of blank audio CDs had surpassed sales of music CDs.[13]

There were some copyright infringement concerns associated with making audio content available for downloading on the Internet. Napster had raised the ire of the music recording industry, and producers of audiobooks saw similarities. Apple had recently launched the Icons music service and on-line iTune store, allowing consumers to pay per song for music files. Katz commented:[14]

> The download culture received a tremendous boost. The launch by Apple of the Icons music service apparently accounted for a million legally sold and downloaded music files in the first week of operation. Emergence of viable legal music services will increase the population of legal audio for the consumer. It will increase the distribution of digital audio devices and lower their costs.

In contrast to Audible, many providers of audiobooks relied on the physical distribution of tapes and CDs through bookstores or mail order. Carrie Kania of HarperAudio talked about audio downloading on the Internet:[15]

> We're very early in that game. We want to do what's best for the authors. At this point we would make select titles available, stressing quality over quantity, and work with a retail partner. But the whole world could change again in six months, so we don't want to be locked into anything, either.

Tim Ditlow, publisher at Listening Library, said in 2001:[16]

> We have a rich treasure trove of content and as the technology evolves, we're there; we could convert quickly. But we also have a moral responsibility to authors and agents not to take any risks with delivery systems.

ENVIRONMENT

From 1995 to 2000, Internet businesses enjoyed great success fueled by over-inflated expectations and media hype. By the second half of 2000, the Internet bubble burst. A roundzero.com article described the situation in January 2001:[17]

> In the latter part of 2000, 210 dot-coms shut their doors, taking down with them $1.5 billion in invested capital. Since only the cash-flow positive will survive, remaining entities have curbed excess spending and focused squarely on revenue. . . . In the last year, companies even remotely connected with the Internet or technology in general already have lost between 50-90 per cent of their market caps. The Internet still represents an enormous opportunity. Companies with sound business models, proven management teams, and strong value propositions (the same elements that historically determine success) not only will survive, but thrive.

By May 2003, Internet companies had not returned to the glory days of the late 1990s and were attempting to build businesses with long-term viability. The environment made it difficult for Internet ventures to attract funding.

AUDIBLE.COM HISTORY

Audible was founded in November 1995 by Donald Katz, an author and business journalist, who saw the opportunity to provide digital content on the Web for playback on personal computers (PCs) or mobile devices.[18] The company began by marketing and producing AudiblePlayer, a hand-held device for downloading audio from the Internet. It also aimed to corner the market for audiobooks.

In the first three years of operation, Audible had attracted an impressive list of business partners. The underwriters were Credit Suisse First J.P. Morgan, Volpe Brown Whelan and Wit Capital. It received venture capital through Patricof & Co. Ventures, Kleiner Perkins, Ironwood Capital, AT&T and, by 1999, Microsoft.[19]

In 1997, when Audible started to sell its own player and services, it posted revenues of US$60,000.[20] In 1998, revenue grew to $376,000 and had reached $1.7 million by 1999. On April 30, 1999, Audible filed for a $46 million initial public offering (IPO). By the end of 2002, Microsoft was the largest shareholder with one-third of the stock.[21]

With continued expenses exceeding revenue, share prices declined. Audible's stock moved from the NASDAQ National Market to the NASDAQ Small Cap Market in August 2002, and then to the Over-the-Counter Market in February 2003 because it had closed below the $1.00 per share requirement for 180 consecutive days.[22] In May 2003, the stock price was approximately $0.50. Exhibit 1 shows Audible's stock chart from 2000 to 2003.

SHAREHOLDERS[23]

Microsoft was the largest shareholder at the end of 2002, with 35.1 per cent of Audible's shares. The Special Situations Fund, a private equity firm controlled by two individuals not associated with the management or board of directors of Audible, operated four funds accounting for 15.9 per cent ownership of Audible. Amazon had 5.9 per cent, Random House 4.4 per cent, and executive officers and directors together owned 11.1 per cent, including Katz with six per cent, Robert Kramer, the president, with 1.9 per cent and Kaplan, the CFO, with 2.3 per cent.

EXECUTIVE AND EMPLOYEES[24]

Katz, the chief executive officer, had worked for 20 years as an author, business journalist and media consultant. Robert Kramer, the president, had been promoted from his chief technology officer post in July 2001. Kramer had been an executive with American Management Systems. Andrew Kaplan, vice-president and CFO, joined the company in 1999, and had previously served as CFO of The Thompson Corporation,

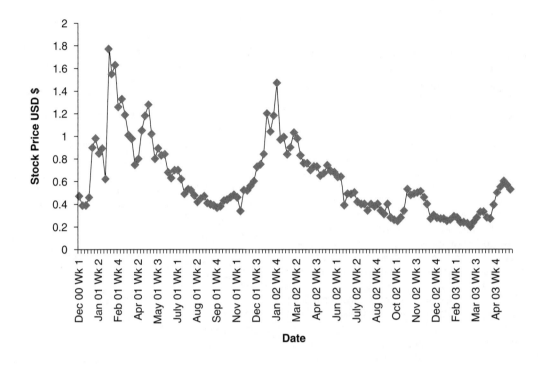

COMMON STOCK HIGH AND LOW		
2001	**High**	**Low**
First Quarter	1.78	0.41
Second Quarter	1.40	0.62
Third Quarter	0.68	0.34
Fourth Quarter	0.80	0.36
2002		
First Quarter	1.46	0.75
Second Quarter	0.85	0.32
Third Quarter	0.52	0.30
Fourth Quarter	0.55	0.27
2003		
First Quarter	0.35	0.20

Exhibit 1   Audible's Stock Chart (compared to NASDAQ Composite Index)

Source: Audible Annual Report, December 31, 2002, p. 13.

Vertis, Inc. and Time Life Inc., part of AOL Time Warner.

Audible had 65 full-time employees: 13 in production, 29 in sales and marketing, 20 in development and three in general positions. Originally, the staff had grown to 85 people, but was cut back in March 2002 for cash-flow considerations.

COMPANY GOAL[25]

Audible's goal was to be the leading provider of Internet, subscription-based audio content. To achieve this goal, management promoted the Audible brand and increased Web-site traffic through on-line marketing and strategic alliances with cable operators, CD-burning software providers, retail partners and AudibleReady player manufacturers. Audible sought Internet distribution rights to additional audio content and expanded the format's breadth through offering materials currently not available in audio as well as one-off original topic-specific content.

The company planned to expand the technological functionality of AudibleReady to cell phones, personal digital assistants (PDAs) and other mobile devices. Audible's proprietary software, Audible Manager, made it simpler for customers to control and automate their own audio downloads and selections. The idea was to give customers audio content when, where and how they wanted it.

PRODUCTS AND SERVICES[26]

Audible provided audio content by subscription or one-time purchase via its Web site, audible.com. Audible had its own digital audio player, Otis, manufactured by a third party in Korea. Audible also sold its audio content via Amazon.com and had agreements with many hardware and mobile device manufacturers to include Audible software on their devices.

Audible's library of more than 34,000 hours and 5,000 audiobooks came from major publishers, such as Random House Audio, Harper Audio, Simon & Schuster Audio and Time Warner AudioBooks, as well as smaller content providers.

Audible subscribers paid a fixed monthly fee for subscriptions, ranging from US$4.95 per month for Fast Company, to US$12.95 for a daily such as the *New York Times*. The AudibleListener flat-fee program was available for $14.95 per month with a choice of one magazine, newspaper or radio program plus an audiobook or $19.95 for two audiobooks each month. Consumers received Audible's Otis digital audio/MP3 player as an additional incentive for joining AudibleListener® for one year. Audible's pricing offered advantages over books on cassette or books on CD purchased in store: for one-off purchases, the consumer typically paid 35 per cent less. For subscription-based sales, the consumer could receive up to a 60 per cent discount from the price of cassettes or CDs.

One hour of spoken audio required two megabytes of storage, and download time ranged from one minute, using a high-speed Internet connection to 15 minutes using a 28 kbps modem. Hardware requirements were either a Pentium processor with 200 MHz or more, a Mac OS X, iTunes 3 or above and mobile devices such as Audible's Otis MP3 player or the Pocket PC, Palm Handheld or Apple iPod. The AudibleManager software program restricted the number of times content could be downloaded, so listeners could not easily infringe upon copyright.

Audio books included fiction, non-fiction and educational materials by popular authors, such as Tom Clancy, Stephen King, John Grisham, Mary Higgins Clark, James Patterson, the Dalai Lama, Stephen Hawking, William Shakespeare, and Jane Austen. Subscription material included timely audio editions of print publications, such as the *Wall Street Journal, The New York Times, Forbes, Harvard Business Review, Scientific American* and *FastCompany*. Consumers could choose from a wide range of topics: comedy,

Cost of content and services revenue. Cost of content and services revenue includes the royalties that we pay publishers, as well as the amortization of publisher royalty advances and equity securities issued in connection with Random House Audible. Cost of content and services revenue was $4,970,000, or 44 per cent of content and services revenue, for 2002, as compared to $4,902,000, or 66 per cent of content and services revenue, for 2001. Included in cost of content and services revenue for 2001, was a charge of $709,000 to reflect the net realizable value of royalty advances, as compared to a charge of $80,000 for 2002. The relative cost of content and services revenue decreased for 2002 due to the reduction in unrecoupable royalty advances.

Cost of hardware revenue. Cost of hardware revenue was $2,718,000, or 292 per cent of hardware revenue, for 2002, as compared to $2,858,000, or 221 per cent of hardware revenue, for 2001. This decrease was primarily due to reduced unit costs of hand-held electronic devices in 2002 versus 2001. The increase in cost of hardware revenue as a percentage of hardware revenue was due to providing more customers with an Audible Otis "free of charge" when the customer signed up for a one year commitment to AudibleListener®.

Production expenses. Production expenses are primarily related to hosting and bandwidth costs incurred in the operation of www.audible.com. Production expenses also include staff costs related to Web site operations, audio production and content acquisition. Production expenses were $3,882,000 for 2002, as compared to $5,636,000 for 2001, a decrease of $1,754,000, or 31 per cent. This decrease was primarily due to a reduction in personnel costs and reduced outside services as a result of our streamlining initiative of July 23, 2001.

Development. Development costs are primarily staff expenses related to our information technology and Web site infrastructure. Development costs were $2,271,000 for 2002, as compared to $3,322,000 for 2001, a decrease of $1,051,000, or 32 per cent. This decrease was primarily due to a reduction in outside consultants as well as reduced personnel cost as a result of our streamlining initiative of July 23, 2001 offset in part by expenses associated with a technology license.

Sales and marketing. Sales and marketing expenses were $12,468,000 for 2002, as compared to $15,187,000 for 2001, a decrease of $2,719,000, or 18 per cent. This decrease was due to a reduction in certain advertising costs such as advertising received in connection in barter transactions, web related advertising, tradeshow expenses, warrant charges in connection with a services agreement, reduced personnel costs as well as expenses recognized in connection with our Co-Branding, Marketing and Distribution Agreement with Amazon.com.

General and administrative. General and administrative expenses include legal fees, audit fees, public company expenses, the Company paid portion of medical plan costs, staff costs, insurance, postage, rent, leasehold improvement amortization and telephone costs. General and administrative expenses were $3,647,000 for 2002, as compared to $4,727,000 for 2001, a decrease of $1,080,000, or 23 per cent. This decrease was primarily due to a reduction in personnel costs as a result of our streamlining initiative of July 23, 2001 offset in part by higher professional fees.

Exhibit 2   Operating Expenses

Source: Audible Annual Report, December 31, 2002, pp. 19–20.

spirituality, language learning, academic lectures, public radio programs, and business management materials.

In delivering this content, Audible did not have the traditional and conventional cost constraints of managing an inventory. An excerpt from its Annual Report describes its cost performance in Exhibit 2. Its costs were in five main areas:

- Cost of content—Audible paid royalties to publishers. Most publishers required royalty advances, which in some cases exposed Audible for content that did not sell.
- Cost of hardware—The Otis MP3 Players were manufactured by a third party.
- Production costs—Most of this cost was for hosting and bandwidth costs on the Internet in offering Audible's audio content.

- Development costs—This included the cost of staff to develop and maintain the Web site, the backbone of Audible's business.
- Sales, marketing, general and administrative costs.

Audible's Web site featured organized and searchable lists of content. Audible aimed to create a community where customers could talk with one another and leave comments about audio programs. In its referral program, an individual who recruited a new customer would receive a discount or special products. It offered fundraising campaigns for non-profits. The company targeted businesses through a "library" service, which offered a relevant selection of management journals and magazines included as part of its monthly subscription. Audible believed that both companies and individuals were continually trying to turn car time into productive time.[27]

CONSUMER REACTION

Katz commented about results and consumers in early 2003:[28]

> During the first quarter, Audible continued to achieve steady sequential growth with steadily decreasing operating expenses. Our cost of acquiring customers decreased by 10 per cent over the previous quarter. Meanwhile, we advanced our strategy of increasing distribution and awareness of the Audible service—recently named the "best consumer Web service" by CNET—with new or enhanced marketing and product integration efforts with Apple, Gateway, Palm and other partners.

The CNET review talked about Audible's products in May 2003:[29]

> Audible.com lets you read and keep your hands free at the same time and is perfect for the visually impaired, and it's a handy, inexpensive way to get best-sellers onto your portable MP3 player.

PC World also rated it one of the "Best of Today's Web" in August 2002.[30]

By the end of Q1, 2003, Audible had 229,000 customers, a 60 per cent increase from Q1 2002.[31] The following table shows the total listenership:[32]

Date	Number of Listeners
Dec 1999	13,000
Dec 2000	51,000
Dec 2001	123,000
March 2002	143,000
Sept 2002	182,000
March 2003	229,000

STRATEGIC ALLIANCES

Microsoft

Microsoft had agreements to license Audible's AudibleManager and AudiblePlayer software for $2.0 million a year. In return, Audible agreed to make all of their technologies compatible with Microsoft's Windows Media Technology. Microsoft also had the first right of refusal to purchase Audible.[33] Microsoft's focus for the future was to flesh out its network of Internet products. Windows Media Technology with 40 million users,[34] offered a comprehensive and mainstream entertainment experience, which included features such as a CD player, audio, video player, media jukebox, media guide, Internet radio, portable device music file transfer and an audio CD burner.[35] Audible's content added value to Windows Media Technology.

Dick Brass, vice-president of technology development at Microsoft, commented:[36]

> Microsoft believes in the long-term strength of its [Audible's] business. Spoken-word content is a key growth area for the development of digital media commerce, and we share Audible's vision of a future in which the information and entertainment economy is fundamentally based on digital delivery.

Because of Microsoft's large shareholding and its 10-day first right of refusal on the purchase of Audible, it would be difficult for any third party to try to gain control of Audible. In February 2001, Microsoft purchased 2.6 million preferred shares for $3.75 per share, each convertible to four shares of common stock. Dividends in cash or shares were payable at the rate of 12 per cent annually. At the fifth anniversary of the deal, Audible was required to redeem all remaining outstanding shares at $3.75 plus all accrued and unpaid dividends.[37]

Amazon.com

Audible's relationship with Amazon.com began in January 2000. Amazon strove to be the "Earth's most customer-centric" company, through low prices and massive selection of any product, including books, electronics, computers, software, DVDs, cameras and a host of other goods. Through its merchant.com program Amazon used its infrastructure to sell goods for other companies over the Internet. Amazon had sales of $3.9 billion and more than 7,500 employees.[38]

Audible paid $22.5 million in January 2000 to become Amazon's exclusive provider of digital spoken audio for a three-year contract.[39] Amazon then purchased common stock for $20 million, which offset Audible's debt to Amazon. By 2003, $1.5 million was still remaining to be paid by Audible. The agreement propelled Audible's products and services into the Internet's largest on-line book seller and was important in its strategy to increase its brand awareness.

Random House

The agreement with Random House was based on the formation of Random House Audible, with the intent "to produce spoken word content specifically suited for digital distribution."[40] The agreement signed in May 2000, stated that all titles created by the new formation would be exclusively distributed by Audible on the Internet with the expectation that Audible would "contribute towards funding the acquisition and creation of digital audio titles."[41] The agreement permitted Audible to have immediate access to Random House's titles.

Erik Engstrom, president and chief operating officer of Random House, said:[42]

> Random House believes downloading of digital audio content to be the most significant engine of growth for the spoken word and audiobook industry in the future.

In October 2001, Books on Tape, one of Audible's largest competitors, was acquired by Random House.[43] With the expansion of its audio division through this acquisition, Random House Audio had the ability to decide whether it would make the digital rights available to Audible.

Device Manufacturers

Audible had marketing agreements with Apple Corp., Card Access Inc., Casio Inc., Compaq Computer Corporation, Handspring, Hewlett-Packard Company (HP), Microsoft Corporation, RealNetworks, Inc., SONICblue Incorporated's Rio Audio Group, Sony Electronics, Texas Instruments and VoiceAge Corp.[44] All of the manufacturers received a percentage of revenue for a period of one to two years if they referred their customers to Audible's products and services.[45] Audible was also experimenting with one-month free trials with devices such as Apple's iPod, Palm pilots or HP's pocket PC, offered in stores and on Pocket PC, Palm and iPod Web sites. A high number of trial users were converting to fully paid members.[46]

Katz explained Audible's growing relationship with Apple:[47]

> . . . users of our Mac-based Otis MP3 players have grown to represent a double-digit percentage of our customer base, a figure high above Apple's platform penetration of the general computer market place. And this has [been] from only the few weeks' exposure and distribution efforts that Apple and Audible teams have planned together. The Audible links inside the Apple.com Web site are by far the most productive Web exposure elements we've ever had. We expect to enter a new phase of awareness building with Apple and with key retailers of Apple products online and in physical stores.

Distribution and Marketing Alliances

In order to attract new customers, Audible was working on different agreements with partners from direct marketing companies through to bricks and mortar computer retail outlets such as Gateway. Katz commented on partnerships that would help adoption of Audible's services:[48]

> A very important Q2 partnership . . . is our new relationship with Gateway Computer. Within the last two weeks all of Gateway's retail stores began displaying Audible's Otis MP3 player as a $99 product which includes the purchasers' first month of our basic listener membership.
>
> Another distribution outlet . . . is broadband services providers. A good example of a strong brand franchise that covers a large customer base is Roadrunner. It has over 2.5 million customers. The co-marketing deal with Roadrunner [is an] integrated online email and direct mail campaign promoting the Audible service. [Together] we'll be creating an audio hub inside the Roadrunner Web site. Using an internal Audible application we call FreeBird, we will be automatically distributing timely audio samples to Roadrunner as a means of exposing their users to the power and value of the Audible listening experience.

CONTENT PROVIDERS
AND AUDIO PRODUCERS

Audible created a new market and provided a new source of revenue for publishers of newspapers, magazines, journals, newsletters, professional publications and business information, since some of the content was too time sensitive for distribution on cassette or CD. As well, Audible was able to easily store archived or out-of-print content in digital form.[49]

Content producers (e.g., Random House Audio, HarperCollins Audio, Simon & Schuster Audio and AOL Time Warner Audio) were wholly owned subsidiaries of their respective publishing parents, which were part of major entertainment giants.

Random House Publishing had revenues of over US$2 billion. Its parent, Bertelsmann, was privately owned and had sales of $19 billion. Random House was the largest trade book publisher in the world and its audio division, at 5000 titles annually, was the market leader. It grew internally and through the acquisition of Listening Library and Books on Tape. Random House Audio had the exclusive rights to Harry Potter audio in the United States. It had a dedicated children's sales force, the No. 1 position in the children's market,[50] and a large share in the library/educational market. There were specialty divisions which focused on business management and inexpensive audio.[51]

Harpers Audio was owned by Harper Collins with revenues of more than $1 billion. It produced around 3,000 books a year. Its parent company, NewsCorp, had revenues of $16 billion a year.

Simon & Schuster had revenues of $648.7 million in 2002 and produced more than 2,000 books a year. It was owned by Viacom (with US$25 billion in sales), whose other divisions included Paramount, MTV and Nickelodeon. Simon & Schuster published many of its prominent works in audio editions and published original content in order to build reader communities on its Web site.[52]

Time Warner's Book division produced $400 million in revenues through traditional channels and the Book-of-the-Month Club, which was a 50-50 joint venture with Bertelsmann Doubleday books. AOL Time Warner was looking to sell off its book division. Like its competitors, Time Warner Books actively pursued releasing popular titles on audiobook in CD and cassette formats.

COMPETITION

Competition for Audible was either audio content on cassette or CD or on the Internet via digital download. Audible competed with traditional and on-line retail stores, catalogues, clubs and libraries that were involved in the selling, renting and loaning of audiobooks on cassette or CD.[53]

It was estimated that 38 per cent of audiobooks were borrowed from libraries, 37 per cent were purchased, 10 per cent were received as gifts, nine per cent were borrowed from individuals and six per cent were rented.[54]

Retail Stores

Large U.S.-based retail bookstores, such as Borders, Barnes & Noble, their on-line sales business and others, carried audiobooks. Borders and Barnes & Noble led the way in book and audiobook sales, but faced competition from mass merchant retailers such as Wal-Mart, Costco, Sam's Club and Target. Audiobooks represented only a small proportion of book titles sold through bookstores and mass merchants. Book superstores were becoming more of a trend in book retailing, and as a result, smaller, independent booksellers faced an increasingly hostile competitive environment. Retail shops typically experienced strong sales at Christmas and during the summer when families were traveling in cars for long periods of time.

Barnes & Noble was the number one bookseller in the United States, at $5.3 billion in sales through almost 900 stores, of which 630 were superstores and 260 smaller mall formats.[55] It owned 38 per cent of its on-line book business. Bertelsmann, who owned Random House, had an interest in Barnes & Noble, even though Barnes & Noble was planning on purchasing it back in September 2003.[56] Borders had sales of $3.5 billion and operated 1,250 retail stores. Borders sold its product on the Internet through its Amazon-operated Web site.[57]

Books on Tape, MediaBay and Internet Firms

Books on Tape

Although purchased by Random House in 2001, Books on Tape continued to sell and rent recorded versions of books on cassettes, CDs and MP3-CDs. It had 5,000 titles on its Web site and added approximately 25 new releases each month. Books on Tape sold directly through its Web site, by catalogue and to libraries. It rented its products for 30-day periods at relatively low prices.

MediaBay[58]

MediaBay distributed, published and broadcast spoken audio content, with an inventory of 50,000 hours acquired under license from major publishers such as Random House Audio, Simon & Schuster and Harper Audio. Royalty payments were often paid in advance. MediaBay's 2.9 million customers purchased through catalogues, direct mail, retail outlets, Amazon.com and through its own web sites. MediaBay ran an Audiobook Club with 2.5 million members. In 1999, MediaBay purchased its two main book club competitors: Columbia House Audiobook Club, from Time Warner and Sony and Doubleday's Audiobooks Direct Club, from Bertelsmann. MediaBay offered four audiobooks at $0.99 as an incentive for new members, after which members had to purchase one or two more audiobooks valued from $10 to $40 per unit. MediaBay sought customers through direct mail and the Internet. It estimated that the cost to obtain a new member had decreased from $50 per person in 2000 to $12 in 2002, due to attracting 360,000 members on-line. MediaBay had begun to offer minimal digital downloads of audio content through its Web sites.[59]

Other Internet Companies[60]

Internet companies such as Pressplay, MusicNet, Listen.com and Full Audio offered spoken audio content and music over the net on a pay-to-listen basis. It was possible that major portals such as Yahoo!, America Online or MSN would begin to charge for audio content. Content providers currently supplying Audible could launch their own direct-to-consumer services and products.

Audible commented on its competitive position in the 2002 Annual Report:

> Many of these companies have significantly greater brand recognition and financial, technical, marketing and other resources than we do. We also expect competition to intensify and the number of competitors to increase significantly in the

	1998	1999	2000	2001	2002
Revenue					
Total Content and Services	$132,357	$477,675	$2,519,345	$7,461,971	$11,287,687
Hardware	$243,733	$313,627	$1,273,117	$1,293,533	$931,785
Other	$—	$951,303	$756,518	$315,909	$150,067
Total Revenue	**$376,090**	**$1,742,605**	**$4,548,980**	**$9,071,413**	**$12,369,539**
Operating Expenses					
Cost of contents & services revenue	$372,114	$812,062	$3,667,799	$4,901,866	$4,970,017
Cost of hardware revenue	$555,575	$307,395	$2,571,994	$2,858,495	$2,717,542
Write-down related to hardware	$952,389	$—			
Production expenses	$1,639,420	$3,397,297	$6,457,638	$5,635,977	$3,882,320
Development	$1,641,458	$2,680,108	$4,444,531	$3,322,133	$2,270,912
Sales and marketing	$1,453,196	$6,108,988	$16,052,207	$15,187,584	$12,467,569
General and administrative	$1,838,365	$3,015,227	$5,548,085	$4,726,694	$3,647,415
Total operating expenses	**$8,452,517**	**$16,321,077**	**$38,742,754**	**$36,632,749**	**$ 29,955,775**
Loss from operations	$(8,076,427)	$(14,578,472)	$(34,193,274)	$(27,561,336)	$(17,586,236)
Total other income, net	**$(61,647)**	**$1,102,161**	**$1,601,830**	**$565,565**	**$85,158**
Loss before state income tax benefit			$(32,591,444)	$(26,995,771)	$(17,501,078)
State income tax benefit			$316,310	$326,898	$313,580
Net Loss	**$(8,138,074)**	**$(13,476,311)**	**$(32,275,134)**	**$(26,668,873)**	**$(17,187,498)**
Basic and diluted net loss Per common share	$(1.15)	$(0.85)	$(1.21)	$(1.03)	$(0.61)
Weighted average shares outst	7,096,945	15,890,528	26,643,589	26,917,513	30,508,217

Exhibit 3(a)   Financial Statements, Statements of Operations (For Years Ending December 31)

Source: Annual Report, 2002.

future as technology advances provide alternative methods to deliver digital audio content through the Internet, satellite, wireless data, digital radio or other means.

Dilemma

Since its inception, the company had made great headway with its products and had been experiencing increases in its number of customers. Concerning its partnership strategy, a company representative stated:

We continue our alliances with very large partners who require assurances that Audible will survive when they consider integration of Audible's technology with their devices. Audible needs a more neutral stance with regard to its large partners—devolving the level of financial relations with Microsoft. That said, our business relations are still strong in terms of partnering.

What actions could Audible pursue if it wanted to operate as a going concern? See Exhibits 3(a) to 3(c) for financial statements. Who could Audible look to for further financing? A course of action would have to be decided upon quickly because cash was running out.

ASSETS	2001	2002
Current Assets:		
Cash and cash equivalents	$7,627,802	$2,822,080
Accounts receivable	$153,122	$189,263
Royalty advances	$56,682	$58,425
Prepaid expenses	$661,192	$736,823
Inventory	$449,220	$77,262
Note receivable due from stockholder, current	$10,000	
Total Current Assets	**$8,958,018**	**$3,883,853**
Property and equipment, net	$1,990,670	$633,400
Note receivable due from stockholder, noncurrent	$35,000	
Other assets	$15,805	$90,805
Total Assets	**$10,999,493**	**$4,608,058**
LIABILITIES AND STOCKHOLDERS DEFICIT		
Current liabilities:		
Accounts payable	$1,519,586	$1,077,509
Accrued expenses	$1,635,140	$2,952,314
Royalty obligations - current	$896,950	$598,500
Accrued compensation	$710,148	$279,579
Advances - current	$517,813	$476,053
Accrued dividends on redeemable convertible preferred stock	$730,612	$125,257
Total Current Liabilities	**$6,010,249**	**$5,509,212**
Deferred cash compensation	$93,550	$90,550
Royalty obligations - noncurrent	$48,500	$25,000
Advances - noncurrent	$77,780	$19,448
Redeemable convertible preferred stock	$10,318,902	$12,289,976
STOCKHOLDERS' DEFICIT		
Convertible Series B preferred stock	$—	$1,137,500
Common stock	$275,470	$316,779
Additional paid-in capital	$93,728,564	$98,033,060
Deferred compensation	$(467,600)	$(174,488)
Deferred services	$(5,416,667)	$(416,667)
Notes due from stockholders for common stock	$(294,456)	$(289,545)
Treasury stock at cost: 676,725 and 689,225	$(179,990)	$(184,740)
Accumulated deficit	$(93,194,809)	$(111,748,027)
Total Stockholders' Deficit	**$(5,549,488)**	**$(13,326,128)**
Total liabilities and stockholders' deficit	$10,999,493	$4,608,058

Exhibit 3(b)   Balance Sheet (For Years Ending December 31)

Source: Annual Report, 2002.

	2001	2002
Cash flows from operating activities:		
Net loss	$(26,668,873)	$(17,187,498)
Depreciation and amortization	$1,825,466	$1,506,815
Services rendered for common stock and warrants	$7,182,106	$6,153,998
Services rendered for preferred stock		$547,500
Noncash compensation charge	$333,375	$293,112
Noncash bonus in satisfaction of note rec from stockholder		$40,250
Deferred cash compensation	$(117,515)	$(3,000)
Noncash barter revenue exchanged for ppd advertising	$(213,788)	
Changes in assets and liabilities:		
Interest receivable on short-term investments	$95,336	$1,260
Accounts receivable, net	$40,630	$(36,141)
Royalty advances	$790,714	$(1,743)
Prepaid expenses	$16,727	$(76,891)
Inventory	$(331,050)	$371,958
Other assets	$21,705	$(75,000)
Account payable	$(234,854)	$(442,077)
Accrued expenses	$(705)	$1,907,174
Royalty obligations	$(329,250)	$(321,950)
Accrued compensation	$(51,886)	$(430,569)
Advances	$142,117	$(100,092)
Net cash used in operating activities	**$(17,499,745)**	**$(7,852,894)**
Cash flows from investing activities:		
Purchases of property and equipment	$(997,344)	$(149,545)
Redemptions of short-term investments	$1,957,733	
Notes receivable repaid by stockholders	$5,000	
Net cash provided by (used in) investing activities	**$965,389**	**$(149,545)**
Cash flows from financing activities:		
Proceeds from issuance of Series A redeemable convertible preferred stock	$10,000,000	
Proceeds from the sale of common stock		$3,186,250
Payments received on notes due from stockholders for common stock	$66,085	$4,911
Proceeds from exercise of common stock options		$5,556
Payment of principal on obligations under capital leases	$(47,187)	
Cash payment for purchase of treasury stock	$(5,767)	
Net cash provided by financing activities	**$10,013,131**	**$3,196,717**
Increase (decrease) in cash and cash equivalents	**$(6,521,225)**	**$(4,805,722)**
Cash and cash equivalents at beginning at year	**$14,149,027**	**$7,627,802**
Cash and cash equivalents at end of year	**$7,627,802**	**$2,822,080**

Exhibit 3(c)   Statement of Cash Flows (For Years Ending December 31)

Source: Annual Report, 2002.

NOTES

1. This case has been written on the basis of published sources only. Consequently, the interpretation and perspectives presented in this case are not necessarily those of Audible.com or any of its employees.

2. Audible Annual Report, December 31, 2002, *www.sec.gov*, accessed July 15, 2003, p. 1.

3. Audible Quarterly Report, March 31, 2003, *www.sec.gov*, accessed July 15, 2003, p. 6.

4. "Audible Inc. Q1 2003 Earnings Conference Call," *Fair Disclosure Financial Network*, May 12, 2003, pp. 2-3.

5. Audible Annual Report, December 31, 2002, *www.sec.gov*, accessed July 15, 2003, pp. 3-4.

6. Barnes & Noble Annual Report, January 30, 2003, *www.sec.gov*, accessed July 15, 2003, p. 6.

7. Phillip Honstein, "Publishing Audiobooks in the Information Age," *Emerson College*, October 2, 2000.

8. Shannon Maughan, "Checking up on Children's Audio," *Publishers Weekly*, June 11, 2001.

9. Ibid.

10. Ibid.

11. "April 2003 Internet Usage Statistics," Nielsen/Net Ratings Inc, available at *www.itmanagement.earthweb.com*, May 12, 2003.

12. Audible Annual Report, December 31, 2002, *www.sec.gov*, accessed July 15, 2003, p. 4.

13. Ibid.

14. "Audible Inc. Q1 2003 Earnings Conference Call," *Fair Disclosure Financial Network*, May 12, 2003, p. 8.

15. Shannon Maughan, "Checking up on Children's Audio," *Publishers Weekly*, June 11. 2001.

16. Ibid.

17. "Internet 2001: Year of Real Opportunity or Year of the Not-Com?" *roundzero.com*.

18. Audible Annual Report, December 31, 2002, *www.sec.gov*, accessed July 15, 2003, p. 34.

19. "Audible Files for $46 Million IPO," *PR Newswire*, April 30, 1999.

20. Audible Annual Report, December 31, 2001, *www.sec.gov*, accessed July 15, 2003, pp. F1-5.

21. Ibid.

22. Audible Quarterly Report, March 31, 2003, *www.sec.gov*, accessed July 15, 2003, p. 16.

23. Audible Annual Report, December 31, 2002, *www.sec.gov*, accessed July 15, 2003.

24. Ibid, p. 34.

25. Ibid, p. 6

26. Ibid, pp. 4-9.

27. Phillip Honstein, "Publishing Audiobooks in the Information Age," *Emerson College*, October 2, 2000.

28. "11 Per Cent Content Revenue Growth Over Fourth Quarter 2002 . . . ," *PR Newswire*, May 12, 2003.

29. "Premium Audio Download Service Cited for Stupendous Amount of Digital Audio Content," *PR Newswire*, May 2, 2003.

30. Ibid.

31. "11 Per Cent Content Revenue Growth Over Fourth Quarter 2002 . . . ," *PR Newswire*, May 12, 2003.

32. Audible Quarterly Report, March 31, 2003, *www.sec.gov*, accessed July 15, 2003, p. 18.

33. Audible Annual Report, December 31, 2001, *www.sec.gov*, accessed July 15, 2003, p. F17.

34. "Microsoft Audible Expand Strategic Relationship around Premium Spoken Audio Content," August 16, 1999, available at www.microsoft.com, accessed July 15, 2003.

35. *www.microsoft.com*, July 30, 2003.

36. "Audible Inc. Announces New Investment from Microsoft," *PR Newswire*, February 9, 2001.

37. Audible Annual Report, December 31, 2002, *www.sec.gov*, accessed July 15, 2003, p. 17.

38. Amazon.com Annual Report, December 31, 2002, *www.sec.gov*, accessed July 15, 2003, pp. 1-2.

39. Audible Annual Report, December 31, 2002, *www.sec.gov*, accessed July 15, 2003, p. 17.

40. Ibid.

41. Ibid.

42. "Random House to Invest in Audible through Random House Ventures," Audible News Release, May 11, 2000, *www.audible.com*, accessed July 15, 2003.

43. Books on Tape Company Capsule, June 8, 2003, *www.hoovers.com*, accessed July 15, 2003.

44. *www.audible.com*, accessed June 5, 2003.

45. Audible Annual Report, December 31, 2002, *www.sec.gov*, accessed July 15, 2003, p. 9.

46. Audible Investor Conference Call with Andy Kaplan and Jonathon Korzen, September 2003.

47. "Audible Inc. Q1 2003 Earnings Conference Call," *Fair Disclosure Financial Network*, May 12, 2003, p. 5.

48. Ibid.

49. Audible Annual Report, December 31, 2002, *www.sec.gov*, accessed on July 15, 2003, p. 10.

50. Moira McCormick, "Harry Potter to Cast Spell over Audio," *Billboard*, October 9, 1999.

51. *www.randomhouse.com*, accessed July 13, 2003.

52. Viacom Annual Report, December 31, 2002, *www.sec.gov*, accessed July 15, 2003, pp. 1-21.

53. Audible Annual Report, December 31, 2002, *www.sec.gov*, accessed July 15, 2003, pp. 9-10.

54. Shannon Maughan, "Checking up on Children's' Audio," *Publishers Weekly*, June 11, 2001.

55. Barnes & Noble Company Capsule, *www.hoovers.com*, July 30, 2003.

56. Ibid.

57. Borders Group Company Capsule, July 30, 2003, *www.hoovers.com*, accessed July 15, 2003.

58. MediaBay Annual Report, December 31, 2002, *www.sec.gov*, accessed July 15, 2003, pp. 1-5.

59. Ibid.

60. Ibid.

CANADIAN CLOSURES (A)

Prepared by Davin Li under the supervision of Professor Louis Hébert

Version: (A) 2001-06-05

On April 9, 1993, Bernard Kayvon, general manager (GM) of Canadian Closures had just arrived in his Mississauga office when his telephone rang. It was Tom Brockner, his manufacturing manager: "I'm afraid we have a problem. There's something wrong with the lacquer on the crowns produced during the last shift. We don't know what's wrong, but they didn't pass the copper sulphate test . . ."[1] Kayvon exclaimed: "That shipment's worth over $500,000. . . ." His response met with silence. "Put a hold on the entire shipment, I'll get back to you."

After putting down the phone, he slumped into his chair. He had been hired two months earlier to head this bottlecap (crown) producing joint venture between Johnson & Guy Plc and Macklin, one of Canada's leading brewers. His mandate was to solve customer complaints, improve quality, and lead the company toward profitability. The joint venture's only client, Macklin Breweries, was becoming impatient with the constant barrage of quality problems at their plants, for which they were blaming Canadian Closures' crowns. Already, 75 million crowns had been rejected and they wanted to be reimbursed. On top of these problems, the relationship between the partner firms was also becoming increasingly tense. In spite of it all, Bernard knew that he had to do what was best for Canadian Closures.

THE CANADIAN BEER INDUSTRY

The brewing industry had been a significant part of Canada's economy. In 1993, it contributed $10 billion to the economy, approximately 1.5 per cent of the Canadian gross national product. The 1993 television advertising expenditures made by the largest breweries were estimated at $100 million. Furthermore, the industry employed, either directly or indirectly, 179,929 people or 1.3 per cent of working Canadians. The Canadian beer industry consisted of two major companies, a score of smaller regional breweries, and several microbreweries. The two largest players were Labatt and Molson, which accounted for about 90 per cent of all Canadian beer sales. The remaining 10 per cent belonged to regional and microbreweries, and to an even lesser extent to imports.

Consumers

The changing demographics and preferences of the Canadian population during the 1980s and 1990s greatly altered the industry's key success factors. Growth no longer came from the attitudes towards alcohol being a desired part of social and cultural activities. In fact, beer consumption levels either stagnated or declined because of an aging population who were more concerned about living healthier lives, an increased awareness about the dangers of drinking and driving, and the growing popularity of substitutes like wines, coolers, soft drinks, mineral water and juices. A recent study cited that per capita domestic beer consumption slid from 77.09 litres in 1989 to 69.27 litres in 1992.[2]

The breweries relied on advertising and marketing campaigns, a wider product selection, and new packaging techniques to increase total beer consumption. Lower prices were achieved by reducing the amount of barley and hops used in beer with less expensive substitutes like wheat, rice and corn. In turn, regional and microbreweries flourished due to the customer's need for stronger tasting brews that avoided the use of preservatives and used less carbonation. National brewers also spent enormous amounts of money to target consumer groups such as young professionals and college/university students with lifestyle ads showing physically attractive people having fun. This strategy consisted of designing a beer bottle that appealed to the group, and launching a massive advertising blitz geared to the target group's "lifestyle." Many members of the community objected to these ads since they were blamed for luring more youth to drink alcohol.

Similarly, advertising and promotional campaigns were used to attract new drinkers. From promoting tennis tournaments to baseball teams, the privilege of sponsoring high profile sporting events was intensely fought over by the major Canadian breweries. When brewers realized that consumers valued distinct flavors and healthier products, they launched several new product lines to meet that need. Dry beers were introduced to satisfy consumers who wanted a sweeter brew and a slightly higher alcohol content. Light and non-alcoholic beers were introduced to satisfy those who wanted products with a lower calorie and alcohol content.

In the mid 1980s, Canadian brewers discovered that packaging changes could spark consumer interest in their brands. More consumers were drinking sophisticated-looking, imported beers. As a result, breweries switched from the traditional brown, short necked, stubby bottles, to over 15 different shapes, colors and sizes of long-necked bottles. By 1986, only 10 per cent of Canada's beer was still bottled in "stubbies." Although the introduction of "long necks" cost over $100 million, the brewers absorbed the expenses and accepted reduced profits. Significant changes in packaging included the first twist-off crowns introduced by Labatt in 1985, the bottom beer bottle opener introduced by Carling O'Keefe in 1987, and the announcement of a Canadian-Australian joint venture to create plastic beer bottles for the British market in 1990. Packaging changes like these usually resulted in significant gains in market share.

In particular, Labatt's introduction of twist-off crowns to Canadian consumers had resulted in a significant national market share gain. The introduction of twist-off crowns for the "Blue" beer had experienced unprecedented market share success. Labatt had quickly followed with the same crowns for its "Blue Light" and was contemplating using them for its entire product line. In a newspaper interview, an executive added: "People in bars have begun asking for their bottles unopened . . . they enjoy the fun of taking the caps off themselves."

Still, despite the industry's attempts to increase beer consumption, levels remained flat. Every brewery was forced to fight with each other for every market share per cent. It was estimated that each national market share percentage point gained contributed $10 million in operating profits. For this reason, the competition for market share was intense. Every attempt in differentiating through price, advertising, marketing, product line or packaging type was quickly copied throughout the industry. However, a first mover advantage could result in a significant increase in market share, making rapid differentiation a vital key to success.

Government Regulations

Due to federal and provincial government interventions, the Canadian brewing industry evolved as several regionally based markets. Regulations discouraging the sale of beer produced in other provinces included the application of provincial import duties on beers produced outside of the province. To avoid losing significant market share, national brewers were compelled to build breweries within each province. These same regulations also kept regional breweries such as Moosehead of New Brunswick from expanding outside their home provinces. Because provincial governments required all breweries to set up provincial plants, none of the Canadian breweries could achieve economies of scale. It was estimated that a brewery needed the capacity to produce approximately four million to five million hectolitres[3] of beer annually in order to minimize its costs.[4] In comparison, the average size of a brewery in Canada produced only 1.24 million hectolitres.[5] The provincial governments also heavily regulated the beer distribution system. However, each province was different. In Ontario and most other provinces, breweries could sell through their own private retail stores and government-run outlets. In Quebec and Newfoundland, beer was sold in corner grocery stores.

The federal and provincial governments also influenced the price of beer by levying taxes that were equivalent to 53 per cent of the retail price paid by the end-consumers. These beer taxes had increased 222 per cent since 1980. High Canadian barley prices also led to higher Canadian cost structures. A study estimated that Canadian beer drinkers would save $50 million annually if the government allowed domestic brewers to buy malt on the open market. Canadian brewers were forced to buy their barley malt from the Canadian Wheat Board at set prices. Foreign competition, such as U.S. breweries, had a huge cost advantage because the higher priced barley acted like an extra tax.

U.S. Imports

Another factor that influenced the long-term viability of the Canadian brewing industry was the threat of cheaper American imports. American imports enjoyed lower cost structures because of larger cost-minimizing breweries and lower priced barley. To illustrate, only one of the largest plants in the United States could have supplied all of the beer consumption in Canada. Because of these considerations, the government placed heavy tariffs on imported beer so Canadian products were competitively priced. Whether these tariffs would exist in the future was still under debate.

Packaging System

The Canadian brewing industry evolved in a way that favored more costly packaging, resulting in higher cost structures. Returnable glass bottles comprised about 81 per cent of the packaging type used, while aluminum beer cans made up the rest. Because bottles were heavier and required a bottle return system, they were more costly than cans to ship and maintain. Hence, they resulted in higher retail beer prices than those within a system that used mainly aluminum cans such as the U.S.

THE CROWN

Although many consumers considered the crown to be a relatively unimportant part of the packaging, it served a significant function. Canadian Closures' Technical Manual described in the following terms the purpose of the crown:

> One of the final components to go on a bottle, the crown must not only be secure enough to withstand the handling of transportation and application, not only come off quickly and easily to customer satisfaction, but above all, it must ensure that the flavor of the bottle's content is both retained and in no way contaminated. A rather large accomplishment for what appears to be just a bit of painted metal.

Throughout its 90-year history, the crown underwent many changes. Such innovations included alterations in height-size, convenience features such as tear-offs, flip-offs and twist-offs, and different material contents such as solid cork, composition cork, plastic liners, and foil and vinyl spots. And like most other products, these innovations were made to successfully meet the changing needs of the customers. In 1990, more than 25 billion steel crowns were used to cap beer and soft drinks every year in Canada and the United States.[6]

There were two major categories of crowns: pry-off and twist-off. They were made of mostly tin-free steel and matte finish tin plate (which had a brighter finish) that were supplied by traditional steel manufacturers. Typically, breweries saw crowns as a commodity and they demanded little from their crown suppliers. For this reason, low quality levels were pervasive throughout the industry.

In 1990, Crown, Cork, & Seal (CCS) had acquired several smaller competitors. Alone, it accounted for almost 60 per cent of the North American industry's production capacity that was estimated to be 40 billion crowns. Three other firms, all based in the U.S., accounted for the rest of the supply. The Canadian and U.S. crown market had eight major customers in 1993. In Canada, the three national breweries consumed approximately the same number of crowns (See Table 1).

THE CROWN MANUFACTURING PROCESS

Two types of steel are normally used to manufacture crowns: tin-plated steel and tin-free steel. The thickness of the tin-plated and tin-free steel is required to be 0.0087 inches plus or minus 0.00079 inches in order to guarantee seal efficacy upon application. Steel coils are first transformed into 28x34 inch sheets. A size coat of clear or aluminum-pigmented vinyl is applied to the external service to improve the adhesion of ink. A vinyl sanitary lacquer is then deposited on the interior surface to provide a base for the plastic liner. After this, either a single-color printing for most applications, or multicolor decoration for others, is applied. A varnish coat protects the exterior surface.

Discs are punched from the flat steel, then fed into shell-forming dies, where flutes are pressed in the flaring skirts of the shallow shells. In bottle sealing, the flutes are crimped against a protecting ring on the container mouth. The typical crown dimensions are 1.264 inch diameter plus or minus 0.008 inches and a 0.235 inch height plus or minus 0.005 inches.

Next, powdered polyvinyl chloride (PVC) is extruded, heated to the molten state, and accurately metered pellets of the compound dropped into the centres of the now heated crown shells. Moulding or a flow-in technique forms the liner, and the curing of this sealing gasket follows. Crowns are inspected by a computerized system and defects are promptly removed. Crowns are then counted electronically and packed into corrugated boxes, each holding 10,000. Palletizing the boxes for shipment to customers is the last step in the sequence of crown manufacturing.

THE CREATION OF CANADIAN CLOSURES INC.

Johnson & Guy was a 75-year old conglomerate based in London, England with net sales of $2.4 billion and profits of $100 million in 1993. Its extremely diversified interests ranged from food

Table 1

1993 CANADIAN MARKET		1993 U.S. MARKET	
Company	Demand (in billions)	Company	Demand (in billions)
National breweries	5.0	Anheuser-Busch	7.9
Others	0.5	Miller	4.2
		Coors	1.9
Soft Drinks & Coolers	0.2	Soft Drinks & Coolers	2.0
TOTAL	**5.7**		**16.0**

and fermentation products (yeast, spices, cake mixes) to hardware (home renovation, building and plumbing) to shipping, and automotive parts. Its operations stretched over the United Kingdom, Australia and New Zealand.

Melbourne Closures was the subsidiary of a larger Australian group acquired by Johnson & Guy. It had sales of $20 million and five years earlier, it had designed a "swift-off" crown. The swift-off crown was an improvement over the normal conventional pry-off and twist-off versions because it lacked the sharp edges of the North American crowns, and was easier to turn. After successfully expanding throughout Australia and New Zealand, George Tyler, the GM of Melbourne Closures, began looking for other markets to expand into. Hoping that his swift-off would catch on in North America, just as it did in Australia and New Zealand, Tyler sent out a letter proposing the use of his patented crown to every major North American brewery. Only one firm expressed interest: Macklin, one of Canada's leading breweries.

When Macklin received George Tyler's letter, it was in the midst of a fierce battle for market share with its two major competitors, Molson and Labatt. Macklin Breweries was one of Canada's oldest firms, with sales close to $2 billion. With the stagnation of the Canadian beer market, just like its competitors, it implemented a diversification strategy during the 1980s. Macklin expanded its ownership interests into various consumer product firms. By the 1990s, Macklin and its competitors began refocusing their activities on brewing and divested out of several of their non-core activities.

To follow its archrivals, as well as the changing desires of Canadian consumers, Macklin launched a variety of new brands and packaging features. For instance, it introduced its own dry product, a non-alcoholic beer and a lower calorie level light and dry combination. Labatt had been the first brewery in North America to introduce the twist-off crown in 1984 and had enjoyed significant gains in national market share. Macklin management thought that Melbourne Closures' patented swift-off technology could be an important differentiating factor.

The Joint Venture

Representatives from Macklin, Johnson & Guy and Melbourne Closures met in the summer of 1990 to discuss the possibility of a joint-venture crown manufacturing company based in Canada. Both firms quickly reached an agreement and created Canadian Closures Inc. Parent companies agreed on a 50/50 structure for the joint venture with an initial investment of $2 5 million. This structure meant that they would support the business equally and that all decisions needed to be agreed upon unanimously. They decided to base the company in an old crown-making plant in Mississauga, Ontario. The refurbishment of the facilities and the new equipment raised the investment by $6 million.

Macklin and Melbourne believed they had much to gain from this joint venture. Macklin was to provide an existing market for the crown with an exclusive preferred supply agreement. Melbourne contributed its patented swift-off technology, technical support during the initial plant set-up and early operations, and, in addition, it was responsible for the administration of the joint venture. Macklin expected an increase in market share through innovative packaging, thus improving overall profits. A complementary licensing agreement permitted Melbourne to receive a minimum of $250,000 in royalties annually for the use of its technology, in addition to its share of profits.

George Tyler also had his eye on expanding further into the rest of North America because: "It would probably be most efficient to use the Mississauga plant as a springboard into the world's biggest packaging market." The general manager of Canadian Closures was to be jointly appointed and would officially report to a board of directors comprised of an equal number of executives from both partners. The board consisted of the chairman, president, vice-president of operations, and vice-president of finance from the Macklin side. The general manager of Johnson & Guy's Food Division, George Tyler, and two legal representatives from Australia made up the Johnson & Guy side. Macklin's vice-president Finance and George Tyler were the general manager's contact persons.

An England-born and long-time employee of Melbourne, Tom Brockner, was hired as the first general manager of Canadian Closures in December 1990. A mechanical engineer by training, Brockner was responsible for getting the company operational and productive by April 1991. Macklin's president explicitly stated that it wanted to use the swift-off crowns for all of its brands by May 1, 1991. Given this time constraint, Brockner worked intensively with his production employees to get the job done from day one.

Although the plant shipped its first batch by Macklin's specified date, Canadian Closures' infancy was not without problems. Canadian Closures was responsible for supplying crowns to all 10 Macklin brewing plants in Canada. Quality problems such as the discoloration of the company logos resulted in Macklin rejecting several large shipments of Canadian Closures crowns. Macklin breweries also reported that some shipments of crowns failed to pass tests examining seal efficacy. The effectiveness of the seal was paramount in ensuring that the beer's taste and shelf life were within normal parameters. Numerous claims and complaints were registered with Canadian Closures' administrative office that operated with the same skeleton crew than at the start-up.

In February 1992, Canadian Closures' board of directors concluded that Brockner was unable to solve the current problems. Immediately, the search for a new general manager began. And the board had a very clear idea about what that new GM's mandate should be. First, he had to resolve the complaint situation. Second, he had to improve the quality of Canadian Closures' crowns. Third, he had to improve Canadian Closures' profitability. In March 1993, Mr. Bernard Kayvon was hired as Canadian Closures' new GM. Kayvon's diversified professional experience made him well suited to the position at Canadian Closures. An accountant by training, he had spent over 25 years working in general management, operations, manufacturing and comptroller functions in industries ranging from electrical connectors to pharmaceuticals and packaging. Although he was unfamiliar with

the crown business, the board of directors was confident that he would be able to adapt.

THE ARRIVAL OF A NEW GENERAL MANAGER

Bernard Kayvon was determined to make Canadian Closures a success. But the price of taking this opportunity was high. He had left a vice-president position in a well-known company for one reason alone: "to be the top dog." And because his former company was family-owned, he knew that he would never have that opportunity there. Nonetheless, he realized that the price of failure was just as high. He was 41 years old and if he did not turn Canadian Closures around, it would be very difficult to "start all over again."

Kayvon had his work cut out for him. To top it off, on the first day of the job he was given the responsibility of informing Tom Brockner that he was fired as general manager, but Kayvon convinced him to stay on as technical director. Soon after, the facility suffered from various problems such as logo discoloration, packaging inadequacies, crown defects and equipment breakdowns. No system to deal with these complaints or potential problems was in place and production employees had, until now, received minimal training. Some technical assistance from Melbourne engineers was possible, but they could not solve all the operational issues at a distance. Kayvon quickly realized that he could not depend on its parent firms. Brockner was instrumental in helping Kayvon become more familiar with the industry and Canadian Closures' machinery.

Benchmarking the venture's results against the very detailed business plan prepared by George Tyler in 1990 revealed that problems went beyond manufacturing. Material costs, including steel that made up 55 per cent of the total, were one-third above targets. The joint venture (JV) was also dependant on a subcontractor to perform the initial lacquer coating of the steel for eight months of the year; an expense totalling $400,000. In addition, the JV contract stated that Macklin would pay a "competitive price" for Canadian Closures' crowns. However, the partners had not agreed upon what a competitive price was and the prices in the supply agreement were a few years old. Also, the financial resources, additional engineering staff, and technical resources planned had not yet been fully realized.

With the degradation of the situation, it was with little surprise that conflicts and tensions were developing between the parent companies and between them and the venture's personnel. Relationships with contact managers were deteriorating fast. Kayvon could not turn to Macklin for any help in solving Canadian Closures' quality problems. "How could you tell your only customer you were having operational problems making the crowns that they were depending on you to supply?" was the dilemma Kayvon faced. He had also to deal with unremitting demands for financial information and forecasts from Melbourne that overwhelmed the venture's administrative staff. As for the board of directors, no formal meetings were scheduled. Kayvon's contact with the board was limited to conference calls where the agenda was dominated by approvals of auditors, audited statements and pension fund changes. No discussion of the venture's problems had been productive so far.

THE SITUATION IN APRIL 1993

Although Canadian Closures received complaints from all 10 breweries, three plants registered the bulk of the rejected crown shipments. The three plants were based in Kingston, Ontario; Winnipeg, Manitoba; and Moncton, New Brunswick. Like his predecessor, Kayvon did not understand why these three particular plants were always registering complaints. "I have no idea why these breweries are having all these problems . . . we send out the exact same crowns to all the breweries across Canada." Assistance from Melbourne was not really an option. In the early days of the venture, Tyler and a Melbourne engineer had joined in a visit of a brewery that repeatedly suffered from crown-related problems. Very quickly the atmosphere became confrontational and each side

was throwing insults and blames at the other side. The visit had to be cut short before a fight started.

Heightening tensions in Macklin's senior management were also distressing Kayvon. In spite of the sustained 1.5 per cent national market share they gained from introducing the swift-off, its novelty had already lost its lustre. Their senior executives stated that it had no intention of adding any more money to its current investment in Canadian Closures. There were rumors that they were considering changing crown suppliers because of Canadian Closures' quality problems and its sub-industry profit levels. However unrealistic and optimistic had been the initial business plan, Kayvon was convinced that the parent firms perceived Canadian Closures' performance levels as being below industry standards. In the prior year, it has showed losses of $350,000 on sales of $10.2 million and only more losses were planned for the near future.

Kayvon sat in his chair and looked out the window of his office. Claims regarding the 75 million crowns were worth over $350,000. Recognizing these claims would be sacrificing Canadian Closures' profit objectives, which both parent firms demanded he reach. In turn, rejecting Macklin's requests would antagonize the venture's only client for a long time, if not for good. And now he had to put over $500,000 in crowns on hold and stop production until Canadian Closures could determine the source of the lacquer problem. He looked at the clock. It was 9:16 a.m. He knew it was going to be a very long day.

NOTES

1. When crowns (or bottlecaps) do not pass the copper sulfate test, seal efficacy cannot be guaranteed, and there is a high likelihood of corrosion or rust formation on the interior of the crown.

2. Brewers Association of Canada, *Statistics,* www.brewers.ca/stats_per_capital.htm

3. A hectolitre (hl) is equivalent to 1,000 litres (L).

4. Ager, David et al., *Labatt Ice (Ivey Case Study),* September 15, 1998.

5. Ibid.

6. Canadian Packaging Magazine.

CAMECO IN KYRGYZSTAN:
CORPORATE SOCIAL RESPONSIBILITY ABROAD

*Prepared by John Scarfe and Richard Johnston
under the supervision of Professor Tima Bansal*

Version: (A) 2006-02-08

On May 20, 2001, a truck carrying 20 tons of sodium cyanide overturned en route to a Cameco mine site in Kyrgyzstan, spilling some of the chemical into the Barskaun River. Although the environmental damage was insignificant, management of the crisis was reactive and carried out poorly. Relationships within the nearby communities were at an all-time low.

Cameco, a Canadian corporation and the world's largest uranium mining company at the time, had formed a joint venture with the Kyrgyzstani government called the Kumtor Gold Company (KGC). Kumtor was to develop and operate a gold mine in the Tien Shan Mountains of eastern Kyrgyzstan. Its headquarters were in Bishkek, Kyrgyzstan.

Ray Duret had been promoted in June 2001 to vice-president of human resources and corporate relations at Kumtor. Previously, he had served as manager of human resources at Cameco's head office in Saskatoon, Saskatchewan, Canada. In his earlier role, Duret had been involved in northern relations within Canadian uranium mining operations, located primarily in northern Saskatchewan. Cameco had successfully developed working relationships with the people in nearby communities, mainly aboriginals of Cree and Dene descent. Consequently, Cameco could count on some local support to facilitate obtaining environmental approval for new mines.

It was now August, 2001 and Duret wondered whether the Saskatchewan model of social responsibility could be applied in the Tien Shan Mountains of Kyrgyzstan, especially in light of the spill. And, with Cameco contemplating a gold mine in Mongolia, Duret knew that if Cameco's model of corporate social responsibility could be applied to other countries, the new venture could start on the right foot.

THE URANIUM INDUSTRY

Uranium, the heaviest of the naturally occurring elements, is plentiful in the Earth's crust, and is even more common than tin. Northern Saskatchewan had the world's richest concentrations of uranium, which were found in ore bodies around the Athabasca Basin.

Uranium was used primarily as fuel in nuclear reactors. In 1998, more than 400 reactors worldwide produced 17 per cent of the global demand for electricity; in the United States, nuclear power supplied 20 per cent of the demand. One kilogram of uranium contained the same amount of energy as 35 tonnes of coal or 150 barrels of oil.

Cameco's main competitor was Cogema, owned by the French government and completely vertically integrated in the nuclear fuel cycle. Seventy-five per cent of France's electricity was produced by nuclear plants, and Cogema ran most of them. As with most European utilities, Cogema was under political pressure from the Europeon Union (EU) to privatize. With growing acceptance of nuclear power and growing environmental backlash to fossil fuel electricity generation, many in the industry spoke of a "nuclear renaissance."

BACKGROUND TO CAMECO

Cameco Corp. was formed in 1988 with the amalgamation of Eldorado Nuclear and Saskatchewan

Mining and Development Corporation (SMDC), both owned by the Canadian and Saskatchewan governments. Shortly after its inception, the company was privatized, and its shares listed on the Toronto and New York stock exchanges. With control and ownership of the world's largest reserves of high-grade ore, Cameco was thought to have had the lowest cost of production, although this was unconfirmed, given the limited information of Soviet production. In 1998, Cameco produced 20 per cent of the world's uranium.

The company was vertically integrated in the nuclear fuel cycle, involved with the exploration, mining, milling, refining, conversion and power generation parts of the fuel cycle. It had uranium mining interests in the United States and a refinery and conversion facility in Ontario. In 2001, Cameco bought a 15 per cent interest in the Bruce Power Partnership (Bruce Power), which was formed to lease and operate the Bruce Nuclear Power station, formerly operated by the Ontario government. This brought Cameco alongside British Energy, which owned 80 per cent of the lease.

To further leverage its mining capabilities, Cameco Corp. formed Cameco Gold Inc., headquartered in Toronto. In 1992, Cameco formed the Kumtor Operating Company (KOC), a joint venture with the Kyrgyzstani government, to mine gold. And, in March 2001, Cameco announced an investment in Mongolia's Boroo Gold deposit, which was expected to begin production by 2003. The company had explored for uranium and gold in other locations in North America, Australia and Asia. Its five-year financial summary is shown in Exhibit 1.

The locations of major communities and Cameco mines in Saskatchewan are shown in Exhibit 2. Cameco was the majority owner of the Key Lake, McArthur River, Cigar Lake and Rabbit Lake mines.

Northern Saskatchewan: Sociopolitical Background

The Saskatchewan government designated a 250,000-square kilometre section of the province as the Northern Administrative District (NAD). In 1998, the population of the Northern Administrative District was approximately 35,000 or three per cent of the provincial total, even though it covered geographically half of the province. The people, 80 per cent of whom were of Woodland Cree, Dene or Métis descent, lived in 35 municipal communities and 12 First Nations reserve communities scattered throughout the area.

Until the 1950s, most of the area's people relied heavily on the land to support daily living, as they had for generations. Although trapping was still important to Canada's native people, the demise of the fur trade had devastated their income source and taken away their traditional way of life and independence.

Still, many aboriginal communities continued to rely on traditional hunting and gathering skills for survival, so formal education was not always a priority. Until recently, a native child's first exposure to the education system was through residential religious schools. To receive this education, however, children were often separated from their families for long periods of time, and reports of child abuse had started to surface. As more schools were built in the communities and more local people became teachers, the quality and social value of education improved.

The people of the Northern Administrative District had significant problems with poverty, unemployment, illiteracy, welfare dependency, poor business infrastructure, and a myriad of associated social ills that were often prevalent within the aboriginal communities. Surveys by Statistics Canada indicated that the region's rate of alcohol consumption was significantly greater than the Canadian norm. According to Health Canada, the area had more than twice the normal incidence of tuberculosis.

The Canadian government's 2001 Northern Saskatchewan Training Needs Assessment Report, used by educational institutes to focus their resources, identified a number of issues:

- One-third of the aboriginal population lived in reserve communities.
- Low-income private households formed 34 per cent of the total, compared to 18 per cent provincially.

Commodity Market Prices (annual average)	2001	2000	1999	1998	1997
Uranium (spot price in US$/lbs U₃O₈)	$8.77	$8.21	$10.23	$10.32	$12.04
Gold (market price in US$/oz)	270.94	279.08	278.88	294.24	330.98
Operations					
Revenue	$700.80	$688.90	$741.60	$718.90	$642.90
Earnings (loss)[1] from operations	94.80	(45.70)	79.30	104.50	151.00
Net earnings[1] before special items	55.90	44.50	42.30	67.50	82.00
Net earnings (loss)[1]	55.90	(87.20)	71.20	43.70	82.00
EBITDA[2]	234.00	213.60	252.00	245.50	265.70
Cash provided by operations	116.20	224.30	249.40	236.80	162.10
Capital expenditures	58.30	84.10	201.10	702.30	307.70
Financial Position					
Total assets	$2,947.30	$2,800.50	$2,964.10	$2,938.60	$2,270.70
Total debt	354.00	294.30	359.20	601.40	286.70
Shareholders' equity	1,822.90	1,780.50	1,922.30	1,903.30	1,692.20
Financial Ratios					
Current ratio					
(current assets/current liabilities)	4.3:1	3.6:1	3.3:1	2.4:1	2.0:1
Return on common shareholders' equity	3%	−3%	4%	3%	6%
Net debt to capitalization	15%	13%	14%	23%	9%
Cash from operations/total net debt	36%	86%	80%	42%	92%
Common Share Data ($ per share)					
Net earnings before special items	$1.01	$0.81	$0.72	$1.18	$1.51
Net earnings (loss)	1.01	(1.57)	1.24	0.76	1.51
Cash provided by operations	2.10	4.04	4.35	4.13	2.98
Dividends	0.50	0.50	0.50	0.50	0.50
Book value	29.24	28.77	30.51	29.77	29.46
TSE Market - high	43.00	28.25	40.50	48.75	60.00
- low	23.75	14.50	20.75	24.05	40.00
- close	39.25	26.25	21.95	27.45	46.40
- annual volume (millions)	45.70	35.30	30.50	24.30	33.00
Shares outstanding (millions)					
Weighted average	55.40	55.50	57.40	57.30	54.40
Year end	55.70	55.50	57.20	57.70	57.40
Production (Cameco's Share)					
Uranium concentrates					
(million lbs U₃O₈)	18.80	16.60	16.80	27.50	19.30
Uranium conversion (UF₆ and UO₂) (000s tU)	11.00	9.30	11.20	11.20	12.60
Gold (oz)	250,907	223,339	203,508	244,385	202,454
Employees	2,948	2,924	2,843	2,902	2,469

Exhibit 1   Five Year Financial Summary (Cdn$ millions except prices and per share amounts)

Source: Company files.

1. Attributable to common shares.

2. Earnings before interest, taxes, depreciation and amortization, writedowns, gains on asset sales and other income.

Exhibit 2   Major Communities and Uranium
Mine Sites in Saskatchewan

Source: Company files.

- One-third of the population had an education level of less than Grade 9.
- Forty-five per cent of the adults had dropped out of the labor force. The remaining 55 per cent had unemployment rates at three times the provincial average.
- On average, a greater percentage of teenage girls became teen mothers (25 per cent compared to 10 per cent provincially). Births to girls aged 10 to 14 were 6.3 times the provincial rate.
- The number of teens attending school was less than provincial or national averages.

There were, however, some signs of improvement. Between 1996 and 2001, there had been a 31 per cent decline in the number of people receiving social assistance in the region.

Enrolment in provincial schools had increased by three per cent, and First Nations enrolment had increased by 100 per cent.

In Saskatchewan, 28 of 70 First Nations groups had not received the land they were promised under treaties with the federal and provincial governments. The two governments tried to resolve the issues through the Treaty Land Entitlement Framework Agreement. In 1992, 25 of the groups signed the agreement, which entitled them to Cdn$516 million over 12 years to buy 1.95 million acres. Treaty issues grew more contentious as First Nations peoples made demands and the Canadian government looked for cost-effective yet equitable solutions. With mounting court victories for aboriginal peoples, resource companies were compelled to step up negotiations with native peoples. Proactive companies began to establish relationships with Canada's First Nations.

Community consultation was an essential part of Cameco's strategy. Aboriginal people told Cameco that they wanted economic opportunities for themselves and their children while the mines were active and, after the mines were gone, they wanted to possess the skills and facilities necessary to fully participate in the Canadian economy. Also important was their desire to continue to live off the land, both during and after the mining project. They wanted assurance that no harm would come to the environment. Cameco was willing to operate within these guidelines.

Cameco in Northern Saskatchewan

In the Uranium City area of northern Saskatchewan, uranium had been mined since 1952. Most of it was used to supply the American nuclear arsenal. By the 1990s, demand for weapons-grade uranium had diminished substantially, and the large stockpiles of the material, including the very large stockpiles in the ex-Soviet Union, were being converted to reactor fuel.

In the early days of uranium mining, average ore grades ranged from 0.17 per cent to 0.50 per cent uranium. Exploration in the late 1970s uncovered a number of higher-grade deposits on the perimeter of the Athabasca Basin sandstone formation in northern Saskatchewan. With zones that sometimes averaged over 50 per cent uranium, these deposits soon made the older mines—at Uranium City, Elliot Lake in Ontario and several U.S. locations—uneconomical.

After its formation in 1988, Cameco quickly took control of several high-grade deposits in northern Saskatchewan and continued its aggressive exploration program. In 2000, it had 500 million pounds of uranium proven and probable, 165 million pounds measured and indicated, and another 275 million pounds of inferred reserves. Western world consumption was 144 million pounds in 2001.

Cameco's uranium mining operations were on provincially owned land, and the province governed mining activities through surface leases. Cameco, however, tried to be sensitive to the activities of local aboriginal people who owned the surface and mineral rights on reserve land, which included unlimited fishing and hunting.

Social responsibility was an important aspect of Cameco's policies in northern Saskatchewan. To ensure it acted in a sensitive, inclusive and socially appropriate way, Cameco developed a complex set of economic, social and community-relations programs. Cameco's social responsibility policy is shown in Exhibit 3.

The company undertook several programs throughout northern Saskatchewan, including business development, environmental quality committees, trainee programs, and donations to schools and local communities. Total program costs in 2000, detailed in Exhibit 4, were estimated to be Cdn$5.2 million.

Of the mining industry's many potential social and economic benefits, employment was the priority for local aboriginal people. Most workers reached the mine sites by airplane from a number of pick-up points. A seven days in, seven days out schedule allowed them to be at home communities while not at work. In 1998, the average mine site employee earned Cdn$55,000 yearly. In 2001, the underground workforce at Cameco's McArthur River site was more than 80 per cent aboriginal. Greater than 50 per cent of Cameco's total Northern workforce

was of aboriginal descent. In comparison, mining companies in Northern Ontario, as well as the Syncrude project in Fort McMurray, employed aboriginals at levels of 10 per cent or less.

To help develop the community, Cameco preferred to do business with local suppliers, despite the higher expense related to few economies of scale, high turnover, weak management, and insufficient distribution facilities and support infrastructure. The well-established national suppliers, such as the airline and the explosives companies, did not receive special compensation from Cameco. The company hoped that local suppliers would become similarly competitive and that the local area would remain economically viable long after the mines withdrew.

Cameco's relationship with Northern Resource Trucking (NRT) illustrates the company's strategy for local business development. In 1994, in exchange for an exclusive six-year hauling contract, NRT obliged Cameco's request to structure its equity to include 71 per cent northern aboriginal ownership from nine First Nations and three Métis communities. In 1999, NRT employed 140 people and reported annual revenue of Cdn$18 million. Typical of Cameco's approach to suppliers, the NRT deal demonstrated Cameco's awareness that economic benefits derived from service suppliers generally outweigh those of merchandise suppliers. Suppliers of products manufactured outside of the region add only a small fraction of the value to the product; thus, relatively little margin is retained in the region. Service suppliers, on the other hand, retain in the region all the value added from equipment rental and labor.

With local populations growing more politically astute and government regulators growing more rigid, Cameco's Northern Policy was essential to the company's goals of long-term stability and obtaining a social licence to operate. Without co-operation from both the regulators and the community, operating expenses could skyrocket, as Cogema Resources found out when the licensing process went awry at its McClean Lake operation. Not only did the Northern Policy help reduce operating expenses, it also proved valuable

(Text continued on page 293)

Cameco conducts all of its activities in an economically safe, environmentally and socially responsible manner that meets or exceeds the expectations that society has of business. To this end, we are committed to the following general business principles:

- Striving to be a leading performer amongst our peers with regards to shareholder value, safety and environmental protection, business ethics, community support, community economic development, corporate governance, human rights and the work environment;
- Minimizing the potential for adverse impacts that may arise from our operations to levels as low as reasonably achievable, social and economic factors taken into account;
- Optimizing the potential for positive impacts to arise from our operations to levels as high as reasonably achievable, social and economic factors taken into account; and
- Continually improving the management of our operations so we may respond to the economic, environmental and social expectations of our employees, communities, shareholders, governments and the public.

In adopting these principles, Cameco recognizes a continuing commitment to behave ethically and contribute to society through the creation of wealth, employment and the sale of its products and services on a long-term basis.

In support of these principles, Cameco will:

- Strive to achieve the highest sustainable growth in value to meet the needs of the enterprise and its stakeholders today, while contributing to the maintenance or enhancement of overall assets (economic, environmental and social) available to future generations;
- Identify and quantify risk factors which may materially impact our economic performance;
- Account for liabilities that may arise out of our operations, mitigate such liabilities in a responsible manner and provide sufficient financial resources to responsibly manage them;
- Remain economically competitive so we may contribute to the long-term secure supply of primary products to our customers through exploration, development, acquisitions and reinvestment;
- Implement and maintain an environmental policy and supporting programs which allow the company to honor its commitments to protecting the environment, including the adoption of formal environmental management systems;
- Continually improve efficiency of resource use, waste reduction and water conservation efforts;
- Safeguard valued environmental qualities through environmental assessment before starting a new project and before decommissioning the site of an operation;
- Implement and maintain a health and safety policy and supporting programs which allow the company to honor its commitments to health and safety in the work environment and the protection of the public, including the adoption of formal health and safety management systems;
- Continually improve the quality of its human resource management and be an employer-of-choice through progressive wages and benefits, recruitment and employment practices, training and education programs and other fair labor practices; and
- Continually improve social responsibility through investments in community capacity building, labor force development, and business-to-business partnerships.

APPLICATION AND ACCOUNTABILITY

This policy applies to all operations controlled[1] by Cameco and its subsidiaries. The establishment and review of this policy and the supervision of it implementation by management is the responsibility of the board of directors of the corporation. The chief executive officer shall be responsible to ensure compliance with this policy and implementation of its supporting programs and to monitor, from time to time, the status of the implementation of this policy.

The senior management of each division, department, operation and subsidiary is accountable for and has the necessary authority for the establishment, maintenance and implementation of documented programs, plans and procedures that support this policy.

All employees are accountable for the performance of their jobs in conformance with this policy.

Exhibit 3   Cameco Social Responsibility Policy Statement

Source: Company documents

1. "Controlled" means owning a greater than 50 per cent interest or where there is sole operational control. Where Cameco has 50 per cent or less interest in an entity, or does not have sole operational control, it shall proceed in good faith to use its influence to the extent reasonable to cause the entity to adopt practices consistent with this policy.

Program Name	Cameco's Cost
Northern Business Development*	$3,738,600
Athabasca Economic Development and Training Corporation	Nil
Junior Achievement	8,500
Athabasca Working Group & Site Visits**	42,493
Environmental Quality Committees (EQC)	Nil
Donations	100,000
Community Vitality Monitoring Partnership	20,000
Multi-party Training Plan	
– Athabasca Education Awards	5,366
– Northern Scholarship Program	30,000
– Northern Summer Student Program	521,192
– Candidate Assessment	1,680
– Trainee monitoring	14,100
– Apprenticeship Program	254,968
– Student mine tours	24,768
– School presentations	14,114
– Donations to schools	24,375
– School equipment	1,300
– Education leave for Northern employee	14,000
– Cooperative Education Programs	285,920
– CAPES	340,000
– Rabbit Lake Workplace Education Program	53,920
Subtotal	$1,294,783
Total	**$5,208,476**

* Premium paid for $102 million of northern goods and services.
** (i.e. school and EQC tours)

EMPLOYMENT

1. Northern Employment

This was Cameco's largest program. It ensured that RSN's (Resident of Saskatchewan's North) were given hiring preference with both Cameco and its contractors. It was very difficult to determine the cost of this program to Cameco. As of December 31, 1999, 44.2 per cent of Cameco's northern mine operations work force were RSNs. In the McArthur River mine, over 70 per cent of the underground work force was of aboriginal descent. Mines in Northern Ontario did not exceed 10 per cent.

2. BUSINESS

Northern Business Development

As an integral part of Cameco's corporate policy and surface lease commitments, the company afforded preferential consideration to northern businesses in both the service and merchandise sectors. Usually these commitments amounted to a premium over other available suppliers. Premiums varied from nothing to five per cent, depending on the supplier. From 1990 to 1999, the total purchases had steadily increased from $10 million to $115 million. This represented 39 per cent of Cameco purchases in Saskatchewan.

Exhibit 4   Summary of Northern Initiatives and Their Costs - 2000

3. TRAINING AND EDUCATION

Junior Achievement

This program was designed to encourage students to stay in school by educating them to understand the personal and economic costs involved in dropping out of school. The cost to Cameco in 1999 was $8,500. This program was done in conjunction with Cogema Resources and various school divisions. The number of Grade 12 graduates from the region continued to increase although the success of this program was very difficult to measure.

Multi-party Training Plan (MPTP)

The goals of this program were to enhance economic development in the north and maximize the employment potential of the people living in this area by upgrading their skills to meet industry standards. Cameco's contribution to this program since 1993 had been more than $4 million. From July 1998 to June 1999, the cost was $1,186,783. This cost included company support for Northlands College programs in basic education, technical and trades in northern Saskatchewan. Northlands College is headquartered in La Ronge and had several teaching facilities throughout northern Saskatchewan. It also included company support for scholarships, summer students, educational leave and some donations to students. The plan had been successful in increasing the number of northern residents in all occupations, particularly trades, technical, professional and supervisory positions. Several other companies and government organizations were partners in this program. Some of the programs included in the MPTP are listed below:

Athabasca Education Awards

These cash awards were given to Grades 7 to 12 students of the Athabasca Basin on an annual basis to encourage them to graduate from Grade 12. This program cost Cameco $5,000 annually. The number of Grade 12 graduates from the region continued to increase.

Northern Scholarship Program

This program provided assistance to northern students enrolling in post secondary institutions. Special consideration was given to those students pursuing careers in mining. Cameco awarded $30,000 in scholarships annually. A number of the recipients of these scholarships had become Cameco employees.

Northern Summer Student Program

A select group of northern students were given summer employment at a variety of the company operations. Priority was given to students pursuing careers in the mining industry. Costs were part of each individual department in which they were employed. No premium was paid for northern students versus southern students, other than costs incurred in recruiting, which were minimal. The wage costs for summer students were included in the Multi-party Training Plan costs; for 1998 to 1999, the cost was $521,192.

CAPES (Cameco Access Program for Engineering and Sciences)

The objective of this program was to increase the number of northerners in engineering and science professions. This was to be achieved by increasing awareness of engineering with elementary and secondary students, supporting the needs of those entering this field, and collaborating with the universities to better facilitate northern students. In 2000, there were six students completing their first year engineering studies at Northlands College in La Ronge, five students on campus at the University of Saskatchewan, and eight to 10 applicants expected in September 2000. Also, several northern-based university education students were part of this program. It was intended that they would bring a stronger math and science component to northern elementary and high schools. In 2000, there were 12 students registered in the first year of the program, with six expected to continue into the second year. Cameco had committed to spending $1 million over five years from 1997 to 2002. Other partners in this program were various secondary and post secondary institutions.

Exhibit 4 (Continued)

Rabbit Lake Workplace Education Program

This program was initiated at the Rabbit Lake mine site as a means to upgrade the educational skills of personnel, with special emphasis on those in the apprenticeship program. It had been in existence since 1996 and was administered by Northlands College. In 2000, the total cost was $30,000, shared by Cameco and various Government agencies. The program was successful in that the apprentices had better success in the scholastic areas of their formal training. The program was duplicated at the Key Lake mine site.

4. COMMUNITY RELATIONS

Athabasca Economic Development and Training Corporation

This group was set up to help encourage economic development and training in the Athabasca region. Cameco did not sponsor this organization, other than participating in their meetings. It was sponsored by various government agencies.

Athabasca Working Group

This group was set up to form an agreement — Impact Management Agreement (IMA) — between the communities of the Athabasca region and the mining companies to address concerns regarding environmental protection, employment training and business development, and benefit sharing. The agreement was signed in 1999. The amount spent implementing the agreement and administering the affairs of the group in 1999 was $42,493, this included several northern-based site visits such as school tours, etc.

Environmental Quality Committees (EQC)

To assure northern people that the mines were operating in a safe and compliant manner, government in several regions of northern Saskatchewan formed these committees. The provincial government covered operating costs. Cameco contributed by making expertise available and sponsoring annual site tours by paying for flights and expenses.

Donations

Cameco made donations to several organizations through its Northern Affairs office in La Ronge. The yearly budget was $100,000. These donations were meant to contribute to the quality of life in the communities and support educational and business initiatives.

Community Vitality Monitoring Partnership

This partnership was set up to gather information on environment, health, economic/social infrastructure, communication dynamics and relationships, and special topics (such as youth out migration and poverty). It originated to fulfil an obligation made during the Environmental Impact Statement (EIS) Panel hearings for McArthur River and Cigar Lake. The purpose of the initiative was to investigate the impacts of mining developments on the health and social well-being of northern communities. The group was planning several research initiatives, the first of which was on out migration. "Out migration" was a facet of community vitality and health. When people leave northern communities, this influences the social and economic context of the remaining community members and eroded family ties. This program was a partnership between industry and several provincial government agencies. Cameco spent approximately $20,000 in 2000 on this program.

Exhibit 4 (Continued)

Source: Company files

when Cameco developed subsidiaries internationally. Equipped with an existing model for local development, the subsidiary would more likely be seen as socially responsible. A history of good deeds could mean the difference between a roadblock and a green light for the project.

Within Cameco's budget for northern initiatives, spending on training and public relations was clear and easy to allocate. With business development initiatives, however, decisions were tougher. Executives deliberately set a fairly loose definition of "northern business" in order to deter eager companies from finding loopholes. Some would merely establish local toll free numbers with call forward or would set up northern post boxes and bank accounts, or use relatives' names on ownership documentation. Cameco insisted on northern ownership, management, and employees—then it would decide whether a company was truly northern. While Cameco continually encouraged larger suppliers to become "more northern," it often found better value with small suppliers. Usually more visible and involved in the community, small business owners participated in community affairs and spent their money locally. They offered vital support to Cameco's plans, for expansion and development.

With communities nearby, mine sites could often use locally stocked supplies and thus carry lower inventories and reduce capital costs. Other benefits included lower overhead costs and easier mobilization of contractors. Transporting personnel was also less expensive, as most workers from outside the region had to commute by airplane.

Not only did Cameco shop locally, it included a representative of the community on its board of directors. Chief Harry Cook of the Lac La Ronge Indian Band, one of Canada's most commercially successful bands, had been a member of the board since 1992.

As northerners and Cameco personnel grew more knowledgeable and familiar with the uranium industry, the company became less vulnerable to outside detractors such as Greenpeace, which gained no ground in the region. With community interaction and policies to enhance employment, business, training and education opportunities for local people, Cameco could help entrench local support for uranium mining.

Through the Northern Policy, Cameco expressed and acted on its social and economic responsibilities. These, in turn, informed and permeated the company's strategic objectives, corporate policies, vision and value statements, and individual performance objectives of its senior executives. Other Canadian and international companies, notably Syncrude in the Fort McMurray area and Ekati Diamond in the Northwest Territories, modeled their operations on Cameco's trend-setting initiatives.

Kyrgyzstan: Sociopolitical Background

In 1998, two-thirds of Kyrgyzstan's five million people lived in rural areas. They had been nomadic peoples until Soviet rule forced them into collectives. They had strong family ties, values and loyalties. With so many failed expectations from the Communist era, the people were reluctant to trust outsiders. Cameco tried to build trust by living up to commitments and enhancing the local economy, but it was a slow process.

Kyrgyzstan gained independence from the Soviet Union in 1991. Officially a constitutionally governed republic with a single president, the country had known only one leader, President Askar Akayev. Akayev had maintained political longevity by expanding presidential power. As his enthusiasm for democracy waned, so did parliamentary reform, freedom of the press and political opposition.

The government hoped to stop the exodus of Russian nationals who made up a large part of the skilled and professional workforce. Laws were enacted to make Russian an official language and to promote dual Russian-Kyrgyzstani citizenship. Infuriated Kyrgyzstani nationalists regarded these policies as more Russian colonialism. Still, Kyrgyzstan counted on Russia for most cross-border trade. Relations with China, on the other hand, were improving and trade had increased between the two nations.

Islamic militants inhabited the southern regions around Osh and Jalal-Abad, and their presence in the rest of the country had been rising. But, with the war in Afghanistan and the American lease of a military base near Bishkek in 2001, the threat had diminished. Forty aircraft and between 3,000 and 4,000 military personnel were stationed at the base. Maps of Kyrgyzstan are presented in Exhibit 5.

With literacy rates estimated at 99 per cent, the Kyrgyzstani people clearly valued and sought formal education. Government cutbacks had hampered the education system, and teachers struggled with low wages and inadequate teaching materials. The Soviets had left a relatively good medical system. It was now in serious decline and paid services were on the rise. Birth rates had also declined.

Government employees were poorly paid and bribes were an essential part of Kyrgyzstani people's income. GDP per person increased by five per cent to US$267 in 2000. The inflation rate was seven per cent, a relatively low level for the region. President Akayev had retained tight control of the economy, and reforms had progressed much further than in neighboring countries. Industry privatization had increased, the budget deficit had fallen and private ownership of land was increasing. In spite of this optimism, in 2000 the Economist Intelligence Unit reported on the country's poor investment environment and corrupt regulatory framework. In general, Kumtor management felt that, in spite of much talk about change, the government was simply unwilling to take steps toward it.

Cameco in Kyrgyzstan

In December 1992, Cameco Corporation and State Concern Kyrgyzaltyn (a Kyrgyz state-owned company) formed a joint venture company, the Kumtor Gold Company (KGC) to develop the Kumtor deposit. This entity was owned one-third by Cameco and two-thirds by the Kyrgyzstanis. Cameco had control of the company by naming two of the three members of the Executive Committee for a 10-year period after commercial production. The Kumtor Gold Company appointed the 100 per cent owned Cameco subsidiary, the Kumtor Operating Company (KOC), as project operator. Kumtor poured the first gold bar in December of 1996. By 1998, it was producing 733,155 ounces of gold, making it the eighth-largest gold mine in the world. There were more than 1,500 full-time employees, of whom 90 per cent or more were Kyrgyzstani nationals. In 1999, Kumtor employed 127 expatriates. Expatriate rotational

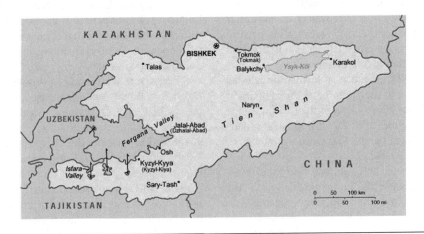

Exhibit 5   Map of Kyrgyzstan

Source: www.cia.gov/cia/publications/factbook/geos/kg, accessed October 2003.

Item	Value
Total Tax Benefits	
Concession Tax	$5,148,000
Road Tax	1,357,000
Royalty Tax	918,000
Tamga Power Line Payment	
Principal	$3,244,185
Interest	1,692,713
Power Usage	3,795,570
Training Costs	726,707
Public Assistance	
Corporate Contributions	$380,143
Scholarships	202,707
Net National Payroll	
To employees	$4,920,196
To Gov't Income Tax	1,055,233
To Gov't as Welfare & Pension Fund	723,404
Purchase of Materials	4,068,984
Total	**$27,649,992**

Exhibit 6   Benefits to the Kyrgyzstani Republic—1999

Source: Company documents

employees worked 28 days in, 28 days out, and were flown home for their time off. Expatriate resident employees worked the Monday to Friday schedule. Expatriate management typically worked two-year contracts with generous holiday time.

Working conditions at the site were harsh. The deposit was located in a remote part of the Tien Shan Mountains at an average altitude of 4,000 metres and an average temperature of -5C. Kumtor's head office was in Bishkek, the capital of Kyrgyzstan, about 250 kilometres to the northwest. See Exhibit 5 for maps and locations.

Kumtor was the largest foreign investment project in the country. In 1999, it represented 10 per cent of the country's GDP and 36 per cent of its exports. A number of other benefits are shown in Exhibit 6. Cameco expected that by 2007 all economically recoverable ore would have been milled.

Initial expectations of the financial returns on the project were high. When feasibility studies were done, the price of gold was over US$400 per ounce but had dropped considerably. As managing partner, responsibility for the project's less-than-expected results was laid on Cameco.

Since its inception, Kumtor had developed a number of corporate responsibility programs. Policies were directed to maximize benefits to the Kyrgyzstani Republic, the people of Kyrgyzstan and the communities nearest to the project. Kumtor intended to replace expatriate workers with national employees as rapidly as feasible. The Expatriate Staffing Plan projected a reduction of expatriates from 204 to 83 in a five-year period ending December 31, 2003.

Kumtor also initiated a training, education and awards program. An off-site training centre was established during the project construction phase to provide pre-employment training mainly to heavy equipment operators, mill operators and maintenance personnel. Kumtor gradually phased out the centre and assigned training responsibilities to the mine site once it was operational. Through a variety of classroom and on-the-job training initiatives, the company further improved the skills and career prospects of its Kyrgyzstani workforce. The training initiative included the creation of shadow positions to help replace expatriates in supervisory and management positions.

National employees occupied a large majority of the technical, professional, supervisory and middle-management positions. Because the mine introduced Western technology and equipment for which national maintenance personnel were not available, 60 per cent of the expatriates were tradespersons, mill operators or trainers. Extensive on-the-job training was carried out for national tradespersons.

Kumtor contributed US$200,000 annually to the Kyrgyzstani government's Workforce of the 21st Century program, which sponsored university students to study abroad. Kumtor had contributed US$1 million and had committed to another US$1 million. Kumtor directly sponsored selected national employees to study at North American universities. Others received short-term technical training in Canada. Residents could apply for one of 16 annual scholarships to help them pursue post-secondary education within the Kyrgyzstani Republic. Kumtor sponsored 142 national employees taking evening and correspondence classes at local technical schools or universities. This program allowed participants an annual average of four weeks off with pay to prepare for exams. Kumtor was involved in three CIDA Educational Development projects aimed at improving technical and university training. Kumtor provided direct and in-kind funding in excess of US$200,000.

The Kumtor workforce was unionized. All national employees, including national supervisors and managers, could join the union, and approximately 65 per cent of the total workforce did so. Those at the mine site, representing the vast majority of employees, worked a rotating schedule of 14 days in and 14 days out and received compensation superior to any local industries, including mining.

Kumtor's policies also focused on community and business development. The company sourced most of its materials and supplies from inside the Kyrgyzstani Republic. Due to Kyrgyzstan's weak economy in 1998, Kumtor gave loans and prepayments to existing suppliers so their factories could start production. Advance payments allowed contractors to acquire equipment to perform the required services. In the communities nearest the project, Kumtor helped create small businesses to produce needed materials and supplies such as wooden pallets, survey stakes, ore sample bags and metallic wheel chocks.

The Spill and Crisis Management

On Wednesday, May 20, 2001, at 12:10 p.m., a convoy of five transport trucks approached a bridge on the Barskaun River. Accompanied by two security vehicles, they were en route to the Kumtor mine site. Each truck carried a six-metre sea container holding 20 tons of sodium cyanide briquettes used to process gold. Eight kilometres above the village of Barskaun (population 7,000) the fourth truck rolled over and fell into the river with its cargo. The damaged container released 1,762 kilograms of sodium cyanide into the

water. The truck driver broke a leg and arm. Within six hours the truck had been removed and the accident site cleaned up. Some of the diluted cyanide entered watering ditches and reached the towns of Barskaun and Tamga.

Humans are very sensitive to cyanide. Exposure to high doses of cyanide has immediate, obvious and lethal effects. A fatal dose is one to three milligrams per kilogram of body weight. In non-lethal doses, sodium cyanide is quickly removed from the body through self-detoxification with no delayed, cumulative or long-lasting ill effects. Sodium cyanide occurs naturally in most stone fruits (cherries and apples, for example) and some vegetables such as cabbage and turnip. It is also found in tobacco and vitamin B12. Fish are 1,000 times more sensitive to cyanide than humans. The fish populations of Barskaun Bay on Lake Issyk-Kul were noted to be healthy shortly after the spill.

Initially the Kyrgyzstani government reported two deaths and 2,535 illnesses. One of the two fatalities was later attributed to cancer while, in the second case, the victim had a history of heart and lung ailments. Kumtor representatives were not allowed to take flesh samples for independent analysis. At no time did the levels of cyanide reach fatal levels in the communities. It was possible that a few people had ingested small amounts of sodium cyanide, but any exposure would have occurred only for a few hours immediately after the spill.

As a goodwill gesture, Kumtor agreed to pay the families of the claimed fatalities enough to cover funeral expenses and other costs, and to construct a modern water supply system for the villages of Barskaun and Tamga. In the interim, drinking water was to be trucked into the villages. To mitigate community concerns, Kumtor also committed to pay 1,000 soms[1] for every villager over the age of 10, and 500 soms for each child. These payments, along with a number of other compensation programs, were expected to total more than US$500,000. One of the most significant measures taken was to establish a health clinic in Barskaun to deal with "perceived" cyanide related illnesses.

In the last week of May, Richard Mann, Canada's ambassador to Kazakhstan, in co-operation with the Kyrgyzstani deputy prime minister, helped assemble a commission of Russian and Canadian experts to study the impact of the spill. The commission members were:

- Thomas Hynes, Environmental Specialist, Natural Resources Canada, Ottawa, Canada
- John Harrison, Health Advisor, Health Canada, Ottawa, Canada
- Evgene Bonitenko, Medical Toxicologist, EMERCOM, Russia
- Tamara Doronina, Chemist, Moscow Chemical Institute of Chemical Materials, Russia
- Harry Baikowitz, Chemist, Bodycote Technitrol, Pointe-Claire, Canada
- Michael James, Medical Consultant, Medisys, Toronto, Canada

The commission's report was concluded and made public on June 9, 2001. It stated:

- No one died as a result of the spill.
- There was no possibility of harmful exposure to cyanide in the air.
- Potential exposure to cyanide in the Barskaun River was limited to 16 people, and there was no medical evidence to support claims of harm to humans.
- A number of dead fish were found in a small bay leading into Lake Issyk-Kul, but fish populations rebounded in a matter of days. There was no short- or long-term damage to Lake Issyk-Kul.
- Damage to local crops was due to lack of water, not cyanide exposure.

- The temporary evacuation of 5,300 people from the region had been unnecessary and had intensified the panic in the community.

These findings were confirmed by another report conducted by the World Health Organization (WHO).

LOOKING FORWARD

Ray Duret knew that Cameco would continue to look for more opportunities in Kyrgyzstan, central Asia and the rest of the world. Further, in northern Saskatchewan, Cameco had successfully gained a competitive advantage by developing relationships with local communities, and it wanted to experience the same in Kyrgyzstan. Duret needed to develop a short-term plan to manage the issues surrounding the spill and the subsequent deterioration of relationships. He also needed to think more broadly about the company's long-term strategy in applying its social responsibility policy to Kyrgyzstan. He pondered his options, reflected upon Cameco's history and wondered where to start.

NOTE

1. Basic unit of Kyrgyzstani currency.

WIL-MOR TECHNOLOGIES: IS THERE A CRISIS?

Prepared by Andrew C. Inkpen

Version: (A) 2000-01-11

In February 1997, David McNeil, CEO of Wilson Industries Inc. (Wilson) met with Ron Berks, the president of Wilson's North American Automotive Division. "Ron, the situation with the Wil-Mor joint venture (JV) does not seem to be improving," said McNeil. "After three years it is still losing money. What's going on down there?" Berks, a JV board member and the Wilson executive who initiated the JV formation, realized there was a problem but was not sure what to do. Not only were the JV managers not concerned, but they were talking about expansion. Wilson's Japanese JV partner did not even want to discuss profitability; all they seemed to care about was lowering costs and keeping the JV's largest customer happy. McNeil emphasized that something had to be done, adding, "When we formed this venture you predicted it would reach break-even by the second year of operation. We are not even close to that after three years."

WILSON INDUSTRIES INC.

Wilson, a Detroit-based company founded in 1923, was a manufacturer of plastic and metal parts for the automotive and appliance industries. Total sales in 1996 were $480 million of which $290 million came from the North American Automotive Division. The Automotive Division produced components for engines, transmissions, and power steering systems. Ford and Chrysler accounted for 80 per cent of Wilson's sales with the remainder going to General Motors. For several years, the Automotive Division's sales had remained flat and profits had been decreasing.

In recent years, Wilson had taken steps to internationalize its automotive operations. In 1986, exports began to Germany and a small plant was purchased in England. Besides Wil-Mor, a JV was launched in 1990 to distribute Wilson products in Australia.

THE AUTOMOBILE INDUSTRY

The North American automobile industry changed dramatically in the last two decades of the 20th century. The primary impetus for much of the change was the emergence of the Japanese automakers as leading competitors and domestic producers. In 1981, there were no Japanese assembly plants in North America. In 1990, there were nine Japanese-operated assembly plants in the United States and three in Canada. These plants produced 1.8 million cars in 1990, more than 20 per cent of total North American production. By 1997, output from the Japanese assembly plants, referred to as transplants[1], was getting close to three million cars per year. Including imports, the three largest Japanese firms, Honda, Nissan, and Toyota, collectively had a 27 per cent share of the U.S. passenger car market. In contrast, the Big Three (Chrysler, Ford, and General Motors) had seen a steady decrease in share. From 1993 to 1997, the Big Three share had dropped from 66 per cent to about 61 per cent.

Although Nissan was experiencing financial difficulties and was rumored to be a takeover candidate, Honda and Toyota continued to increase capacity and establish new industry standards for design and production efficiency. Both firms were becoming full-fledged North American producers capable of designing, engineering, and assembling vehicles entirely in North America. In 1998 Toyota planned to introduce a U.S.-designed full-size pickup truck produced in a new plant in Indiana. This truck would attack the Big Three in their primary profit sanctuary of light trucks. In late 1997 Honda expected to introduce the newest iteration of the best-selling Accord model. The new Accord was planned to arrive exactly four years after the previous new model, a consistent development cycle that none of the Big Three had yet managed to imitate.

All of the Japanese producers in North America were committed to increasing local content and reducing reliance on imported parts. By the mid-1990s, with the Japanese yen appreciating more than 50 per cent since 1990, the Japanese producers were ramping up their efforts to increase their number of U.S. suppliers.

Automotive Suppliers

The typical car is made up of more than 10,000 parts. In the initial years of the automobile industry, carmakers tried to produce as many parts in-house as possible. By the 1950s, outsourcing of parts from independent suppliers had become commonplace. Suppliers were given blueprints and asked to bid on parts contracts. The lowest bidder generally was awarded the contract, usually for one year. In the 1990s, the world's automobile companies were all using outsourcing as an increasingly important element of production.

The shifting importance of outsourcing developed in the 1980s as the Big Three increased their outsourcing and made substantial cuts in the number of suppliers they dealt with. The customer-supplier relationship shifted to a structure based on tiers of suppliers. The first tier suppliers dealt directly with the vehicle manufacturers and, increasingly, participated jointly in the design of new systems and parts. The first tier suppliers coordinated the operations of many smaller second tier suppliers who, in turn, worked with their own sub-suppliers. The advantage of this multi-layer approach, used by the Japanese producers for many years, was that the automakers could deal with a limited number of companies and work closely with them in design and engineering.

Besides the move toward outsourcing and multi-tiered supplier arrangements, several other trends characterized the supplier industry. One, automakers were pushing their suppliers toward just-in-time delivery systems and increased investment in design and engineering capabilities. Two, mergers were becoming prevalent in the supplier sector, largely because of the heavy demands for research and development, new equipment, and employee training. This trend was reflected in the increasing international consolidation of automotive suppliers. Large suppliers, such as Johnson Controls, Lear, Magna, and Bosch, were increasingly focused on automotive systems, rather than just parts. With systems, such as seats or car interiors, suppliers took on more responsibility for design and engineering and worked closely with the automakers throughout the design and development product life cycle stages. Three, suppliers were moving away from their traditional focus on home markets toward foreign investment. For example, close to 300 Japan-based supplier firms had operations in North America, most of which had arrived in the late 1980s and early 1990s.

The arrival of the transplant automakers was the major reason Japanese suppliers were locating in North America. However, many of the Japanese suppliers were making inroads into the domestic automakers as well. The implications were clear: like the situation with automaking capacity, excess capacity at the supplier level was becoming a reality. The overcapacity and competition from foreign-based component suppliers were creating increasingly difficult conditions for North American automotive suppliers, and particularly smaller suppliers, like Wilson. The industry view was that over the next few years, many of the remaining smaller suppliers would either be acquired by the large multinational firms or would be forced to exit the automotive industry.

The Japanese Transplants

With their traditional North American market eroding, many suppliers, including Wilson, saw a potentially lucrative market in supplying the transplants. The transplants were committed to North American content and were rapidly building up their manufacturing capacity. Unfortunately, becoming a supplier to a transplant firm had proved to be very difficult for many North American-based firms. North American companies were often unfamiliar with the rigors of Japanese just-in-time inventory systems and demands for flexible production. A further problem frustrating the efforts of North American suppliers was that, unlike their North American competitors, the Japanese automakers rarely changed suppliers. For example, Toyota's supplier base in Japan had remained virtually unchanged since the 1950s. Many of the Japanese suppliers were partially owned by the automakers and, as part of a keiretsu, had a relationship that was much stronger than a North American supplier relationship. The president of Nissan's U.S. operations explained:

> Nissan's mix of U.S. suppliers and Japanese suppliers is not likely to change much. Given our philosophy, once you become our supplier you're our supplier forever on that part, unless you mess up so bad we can't fix you.[2]

The Japanese firms put much more emphasis on trust and cooperation in the supplier relationship. As one supplier executive commented:

> The North American supplier relationship is often adversarial. The supplier usually works with the blueprint provided by the automaker. You manufacture according to the blueprint and if the part doesn't fit, "you tell your customer to stuff it." With Honda our relationship is supportive as long as we deliver the product. And, the blueprint is only the starting point. The part must fit the car; if it doesn't, Honda will say, "What can we do together to make it fit?" If you ship 150 bad parts to General Motors, they will tell you that you have a problem and you better fix it fast. Honda may say you have a problem, but they will also say, "How can we help you fix it?" The Japanese customer will not use its power to threaten or harass the supplier. Once the marriage is formed, they will try to make it work.

In North America, the threat that supplier contracts could be cancelled or moved in-house had created a system in which, according to some observers, neither party fully trusted the other. By contrast, the Japanese approach was based on long-term relationships, mutual discussion and bargaining. While suppliers were expected to decrease prices over the term of the contract, joint activities between supplier and automaker were critical to the relationship. According to one study, "The (Japanese) system replaces a vicious circle of mistrust with a virtuous circle of cooperation."[3]

Of course, the Japanese automakers could, and did, fire their suppliers. When it became obvious that a supplier could no longer meet the exacting quality standards or improve on cost and quality, the Japanese customer was as likely to look for a new supplier as an American customer. The difference was that the Japanese automaker would expend more effort in assisting the supplier than was typical in the North American context. In addition, the Japanese companies usually kept their suppliers better informed about their performance relative to other suppliers.

THE JV FORMATION

In the early 1990s, Ron Berks was convinced that the transplant share of the North American market would continue to grow. He began to explore the possibility of becoming a supplier to the transplant firms. He made several trips to Japan and initiated discussions with Honda America in Ohio. However, after several years of fruitless efforts, he became convinced that without an established reputation, access to the Japanese transplants was very difficult. One way to speed up this access was to establish a relationship with a Japanese firm.

In the meantime, the Japanese presence in the automobile industry continued to grow. The transplant automakers encouraged their Japanese suppliers to build plants in North America in order to maintain established customer relationships and also, because of political pressure, increased domestic content was a priority. Trepidation about starting a new facility in North America and pressure from the Japanese automakers to involve local firms in the supply chain encouraged many Japanese suppliers to form JVs with American partners. As well, a large number of Japanese suppliers entered the North American market on their own.

Nevertheless, through the early 1990s, the Japanese automakers continued to source components from Japan. But, with the continuing rise in the value of the yen, there was a new effort to localize the supplier base. The strengthening of the yen made it more economical to produce in the United States and local production supported the Japanese automakers' commitment to lean production and just-in-time delivery. All of the Japanese producers were carefully reviewing their purchasing programs to determine what component production could be shifted out of Japan. For example, Toyota's Georgetown, Kentucky facility increased its purchases of U.S.-made parts from $700 million in 1990 to more than $2 billion in 1995.

In late 1991, Berks first considered the feasibility of forming a JV. An obvious choice for a JV partner was Morota Manufacturing Company Ltd. (Morota). For several years, Wilson had been involved in a licensing agreement with Morota. Morota, founded in 1950, was a manufacturer of small electric motors for products such as sewing machines and small appliances and also produced various components for engines and transmissions for the automobile industry. Morota had sales of $480 million in 1996 with $276 million to the automobile industry. About 70 per cent of the automobile sales were to Toyota with the remainder going to Nissan, Honda, and Mitsubishi. Although Toyota did not own equity in Morota, the two firms had a very close relationship that had begun in the 1950s. Except for a JV in Korea, Morota had limited international experience.

Berks knew that Morota wanted a plant in North America because Toyota could no longer justify importing Morota components from Japan. In early 1992, he contacted the president of Morota and set up a meeting in Japan for July. Berks learned at the meeting that Morota was being encouraged by Toyota to form a JV in North America. He also learned that Morota was "internationally naive and probably scared to death to come to the U.S. They were particularly worried about dealing with an American workforce." At the meeting, the two firms agreed to work toward forming a JV.

The JV Agreement

JV discussions between Wilson and Morota started in late 1992 and six months later a JV agreement was signed. The JV was named Wil-Mor Technologies, Inc. (Wil-Mor). Initially, Berks had hoped that Wilson would have about 70 per cent ownership. However, although the Morota executives would not say so explicitly, Berks sensed that there would be problems with Toyota if Wilson had a majority position. Berks, therefore, agreed to 50/50 ownership. The JV agreement specified that Wilson would be responsible for locating a plant site and managing the workforce. Morota would be responsible for the equipment acquisitions and installation. Morota would provide initial engineering support and help train the workforce, both in Japan and the U.S. Morota would also work with Toyota to ensure that the JV had contracts when the JV became operational.

The JV president would be nominated by Morota and the general manager would be nominated by Wilson. These two managers would be responsible for the JV startup. The JV board would include three executives from each firm. From Wilson, there would be Berks, an Automotive Division vice president, and the JV general manager. Morota's representatives would include Morota's president, its executive vice president, and the JV president.

Berks was very enthusiastic about the JV's potential. After the JV announcement in early 1993, his opinion was that the joint venture was a very important strategic move for Wilson. The JV was seen as an extension of Wilson's existing operation that would help increase market share and provide access to a growing segment of the market. The JV would also help Wilson learn from its Japanese partner. There was even some thought that in a few years, the JV would be able to export parts back to Japan.

Startup

Berks thought that an experienced American manager should be general manager. He selected 58-year-old Dan Johnson, a Wilson employee for 30 years and most recently a plant manager. The president, Akio Sakiya, was 55 years old and had spent his entire career with Morota. Although an engineer by training, he was vice president finance prior to becoming the JV president.

Johnson was given the task of selecting the plant site. He chose Elizabethtown, Kentucky, a small town south of Louisville and close to the Toyota plant in Georgetown. The initial investment in the JV was $20.2 million. Each partner contributed $4 million; the other $12.2 million was borrowed by the JV and guaranteed by the partners.

The JV plant was based on the manufacturing system used by Morota. Most of the equipment in the plant was Japanese. Morota put together a Japanese team of engineers and technical specialists. This team was responsible for installing the equipment, getting the process started, and training the workforce. The workforce was hired by Johnson and Sakiya. Their emphasis was on young people with little or no manufacturing experience (from Morota's perspective, "no bad habits."). Both partners wanted to keep the JV union-free.

The JV began operations in early 1994 with contracts from Toyota. All contracts were for engine component parts, identical to parts made in Japan by Morota and functionally similar to parts made by Wilson for its Big 3 customers. The initial startup was done very slowly and for some months there was only enough work for about two-three days a week. The startup, slower than Wilson would have liked, was based on Morota's attitude of "training before operating."

JV Management

Besides the president and general manager, JV management came from both partners. Wilson provided the operations manager, human resource manager, controller, and a marketing manager. None of these managers had any Japanese language capability or experience with the transplants. Morota provided the engineering manager, the quality manager, and a marketing manager (see Exhibit 1 for an organization chart). None of these managers had any prior international experience and, except for the marketing manager, had only limited English language skills. The Japanese managers, including the president, had three- to five-year visas. At the end of the visa terms these managers would be rotated back to the Japanese parent. The American managers were in the JV for an indefinite period. The partners hoped that eventually the Japanese managers could be replaced by American managers promoted from within the JV.

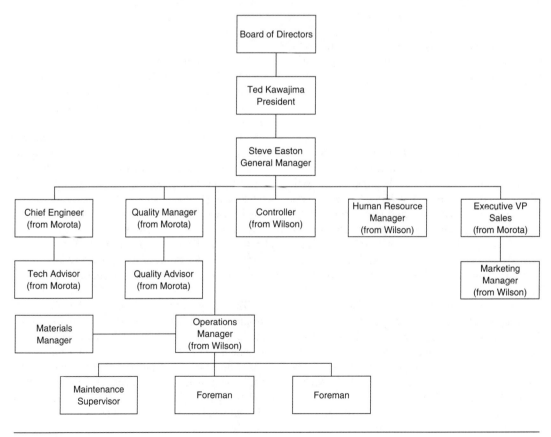

Exhibit 1   Organizational Chart

The JV did not begin smoothly. The Japanese managers insisted on complete technical responsibility. Johnson, the general manager, was not allowed to assist in the technical setup. This caused several problems because the Japanese were unfamiliar with many of the basic aspects of establishing a new plant, especially one in North America. The Japanese insisted on running the operation their way. They used a Japanese approach in selecting suppliers. Johnson estimated he could have saved the JV about $300,000 a year if a North American approach had been used to select suppliers. However, the Japanese insisted that, if possible, suppliers should be selected not just on the basis of price but because they had established themselves as capable suppliers to Wilson or Morota.

When the JV started, the Japanese managers were initially skeptical about the ability of an American workforce to produce a quality product. They wondered: Can they run the machines properly? Do they know what a good product is? The Japanese managers drove the workers very hard at the outset. Several times Sakiya became furious with what he saw on the shop floor and berated the workers in Japanese.

Johnson became convinced that the Japanese managers were deliberately excluding him from the management process. The Japanese managers would regularly hold meetings and exclude the Americans. When meetings were held with both Americans and Japanese present, they would last for hours because of the necessity to translate from English to Japanese. In addition, the Japanese managers corresponded daily by fax with their head office in Japan and would meet socially in the evenings and on weekends. The inevitable result was two distinct management "camps": the Americans and the Japanese.

By March 1995, it was obvious to Ron Berks that there were serious management problems in the JV. Although the contracts with Toyota seemed to be working out well, the plant was still running at far less than capacity. Very few decisions in the JV were "joint" because the Americans and Japanese rarely talked to each other. The American managers were looking after areas such as materials sourcing, human resources, accounting and finance. The Japanese managers concentrated on product design, quality, pricing and sales.

Berks discussed the situation with Morota's president. They decided to replace the JV president and the general manager. The new general manager, Steve Easton, was 46 and a former Wilson plant manager who had recently been working at Wilson headquarters in an international development position. The new president was 51-year-old Ted Kawajima, an engineer with several years of international experience and an excellent command of English.

The New Management Team

The new management team got off to a much better start than the previous one. Both Easton and Kawajima were avid golfers. They began playing golf together regularly and involved several of the other managers. Gradually, the tension between the American and Japanese "camps" began to ease. Although the regular faxing between the JV and Japan continued, meetings of Japanese managers became less frequent.

The JV was also successful in winning new contracts with Toyota and was quoting on some work for Mazda and Ford. By early 1996, Wil-Mor had successfully bid on several General Motors contracts. The JV customer mix was now about 80 per cent Toyota and 20 per cent General Motors. The JV was actively seeking new customers and was encouraged by Toyota to do so.

Annual sales in the JV were now close to $30 million. Employment had reached 300 and the plant was close to capacity. Although the JV was still losing money, Easton and Kawajima were considering a possible expansion.

Head Office Concerns

Ron Berks was pleased by the improved managerial situation in the JV but was troubled by a financial situation that did not seem to be improving. He knew at the outset that it would take a few years for the JV to become profitable. However, based on Morota's estimates, he thought that the JV could at least be at breakeven by the end of 1995 and making a profit by 1996. In early 1997 the JV was still losing about $100,000 a month.

Even more troubling was the fact that at the most recent JV board meeting in November 1996, the Morota executives did not seem concerned that the JV was losing money. In fact, they seemed pleased that the losses were not greater. At the board meeting, when Berks questioned the JV's performance, Kawajima replied that the JV was meeting expectations and was exceeding Toyota's quality standards. He went on to say that the JV still had to get its costs down and had some way to go before quality was at a level consistent with that in Morota's Japan plants. When Berks angrily asked how many years it would be before there was a profit, Kawajima replied that:

Profit is obviously important but to achieve profitability there has to be a satisfied base of customers. We have achieved a good record with Toyota and now we are trying to build a relationship with General Motors. I think that we are in a very strong position.

Berks left the board meeting without a clear understanding of the Japanese expectations about profits in the JV. They seemed concerned only about the quality of the product and not about making money.

Easton's Perspective

Steve Easton knew that Berks, his boss, was concerned about the JV performance. He explained:

There is an unresolvable conflict in the relationship between the partners. Morota is willing to lose money in the JV for as long as it takes to build up market share and quality in North America. Right now, their primary focus is on customer service and product improvement, not profit. They intend to be in this market for the long term and they know that Toyota plans to increase its North American capacity. Morota is determined to make money in North America but is willing to be patient. They believe that if there is a quality product and low costs, profit will take care of itself. They cannot answer the question about when the JV will be profitable because it is not consistent with their philosophy. Their approach is that prices are not the issue; costs must be improved first.

When the JV was formed, the partners thought that they were in sync about prices and profit margins that might be expected. Clearly, that was an incorrect assumption. Wilson wanted to make a quick buck; they were skeptical of making long-term investments. They saw the JV as a way to make some money. They expected a profit in two or three years. Morota expected the JV to lose money for about five or six years. However, they never communicated this to Wilson and the business plan was very unclear on partner expectations. Wilson prepared the pro-formas and based on my conversations with Ron Berks, no one at Morota raised any serious objections when we were negotiating the final agreement.

This perspective was echoed by an industry analyst's comments:

The Japanese invest in a country first and anticipate the payoff later. They have staying power.

Easton suspected that part of the problem was that Berks did not do his homework when the JV was formed. He commented:

The JV was started on blind faith. Each partner had some expectations about the other which have not been met. Wilson expected faster production and higher efficiency. The only thing certain at the outset was that Toyota would be a customer. Berks expected that a share of Toyota's business would be great to have and that it would be profitable. Unfortunately, nobody in Wilson had any idea of the potential profitability of supplying the transplants.

The reality is that we are unable to get the same kind of profit margins with Toyota as we can with the Big 3. We make more money on the parts we sell to GM than on the parts we sell to Toyota. A lot of suppliers are starting to say that transplant business is not good business because the prices are too low.

Easton also sensed that there was some resentment in Wilson toward the JV and an unwillingness to acknowledge openly that the JV provided an excellent learning opportunity:

> I have given other Wilson managers an open invitation to visit the JV and see what we are doing. There has been some response to my invitations but there seems to be some resentment toward us. When I attend corporate meetings at Wilson, I show people what we are doing and it is clear that the JV is outperforming the other Wilson plants on a quality basis. In terms of reject rates, we beat Wilson by 10 times. Wilson talks about quality but we do it. I don't like to brag about our success in the JV but what I would like to see is an interest by the other Wilson managers in finding out why the JV is able to do so well.
>
> The JV and the relationship with Toyota has put Wilson in a position to start questioning their capabilities. Berks would like to have Toyota as a customer so he invited Toyota purchasing managers to visit the Wilson plants. Toyota reported back to Wilson and the report was scathing. Berks's attitude was "these guys are just unreasonable."
>
> Berks has acknowledged that some changes at Wilson may be necessary but he has avoided the serious questions. The reality is that Wilson would have to cross a lot of hurdles to get any Toyota business. However, the senior management at Wilson don't know that and would be surprised to find out. They have not addressed it and it is not a priority because of their existing business. My own belief is that Wilson has not grasped what world class manufacturing is.

On the relationship between the partners, Easton commented:

> Kawajima and the Morota executives realize that Berks is not pleased with the JV performance. However, they view their relationship with Wilson from a long-term perspective. They intend to succeed in North America and assume that Wilson thinks the same way. Should Wilson express some desire to end the JV, Kawajima and the other Morota executives would be shocked and take it as a serious affront. From their perspective, strengthening the relationship between the partners is critical to the success of the JV.

THE CURRENT SITUATION

The meeting with David McNeil left Berks in a difficult position. Berks was aware that at Wilson headquarters, there was growing opposition to the JV because it was not making money. Some managers were even starting to question Morota's capabilities, arguing that if they can't make money when they have a new plant and a guaranteed customer, how can we ever hope to learn anything from them?

McNeil wanted to see a JV return on investment at least as high as the other Wilson plants but Berks did not know when that would happen. At a meeting with Easton the previous week, Easton had assured him that Wil-Mor had the potential to be a leading supplier to both the transplants and the Big 3. Easton had also said that an expansion would soon be necessary. Berks knew that McNeil would never approve further capital investment until the JV started showing a profit. However, Easton argued that without expanding, the JV would lose market share and would probably take even longer to become profitable.

Ron Berks wondered what should be done about the JV. Maybe Wilson should cut its losses and get out of the JV. Or, perhaps it would be better if Wilson lowered its ownership interest to about 20 per cent. That would reduce Wilson's share of the losses and would allow Wilson to maintain its relationship with Morota. Whatever the decision, Berks knew that McNeil was expecting something to be done very soon.

NOTES

1. Transplant was the generic term used for foreign direct investment in the automotive industry. Besides the Japanese firms, BMW (in South Carolina) and Mercedez-Benz (in Alabama) also had transplant operations.

2. *Ward's Auto World*, February 1991, P. 29.

3. James P. Womack, Daniel T. Jones, & Daniel Roos. *The Machine that Changed the World*. (New York: Rawson Associates, 1990), 150.

THE WUHAN ERIE POLYMERS JOINT VENTURE

Prepared by Professors Thomas Begley, Cynthia Lee and Kenneth Law

Copyright © 2003, Northeastern University, College of Business Administration   Version: (A) 2003-03-17

Hanging up the phone, Stanley Wong felt both pleased and chagrined. His request for a transfer back to the Gary, Indiana, U.S. (Erie) headquarters of the Performance Polymers Division of Erie Specialty Chemicals had been approved. Three years earlier, Wong, a Hong Kong native, had been appointed general manager of the Wuhan Erie Polymers (WEP) joint-venture plant in Wuhan, Hubei Province, China. One year ago, he was given added responsibilities as division manager of the China Region for Performance Polymers. A return to Gary was best for his family, who had stayed in the United States when he went overseas; yet, after devoting his energy to Erie's success in rapidly expanding its specialty chemicals businesses in China, Wong felt the job was not finished.

Since his transfer date was still a few months away, Wong would have time to prepare his units for the change. His main task would be to nominate a successor. James Golding, president of Erie's Region China, had instructed Wong to work directly with corporate human resources in Gary to identify the best person. Although the vice-president of human resources would have the final say, Wong's recommendation would carry much weight. Talented leadership was required in any organization; however, the prominence, deference and respect Chinese employees accorded their leaders made the right selection paramount to the joint venture's continued development. The human resources department sent six résumés for consideration. As he mentally evaluated potential replacements, Wong wondered which one would soon be occupying the chair in which he presently sat.

ERIE SPECIALTY CHEMICALS, INC.

Erie Specialty Chemicals, based in Cleveland, Ohio, developed and produced specialty chemicals. The company's five divisions, Performance Polymers, Consumer Care, Additives, Textile Dyes and Pigments, had sales in 79 countries, manufacturing plants in 18, research and development facilities in six and total 2001 revenues of US$4.2 billion. The Performance Polymers Division's US$1.4 billion in revenues comprised 33 per cent of the company total.

Starting in the 1980s, Erie had moved aggressively into China, which provided a potentially vast new market for specialty chemicals to support its rapidly expanding industrial capacity. By 2001, the company's 12 wholly owned or joint venture plants in the Asia Pacific region generated 15 per cent of total sales. Executives expected China to play a key role in the company's goal to generate 25 per cent of its sales in Asia within the next 10 years. To date, Erie had invested US$250 million in four joint ventures employing 1,250 people in the country. (The organization chart for Erie's Region China, which included Hong Kong and Taiwan, is shown in Exhibit 1.)

The specialty chemicals business had become very competitive as new entrants emerged from developing countries. Lower production costs enabled these entrants to set aggressive prices, forcing Erie and other established companies into margin-squeezing price cuts. In response, Erie had implemented ambitious cost-cutting programs. At the same time, to differentiate itself the company invested heavily in research and development (R&D) for product innovation, emphasized quality and located production close to customers to increase responsiveness and reduce delivery time. Executives sought to position Erie as a local company focused on developing China's internal markets, not an expatriate-run foreign multinational. Although expatriates currently occupied several key positions, cultivating a strong management team of native Chinese was a high priority.

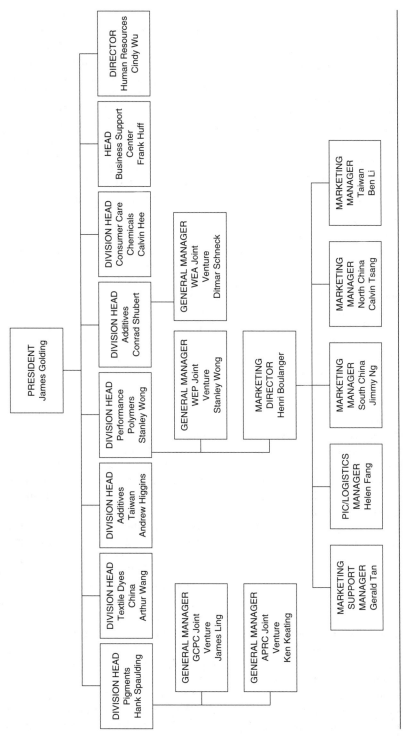

Exhibit 1   Erie Specialty Chemicals Region China Organization Chart

Source: Company files

THE WUHAN ERIE POLYMERS CO., LTD. JOINT VENTURE

To expand its production in China, Performance Polymers had joined with Wuhan Plastics Factory to form Wuhan Erie Polymers (WEP). A leading Chinese state-owned enterprise and the biggest hard-plastics producer in the Wuhan region, Wuhan Plastics employed approximately 1,800 people. Compared to other state-owned enterprises, it produced high-quality products, including about 50 per cent for export, and had recently obtained ISO 9002 certification (Exhibit 2 shows WEP's organization chart).

Through the joint venture, Erie Polymers hoped to exploit the fast-growing market for high-quality resins and hardeners in the Asia Pacific region and to establish the first multinational polymer plant in China. Wuhan Plastics' objectives were, in order of importance, to access modern manufacturing knowledge, to learn Western management skills and to earn foreign exchange. WEP sold most of its resin production to western companies in China and exported the rest worldwide. Although the initial agreement set Erie Polymers' ownership at 55 per cent, its resource investments prompted a revised ratio of 80 per cent Erie and 20 per cent Plastics.

The Wuhan plant provided no cost advantage, nor had the company expected one. Higher labor costs in the United States were offset by higher labor productivity. Compared with a sister plant in Gary, the Wuhan plant employed equally modern equipment and technology while using more advanced computer systems.

STANLEY WONG

Stanley Wong, division manager, China Region and general manager, WEP Joint Venture, had managed the team that negotiated the joint venture's (JV's) original agreement. He then moved to China in 1998, became WEP's general manager, and served as vice chairperson of the JV, which was chaired by an executive from the Chinese partner. Wong graduated from the University of Hong Kong with a bachelor of science degree (Hon) in chemistry and physics in 1973. He began as a sales associate, then was employed as a manager in the Polymers Division's Hong Kong office from 1976 until 1983. Later he attended management training in Cleveland, Ohio, and Birmingham, England, before returning to Hong Kong as division general manager from 1987 through 1992. In 1993, he immigrated to the United States with his family, where he was employed as a manager in the International Marketing Department in Gary, Indiana, until his posting to China.

PERFORMANCE POLYMERS DIVISION

The Performance Polymers Division sold epoxy resins, hardeners, specialty auxiliaries and formulated systems that were manufactured in the United States, Germany, Great Britain, Japan and the Netherlands. The division developed high value-added products through the application of advanced chemical know-how. Polymer products were used in numerous industries, including coatings, structural composites, electronics, electrical engineering, transportation, aerospace, adhesives and tooling. Contrasted with bulk chemicals, the division manufactured relatively small batches, often tailored to a customer's needs, and charged a premium. All sites adhered to international quality control standards and were ISO 9001 certified.

Similar to other division plants, WEP sought consistently high quality, price-competitive products delivered rapidly and reliably. The plant operated according to world-class manufacturing standards and was expected to contribute to the company's cost leadership position through process improvements that lowered costs and improved quality. Since the same equipment could be used to manufacture several products, rapid change-over was important. Typically, chemical engineers at the plant developed product specifications, and quality control chemists applied the formulations and monitored quality. Line workers' informal skills at adjusting

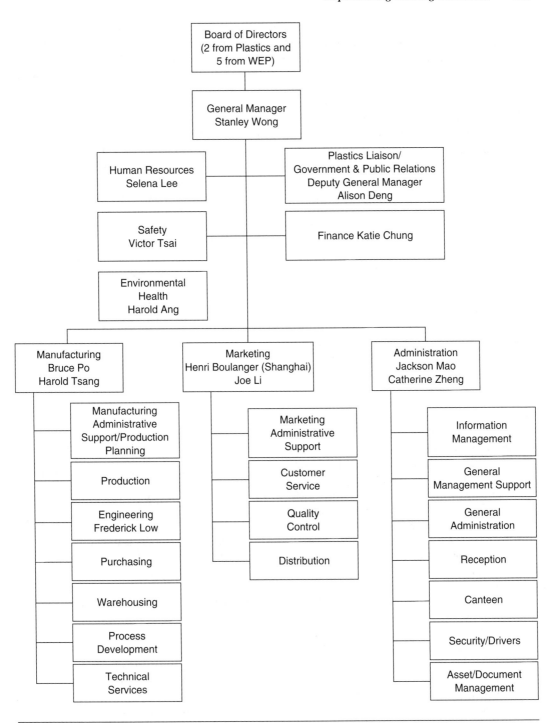

Exhibit 2   Wuhan Erie Polymers Organization Chart

Source: Company files

computer settings and production equipment to raw material mix contributed to productivity and quality. WEP sourced much of its raw material from China.

In the production process, raw materials were made soluble then mixed in 40-cubic-meter vats to react chemically. Polymers were formed, filtered by huge presses, washed and transported to band dryers. The dry crude product was then blended to give constant quality, ground by big milling machines into a very fine powder, packed and stored for shipment. Blending, weighing, temperature control, moisture content, time and pH control were all monitored by computer. State-of-the-art labs facilitated process development, customer technical service and quality control.

WONG'S RESPONSIBILITIES

Wong's activities at the plant evolved through two phases. During the first phase, he monitored plant construction, obtained environmental and import permits, sought taxation relief, tackled such financial concerns as foreign exchange procedures and payments for suppliers, selected and trained key staff, and co-ordinated activities between Chinese and American engineers. In the post-startup phase, Wong concentrated on developing his management team through training, team building and personal communication. His primary objective was to build a strong organizational culture that integrated Chinese and American values in the pursuit of excellence. He also oversaw plant operations and responded to safety issues.

In both phases, Wong interacted weekly with the JV partner and government officials. Through a close relationship with the Wuhan Plastics director and infrastructure manager, he sought to solidify their commitment to provide utilities for the plant. Frequently, Wong and Wuhan Plastics executives jointly contacted government departments. In one instance, he invited the management of Wuhan Plastics to participate in an off-site team-building event. Wong's most frequent interactions were with the Wuhan municipality Vice Mayors for Foreign Trade and Economic Relations, managers from the Environmental Protection Agency, state bank managers, customs officers and Planning Bureau directors.

Wong attended at least one social function a week, including dinners with partners and government officials, and opening ceremonies for Erie's joint ventures, as well as those of other multinationals. He also attended both monthly meetings with managers of other foreign JVs to exchange information and business promotion functions in which the government used WEP's success in China employing advanced technology to woo additional foreign investment. Wong even hosted dinners and outings where he entertained top Chinese leaders and visiting Erie executives.

After Wong's appointment as division general manager, his responsibilities expanded to include:

- motivating the marketing and sales staff, setting sales targets, visiting customers with salespeople and ensuring responsive customer services;
- establishing divisional production objectives with James Golding, Region China president, then apportioning responsibility to the plants in China and Taiwan to meet these objectives;
- monitoring such financial indicators as profitability, cash flow and asset management; and
- overseeing employment planning for the division, encouraging management development and resolving personnel problems.

In addition, his ambassadorial duties greatly increased, as did his responsibilities for government relations and negotiations for new JVs. Mindful of the Chinese practice of "renqin," meaning the exchange of favors between people or "rubbing each other's back," he tried to respond to requests for assistance.

Initially after becoming division manager, Wong continued to devote about 60 per cent of his time to WEP. Once satisfied that his managerial team was performing well, he apportioned more of his time to divisional tasks, especially assisting the marketing and sales staffs sell polymer products.

Aside from one to two weeks per month spent at the plant, Wong traveled extensively. He visited customers all over China, held divisional meetings in Shanghai, Guangzhou, Beijing and Hong Kong, attended corporate management meetings in Hong Kong and Taiwan and returned to Gary three times a year to meet headquarters executives and vacation with his family. In addition, he traveled frequently to Xiangtan, Hunan Province to shepherd negotiations for another joint venture.

CREATING A DISTINCTIVE CULTURE FOR THE WEP PLANT

As an ethnic Chinese who understood the gap between Chinese and Western business practices, Wong showed sensitivity to Chinese culture while also pursuing the business goals of his Western multinational employer. Wong believed, "The essence of traditional Chinese cultural values can be boiled down to a single core value, i.e., 'social stability,' achieved through harmony among people." By contrast, Erie's corporate culture displayed the individualistic values common to Western countries (Exhibit 3 presents the company's vision statement and values).

Erie sought to inculcate all employees with its core values: directness with advice and opinions, open communication across hierarchical levels, questioning decisions, accountability, a bottom-line orientation, explaining the rationale for managerial decisions and transparency with financial data. According to Sharon Lieder, the U.S. director of training, "Erie wants employees who will stand up for their ideas and push each other to defend them, regardless of rank or position. How else can a company foster the innovation that is so necessary in today's business environment?" As a chemicals business, the culture also emphasized quality consciousness and concern for safety.

Wong faced a major challenge in trying to integrate Erie and Chinese cultures at WEP (Exhibit 4 describes several key Chinese values). Erie's emphasis on autonomous decisions and constructive confrontation ran counter to the Chinese belief in obeying superiors and

maintaining harmonious interpersonal relations. Since Wong believed principles such as autonomy and feedback provided the best road to high productivity, he wanted to quickly instill them in employees. Acknowledging the power of traditional Chinese values, he decided, however, not to tackle thousands of years of Chinese culture in one fell swoop. Although he admired Americans' belief that they could overcome any obstacle, he had frequently seen U.S. expatriates encounter problems because of their unwillingness to accommodate the local culture. He worried that a dramatic change in value systems might confuse and upset employees, create resistance and lower productivity.

Wong had concluded that Chinese employees would never become fully westernized, nor should they. Rather, he sought to create a unique culture that synthesized Chinese with Western values and organizational practices:

> I have tried to highlight the "good" and eliminate the "bad" from both cultures. I emphasized a spirit of responsibility, questioning, open communication, a business orientation and a safety culture, all of which were largely absent from Chinese organizations. At the same time, I promoted a spirit of teamwork through good relationships that has always been highly valued in China. I tried to remove the negative elements from the West such as bluntness, not giving face, impatience, and placing self before team.

He believed in the ability of Chinese employees to think for themselves. One of his main motives for going to China was to increase the technical and managerial skills of the Chinese workforce, which were in short supply. Since the plant opened, Wong had consistently pushed employees to develop a sense of empowerment, in accordance with Erie's emphasis on autonomy. He had studiously avoided advocating constructive conflict, however, a second important Erie cultural value, because he believed that harmonious relationships and concern for face were too central to Chinese culture to risk violating them through direct confrontation. In his role as general manager, he was shown tremendous respect and deference. Wong tried to model autonomous

Who We Are

Erie Specialty Chemicals is a global leader in the discovery, development, manufacture and marketing of innovative specialty chemicals. Our products hold leading positions in their chosen market segments. We add value beyond chemistry for our customers, employees and shareholders through our state-of-the-art environmentally compatible technologies and proven international marketing expertise.

Vision

Deliver Value

We deliver value for customers, employees and shareholders. Value is created though innovation, productive relationships with customers, and speed and simplicity in everything we do. We achieve this in balance with our responsibilities to society and the environment.

Perform to Win

We appreciate and recognize competence and performance. As empowered individuals and teams in a networked company, we focus on results. The perceptions and actions of our stakeholders are crucial for our success.

Shape the Future

We shape the future of our company and industry. We take the initiative and make things happen, always embracing change as a source for new opportunities.

Values

Performance

We demand and appreciate high performance. We set aggressive standards and targets. We recognize and celebrate success. We are quick to compete for a pre-emptive share of global opportunities. We are not satisfied just to meet goals, exceed last year's result or maintain our current market share. We judge performance by considering financial results, initiated improvements and how well we do in attracting, developing and retaining highly qualified and effective people.

Customer Focus

We are passionate about contributing to the success of our customers. We build mutual success through partnership. We strive for speed, simplicity and operational excellence. We fight costs and delays in all areas.

Innovation

We drive for innovation across organizational boundaries within and beyond our organization. We encourage comparisons with best-in-class organizations. We foster target-oriented team work. Change and mistakes are opportunities to learn, improve and increase our competence.

People Potential

We respect, stimulate and develop the potential of our people. We are constantly aware of the fact that potential is easily underestimated and under-utilized. We support diversity as it enriches the potential of our worldwide organization.

Environmental and Social Responsibility

We act responsibly in environmental and social matters.

Integrity and Open Communication

We build trust through integrity and open communication. Integrity means speaking and acting honestly and truthfully. Integrity honors commitments and promises. It is based on trust and competence and rejects politics.

Exhibit 3   Erie Specialty Chemicals Vision and Values Statements

Confucianism heavily influenced Chinese employees. Traditional Chinese values emphasized harmony, discipline, obedience to authority and primacy of personal relationships over task accomplishment. Respectful obedience to superiors and parents, duty to family, loyalty to friends, humility, sincerity and courtesy were part of the accepted code of social conduct. At home and work, age, rank and status held sway. At work, immediate supervisors were close in power and status to their direct reports, but a large gap existed between these groups and senior managers. Due to the paternalistic nature of Chinese companies, senior management intervention often was sought for problems that would be handled readily at lower levels in Western organizations.

Chinese culture also emphasized preservation of face and avoidance of conflict or confrontation. Employees commonly tried to solve problems on their own rather than ask for help because admitting lack of knowledge engendered a loss of face. Similarly, Chinese employees routinely agreed to follow any order given by their supervisor. The supervisor then might assume everything was in order only to find out later that nothing had been accomplished. Employees who did not understand an order or know how to perform a task would conceal this fact lest they lose face for perceived incompetence. To preserve harmony and avoid confrontation, employees covered up problems for one another so they would not come to management attention. Personal problems, in particular, were kept hidden.

Under Communism, the "iron rice bowl" concept promised jobs for life. Because productivity was not emphasized, employees usually did not work hard. Since management's primary responsibility was to oversee production, areas such as marketing, finance and human resource development were underdeveloped. A focus on obeying superiors and absence of areas in which risk was a major factor produced a risk-averse approach to management, which reinforced the Chinese tendency toward conformity.

Good personal relationships or *quanxi* were very important in China. Quanxi, described as the informal connections needed to obtain privileged access to scarce resources, was especially important. Company relationships depended on trust between the parties rather than legal regulation.

Exhibit 4   Chinese Cultural Values Affecting Current Workplace Behavior

decision-making for his managers. He regarded poor decisions by inexperienced Chinese managers as simply part of the learning process:

They will not grow if you do not give them opportunities to practice making important decisions. Everyone makes mistakes. The important point is to learn from your mistakes and avoid stepping into the same trap next time. I hold people accountable for results. These are high-quality, smart, capable managers. When they are responsible for decisions, they will be careful to make high-quality ones. When managers ask for my opinion, I simply ask them to discuss their viewpoints. The key is to trust them.

Wong acknowledged the Chinese expectation that senior management would involve themselves in problems at lower levels of the organization:

Thirty per cent of my time is spent on problems brought to me by individual employees. The objective here is to socialize our Chinese employees to the Western or Erie philosophy. However, the reason I engage myself in these matters is that in China problems usually are dealt with by the person in authority.

He saw this approach as a means to foster a trusting organizational culture. "For me, the first priority was really trust," he explained. "Without it, empowerment and teamwork cannot work."

EMPLOYEE REACTIONS

Consistent with the company's aim to localize, the joint venture was staffed mainly by local Chinese. Wong, Catherine Zheng in information technology and Katie Chung in finance were originally from Hong Kong. Jonathan Beck, an American engineer assigned to WEP as a technical consultant, was not part of the formal chain of command. Henri Boulanger, a French-Canadian whose position as director of marketing for the Polymers Division included responsibility for WEP, was located in Shanghai. Since the qualities Wong sought in his managers (willingness to learn and change, and openness to ideas) mainly characterized younger Chinese, the WEP staff was young (Exhibit 5 lists WEP management team characteristics). All Chinese managers had a bachelor's or master's degree from a local university, two to 20 years of work experience and good English-language skills, which were needed to progress within Erie.

The management team had closely observed Western culture working alongside employees in Erie's Gary, Indiana, plant during the year prior to WEP's startup. In addition to technical knowledge, the newly hired management team received training in cross-cultural skills and an introduction to Erie's culture and vision for worldwide operations, with particular focus on China. The entire WEP workforce below the managerial level was Chinese. Through training modules offered on Friday afternoons, employees learned Erie's values and culture, as well as English and general business skills.

Reflecting on the comparison between WEP under Stanley Wong and the typical state-owned firm, Selena Lee, WEP's head of human resources, observed:

Employees in WEP are young and more easily influenced by the culture Stanley has tried to create. They have been encouraged to speak their minds and most of what they have said has been heard. So you see more trust and open communication at WEP than a state-owned firm. Because they have been heard and cared for, WEP staff feels they are respected, which increases their confidence and pride in what they are doing. In most state-owned firms, people behave more carefully. You need to be aware of your position and the situation around you. You must not stand out or offend somebody in a superior position. Because of the higher stress and lower pay, employees in those firms more frequently grumble behind their bosses' backs but are reluctant to express their discontent openly.

Name	Position	Age	Gender	Years Experience	Education
Harold Ang	Ecology Officer	31	Male	8	Bachelors
Katie Chung*	Finance Manager	27	Female	7	Bachelors
Alison Deng	Deputy General Manager	46	Female	20	Bachelors
Selena Lee	Head, Human Resources	30	Female	8	Bachelors
Joe Li	Deputy Manager, Marketing	33	Male	8	Masters
Frederick Low	Head, Engineering	31	Male	7	Masters
Jackson Mao	Manager, Administration	31	Male	11	Bachelors
Bruce Po	Manufacturing Manager	32	Male	10	Bachelors
Victor Tsai	Safety Officer	30	Male	2	Masters
Harold Tsang	Production Manager	28	Male	5	Masters
Catherine Zheng*	Manager, Information Technology	27	Female	6	Bachelors

Exhibit 5   Characteristics of the WEP Management Team

*Expatriate from Hong Kong

Wong's notions of empowerment generated strong reactions from his managers when first introduced.

> At the beginning, many of them were quite reluctant to make decisions because of their deep-rooted experiences in state-owned enterprises of being submissive to the directions set by the leaders.

According to employees, Wong greatly stressed role-modeling, paternalism and teamwork. Said one employee:

> He treats and nurtures the employees as his own children. He invites them to his home for dinner, plays basketball games with them and eats lunch with them in the company-sponsored canteen.

Bruce Po, the manufacturing manager, stated:

> The key factor to our success as a joint venture has been the way Stanley treats our employees. He provides much training during working hours without worrying about lost productivity. He has not been concerned with other companies poaching trained employees because the trust he has built and empowerment he has provided have developed a sense of loyalty and commitment from us.

Although some WEP managers had increased their skills in autonomous decision making, others continued to show reluctance to make decisions. As Bruce Po illustrated:

> When Stanley is away, I have to make important decisions together with Alison Deng, who is the acting general manager for Stanley. However, Alison is very conservative and not willing to commit to any important decisions. Most of the time, I have to wait for Stanley to come back in order to get things done. This has slowed our progress significantly on certain occasions in the past.

One employee expressed the need for Wong's presence as a decision-maker thus:

> Problems dealing with suppliers, selection interviews, authorization signatures, internal co-ordination and administrative logistics require his attention and approval. It is difficult for us to determine what to do during his absence.

Despite ongoing attempts to improve managerial skills, WEP still had a relatively young, inexperienced staff, shaped by the dual legacies of early career experiences in state-owned enterprises and the Confucian cultural belief system in which they were raised. Wong believed the management team had not yet adopted enough of the Western management orientation essential for effective corporate management.

Plant turnover had been less than two per cent per year. Productivity, which had surpassed first-year goals, was approaching that of the plant in Gary, Indiana. Wong's boss had recently decided to completely integrate the plant into Erie's global supply chain.

NOMINATING A SUCCESSOR

Looking to the future, Wong anticipated changes in the plant manager and division manager positions. With the rapid expansion of Erie business ventures in China, division managers would need to become even more involved in JV negotiations and plant construction, including intense, frequent socializing with government officials and executives in Chinese state-owned enterprises to build relationships. As the company expanded operations in China, it would also be necessary to concentrate on strategic issues. Two vital concerns were the ongoing shortage of Chinese managers qualified to operate in western enterprises and fierce competition for the services of the few available. Internally groomed management talent was of prime importance to staff the company's ever-increasing needs. In the plant manager's position, Wong anticipated responsibilities to move away from relationship-building with both government officials and the JV partner and move toward internal plant management. With a functioning plant, the manager could concentrate on reducing production costs and "de-bottlenecking" processes, working with marketing to increase sales, fine-tuning the organization and continuing staff development.

Most WEP employees worried about what would happen after Wong left. Alison Deng, the deputy general manager, expressed the beliefs of many employees:

> Stanley is a very good general manager. We do not know who would be his successor. But it seems that no one can ever replace him. We are especially reluctant to see a non-Chinese expatriate being sent from Gary to be in charge of this operation. Verbal communication between managers and workers is critical in China. A manager who can only speak English would not be able to communicate effectively with his Chinese subordinates. We just

wait and cross our fingers, although I am not optimistic about the new general manager.

To organize his thoughts regarding a successor, Wong drew up a list of the major functions and responsibilities of each role. Next, he profiled the desired qualities of a successor, which included the capability to advance his vision (see Exhibit 6). Finally, he evaluated the slate of candidates against the job requirements and desired characteristics (see Exhibit 7). No one on the list encompassed the same characteristics that he brought to the job. With the possibility his

---

Stanley Wong's Responsibilities

Managing the Polymers Division

- Provide leadership for the strategic direction of the division in Region China
- Build up the organization and develop the infrastructure for the division
- Manage personnel issues within the division
- Ensure sales expansion
- Ensure effective asset utilization

Strengthening WEP

- Build up the organization of WEP through recruitment, training and value system establishment
- Communicate effectively with Chinese employees
- Support and control the management team's efforts to increase factory production
- Manage relationships with Plastics and Chinese government officials
- Integrate sales activities between the Performance Polymers division and WEP

Other major functions

- Provide Chinese expertise to support the Nanjing joint-venture project
- Assist James Golding, regional president, on corporate issues, e.g., incinerator, waste-water treatment, HR projects and the general direction of Erie's development in China
- Serve as a board member of WEP and Wuhan Erie Additives
- Act as an ambassador of Erie Specialty Chemicals in Wuhan

Desired Qualities of Stanley Wong's Successor

- Strong people skills (the most critical requirement for working in China)
- Knowledge of Chinese culture and language
- Vision and strategic business skills
- Ability to synthesize Chinese and Western cultures
- Knowledge of Performance Polymers
- Familiarity with Erie values
- Stamina for hard work
- Willingness to live in China
- Ability to stand up to frustration
- Over age 40 (to command respect from Chinese colleagues, customers and partner)

Exhibit 6   Stanley Wong's Responsibilities and Desired Qualities for His Replacement

Henri Boulanger—marketing director, Polymers Division, age 46, male, French.

Education: Bachelor's degree in management from the University of Ottawa, Ottawa, Canada.

Work history: 24 years experience. In sales and sales management with Rhone-Poulenc from 1974 to 1982. Last 16 years at Erie, in sales management from 1982 to 1985, then last 13 years in marketing. Marketing manager for a small line of hardeners in Canada, 1985 to 1988, then for resins in the U.S., 1988 to 1991. The last seven years as marketing director for the expanding Chinese polymers business, 1991 to 1995, from Hong Kong and since 1995, from Shanghai.

Personal qualities: Very intelligent, energetic, experienced in marketing and sales. Emotional and quick-tempered. Gets along very well with his Chinese subordinates. Lacks Chinese language skills, potentially limiting his ability to communicate at the plant. Very effective in current position introducing Western marketing techniques and networking with corporate headquarters.

Alison Deng—deputy general manager, WEP, age 46, female, P.R.C. Chinese.

Education: Bachelor's degree in chemistry from Wuhan Technical University.

Work history: 20 years experience, 17 with Wuhan Plastics Factory first as senior chemist then project manager, then department head. Department head of production technology for two years, then technical development for four years, then foreign trade for two years. Primary responsibility for negotiating the joint venture with Erie. Last three years as deputy general manager of WEP.

Personal qualities: Very hard-working, detail-oriented, conscientious, tough with her subordinates. Exercised primary responsibility at Wuhan Plastics for handling employees with problems, a critical competency at WEP. Little skill in English language. Her approach to management adheres closely to traditional Chinese Confucian practices learned in her years at Wuhan Plastics Factory.

Dr. Thomas Klemm—head, resin technology development department, Erie Specialty Chemicals in Cleveland, age 41, male, American.

Education: Bachelors degree in biochemistry from the University of Maryland; Ph.D. in chemistry from the University of Delaware; MBA from Cornell University, all in the United States.

Work history: 11 years experience. Head of an independent research institute for two years. Technical management for Erie Specialty Chemicals for past nine years in Cleveland headquarters, seven in middle management, the last two in senior management.

Personal qualities: Highly regarded by Erie top management, who want him to obtain significant management experience in a challenging overseas assignment. Positioned on a fast track to career advancement. Known as task-oriented, little time for relationship-building. Under his charge, technology development has produced impressive results. Lacks Chinese language skills.

Benson Leung—business group manager, Erie Additives, Hong Kong, age 42, male, Hong Kong Chinese.

Education: Associates degree in textile technology, Hong Kong Polytechnic.

Work history: 21 years experience. Entire career with Schmidt then Erie Specialty Chemicals, most in the Additives Division. Sales and technical positions in Hong Kong for first 11 years, then three years as country manager for Erie in China, four years as head of Erie in Taiwan, last three years in current position.

Personal qualities: Good communicator and salesperson, very approachable. Good skills in both Chinese and English. Managerial experience in Erie's China operations. Poor strategic thinking and conceptual skills. Lacks deep understanding of P.R.C. Chinese culture. Aims to please rather than deal with hard truths.

Bruce Po—manufacturing manager, WEP, age 32, male, P.R.C. Chinese.

Education: Bachelor's degree in organic chemistry from Central Hubei University. Currently pursuing masters degree in business part-time at Wuhan University.

Exhibit 7   Summary of Qualifications of Candidates to Succeed Stanley Wong   *(Continued)*

Work history: 10 years experience. First seven years at Wuhan Plastics Factory as a chemist, in the R&D Department, a manufacturing plant, then the Production Technology Department. Past three years at WEP, first year in training at Gary, Indiana, last two years in current position.

Personal qualities: Intelligent, experienced in chemical production, committed, hard-working. Still learning Western business and management practices, has had little networking with headquarters colleagues, which may hinder desired support from headquarters. Quiet, may come across as passive, yet confrontational.

Yoshi Tanaga—plant manager, Erie Polymer Division in Japan, age 48, male, Japanese.

Education: Bachelors degree in chemistry from Kyoto University, Japan.

Work history: 26 years of experience, all in Polymers at Erie. First 12 years as chemist, senior chemist, then associate project manager in Japan. Eight years as a technical sales consultant in Hong Kong with extensive travel in the P.R.C. and other parts of Asia. Last six years as plant manager, two in the Isohara, Japan plant and the last four in the Yokohama, Japan plant, the largest Erie production facility in Asia.

Personal qualities: Very honest, hard-working, committed, direct and open. Liked by both his subordinates and headquarters management. Steady as a rock with good human skills. Lacks strategic thinking skills. Intermediate level of Chinese language skills.

Exhibit 7 (Continued)

successor could have significant liabilities, Wong also needed to consider how operations or policies might be adjusted to fit a successor's profile. Possible compromises to the plant's culture might be required if his successor was not equipped to carry it forward.

Since most employees appreciated Wong's leadership style, the new WEP general manager would face a very challenging job. Wong believed, however:

The new general manager can come up with a new style that suits WEP and be appreciated by our employees. The most important point is to find a way to communicate with Chinese employees, develop them to be effective and efficient managers, and maintain the productivity and profitability of the plant.

While suffering from his daily stress headache, Wong leaned back in his chair. Upon reviewing the résumés, he wondered who would be the best candidate for the job. As he unscrewed the cap from the bottle of Aspirins, he wondered if he should leave a new bottle on his desk as a welcoming gift for his successor.

ABOUT THE EDITORS

Jean-Louis Schaan, Ph.D., is Professor of Strategic Management and International Business and the J. Armand Bombardier Chair in Global Management at the Richard Ivey School of Business. Prior to joining Ivey, he was Director of the University of Ottawa's Executive MBA Program. He is a past winner of the University of Ottawa Award for Excellence in Teaching. His research has focused on strategic alliances and project management. In collaboration with Micheál Kelly, he has conducted studies about the management and implementation in strategic alliances in the high-technology sector. He has been serving in private company board of directors and advisory boards for 15 years, has consulted with public- and private-sector organizations in Canada and Europe, and taught in executive programs in North America, Europe, Asia, and North Africa.

Micheál J. Kelly, Ph.D., is Dean and Professor of Strategic and International Management at the University of Ottawa's School of Management. His research focuses on strategic alliances and venture capital financing of high-technology companies. He is the author of several dozen monographs, articles, and studies related to high-technology management and strategy issues.

Dr. Kelly is a former executive board member and chairman of the Six Countries Program, a European research network on innovation and technology policy. He is also a former board member of the Silicon Valley Roundtable. He is a featured speaker at international conferences and executive seminars on strategic alliances and venture capital and has contributed on both subjects to the *National Post,* CBC's *Venture*, and other major business media. He is a past president of the Canadian Federation of Business School Deans.